Aaron Copland

Other Books Edited by Richard Kostelanetz

On Contemporary Literature (1964, 1969)

The New American Arts (1965)

Twelve from the Sixties (1967)

The Young American Writers (1967)

Beyond Left & Right: Radical Thought for Our Times (1968)

Assembling (Twelve vols., 1970–1981)

Possibilities of Poetry (1970)

Imaged Words & Worded Images (1970)

Moholy-Nagy (1970, 1991)

John Cage (1970, 1991)

Social Speculations (1971)

Human Alternatives (1971)

Future's Fictions (1971)

Seeing Through Shuck (1972)

In Youth (1972)

Breakthrough Fictioneers (1973)

The Edge of Adaptation (1973)

Essaying Essays (1975)

Language & Structure (1975)

Younger Critics in North America (1976)

Esthetics Contemporary (1978, 1989)

Assembling Assembling (1978)

Visual Literature Criticism (1979)

Text-Sound Texts (1980)

The Yale Gertrude Stein (1980)

Scenarios (1980)

Aural Literature Criticism (1981)

The Literature of SoHo (1981)

American Writing Today (1981, 1991)

The Avant-Garde Tradition in Literature (1982)

Gertrude Stein Advanced (1989)

Merce Cunningham: Dancing in Time & Space (1992)

John Cage: Writer (1993)

Writings About John Cage (1993)

Nicolas Slonimsky: The First Hundred Years (1994)

The Portable Baker's Biographical Dictionary of Musicians (1995)

A Frank Zappa Companion (1997)

Writing on Glass (1997)

A B. B. King Companion (1997)

AnOther E. E. Cummings (1998)

The Gertrude Stein Reader (2002)

The Virgil Thomson Reader (2002)

Aaron Copland
A Reader
Selected Writings 1923–1972

Edited, with an introduction,
by Richard Kostelanetz

Assistant Editor Steve Silverstein

ROUTLEDGE
NEW YORK AND LONDON

Published in 2004 by
Routledge
29 West 35th Street
New York, NY 10001

Published in Great Britain by
Routledge
11 New Fetter Lane
London EC4P 4EE

Routledge is an imprint of the Taylor & Francis Group.
Printed in the United States of America on acid-free paper.

10 9 8 7 6 5 4 3 2 1

Library of Congress Cataloging-in-Publication Data
Copland, Aaron, 1900-1990
    [Literary works. Selections]
    Aaron Copland : a reader : selected writings 1923–1972 / edited, with
an introduction, by Richard Kostelanetz ; assistant editor, Steve
Silverstein.
        p. cm.
Includes bibliographical references and index.
    ISBN 0-415-93940-2 (hardback : alk. paper)
1. Copland, Aaron, 1900- 2. Music—History and criticism. I.
Kostelanetz, Richard. II. Title.
    ML410.C756A25 2003
    780—dc21

                                        2003008835

For Elizabeth Sessions

Contents

Acknowledgments

A note on the text: Except for obvious typographical errors, all of the material in this volume is reprinted as it originally appeared. The reader may notice some inconsistencies in the spelling of foreign composers' names due to changing standards during the 20th century.

"Composer from Brooklyn: An Autobiographical Sketch," reprinted from *The Magazine of Art* (1939) and *The New Music* (Norton, 1968).

"How We Listen," reprinted from *What to Listen for in Music* (McGraw-Hill, 1939).

"Musical Structure," reprinted from *What to Listen for in Music* (McGraw-Hill, 1939).

"Tone Color," reprinted from *What to Listen for in Music* (McGraw-Hill, 1939).

"Music and the Human Spirit" (1954), reprinted from *Copland on Music* (Doubleday, 1960).

"The American Composer Gets a Break," reprinted from *American Mercury*, 34 (April 1935).

"Music Between the Wars (1918–1939)" (1941, 1968), reprinted from *The New Music* (Norton, 1968).

"Musical Imagination in the Americas," reprinted from *Music and Imagination* (Norton, 1952).

"Jazz Structure and Influence," reprinted from *Modern Music*, 4 (January–February 1927).

"Workers Sing!" reprinted from *New Masses* (June 5, 1934).

"[Letter to the Editor] Varèse," reprinted as "Letter on Varèse and the League of Composers," from *The New York Times* (August 13, 1972).

"Opera and Music Drama," reprinted from *What to Listen for in Music* (McGraw-Hill, 1939).

"Tip to Moviegoers: Take Off Those Ear-Muffs," reprinted from *The New York Times Magazine* (November 6, 1949).

"Second Thoughts on Hollywood," reprinted from *Modern Music*, 17 (March–April 1940).

"Composer's Report on Music in South America," reprinted from *The New York Times* (December 21, 1947).

"Festival in Caracas," reprinted from *New York Times* (December 26, 1954).

"A Note on Young Composers," reprinted from *Music Vanguard*, I/1 (March–April 1935).

"Effect of the Cold War on the Artist in the U.S.," previously unpublished, from The Copland Collection, Music Division, Library of Congress, by permission of The Aaron Copland Fund for Music, Inc. Copyright © 2003 by The Aaron Copland Fund for Music, Inc.

"Introducing Shostakovitch at Dinner," previously unpublished, from The Copland Collection, Music Division, Library of Congress, by permission of The Aaron Copland Fund for Music, Inc. Copyright © 2003 by The Aaron Copland Fund for Music, Inc.

"When Private and Public Worlds Meet," reprinted from *The New York Times* (June 9, 1968).

"Is the University Too Much With Us?" reprinted from *The New York Times* (April 26, 1970).

"Tanglewood's Future," reprinted from *The New York Times* (February 24, 1952).

"From the '20s to the '40s and Beyond," reprinted from *Modern Music*, 20 (January–February 1943).

"Defends the Music of Mahler," reprinted from *The New York Times* (April 5, 1925).

"The Ives Case," reprinted from *Modern Music*, 11 (January–February 1934) and *The New Music* (Norton, 1968).

"Schoenberg's Expressionism," reprinted from *The New Music* (Norton, 1968).

"Stravinsky's Dynamism," reprinted from *The New Music* (Norton, 1968).

"Béla Bartók," reprinted from *The New Music* (Norton, 1968).

"The Younger Generation of American Composers: 1926–59," reprinted from *Modern Music*, 3 and 13 (March–April 1926 and May–June 1936), *New York Times Magazine*, and *Copland on Music* (Doubleday, 1960).

"America's Young Men of Music," reprinted from *Music and Musicians*, 9 (December 1960).

"George Antheil," reprinted from *Modern Music*, 2 (January 1925).

"The Lyricism of Milhaud," reprinted as "Darius Milhaud," from *Modern Music*, 6 (January–February 1929).

"Thomson and Blitzstein," reprinted as "Virgil Thomson and Marc Blitzstein," from *The New Music* (Norton, 1968).

"Composer from Mexico: Carlos Chávez," reprinted as "Carlos Chávez," from *The New Republic*, 54 (May 2, 1928) and *The New Music* (Norton, 1968).

"Stefan Wolpe," reprinted from *Notes, Journal of the Music Library Association* (December 1948) and *Copland on Music* (Doubleday, 1960).

"A Visit to Snape," reprinted as "Benjamin Britten," from *Tribute to Benjamin Britten on His Fiftieth Birthday* (Faber and Faber, 1963).

"Elliott Carter," reprinted from a 1971 publication by the American Academy of Arts and Letters Inc..

"The Pianist: William Kapell," reprinted as "William Kapell," from *Saturday Review*, 28 (November 28, 1953) and *Copland on Music* (Doubleday, 1960).

"Ralph Hawkes," previously unpublished from The Copland Collection, Music Division, Library of Congress, by permission of The Aaron Copland Fund for Music, Inc., Copyright © 2003 by The Aaron Copland Fund for Music, Inc.

Copland on His Own Works, mostly reprinted from record jackets, concert program notes, prefaces to his scores, and manuscripts.

"*Music for the Theatre*, II," previously unpublished, from The Copland Collection, Music Division, Library of Congress, by permission of The Aaron Copland Fund for Music, Inc. Copyright © 2003 by The Aaron Copland Fund for Music, Inc.

"Notes on a Cowboy Ballet," previously unpublished, from The Copland Collection, Music Division, Library of Congress, by permission of The Aaron Copland Foundation. Copyright © 2003 by The Aaron Copland Fund for Music, Inc.

"Letters on *Appalachian Spring*," reprinted as "*Appalachian Spring*," previously unpublished, from The Copland Collection, Music Division, Library of Congress, by permission of The Aaron Copland Fund for Music, Inc. Copyright © 2003 by The Aaron Copland Fund for Music, Inc.

"Fantasy for Piano," reprinted as "*Piano Fantasy*, I," from *New York Times* (October 20, 1957).

"Composing for *Something Wild*," reprinted as "*Something Wild*," previously unpublished, from The Copland Collection, Music Division, Library of Congress, by permission of The Aaron Copland Fund for Music, Inc. Copyright © 2003 by The Aaron Copland Fund for Music, Inc.

"From a Composer's Notebook," reprinted from *Modern Music*, 6 (May–June, 1929).

"From a Composer's Journal," reprinted from *Copland on Music* (Doubleday, 1960).

"The Teacher and the Pupil," previously unpublished, from The Copland Collection, Music Division, Library of Congress, by permission of The Aaron Copland Fund for Music, Inc. Copyright © 2003 by The Aaron Copland Fund for Music, Inc.

"Journal from Venezuela Visit," previously unpublished, from The Copland Collection, Music Division, Library of Congress, by permission of The Aaron Copland Fund for Music, Inc. Copyright © 2003 by The Aaron Copland Fund for Music, Inc.

"Latin America Tour Journal," previously unpublished, from The Copland Collection, Music Division, Library of Congress, by permission of The Aaron Copland Fund for Music, Inc. Copyright © 2003 by The Aaron Copland Fund for Music, Inc.

"Letters," some previously unpublished, from The Copland Collection, Music Division, Library of Congress, by permission of The Aaron Copland Fund for Music, Inc. Copyright © 2003 by The Aaron Copland Fund for Music, Inc.

Conversation with Edward T. Cone (1967), reprinted from *Perspectives of New Music* by permission of Edward T. Cone.

Epigraphs

I remember once we had Aaron Copland talk, and all the students were surprised at his radical mind. They couldn't put it together with what they thought his music was.

—Morton Feldman, "Darmstadt Lecture" (1984)

There were four powerful women who, in this prefeminist era, ran the bureaucratic side of New Music: Claire Reis, who had invented the League of Composers in 1923; Minna Lederman, who started the dazzling Modern Music magazine, verbal artery of "the cause" until its demise in 1946, . . . ; Louise Varèse, wife and biographer of Edgard the innovator, excellent translator of Rimbaud, and parental figure to all; and Alma Morgenthau, sister of Henry Jr. and mother of Barbara Tuchman, who gave money. What these women said went. Claire, Minna, and Alma were each touchingly, because hopelessly, in love with Aaron Copland.

—Ned Rorem, *Knowing When To Stop* (1994)

The characteristics of reticence, of perceptivity and refinement, of expert craftsmanship—all so typically French—are all there; but combined with them is an open-eyed lucidity about the function and meaning of the music that bespeaks a detachment on the part of the composer that is the antithesis of the Romantic attitude.

—Aaron Copland, *The New Music* (1941, 1968)

Everything I write has a motive behind it. I write the same way I perform. I mean you only perform because you want people to fall in love with you.

—Patti Smith, quoted in Legs McNeil & Gillian McCain, *Please Kill Me* (1996)

Someone once astonished me during a discussion period, after I had given a lecture, by asking me what I thought I had accomplished through the years, with my music. To that question my proudest answer would be, "I helped to make art possible in America." Come to think of it, that is what all artists in America do.

—Aaron Copland, from his acceptance speech given in 1956
upon his induction into the American Academy of Arts and Letters

Preface

Many of our best composers have also been skillful writers whose most important essays should be collected in individual volumes. Aaron Copland epitomized the ideal of the composer-writer, who didn't resist speaking and writing intelligently about music, throughout his long career.

One unusual editorial move in this book is placing the subject's classic autobiographical essay before my own introduction, simply because it provides a better introduction to the man's personality and career (and I remain loath to try to do what anybody else has done better).

I'm grateful to Richard Carlin for commissioning this book, to the composer and music writer Steve Silverstein for locating previously unpublished texts, transcribing Copland's handwriting, writing prefaces, and thoroughly assisting me in finishing the book, to Francis Schwartz for helping clarify Copland's journals from his Latin American travels, to Milton Babbitt for lending me his copy of the first issue of *Music Vanguard* (1934), to other colleagues for their advice in making selections, to The Aaron Copland Fund for Music, Inc., John Harbison, President, and Vivian Perlis, Vice President, James M. Kendrick, Wesley York, and Laura Mankin, Esqs., and to Sarah Laskow for proofreading and indexing.

—Richard Kostelanetz

Composer from Brooklyn: An Autobiographical Sketch[1] (1939, 1968)

The best introduction to Copland as both a musician and a writer is his own "Composer from Brooklyn," a masterful exposition that he revised and extended in his lifetime.

I was born on a street in Brooklyn that can only be described as drab. It had none of the garish color of the ghetto, none of the charm of an old New England thoroughfare, or even the rawness of a pioneer street. It was simply drab. It probably resembled most one of the outer districts of lower-middle-class London, except that it was peopled largely by Italians, Irish, and Negroes. I mention it because it was there that I spent the first twenty years of my life. Also, because I am filled with mild wonder each time I realize that a musician was born on that street.

Music was the last thing anyone would have connected with it. In fact, no one had ever connected music with my family or with my street. The idea was entirely original with me. And unfortunately the idea occurred to me seriously only at thirteen or thereabouts—which is rather late for a musician to get started.

I don't mean to give the impression that there was no music whatever in our house. My oldest brother played the violin to my sister's accompani-

---

[1]In the summer of 1939 the *Magazine of Art* invited me to contribute to a series of autobiographies to be written by half a dozen American composers. This sketch was first published in that year. It is presented here with a few slight revisions.—Aaron Copland's note from 1967.

ments, and there were passable performances of potpourris from assorted operas. I also remember a considerable amount of ragtime on top of the piano for lighter moments. But these were casual encounters. No one ever talked music to me or took me to a concert. Music as an art was a discovery I made all by myself.

The idea of becoming a composer seems gradually to have dawned upon me some time around 1916, when I was about fifteen years old. Before that I had taken the usual piano lessons, begun at my own insistence some two years previously. My parents were of the opinion that enough money had been invested in the musical training of the four older children with meager results and had no intention of squandering further funds on me. But despite the reasonableness of this argument, my persistence finally won them over. I distinctly remember with what fear and trembling I knocked on the door of Mr. Leopold Wolfsohn's piano studio on Clinton Avenue in Brooklyn, and—once again all by myself—arranged for piano lessons.

The idea of composing came, as I say, several years later. It was Mr. Wolfsohn who helped me find a harmony teacher when I realized that to be a composer one had to study harmony. At first I had imagined that harmony could be learned by correspondence course, but a few trial lessons cured me of that illusion. So it came about that in the fall of 1917 I began harmony lessons with the late Rubin Goldmark. My new teacher was a nephew of Karl Goldmark, the famous composer of *The Queen of Sheba*. Goldmark had an excellent grasp of the fundamentals of music and knew very well how to impart his ideas. This was a stroke of luck for me. I was spared the flounderings that so many American musicians have suffered through incompetent teaching at the start of their theoretical training.

By the spring of 1918 I had been graduated from high school and was able to devote all my energies to music. It seems curious now that public school played so small a part in my musical training. I neither sang in the school chorus nor played in the school orchestra. Music classes were a kind of joke—we were not even taught to sight-read a single vocal line properly. Perhaps things have changed for the better in that respect. A young person with musical aptitudes would probably find more scope in the regular school curriculum for his or her talents nowadays.

During these formative years I had been gradually uncovering for myself the literature of music. Some instinct seemed to lead me logically from Chopin's waltzes to Haydn's sonatinas to Beethoven's sonatas to Wagner's operas. And from there it was but a step to Hugo Wolf's songs, to Debussy's preludes, and to Scriabin's piano poems. In retrospect it all seems surprisingly orderly. As far as I can remember no one ever told me about "modern music." I apparently happened on it in the natural course of my musical explorations. It was Goldmark, a convinced conservative in musical matters, who first actively discouraged this commerce with the "moderns." That was enough to whet any young man's appetite. The fact that the music was in some sense forbidden only increased its attractiveness. Moreover, it was difficult to get. The war had made the importation of new music a luxury; Scriabin and Debussy and Ravel were bringing high prices. By the time I was eighteen I already had something of the reputation of a musical rebel—in Goldmark's eyes at any rate.

As might be expected, my compositions of that period, mostly two-page songs and piano pieces, began to show traces of my musical enthusiasms. It soon was clear that Goldmark derived no pleasure from seeing what seemed to him to be "modernistic experiments." The climax came when I brought for his critical approval a piano piece called *The Cat and the Mouse*. He regretfully admitted that he had no criteria by which to judge such music. From that time on my compositional work was divided into two compartments: the pieces that really interested me, that were composed on the side, so to speak, and the conventional student work written in conformity with the "rules."

During these student years I missed very much the companionship of other music students. I had a sense of isolation and of working too much by myself. In America today there are undoubtedly other young musicians who are isolated in big and small communities in a similar fashion.

It was a foregone conclusion around 1920 that anyone who had serious pretensions as a composer would have to go abroad to finish his studies. Before the war it was taken for granted that "abroad" for composers meant Germany. But I belonged to the postwar generation, and so for me "abroad" inevitably meant Paris. The hitch was that I knew not a living soul in Paris—or in all France, for that matter.

At about that time, I read in a musical journal of the proposed establishment of a music school for Americans to be inaugurated during the summer of 1921 in the Palace at Fontainebleau. I was so quick to respond to this announcement that my name headed the list of enrollments. My plan was to stay on in Paris for the winter after the closing of summer school. This would give me a chance to acclimatize myself to French ways and at the same time to find a suitable teacher with whom to continue my studies.

Paul Vidal of the Paris Conservatory taught us composition at the Fontainebleau School. He turned out to be a French version of Rubin Goldmark, except that he was harder to understand because of the peculiar French *patois* that he talked. Before the summer was very far advanced, rumors began to circulate of the presence at school of a brilliant harmony teacher, a certain Nadia Boulanger. This news naturally had little interest for me, since I had long finished *my* harmonic studies. It took a considerable amount of persuasion on the part of a fellow student before I consented to "look in" on Mlle. Boulanger's class. On that particular day she was explaining the harmonic structure of one of the scenes from *Boris Godunov*. I had never before witnessed such enthusiasm and such clarity in teaching. I immediately suspected that I had found my teacher.

There were several mental hurdles to get over first, however. No one to my knowledge had ever before thought of studying composition with a woman. This idea was absurd on the face of it. Everyone knows that the world has never produced a first-rate woman composer, so it follows that no woman could possibly hope to teach composition. Moreover, how would it sound to the folks back home? The whole idea was just a bit too revolutionary.

Nevertheless, and despite these excellent reasons, I visited Mlle. Boulanger in the fall and asked her to accept me as her pupil. She must have been about thirty-three years old at that time, and as far as I know, I was her first full-fledged American composition student. I mention this with a certain amount of understandable pride in view of the large number of young American composers who have followed, and are still following, in my footsteps. Two qualities possessed by Mlle. Boulanger make her unique: one is her consuming love for music, and the other is her ability to inspire a pupil with confidence in his own creative powers. Add to this an encyclopedic knowledge of every phase of music past and present, an amazing critical perspicacity, and a full measure of feminine charm and wit. The influence of this remarkable woman on American creative music will some day be written in full.

My one year in Paris was stretched to two and then to three years. It was a fortunate time to be studying music in France. All the pent-up energies of the war years were unloosed. Paris was an international proving ground for all the newest tendencies in music. Much of the music that had been written during the dark years of the war was now being heard for the first time. Schoenberg, Stravinsky, Bartók, Falla were all new names to me. And the younger generation was heard from also—Milhaud, Honegger, Auric, and the other noisy members of the Group of Six. Works by many composers outside France were performed—Hindemith, Prokofiev, Szymanowski, Malipiero, Kodály. It was a rarely stimulating atmosphere in which to carry on one's studies.

Many of these new works were given their première at the Concerts Koussevitzky. Every spring and fall Serge Koussevitzky organized and conducted a series of orchestral concerts at the Paris Opera, where a feast of new compositions was offered. I attended these concerts regularly for three years with my friend and roommate Harold Clurman (later to become director of the Group Theatre in New York). The watchword in those days was "originality." The laws of rhythm, of harmony, of construction had all been torn down. Every composer in the vanguard set out to remake these laws according to his own conceptions. And I suppose that I was no exception despite my youth—or possibly because of it.

During my three years in Paris I had composed several Motets for unaccompanied voices, a Passacaglia for piano, a song for soprano with the accompaniment of flute and clarinet, a Rondino for string quartet, and finally a one-act ballet called *Grohg*, my first essay in the orchestral field. With this baggage under my arm I returned to America in June 1924.

Looking backward to that time, I am rather amazed at my own ignorance of musical conditions in America. I mean, of course, conditions as they affected composers. How a composer managed to get his compositions performed or published and how he was expected to earn his living were equally mysterious. I had left my drab Brooklyn street as a mere student with practically no musical connections. I was returning there in much the same state. As far as I was concerned, America was virgin soil.

The immediate business in hand, however, was the writing of a symphony for organ and orchestra. Nadia Boulanger had been engaged to appear as organ soloist with the old New York Symphony and the Boston Symphony the following winter. Before I left Paris she had had the courage to ask me to supply her with an organ concerto for her American tour. I, on the other hand, had had the temerity to accept the invitation. This, despite the fact that I had written only one work in extended form before then, that I had only a passing acquaintance with the organ as an instrument, and that I had never heard a note of my own orchestration. The symphony was composed that summer while I perfunctorily performed my duties as pianist in a hotel trio at Milford, Pennsylvania.

I returned to New York in the fall to finish the orchestration of the symphony and began to look about me. Without my being aware of it, postwar activities in Europe had affected American musical circles also. Shortly after my departure for France the International Composers' Guild and the League of Composers had begun to familiarize the American public with the output of the new composers of the "left." Like many other composers of so-called radical tendencies, I naturally turned to them for support. Through the good offices of Marion Bauer I was invited to play some of my works for the executive board of the League of Composers. The board voted to accept my two piano pieces—*The Cat and the Mouse* and the Passacaglia—for performance at their November concert. This was the first performance of any of my compositions in my native land. It was followed in January by the performance of the Symphony for organ and orchestra, with Walter Damrosch as conductor and Nadia Boulanger as soloist.

An unexpected incident occurred at this concert, indicative of the attitude toward "modern music" at that period. When the performance of my symphony was over and the audience had settled itself for the next number on the program. Dr. Damrosch turned round and addressed his public as follows: "If a young man at the age of twenty-three can write a symphony like that, in five years he will be ready to commit murder." Fearing that the elderly ladies in his audience had been shocked by the asperities of the new style in music, Dr. Damrosch found this way of consoling them. That, at any rate, was my interpretation of his little speech. In any event, his prophecy luckily came to nothing.

The performance of the symphony brought me into personal contact with the conductor whose concerts I had admired in Paris. Serge Koussevitzky was serving his first term as conductor of the Boston Symphony that winter. Here was a stroke of extraordinary good fortune for me and for American music generally. For Koussevitzky brought with him from Paris not only his conductorial prowess but also his passion for encouraging whatever he felt to be new and vital in contemporary music. Throughout his long tenure in Boston he consistently championed young American music while continuing to introduce novelties from Europe. We Americans are all in his debt.

Koussevitzky made no secret of his liking for my symphony. He told me that he had agreed to conduct a chamber orchestra in an all-modern concert for the League of Composers the following winter. It was his idea, agreed to by the League, that I be commissioned to write a new work for that concert. It seemed to me that my first winter in America was turning out better than I had had reason to expect.

But one rather important item was being neglected—my financial setup. For lack of a better solution I had decided to make a living by teaching. In the fall I had opened a studio on West Seventy-fourth Street in Manhattan and sent out the usual announcements. Unfortunately the effect of this move was nil. It produced not one pupil. By the time the Symphony had been played in Boston the situation was acute. Something had to be done. It was Paul Rosenfeld who came to the rescue. While still a student in Brooklyn, I had read his appreciations of contemporary music in the *Dial*. The morning after the performance of the piano pieces at the League concert, he called me up to tell me how much he liked them. (I couldn't have been more surprised if President Coolidge had telephoned me.) It was 1924; money was plentiful and art patrons were numerous. Through a mutual friend Rosenfeld was asked if he could not find a musical Maecenas to come to the aid of an indigent young composer. Rosenfeld said he could, and did. Shortly afterward, the Guggenheim Memorial Foundation was established for a preliminary trial year, and I was awarded the first fellowship extended to a composer. This was renewed the following year, and so financial stability was assured until the fall of 1927.

Now I was free to devote my entire energies to the composition of the new work for Koussevitzky's League concert. I was anxious to write a work that would immediately be recognized as American in character. This desire to be "American" was symptomatic of the period. It made me think of my Symphony as too European in inspiration. I had experimented a little with the rhythms of popular music in several earlier compositions, but now I wanted frankly to adopt the jazz idiom and see what I could do with it in a symphonic way. Rosenfeld suggested the MacDowell Colony as a good place to work during the summer months. It was there that I wrote my *Music for the Theatre*, a suite in five parts for small orchestra.

It was also at the MacDowell Colony that I made the acquaintance of another young American composer in embryo, Roy Harris. I already knew Virgil Thomson and Douglas Moore from my Paris days, and shortly after meeting Harris I came to know Roger Sessions, Walter Piston, and Carlos Chávez. These contacts with kindred spirits among fellow composers led me to take an active interest in the welfare of American composers in general. The first problem to be attacked was the matter of performance. We thought that American compositions were not being performed enough. (They are still not performed enough, it seems to me.) With Roger Sessions I organized a series of concerts, under the name of the Copland-Sessions Concerts, which functioned from 1928 to 1931. American music made up the bulk of our programs—that was our one innovation. Later I was active in organizing several festivals of American music at Yaddo, in Saratoga Springs, New York. These proved to be the first of a series of efforts toward the improvement of the economic and artistic status of the American composer.

The jazz element in *Music for the Theatre* was further developed in my next work, a Concerto for Piano and Orchestra, which I played as soloist with the Boston Symphony in Boston and New York. This proved to be the last of my "experiments" with symphonic jazz. With the Concerto I felt I had done all I could with the idiom, considering its limited emotional scope. True, it was an easy way to be American in musical terms, but all American music could not possibly be confined to two dominant jazz moods—the blues and the snappy number. The characteristic rhythmic element of jazz, being independent of mood, yet purely indigenous, will undoubtedly continue to be used in serious native music.

In 1929, just before the economic crash, the RCA Victor Company offered an award of $25,000 for a symphonic work. This unprecedented sum obviously implied a composition of major proportions. With this in mind, I began work on a big one-movement symphony that I planned to submit for the prize under the title *Symphonic Ode*. Unfortunately, two weeks before the competition was to close officially, I realized that I could not finish my *Ode* in time. In despair at having nothing to offer, I seized upon the old ballet *Grohg*, written in Paris, and extracting three of the movements I liked best, called the whole a *Dance Symphony* and sent it in on the final day. The judges found no one work worthy of the full award and so decided to divide it among five of the contestants. My *Dance Symphony* won me $5,000. The *Symphonic Ode* was finished subsequently and performed as one of the works celebrating the fiftieth anniversary of the Boston Symphony.

In retrospect it seems to me that the *Ode* marks the end of a certain period in my development as a composer. The works that follow it are no longer so grandly conceived. The Piano Variations (1930), the Short Symphony (1933), the *Statements* for orchestra (1935) are more spare in sonority, more lean in texture. They are still comparatively difficult to perform and difficult for an audience to comprehend.

During the mid-'30s I began to feel an increasing dissatisfaction with the relations of the music-loving public and the living composer. The old "special" public of the modern-music concerts had fallen away, and the conventional concert public continued apathetic or indifferent to anything but the established classics. It seemed to me that we composers were in danger of working in a vacuum. Moreover, an entirely new public for music had grown up around the radio and phonograph. It made no sense to ignore them and to continue writing as if they did not exist. I felt that it was worth the effort to see if I couldn't say what I had to say in the simplest possible terms.

My most recent works, in their separate ways, embody this tendency toward an imposed simplicity. *El Salón México* is an orchestral work based on Mexican tunes; *The Second Hurricane* is an opera for school children of high-school age to perform; *Music for Radio* was written on a commission from the Columbia Broadcasting Company especially for performance on the air; *Billy the Kid*, a ballet written for the Ballet Caravan, utilizes simple cowboy songs as melodic material; *The City, Of Mice and Men*, and *Our Town* are scores for the films. The reception accorded these works in the last two or three years encourages me to believe that the American composer is destined to play a more commanding role in the musical future of his own country.

****

1967: The preceding pages were written a good many years ago. In the intervening period I have learned, to my discomfiture, that the writing of an autobiographical sketch in mid-career is fraught with peril. Commentators, pleased to be able to quote literally, are convinced that they have pinned the composer down for all time. The statements quoted may be long out of date, but the quotation marks that surround them make them seemingly unassailable. Thus, the final two paragraphs of my brief memoir have done me considerable harm. The assertion that I wished "to see if I couldn't say what I had to say in the simplest possible terms" and the mention of "an imposed simplicity" were taken to mean that I had renounced my more complex and "difficult" music, turned my back on the cultivated audience that understands a sophisticated musical language, and henceforth would write music solely for the "masses." Quoted and requoted, these remarks of mine emphasized a point of view which, although apposite at the time of writing—the end of the '30s—seems to me to constitute an oversimplification of my aims and intentions, especially when applied to a consideration of my subsequent work and of my work as a whole.

Taken in context, my position at that time is not too surprising. By the end of 1939, the artists of America had lived through a very special ten years, aptly named "the fervent years" in Harold Clurman's perceptive phrase. In all the arts the Depression had aroused a wave of sympathy for and identification with the plight of the common man. In music this was combined with the heady wine of suddenly feeling ourselves—the composers, that is—needed as never before. Previously our works had been largely self-engendered: no one asked for them; we simply wrote them out of our own need. Now, suddenly, functional music was in demand as never before, certainly as never before in the experience of our serious composers. Motion-picture and ballet companies, radio stations and schools, film and theater producers discovered us. The music appropriate for the different kinds of cooperative ventures undertaken by these people had to be simpler and more direct. There was a "market" especially for music evocative of the American scene—industrial backgrounds, landscapes of the Far West, and so forth. This kind of role for music, so new then, is now taken for granted by both entrepreneurs and composers. But in the late '30s and early '40s it was almost without precedent, and moreover, it developed at just the time when the economic pinch of the Depression had really reached us. No wonder we were pleased to find ourselves sought after and were ready to compose in a manner that would satisfy both our collaborators and ourselves.

Even our own government needed us. For the first time the State Department sponsored official visits of American creative artists and performers to foreign countries. In 1941 the Office of the Coordinator of Inter-American Affairs, under the chairmanship of Nelson Rockefeller, invited me to participate in our good-neighbor policy by going to South America for several months. I had acquired some sense of the Latin-American temperament and a fair smattering of Spanish during several visits to Mexico in the '30s. Carlos Chávez in 1932 had sponsored my first visit south of the border with the tempting bait of an all-Copland program for the first time anywhere. But my initial contact in 1941 with the music and culture of seven different South American countries (to which were added Mexico on the way down and Cuba on the way back) was an eye-opener. I met and talked with almost sixty composers, listened to many of their works, and played and discussed with them recent compositions by their North American confreres. In many ways we found our situation and problems to be similar, especially vis-à-vis Europe; our slow development toward musical independence was paralleled by their own experience. This resemblance created a strong bond between us—a bond we both sensed, and one that still attaches me to my South American composer friends. It was further cemented in later years when numbers of the most gifted younger Latin-American musicians came to study at Tanglewood.

I associate this first trip to South America with the completion of my Piano Sonata in Santiago de Chile, during their September national holidays. One month later I gave the work its first public performance in Buenos Aires at a concert sponsored by La Nueva Musica, an organization with aims not unlike those of our own League of Composers. The Piano Sonata is a piece of absolute music, written without conscious reference to any folk origins. This is also true of my Sonata for Violin and Piano, completed two years later, and of my Third Symphony, completed in 1946. *Appalachian Spring* also dates from these years (1944); it is generally thought to be folk inspired, despite the fact that the Shaker tune *'Tis the Gift to Be Simple* is the only actual folk tune quoted. I stress this point because of the mistaken notion that my music of this period is larded with native musical materials. A confusion seems to exist between rhythms and melodies that suggest a certain American *ambiente*, often arrived at unconsciously, and specific folk themes, such as those which in my ballets *Billy the Kid* and *Rodeo* are utilized and developed in a way that I like to think is my own.

Most of *Appalachian Spring* and a good part of my Violin Sonata were composed at night at the Samuel Goldwyn Studios in Hollywood. An air of mystery hovers over a film studio after dark. Its silent and empty streets give off something of the atmosphere of a walled medieval town; no one gets in or out without passing muster with the guards at the gates. This seclusion provided the required calm for evoking the peaceful, open countryside of rural Pennsylvania depicted in *Appalachian Spring*.

During this time Groucho Marx was employed by Mr. Goldwyn, and I used to see him occasionally in the studio lunchroom, where we exchanged pleasantries. One night I was genuinely surprised to come upon him at a concert of modern music in downtown Los Angeles where my Piano Sonata was being given a local première. "Whatever you do," I said with a smile, "don't tell Mr. Goldwyn about this advanced stuff I write, or you might frighten him. After all," I added jokingly, "I have a split personality."

Groucho came right back with, "Well, it's O.K., as long as you split it with Mr. Goldwyn."

Appalachian Spring owes its origin to the fact that in 1942 the well-known music patron Mrs. Elizabeth Sprague Coolidge was taken to a performance of Martha Graham's Dance Company. Stimulated by what she saw, Mrs. Coolidge, with typical generosity, decided to commission three composers of Miss Graham's choice to compose ballets for her. Martha chose Hindemith, Milhaud, and myself. I have since felt that the music I wrote was tailored to the special talents and very special personality of Miss Graham. The ballet took me about a year to complete. I remember thinking at the time: "How foolhardy it is to be spending all this time writing a thirty-five-minute score for a modern-dance company, knowing how short-lived most ballets *and* their scores are." But as sometimes happens, this musical composition took on a fate of its own, quite different from the expectation of its creator. The Suite I derived from the ballet, transcribed for symphony orchestra (the original instrumentation was for thirteen players), won me two well-known prizes and did much to bring my name before a wider public.

During the '40s I began to give talks in various parts of the country about contemporary music and contemporary American music. One of these engagements took me to the Chicago Musical College in the spring of 1946. I recall the visit partly because of a telephone conversation I had with the manager of the touring Cincinnati Symphony. He explained that the conductor, Eugene Goossens, had suddenly fallen ill, and since the Chicago program included the *Suite from Appalachian Spring* he wished to know whether I would be willing to substitute as conductor of my own composition. The proposal was most inviting, but the cold fact was that I had only very sporadically conducted any kind of orchestra, and besides, I didn't know *Appalachian Spring* from the conductor's standpoint; so I was reluctantly forced to reply, "Sorry, but I can't do it."

I date from that episode a determination to learn how to conduct at least my own works. After all, every composer secretly thinks he knows best how his own music should sound. Moreover, I had reason to believe I was something of a performer by nature. I knew that I liked audiences and they seemed to respond to me. But the question was, how do you practice conducting without an orchestra to practice on?

An unexpected solution presented itself in 1947 when I was asked to tour Latin America for the second time. Carlos Chávez invited me to conduct his Orquesta Sinfónica de México in my Third Symphony, and similar opportunities were given me in Montevideo and Buenos Aires. Here was a chance for working out problems away from home, in places where I might expect to enjoy all the advantages of a visiting fireman. Encouraged by the reaction of orchestras and audiences on that tour, I intermittently continued similar "practice" in subsequent years in far-off places like Rome, Trieste, Zurich, London, Paris, Munich—anywhere, as is evident, except the United States.

Finally I felt ready to face an American audience. This time when the telephone rang (in 1956), it was the manager of the Chicago Symphony who was calling, to invite me to conduct the orchestra at Ravinia Park, and I was able to say, delightedly, "Of course, yes!" The concert must have gone off well enough if I can judge by the number of times I was invited back in successive years.

An elderly and wise woman once gave me some excellent advice. "Aaron," she said, "It is very important, as you get older, to engage in an activity that you didn't engage in when you were young, so that you are not continually in competition with yourself as a young man." The conductor's baton was my answer to that problem. Conducting, as everyone knows, is a bug—once you are bitten it is the very devil to get rid of. What makes it worse is the fact that you get better at it all the time—more expert in rehearsing, more economical in gesture, more relaxed in actual performance. By now I have worked with more than fifty symphonic organizations in countries around the world. Sometimes I think my best audiences have been in England and Scotland, where repeated concert appearances and exposure on BBC television and radio have forged a bond that I know will be lasting from my side and I hope will be lasting from theirs.

One of my fondest memories of this late-starting career is associated with Charles Munch and the Boston Symphony Orchestra. Mr. Munch invited me along as guest conductor when the Boston Symphony made its first visit to Japan, the Philippines, and Australia in 1960. I led the orchestra in Osaka, Yawata, Okayama, Shizuoka, Koriyama, Nagaoka, and of course, Tokyo. On nights when Mr. Munch conducted I watched with fascination the impassive faces of Japanese audiences while a Tchaikovsky symphony was being played, trying to understand how so overtly emotional a composer could be of such absorbing interest to people with such a very different temperament as the Japanese. Nothing of their reaction could be read on their faces. The answer came with the burst of thunderous applause at the end of the symphony.

The tour ended glamorously, at least from my standpoint. My final appearance with the orchestra took place in Adelaide, Australia. At the request of the local concert sponsors I found myself conducting Tchaikovsky's Fifth Symphony for the first, and probably last, time. At a reception following the concert, the mayor of Adelaide, enormously impressed by the playing of the Boston Symphony, asked me to tell him frankly how his city might develop such an orchestra. Remembering what our English cousins tell Americans when they are asked how to develop a proper British lawn—"lots of rain and four hundred years"—I replied, "All you need is lots of money and seventy-five years!"

My association with the Boston Symphony, dating back to the playing of *Music for the Theatre* in 1925, took on a new dimension in 1940 with the establishment of the Berkshire Music Center. It was Serge Koussevitzky who conceived the idea of a music school for talented students as an integral part of the Orchestra's summer festival at Tanglewood. It was Koussevitzky who persuaded a somewhat reluctant board of trustees to embark on a venture that was to have important consequences for musical life in America. With the vision and enthusiasm that were characteristic of him, Koussevitzky propagandized the principle that the best students deserve the best teachers—in this instance, the leading players of the Orchestra. His own prime interest, as was natural, was the training of young conductors and of the student orchestra. But instruction in opera, choral singing, chamber music, and composition were also made an integral part of the school's activities, and there was a department for the musical amateur as well. He invited me to serve as permanent head of the Composition Department and asked Paul Hindemith to join us as guest teacher, which he did for the first two summers. For a period of twenty-five years (until my resignation in 1965), I was in contact with a cross section of America's most gifted musical youth. My summers were filled with forums, lectures, conferences, rehearsals, concerts, and composition classes. It was an exciting and a fruitful time.

It is not easy to sum up the total experience of those lively years. Three things stand out in my mind. The first is the inspired leadership of Serge Koussevitzky. Above all, it was his passionate devotion to the art of music and his deep concern for its well-being in America that communicated itself to all those who came into contact with him. A second exhilaration came from watching young talent unfold. Those of us who attended rehearsals of the student orchestra and then heard its performances under the youthful baton of fellow students such as Leonard Bernstein, Lukas Foss, Eleazar de Carvalho, and Lorin Maazel will not soon forget the special air of excitement that flashed through the Tanglewood Shed on such occasions. Finally, in more recent times, the Fromm Festival of Contemporary American Music, sponsored by the composers' friend, Paul Fromm, an enlightened music patron from Chicago, added zest and stimulus to our musical experiences by bringing to Tanglewood young creators of advanced tendencies and exceptional ability.

I plan, at some later time, to write the full story of those Tanglewood years. Not least among my pleasant memories are the weeks spent, after the close of the school term, working on my own compositions amidst the serenity of the Berkshire hills. Thus, *Quiet City* was composed in a barn studio down the road from Tanglewood after the opening season. Six years later I completed my Third Symphony in a tiny converted stable in Richmond, Massachusetts. Another barn in Richmond, with a beautiful view of open meadow and distant mountains, housed me during fourteen summers. It was there that I first consciously tried my hand at twelve-tone composition, in my Piano Quartet of 1950.

As it turned out, the Schoenberg method (not the aesthetic) continued to intrigue me in subsequent works, such as the *Piano Fantasy* (1957) and the *Connotations* for Orchestra (1962). I found twelve-tone writing to be especially liberating in two respects: it forces the tonal composer to unconventionalize his thinking with respect to chordal structure, and it tends to freshen his melodic and figurational imagination. The *Connotations* was my first twelve-tone orchestral work; it was composed on commission from the New York Philharmonic for the opening program in its new hall at Lincoln Center. The acidulous harmonies of my score, sharpened by the shrill acoustics of the new auditorium, upset a good many people, especially those who were expecting another *Appalachian Spring*. It brought to the fore once again a continuing discussion concerning the apparent dichotomy between my "serious" and my "popular" works. I can only say that those commentators who would like to split me down the middle into two opposing personalities will get no encouragement from me. I prefer to think that I write my music from a single vision; when the results differ it is because I take into account with each new piece the purpose for which it is intended and the nature of the musical materials with which I begin to work. Musical ideas engender pieces, and the ideas by their character dictate the nature of the composition to be written. It bothers me not at all to realize that my range as composer includes both accessible and problematical works. To have confined myself to a single compositional approach would have enhanced my reputation for consistency, no doubt, but would have afforded me less pleasure as a creator. The English critic Wilfrid Mellers puts it this way: "There is no fundamental disparity between the two styles; the same sensibility adapts the technique to the purpose in hand." I like to believe that what he says is true.

Editor's Introduction

He represents the ideal for artists functioning in a democratic society. Copland's roles are many and various—citizen, composer, performer, teacher, lecturer, committee member, spokesperson, and, lest we forget one of his favorites, conductor.

—William Schuman, introduction to a reprint
of *What to Listen for in Music* (1988)

No composer of classical music was as successful, in the ways that such artists can be successful, as Aaron Copland. Born 14 November 1900, he grew up in Brooklyn on 630 Washington Avenue in the section now called Prospect Heights. (Curiously, his near-contemporary, the composer Roger Sessions lived at 417 Washington Avenue when he was born, in the section now called Clinton Hill; on 1035 Washington Avenue in Flatbush, the composer John Corigliano, two generations younger, grew up, contrary to Copland's deprecating remarks about "my street").

Copland's family had a dry-goods store and lived above it. After attending the local Boys High School (now called Boys & Girls High), he decided to study music, soon going to Paris, where he took classes with Nadia Boulanger, who taught a succession of young Americans who later became prominent (Virgil Thomson, Elliott Carter, David Diamond, Arthur Berger, Philip Glass). Returning to America in 1922, Copland began an illustrious composing career that soon included commissions from major orchestras; two of the initial fellowships from the Guggenheim Foundation; Hollywood film scores; exclusive recording contracts with the most visible merchandizers of classical music; honorary degrees; friendships with celebrities and musical powerhouses; conducting gigs around the world; recognition in histories of American music; and requests to write articles, speeches, and books. He befriended younger composers, many of whom might have thought it advantageous to portray themselves as his antagonist, some of whom told me decades ago that they regarded "Aaron" as "my best friend among the older composers." No one before or since has been quite as successful in as many ways—not even George Gershwin or Leonard Bernstein. For nearly a century, Copland's name has been synonymous with American high classical music. He typically performed all of his roles gracefully, revealing few signs of struggle or temperament.

His music passed the final test of surviving his death, not only in life, once his Alzheimer's disease became debilitating, but afterward. His works continue to be heard. His *Fanfare for the Common Man* was for many years the opening sound of ABC's *Wide World of Sports*, and it is often heard in commercials; his *Lincoln Portrait*, incidentally commissioned by an orchestra conductor whose surname resembles mine, was heard during the Super Bowl of 2002, in the patriotic wake of 9/11 (2001), where the show's producers ingeniously portrayed the living American presidents reciting Lincoln's lines in succession. Whenever I see the 1940 film *Our Town*, I remained awed by how effective, if unobtrusive, Copland's music is. *The Red Pony*'s (1948) score is often heard by itself, apart from the film. As his more popular pieces have survived, so have his more difficult works. Several recordings of his Piano Variations (1930) are currently in print. According to James Kendrick, the lawyer who represents the foundation bearing Copland's name, annual royalties rank the composer's posthumous income among the top five American classical composers currently in copyright and among the top twenty in the world. Let it not be forgotten that Copland's success overcame two social disadvantages that might have undermined a less determined person—he was Jewish at a time when anti-Semitism persisted not only in Europe but America, and he was gay when homophobia was more persistent than anti-Semitism. And as a sometime Communist fellow traveler he survived the McCarthyism of the 1950s.

As a historian of the arts in America—all the arts—I've come to regard Copland as our single greatest art politician. The honorific measure is, simply, that in no other artistic field has any major American figure made so many moves successfully to advance not only himself but his colleagues. From his professional beginnings in the 1920s, Copland organized concerts; he initiated music festivals; he introduced people to each other; he got rewards from patrons whom he later advised; he made crucial connections for himself and others. Asked to conduct his own music, he also programmed the work of his colleagues. Even though he did not attend a liberal arts college but music conservatories, he wrote prose and yet more prose, not only publicly but privately, about music in general and other composers. Just as he composed music away from home, so he wrote as he traveled around the world not only letters, many letters, but essays. My sense is that essentially Copland wrote words not as a scrupulously disinterested, independent critic but as a cunning advocate of certain vanguard positions and many people, his words often reflecting ulterior motives. Just as many aspire to be major artists, perhaps just as many try to be important arts politicians; no one known to me succeeded at both rare roles as well as Copland.

Along the way he picked up a New York Critics' Circle Award in 1945 for *Appalachian Spring,* a Hollywood Oscar for the film score to *The Heiress* (1950), a Gold Medal for Music from the American Academy of Arts and Letters (1956), a Presidential Medal of Freedom (1964), a National Medal of Arts (1986, USA), a Commander's Cross of the Order of Merit in West Germany, in addition to honorary degrees from Princeton (1956), Brandeis (1957), Wesleyan (1958), Harvard (1961), Rutgers (1967), Ohio State (1970), New York University (1970), and Columbia (1970). The latter collection of academic diplomas was no modest achievement for an American who never even went to college.

As a writer, Copland knew he had to do whatever was necessary for the survival of American classical music in mid-twentieth century. After all, he had an investment to protect. William Schuman, himself a composer who was also a shrewd arts politician, noted, "Before Copland no major composer had ever attempted to explain the craft of music composition to the layperson." True, but Copland's situation was without precedent as the first prominent classical composer in a country where the only prominent classical musicians before him were all performers. Explaining classical music to those barely initiated was only one of several subsidiary tasks he thought necessary for the survival of classical music in America in the mid-twentieth century. In 1956, Copland declared, "Someone once astonished me during a discussion period, after I had given a lecture, by asking me what I thought I had accomplished through the years, with my music. To that question my proudest answer would be, 'I helped to make art possible in America.' Come to think of it, that is what all artists in America do." The modesty of his last line notwithstanding, Copland did "what all artists in America do" better than anyone else, to a degree that is hard to appreciate now. To make a crucial distinction, he had influence rather than power, which comes from running an institution that dispenses favors (e.g., performances) and/or funds. Only at the summertime Berkshire Music Center in Tanglewood, where he directed the composition department for over twenty years, did he have a bully pulpit.

Copland wrote a book-length introduction to classical music, with a title at once inviting and condescending (with the assumption that the reader might know next to nothing), *What to Listen for in Music* (1939), that was translated into various languages, making his name yet more familiar around the world. More than six decades later, this book remains in print in English, having gone through innumerable editions with several publishers. One virtue is its shrewd organization, taking the reader through increasingly difficult issues.

Perhaps recognizing its success would be hard to top, Copland's later books are less introductory. *Our New Music* (1941) is a populist survey aimed more at professional musicians. Much of this writing appeared again nearly three decades later in a shorter, revised book titled *The New Music 1900–1960* (1968). *Music and Imagination* (1952) publishes his Norton lectures delivered at Harvard, while *Copland on Music* (1959) is an incomplete collection of his fugitive writings. Some essays there also appear here. Working closely with the independent musicologist Vivian Perlis, who functioned as an acknowledged ghost-helper, Copland published in 1984 and 1989 a two-volume quasi-autobiography. He died on December 2, 1990, less than three weeks after his ninetieth birthday.

Given his sense of the different sophistication of his various audiences, it is scarcely surprising that the corpus of Copland's writings resembles his music. Whereas some texts are meant to address the broadest possible audience, others are strictly for his colleagues. Whereas some are very short, others are long. Indicatively, with music as well as words, sometimes Copland could write platitudes; other times, intricate detail. One quality characteristic of both his writing and his music is an amiable fluency. He wrote because he read and thus knew from his own experience the possible influence of good writing. For example, among the major authors he read André Gide and Oscar Wilde for guidance with homosexuality. Perhaps the single greatest influence upon his compositions from the early 1940s was *Let Us Now Praise Famous Men* (1941), a book-length collaboration between the writer James Agee and the photographer Walker Evans. Great literature was not lost on Copland.

As a part-time music critic, he wrote about his predecessors as well as his contemporaries, usually with generosity while noticing faults or disagreements. Rarely does any sense of jealousy or competition creep into his remarks about others. One charm of his references written on behalf of composers to the Guggenheim Foundation, with which he had a special relationship as one of its first beneficiaries, is his precise recollections of when he last heard a certain composer's work. Copland kept track of many musicians, Lord knows how, since much of his career happened before the development of the long-playing record. He remembered, because he cared. Nowadays the only arts politicians functioning in the Copland mold customarily work on behalf not of all American artists but a particular group—women, African Americans, tonal composers, etc.

It is scarcely surprising that Copland could write with cunning about his own works and career. In addition to reprinting essays from his earlier books, this *Reader* also includes brief remarks about his own pieces that were used on record jackets and concert programs, often within the frame of someone else's writing. When one set of remarks about his work differ significantly from another, we reprint both versions. For one of his most enduring compositions, *Appalachian Spring* (1945), we reprint the correspondence leading to its creation. Only in this *Reader* are these notes on his own works gathered in one place.

One theme of the principal biography, Howard Pollack's *Aaron Copland* (1999), is that he felt financially insecure until the 1970s, in his own seventies. That development perhaps accounts for why he barely wrote prose after 1970. This *Reader* concludes with a 1967 interview, even though he lived for another twenty-three years. The principal affliction of his later years was Alzheimer's disease, which was first observed in the mid-1970s and was especially tragic in a man renowned for his powerful memory. Afterward Copland would appear in public venues, smiling and avuncular, as public figures aware of their failing memory do, but more substantial professional duties were problematic for him. One classic anecdote has him continuing to conduct an orchestra with his own piece a few seconds after it ended. He made his last appearance as a conductor in 1983, a year after City University of New York named its School of Music at Queens College after him. (This appears to be a unique distinction for an American composer. Only an art colony, by contrast, was named after Edward MacDowell.)

Though Copland lived an exurban life, partially to protect against his own personal popularity, he was customarily present in Manhattan for important musical occasions—not only performances of his own work, but to greet European composers. (I recall Milton Babbitt telling me in the 1960s that Copland advised him to entertain visiting Europeans if you planned to visit Europe yourself.) Copland had secretaries to handle his voluminous correspondence. As a full-time composer who incidentally wrote prose, Copland knew what was necessary in twentieth-century America. There was no one like him before and has been no one like him since.

I
Musical Experience

This section opens with three chapters from Copland's first book, *What to Listen for in Music* (1939), "How We Listen," "Musical Structure," and "Tone Color," which remain classic introductions to each of those sections. The last essay in this section, "Music and the Human Spirit," from 1955, offers another view of how music affects our culture.

How We Listen (1939)

We all listen to music according to our separate capacities. But, for the sake of analysis, the whole listening process may become clearer if we break it up into its component parts, so to speak. In a certain sense we all listen to music on three separate planes. For lack of a better terminology, one might name these: (1) the sensuous plane, (2) the expressive plane, (3) the sheerly musical plane. The only advantage to be gained from mechanically splitting up the listening process into these hypothetical planes is the clearer view to be had of the way in which we listen.

The simplest way of listening to music is to listen for the sheer pleasure of the musical sound itself. That is the sensuous plane. It is the plane on which we hear music without thinking, without considering it in any way. One turns on the radio while doing something else and absent-mindedly bathes in the sound. A kind of brainless but attractive state of mind is engendered by the mere sound appeal of the music.

You may be sitting in a room reading this book. Imagine one note struck on the piano. Immediately that one note is enough to change the atmosphere of the room—proving that the sound element in music is a powerful and mysterious agent, which it would be foolish to deride or belittle.

The surprising thing is that many people who consider themselves qualified music lovers abuse that plane in listening. They go to concerts in order to lose themselves. They use music as a consolation or an escape. They enter an ideal world where one doesn't have to think of the realities of everyday life. Of course they aren't thinking about the music either. Music allows them to leave it, and they go off to a place to dream, dreaming because of and apropos of the music yet never quite listening to it.

Yes, the sound appeal of music is a potent and primitive force, but you must not allow it to usurp a disproportionate share of your interest. The

3

sensuous plane is an important one in music, a very important one, but it does not constitute the whole story.

There is no need to digress further on the sensuous plane. Its appeal to every normal human being is self-evident. There is, however, such a thing as becoming more sensitive to the different kinds of sound stuff as used by various composers. For all composers do not use that sound stuff in the same way. Don't get the idea that the value of music is commensurate with its sensuous appeal or that the loveliest sounding music is made by the greatest composer. If that were so, Ravel would be a greater creator than Beethoven. The point is that the sound element varies with each composer, that his usage of sound forms an integral part of his style and must be taken into account when listening. The reader can see, therefore, that a more conscious approach is valuable even on this primary plane of music listening.

The second plane on which music exists is what I have called the expressive one. Here, immediately, we tread on controversial ground. Composers have a way of shying away from any discussion of music's expressive side. Did not Stravinsky himself proclaim that his music was an "object," a "thing," with a life of its own, and with no other meaning than its own purely musical existence? This intransigent attitude of Stravinsky's may be due to the fact that so many people have tried to read different meanings into so many pieces. Heaven knows it is difficult enough to say precisely what it is that a piece of music means, to say it definitely, to say it finally so that everyone is satisfied with your explanation. But that should not lead one to the other extreme of denying to music the right to be "expressive."

My own belief is that all music has an expressive power, some more and some less, but that all music has a certain meaning behind the notes and that the meaning behind the notes constitutes, after all, what the piece is saying, what the piece is about. This whole problem can be stated quite simply by asking, "Is there a meaning to music?" My answer to that would be, "Yes." And "Can you state in so many words what the meaning is?" My answer to that would be, "No." Therein lies the difficulty.

Simple-minded souls will never be satisfied with the answer to the second of these questions. They always want music to have a meaning, and the more concrete it is the better they like it. The more the music reminds them of a train, a storm, a funeral, or any other familiar conception the more expressive it appears to be to them. This popular idea of music's meaning—stimulated and abetted by the usual run of musical commentator—should be discouraged wherever and whenever it is met. One timid lady once confessed to me that she suspected something seriously lacking in her appreciation of music because of her inability to connect it with anything definite. That is getting the whole thing backward, of course.

Still, the question remains, How close should the intelligent music lover wish to come to pinning a definite meaning to any particular work? No closer than general concept, I should say. Music expresses, at different moments, serenity or exuberance, regret or triumph, fury or delight. It expresses each of these moods, and many others, in a numberless variety of subtle shadings and differences. It may even express a state of meaning for which there exists no adequate word in any language. In that case, musicians often like to say that it has only a purely musical meaning. They sometimes go farther and say that *all* music has only a purely musical meaning. What they really mean is that no appropriate word can be found to express the music's meaning and that, even if it could, they do not feel the need of finding it.

But whatever the professional musician may hold, most musical novices still search for specific words with which to pin down their musical reactions. That is why they always find Tschaikovsky easier to "understand" than Beethoven. In the first place, it is easier to pin a meaning-word on a Tschaikovsky piece than on a Beethoven one. Much easier. Moreover, with the Russian composer, every time you come back to a piece of his it almost always says the same thing to you, whereas with Beethoven it is often quite difficult to put your finger right on what he is saying. And any musician will tell you that that is why Beethoven is the greater composer. Because music which always says the same thing to you will necessarily soon become dull music, but music whose meaning is slightly different with each hearing has a greater chance of remaining alive.

Listen, if you can, to the forty-eight fugue themes of Bach's *Well-Tempered Clavichord*. Listen to each theme, one after another. You will soon realize that each theme mirrors a different world of feeling. You will also soon realize that the more beautiful a theme seems to you the harder it is to find any word that will describe it to your complete satisfaction. Yes, you will certainly know whether it is a gay theme or a sad one. You will be able, in other words, in your own mind, to draw a frame of emotional feeling around your theme. Now study the sad one a little closer. Try to pin down the exact quality of its sadness. Is it pessimistically sad or resignedly sad; is it fatefully sad or smilingly sad?

Let us suppose that you are fortunate and can describe to your own satisfaction in so many words the exact meaning of your chosen theme. There is still no guarantee that anyone else will be satisfied. Nor need they be. The important thing is that each one feel for himself the specific expressive quality of a theme or, similarly, an entire piece of music. And if it is a great work of art, don't expect it to mean exactly the same thing to you each time you return to it.

Themes or pieces need not express only one emotion, of course. Take such a theme as the first main one of the Ninth Symphony, for example. It is clearly made up of different elements. It does not say only one thing. Yet anyone hearing it immediately gets a feeling of strength, a feeling of power. It isn't a power that comes simply because the theme is played loudly. It is a power inherent in the theme itself. The extraordinary strength and vigor of the theme results in the listener's receiving an impression that a forceful statement has been made. But one should never try to boil it down to "the fateful hammer of life," etc. That is where the trouble begins. The musician, in his exasperation, says it means nothing but the notes themselves, whereas the nonprofessional is only too anxious to hang on to any explanation that gives him the illusion of getting closer to the music's meaning.

Now, perhaps, the reader will know better what I mean when I say that music does have an expressive meaning but that we cannot say in so many words what that meaning is.

The third plane on which music exists is the sheerly musical plane. Besides the pleasurable sound of music and the expressive feeling that it gives off, music does exist in terms of the notes themselves and of their manipulation. Most listeners are not sufficiently conscious of this third plane. It will be largely the business of this book to make them more aware of music on this plane.

Professional musicians, on the other hand, are, if anything, too conscious of the mere notes themselves. They often fall into the error of becoming so engrossed with their arpeggios and staccatos that they forget the deeper aspects of the music they are performing. But from the layman's standpoint, it is not so much a matter of getting over bad habits on the sheerly musical plane as of increasing one's awareness what is going on, in so far as the notes are concerned.

When the man in the street listens to the "notes themselves" with any degree of concentration, he is most likely to make some mention of the melody. Either he hears a pretty melody or he does not, and he generally lets it go at that. Rhythm is likely to gain his attention next, particularly if it seems exciting. But harmony and tone color are generally taken for granted, if they are thought of consciously at all. As for music's having a definite form of some kind, that idea seems never to have occurred to him.

It is very important for all of us to become more alive to music on its sheerly musical plane. After all, an actual musical material is being used. The intelligent listener must be prepared to increase his awareness of the musical material and what happens to it. He must hear the melodies, the rhythms, the harmonies, the tone colors in a more conscious fashion. But above all he must, in order to follow the line of the composer's thought, know something of the principles of musical form. Listening to all of these elements is listening on the sheerly musical plane.

Let me repeat that I have split up mechanically the three separate planes on which we listen merely for the sake of greater clarity. Actually, we never listen on one or the other of these planes. What we do is to correlate them—listening in all three ways at the same time. It takes no mental effort, for we do it instinctively.

Perhaps an analogy with what happens to us when we visit the theater will make this instinctive correlation clearer. In the theater, you are aware of the actors and actresses, costumes and sets, sounds and movements. All these give one the sense that the theater is a pleasant place to be in. They constitute the sensuous plane in our theatrical reactions.

The expressive plane in the theater would be derived from the feeling that you get from what is happening on the stage. You are moved to pity, excitement, or gayety. It is this general feeling, generated aside from the particular words being spoken, a certain emotional something which exists on the stage, that is analogous to the expressive quality in music.

The plot and plot development is equivalent to our sheerly musical plane. The playwright creates and develops a character in just the same way that a composer creates and develops a theme. According to the degree of your awareness of the way in which the artist in either field handles his material will you become a more intelligent listener.

It is easy enough to see that the theatergoer never is conscious of any of these elements separately. He is aware of them all at the same time. The same is true of music listening. We simultaneously and without thinking listen on all three planes.

In a sense, the ideal listener is both inside and outside the music at the same moment, judging it and enjoying it, wishing it would go one way and watching it go another—almost like the composer at the moment he composes it; because in order to write his music, the composer must also be inside and outside his music, carried away by it and yet coldly critical of it. A subjective and objective attitude is implied in both creating and listening to music.

What the reader should strive for, then, is a more *active* kind of listening. Whether you listen to Mozart or Duke Ellington, you can deepen your understanding of music only by being a more conscious and aware listener—not someone who is just listening, but someone who is listening *for* something.

Musical Structure (1939)

Almost anyone can more readily distinguish melodies and rhythms, or even harmonies, than the structural background of a lengthy piece of music. That is why our main emphasis, from here on, must be put upon structure in music; for the reader should realize that one of the principal things to listen for, when listening more consciously, is the planned design that binds an entire composition together.

Structure in music is no different from structure in any other art; it is simply the coherent organization of the artist's material. But the material in music is of a fluid and rather abstract character; therefore the composer's structural task is doubly difficult because of the very nature of music itself.

The general tendency, in explaining form in music, has been to oversimplify. The usual method is to seize upon certain well-known formal molds and demonstrate how composers write works within these molds, to a greater or lesser extent. Close examination of most masterworks, however, will show that they seldom fit so neatly as they are supposed to into the exteriorized forms of the textbooks. The conclusion is inescapable that it is insufficient to assume that structure in music is simply a matter of choosing a formal mold and then filling it with inspired tones. Rightly understood, form can only be the gradual growth of a living organism from whatever premise the composer starts. It follows, then, that "the form of every genuine piece of music is unique." It is musical content that determines form.

Nevertheless, composers are not by any means entirely independent of outer formal molds. It therefore becomes necessary for the listener to understand this relationship between the given, or chosen, form and the composer's independence of that form. Two things, then, are involved: the dependence and independence of the composer in relation to historical musical forms. In the first place, the reader may ask: "What are these forms, and why should the composer bother about them in any way?"

The answer to the first part of the question is easy: The sonata-allegro, the variation, the passacaglia, the fugue are the names of some of the best known forms. Each one of these formal molds was only slowly evolved through the combined experience of generations of composers working in many different lands. It would seem foolish for present-day composers to discard all that experience and to begin to work from scratch with each new composition. It is only natural, particularly since the organization of musical material is by its very nature so difficult, that composers tend to lean on these well-tried forms each time that they begin to write. In the back of their minds, before beginning to compose, are all these used and known musical molds which act as a support and, sometimes, a stimulus for their imaginations.

In the same way, a playwright working today, despite the variety of story material at his disposal, generally fits his comedy into the form of a three-act play. That has become the custom—not the five-act play. Or he may prefer the form of the play in a number of short scenes, which has found favor recently; or the long one-acter without intermission. But whatever he chooses, we presume that he begins from a generalized play form. In the same way, the composer each time begins from a generalized and well-known musical form.

Busoni felt that this was a weakness. He wrote a pamphlet to prove that the future of music demanded the freeing of composers from their overdependence on predetermined forms. Nevertheless, composers continue to depend on them as in the past, and the emergence of a new formal mold is just as rare an occurrence as ever.

But whatever outer mold is chosen, there are certain basic structural principles which must be fulfilled. In other words, no matter what your architectural scheme may be, it must always be psychologically justified by the nature of the material itself. It is that fact which forces the composer out of the formal, given mold.

For example, let us take the case of a composer who is working on a form that generally presupposes a coda, or closing section, at the end of his composition. One day, while working with his material, he happens on a section that he knows was destined to be that coda. It happens that this particular coda is especially quiet and reminiscent in mood. Just before it, however, a long climax must be built. Now he sets about composing his climax. But by the time he has that long climactic section finished, he may discover that it renders the quiet close superfluous. In such a case, the formal mold will be overthrown, because of the exigencies of the evolving material. Similarly Beethoven, in the first movement of his Seventh Symphony, despite what all the textbooks say about "contrasting themes" of the first-movement form, does not have contrasting themes—not in the usual sense, at any rate, owing to specific character of the thematic material with which he began.

Keep two things in mind, then. Remember the general outlines of the formal mold, and remember that content of the composer's thought forces him to that formal mold in a particular and personal way—in a way that belongs only to that particular piece that he is writing. That applies chiefly to art music. Simple folk songs are often of an exactly similar structure within their small frame. But no two symphonies were ever exactly alike.

The prime consideration in all form is the creation of a sense of the *long line* which was mentioned in an earlier chapter. That long line must give us a sense of direction, and we must be made to feel that that direction is the inevitable one. Whatever the means employed, the net result must produce in the listener a satisfying feeling of coherence born out of the psychological necessity of the musical ideas with which the composer began.

Structural Distinctions

There are two ways in which structure in music may be considered: (1) form in relation to a piece as a whole and (2) form in relation to the separate, shorter parts of a piece. The larger formal distinctions would have to do with entire movements of a symphony, a sonata or a suite. The smaller formal units would together make up one entire movement.

These formal distinctions may be clearer to the layman if an analogy is made with the construction of a novel. A full-length novel might be divided into four books—I, II, III, and IV. That would be analogous to the four movements of a suite or symphony. Book I might be, in turn, divided into five chapters. Similarly, movement I would be made up of five sections. One chapter would contain so many paragraphs. In music, each section would also be subdivided into lesser sections (unfortunately, no special term denotes these smaller units). Paragraphs are composed of sentences. In music, the sentence would be analogous to the musical idea. And, of course, the word is analogous to single musical tone. Needless to say, this comparison is meant to be taken only in a general sense.

In the outlining of a single movement, it has become the custom to represent the larger sections by letters *A, B, C,* etc. Smaller divisions are usually represented by *a, b, c,* etc.

Structural Principles

The all-important principle is used in music to create the feeling of formal balance. It is so fundamental to the art that it is likely to be used in one way or another as long as music is written. That principle is the simple one of repetition. The largest part of music bases itself structurally on a broad interpretation of that principle. It seems more justified to use repetition in music than in any of the other arts, probably because of its rather amorphous nature. The only other formal principle that need be mentioned is the opposite of repetition—that is, nonrepetition.

Speaking generally, music that is based on repetition for its spinal structure may be divided into five different categories. The first one is exact repetition; the second, sectional, or symmetrical, repetition; the third, repetition by variation; the fourth, repetition by fugal treatment; the fifth, repetition through development. Each one of these categories (with the exception of the first) will receive separate treatment in single chapters later. Each category will be found to have different type forms which come under the heading of a specific kind of repetition. Exact repetition (the first category) is too simple to need any special demonstration. The other categories are split up according to the following type forms:

I. Sectional or symmetrical repetition	*a.*	Two-part (binary) form
	b.	Three-part (ternary) form
	c.	Rondo
	d.	Free sectional arrangement
II. Repetition by variation	*a.*	Basso ostinato
	b.	Passacaglia
	c.	Chaconne
	d.	Theme and variations
III. Repetition by fugal treatment	*a.*	Fugue
	b.	Concerto grosso
	c.	Chorale prelude
	d.	Motets and madrigals
IV. Repetition by development	*a.*	Sonata (first-movement form)

The only other basic formal categories are those based on nonrepetition, and the so-called "free" forms.

Before launching into discussion of these large type forms of repetition, it would be wise to examine the principle of repetition applied on a smaller scale. This is easily done because these repetitional principles apply both to the large sections which comprise an entire movement and also to the small units within each section. Musical form therefore, resembles a series of wheels within wheels, in which the formation of the smallest wheel is remarkably similar to that of the largest one. A folk song is often constructed on lines similar to one of these smaller units and whenever possible will be used to illustrate the simplest repetition principles.

The most elementary of all is that of exact repetition which may be represented by *a-a-a-a*, etc. Such simple repetitions are to be found in many songs, where the same music is repeated for consecutive stanzas. The first form of variation occurs when, in similar songs, minor alterations are made in the repetition to allow for a closer setting of the text. This kind of repetition may be represented as *a-a'-a''-a'''*, etc.

The next form of repetition is fundamental not only to many folk songs but also to art music in its smallest and largest sections. It is repetition after a digression. This repetition may be exact, in which case it is represented by *a-b-a*; or it may be varied and therefore by *a-b-a'*. Very often in music the first *a* is immediately repeated. There would appear to be some fundamental need to impress a first phrase or section on the listener's mind before the digression comes. Most theorists agree, however, that the essential *a-b-a* form is unchanged by the repetition of the first *a*. (In music, it is possible to indicate the repetition by the sign : ‖ , making the formula ‖:*a*:‖-*b*-*a*.) Here is this species of repetition in two folk songs, *Au clair de la lune* and *Ach! du lieber Augustin*:

The very same formula may be found in art music. The first of Schumann's piano pieces in *Scenes from Childhood* is a good example of a short piece made up of *a-b-a*, with the first *a* repeated. Here is the melodic without the accompaniment:

The same formula, with slight changes, may be found as part of a longer piece in the first page of the scherzo from Beethoven's Piano Sonata, Op. 27, No. 2, even the first *a* when immediately repeated, is slightly changed by a certain dislocation in the rhythm; and the final repetition is different by a stronger cadential feeling at the end. (A "cadence" in music is a closing phrase.) Here is the melodic outline:

It would be easy to multiply examples of the *a-b-a* formula, with tiny variations, but my purpose is not to be all-inclusive. The point to remember about these smaller units is that every time a theme is exposed, there is strong likelihood that it will be repeated immediately; and that once repeated, a digression is in order; and that after the digression, a return to the first theme, either exact or varied, is to be expected. How this same *a-b-a* formula applies to a piece as a whole, including the sonata form, will be demonstrated in later chapters.

The only other basic formal principle, that of nonrepetition, may be represented by the formula *a-b-c-d*, etc. It may be illustrated in a small way by the following English folk song, *The Seeds of Love*, all four phrases of which are different:

This same principle may be found in many of the preludes composed by Bach and other of his contemporaries. A short example is the B flat major Prelude from Book I of the *Well-Tempered Clavichord*. Unity is achieved by adopting a specific pattern, writing freely within that pattern, but avoiding any repetition of notes or phrases. We shall be returning to it in the chapter on Free Forms.

To obtain a similar unity in a piece lasting twenty minutes without using any form of thematic repetition is no easy achievement. That probably accounts for the fact that the principle of nonrepetition is applied for the most part to short compositions. The listener will find it used much less frequently than any of the repetition forms, which now must be considered in detail.

Tone Color (1939)

After rhythm, melody, and harmony comes timbre, or tone color. Just as it is impossible to hear speech without hearing some specific timbre, so music can exist only in terms of some specific color in tone. Timbre in music is analogous to color in painting. It is a fascinating element, not only because of vast resources already explored but also because of illimitable future possibilities.

Tone color in music is that quality of sound produced by a particular medium of musical tone production. That is a formal definition of something which is perfectly familiar to everyone. Just as most mortals know the difference between white and green, so the recognition of differences in tone color is an innate sense with which most of us are born. It is difficult to imagine a person so "tone-blind" that he cannot tell a bass voice from a soprano or, to put it instrumentally, a tuba from a cello. It is not a question of knowing the names of the voices or instruments but simply of recognizing the difference in their tone quality, if both were heard from behind a screen.

Instinctively, therefore, everyone has a good start toward getting a fuller understanding of the various aspects of tone color. Don't allow this natural appreciation to limit your taste for certain favorite tone colors to the exclusion of all others. I am thinking of the man who adores the sound of a violin but feels an extreme distaste for any other instrument. The experienced listener should wish rather to broaden his appreciation to include every known species of tone color. Moreover, although I have said that every person can make broad distinctions in tone colors, there are also subtle differences that only experience in listening can clear up. Even a music student, in the beginning, has difficulty in distinguishing the tone of a clarinet from that of its blood brother the bass clarinet.

The intelligent listener should have two main objectives in relation to tone color: (a) to sharpen his awareness of different instruments and their separational characteristics and (b) to gain a better appreciation of the composer's expressive purpose in using any instrument or combination of instruments.

Before exploring the separate instruments for their individual tone qualities, the attitude of the composer toward his instrumental possibilities should be more fully explained. After all, not every musical theme is born fully swaddled in a tonal dress. Very often the composer finds himself with a theme that can be equally well played on the violin, flute, clarinet, trumpet, or half a dozen other instruments. What, then makes him decide to choose one rather than another. Only one thing: he chooses the instrument with the tone color that best expresses the meaning behind his idea. In other words, his choice is determined by the expressive value of any specific instrument. That is true in the case not only of single instruments but also of combinations of instruments. The composer who chooses a bassoon rather than an oboe in certain instances may also have to decide whether his musical idea best belongs in a string ensemble or a full orchestra. And the thing that makes him decide in every case will be the expressive meaning that he wishes to convey.

At times, of course, a composer conceives a theme and its tonal investiture instantaneously. There are outstanding examples of that in music. One that is often quoted is the flute solo at the beginning of *L'après midi d'un faune* (*Afternoon of a Faun*). That same theme, played by any other instrument than the flute, would induce a very different emotional feeling. It is impossible to imagine Debussy's conceiving the theme first and then later deciding to orchestrate it for a flute. The two must have been conceived simultaneously. But that does not settle the matter.

For even in the case of themes that come to the composer in their full orchestral panoply, later musical departments in the course of a particular piece may bring on the need for varied orchestral treatments of the same theme. In such a case, the composer is like a playwright deciding on a dress for an actress in a particular scene. The stage shows us an actress seated on bench in a park. The playwright may wish to have her clothed in such a way that the spectator knows as soon as the curtain rises what mood she is in. It is not just a pretty dress; it's an especially designed dress to give you a particular feeling about this particular character in this particular scene. The same holds true for the composer who "dresses" a musical theme. The entire gamut of tonal color at his disposal is so rich that nothing but a clear conception of the emotional feeling that he wishes to convey can make him decide as between one instrument and another or one group of instruments and another.

The idea of the inevitable connection of a specific color for a specific music is a comparatively modern one. It seems likely that composers before Handel's time did not have a strong feeling for instrumental color. At any rate, most of them did not even trouble to write down explicitly what instrument was desired for a particular part. Apparently it was a matter of indifference to them whether a four-part score was executed by four woodwind instruments or four strings. Nowadays composers insist on certain instruments for certain ideas, and they have come to write for them in a way so characteristic that a violin part may be unplayable on an oboe even when they are confined to the same register.

Each of the separate tone colors that the composer is enabled to use only gradually found its way into music. Three steps were generally involved. First, the instrument had to be invented. Since instruments, like any other invention, usually begin in some primitive form, the second step was the perfecting of the instrument. Thirdly, players had gradually to achieve technical mastery of the new instrument. That is the story of the piano, the violin, and most other instruments.

Of course, every instrument, no matter how perfected, has its limitations. There are limitations of range, of dynamics, of execution. Each instrument can play so low and no lower, so high and no higher. A composer may wish at times that the oboe could play just half a tone lower than it does. But there is no help for it; these limits are prescribed. So are dynamic limitations. A trumpet, though it plays loudly by comparison with a violin, cannot play more loudly than it can. Composers are sometimes painfully aware of that fact, but there is no getting around it.

Difficulties of execution must also be continually borne in mind by the composer. A melodic idea that seems predestined to be sung by a clarinet will be found to make use of a particular group of notes that present insuperable difficulties to the clarinetist because of certain constructional peculiarities of his instrument. These same notes may be quite easy to perform on oboe or bassoon, but it so happens that on clarinet they are very difficult. So composers are not completely free agents in making their choice of tone colors.

Nevertheless they are in a much better position than were their predecessors. Just because instruments are machines, subject to improvement like any other machine, any contemporary composer enjoys advantages that Beethoven did not have as far as mere tone color is concerned. The present-day composer has new and improved materials to work with, besides which he benefits from the experience of his forebears. This is especially true of his use of the orchestra. No wonder that critics who pride themselves on their severity toward contemporary music willingly allow the brilliance and cleverness of the modern composer's handling of the orchestra.

It is important nowadays for a composer to have a feeling for the essential nature of each instrument—how it may best be used to exploit its most personal characteristics. I should like to take, for example, a perfectly familiar instrument—the piano—and show what I mean by using an instrument characteristically. A treatise on orchestration would do the same for each of the instruments.

The piano is a handy instrument to have around—"maid of all work," someone once called it. It can substitute for a large variety of different instruments including the orchestra itself. But it is also a being in its own right—it is also a piano—and as such it has properties and characteristics that belong to itself alone. The composer who exploits the piano for its essential nature will be using it to best advantage. Let us see what that essential nature is.

A piano may be used in one of two ways: either as a vibrating or as a nonvibrating instrument. That is true because of its construction, which consists of series of strings stretched across a steel frame, with a damper on each string. This damper is vital to the nature of the instrument. It is controlled by the piano pedal. When the pedal is untouched, piano tone lasts only as long as the note is pressed by the pianist's finger. But if the damper is removed (by pushing the pedal down), the tone is sustained. In either case, piano tone declines in intensity from the instant it is struck. The pedal minimizes this weakness somewhat and therefore holds the key to good piano writing.

Although the piano was invented around 1711 by Cristofori, it was not until the middle nineteenth century that composers understood how to take advantage of the pedal in a truly characteristic way. Chopin, Schumann, and Liszt were masters of piano writing because they took fully into account its peculiarities as a vibrating instrument. Debussy and Ravel in France, Scriabin in Russia carried on the tradition of Chopin and Liszt, as far as their piano writing is concerned. All of them took full cognizance of the fact that the piano is, on one side of its nature, a collection of sympathetically vibrating strings, producing a sensuous and velvety or brilliant and brittle conglomeration of tones, which are capable of immediate extinction through release of the damper pedal.

More recent composers have exploited the other side of the piano's essential nature—the nonvibrating tone.

The nonvibrating piano is the piano in which little or no use is made of the pedal. Played thus, a hard, dry piano tone is produced which has its own particular virtue. The feeling of the modern composer for harsh, percussive tonal effects found valuable outlet in this new use of the piano, turning it into a kind of large xylophone. Excellent examples of this may be found in the piano works of such moderns as Béla Bartók, Carlos Chávez, or Arthur Honegger. This last composer has an attractive last movement in his Concertino for piano and orchestra which fairly crackles with a dry, brittle piano sonority.

The point I have been making in relation to the piano is valid for every other instrument also. There is definitely a characteristic way of writing for each one of them. The tonal colors that an instrument can produce that are uniquely its own are the ones sought after by the composer.

Single Tone Colors

Now we are in a better position to examine single colors, such as are found in the usual symphony orchestra. Orchestral instruments are generally taken as a norm, for it is those that we are most apt to find composer's score. Later we shall want to know how these single tone colors are mixed to form timbres of various instrumental combinations.

Orchestral instruments are divided into four principal types, or sections. The first section, of course, is of the strings; the second, of the woodwind; the third is the brass; and the fourth is the percussion. Each of these sections is made up of a related group of instruments of similar type. Every composer, when working, keeps these four divisions very much to the front of his mind.

The string section, which is the most used of all, is itself made up of four different types of stringed instruments. These are the violin, the viola, the violon-cello (or cello, for short), and the double bass.

The instrument with which you are most familiar of course, the violin. In orchestral writing, violins are divided into two sections—so-called first and second violins—but only one type of instrument is involved. There is certainly no need to describe the lyric, singing quality of the violin; it is much too familiar to all of us. But you may be less familiar with certain special effects which help to give the instrument a great variety of tone color.

Most important of these is the pizzicato, in which the string is plucked by the finger instead of being played with the bow, thus producing a somewhat guitar-like effect. That, too, is familiar enough to most of us. Less well-known is the effect of harmonics, as they are called. These are produced by not pressing the finger on the string in the usual way but lightly touching it instead, thereby creating a flute-like tone of special charm. Double stopping means playing on two or more strings simultaneously, so that a chordal effect is obtained. Finally, there is the veiled and sensitive tone obtainable through use of the mute, a small extra contraption placed on the bridge of the instrument, immediately deadening the sonority.

All of these varied effects are obtainable not only on the violin but also on all the other stringed instruments.

The viola is an instrument that is often confused with the violin, because it not only resembles it in outward appearance but is held and played in the same fashion. Closer examination would show that it is a slightly larger and weightier instrument, producing a heavier and graver tone. It cannot sing notes as high as the violin's but compensates for that by being able to sing lower. It plays a contralto role to the violin's soprano. If it lacks the light lyric quality of the higher instrument, it possesses, on the other hand, a gravely expressive sonority—seemingly full of emotion.

The cello is a more easily recognized instrument played, as it is, by a seated performer holding it firmly propped between both knees. It plays baritone and bass to the viola's contralto. Its range is one full octave lower than the viola, but it pays for this by not being able to go so high. The quality of cello tone is well known. Composers, however, are conscious of three different registers. In its upper register, the cello can be a very poignant and touching instrument. At the other extreme of its range, the sonority is one of sober profundity. The middle register, most frequently used, produces the more familiar cello tone—a serious, smooth, baritone-like quality of sound, almost always expressive of some degree of feeling.

The last of the string family, the double bass, is the largest of all and must be played standing. Because it is seen in jazz bands, it has recently taken on an importance more nearly commensurate with its size. When was first used in orchestras, it played a very menial role, doing little more than what the cello did (doubling the bass, as it is called) an octave lower. This it does very well. Later composers gave it a part of its own to play, down in the depths of the orchestra. It almost never functions as a solo instrument; and if you have ever heard a double bass try to sing a melody, you will understand why. The proper function of the double bass is to supply a firm foundation for the entire structure above it.

The second section of orchestral instruments comprises those that come under the heading of woodwinds. Once again they are of four different types, though in this case each type has a closely related instrument which belongs in its immediate group, a kind of first cousin to the main type. The four principal woodwinds are the flute, oboe, clarinet, and bassoon. The flute's "first cousins" are the piccolo and the flute in G; the oboe is related to the English horn, which, as one orchestration book has it, is neither English nor a horn but called that nevertheless. The clarinet is related to the clarinet piccolo and bass clarinet; and the bassoon, to the double bassoon.

Recently a new instrument has been added, which is partly a woodwind, called the saxophone. You've probably heard of it! At first, it was only very sparingly used in the usual symphonic orchestra. Then suddenly the jazz band began exploiting it, and now it is finding its way back to more extended use in the symphonic field.

Even if all the instruments of the orchestra are playing their loudest, you can generally hear the piccolo above all of them. In fortissimo, it possesses a thin but shrill and brilliant sonority and can outpipe anyone within listening distance. Composers are careful how use it. Often it merely doubles, an octave higher, what the flute is doing. But recent composers have shown that, played quietly in its more moderate register, it has a thin singing voice of no little charm.

The tone color of the flute is fairly well known. It possesses a soft, cool, fluid, or feathery timbre. Because of its very defined personality, it is one of the most attractive instruments in the orchestra. It is extremely agile; it can play faster and more notes to the second than any other member of the woodwinds. Most listeners are familiar with its upper register. Much use has been made in recent years of its lowest register which is darkly expressive, in a most individual way.

The oboe is a nasal-sounding instrument, quite different in tone quality from the flute. (The oboe player holds his instrument perpendicularly, whereas the flutist holds his horizontally.) The oboe is the most expressive of the woodwinds, expressive in a very subjective way. By comparison, the flute seems impersonal. The oboe has a certain pastoral quality which is often put to good use by composers. More than any other woodwind the oboe must be well played if its limited tonal scope is to be sufficiently varied.

The English horn is a kind of baritone oboe, which is often, by inexperienced listeners, confused in tone color with the oboe. It possesses a plaintive quality all its own, however, which was fully exploited by Wagner in the introduction to the third act of *Tristan and Isolde*.

The clarinet has a smooth, open, almost hollow sound. It is a cooler, more even-sounding instrument than the oboe, being also more brilliant. Much closer to the flute than to the oboe in quality, it has almost as great an agility as the former, singing with an equal grace melodies of all kinds. In its lowest octave it possesses a unique tone color of a deeply haunting effect. Its dynamic range is more remarkable than that of any other woodwind, extending from a mere whisper to the most brilliant fortissimo.

The bass clarinet hardly differs from the clarinet itself, except that its range is one octave lower. In its bottom register, it has a ghostlike quality which is not easily forgotten.

The bassoon is one of the most versatile of instruments. It is able to do a number of different things. In its upper register, it has a plaintive sound which is very special. Stravinsky made excellent use of that timbre at the very beginning of the *Sacre du Printemps* (*Rites of Spring*). On the other hand, the bassoon produces a humorous staccato in the lower register, of an almost puckish effect. And it is always being called upon to make dullish bass parts more resonant by the sheer weight of its tone. A handy instrument it certainly is.

The double bassoon bears the same relationship to it as the double bass does to the cello. Ravel used it to characterize the beast in his *Beauty and the Beast* from the *Mother Goose Suite*. Mainly it helps to supply a bass to the orchestra where it is badly needed, down in its very depths.

The brass section, like the others, boasts four principal types of instruments. These are the horn (or French horn, to be exact), the trumpet, the trombone, the tuba. (The cornet is too much like the trumpet to need special mention.)

The French horn is an instrument with a lovely round tone—a soft, satisfying, almost liquid tone. Played loud, it takes on a majestic, brassy quality which is the complete opposite of its softer tone. If there exists a more noble sound than eight horns singing a melody fortissimo in unison, I have never heard it. There is one other most effective sonority to be obtained from the horn by stopping the tone either with a mute or with the hand placed in the bell of the instrument. A choked, rasping sound is produced when the tone is forced. The same procedure, when unforced, gives an unearthly tone which seems to emanate with magical effect from distant places.

The trumpet is that brilliant, sharp, commanding instrument with which everyone is familiar. It is the mainstay of all composers at climactic moments. But it also possesses a beautiful tone when played softly. Like the horn it has its special mutes, which produce a snarling, strident sonority which is indispensable in dramatic moments and a soft, dulcet, flutelike voice when played piano. Recently, jazz-band trumpetists have made use of a large assortment of mutes, each producing a quite different sonority. Eventually some of these are almost certain to be introduced into the symphony orchestra.

The tone of the trombone is allied in quality to that of the French horn. It also possesses a noble and majestic sound, one that is even larger and rounder than the horn's tone. But it also partly belongs with the trumpet, because of its brilliance of timbre in fortissimo. Moments of grandeur and solemnity are often due to a judicious use of the trombone section of the orchestra.

The tuba is one of the orchestra's more spectacular-looking instruments, since it fills the arms of the player holding it. It isn't easily manageable. To play it at all one must possess good teeth and plenty of reserve wind. It is a heavier, more dignified, harder-to-move kind of trombone. It is seldom used melodically, though in recent years composers have entrusted occasional themes to its bearlike mercies, with varying results. (Ravel's tuba solo in his orchestral version of Moussorgsky's *Pictures at an Exhibition* is a particularly happy example.) For the most part, however, its function is emphasize the bass, and, as such, it does valuable service.

The fourth section of the orchestra is made up of various kinds of percussion instruments. Everyone who attends a concert notices this section, perhaps too much. With a few exceptions, these instruments have no definite pitch. They are generally used in one of three ways: to sharpen rhythmic effects, dynamically to heighten the sense of climax, or to add color to the other instruments. Their effectiveness is in inverse ratio to the use that is made of them. In other words, the more they are saved for essential moments the more effective they will be.

In the percussion group, it is the drum family that is most imposing. These are all rhythm- and noise-makers of various sizes and assortments, from the little tom-tom to the big bass drum. The only drum with a definite pitch is the well-known kettledrum, usually found in groups of two or three. Played with two sticks, its dynamic range goes all the way from a shadowy, far-off rumble to an overpowering succession of thudlike beats. Other noise-makers, though not of the drum variety, are the cymbals; the gong, or tam-tam; the wood block; the triangle; the slapstick; and many more.

Other percussion-group instruments provide color rather than noise or rhythm. These are likely to be of definite pitch, such as the celesta and glockenspiel, the xylophone, the vibraphone, the tubular bells, and others. The first two produce tiny, bell-like tones which are a great asset to the colorist in music. The xylophone is possibly the most familiar of this group, and the vibraphone the most recent addition. Well-known instruments like the harp, guitar, and mandolin are also sometimes grouped with the percussion instruments because of their plucked-string timbre. In recent years, the piano has been used as an integral part of the orchestra.

There are, of course, a number of nonorchestral instruments, such as the organ, the harmonium, the accordion—not to mention the human voice—which we can do little more than list. Needless to add, all these are sometimes used with orchestra.

Mixed Tone Colors

Mixing these separate instruments in different combinations is one of the composer's more pleasant occupations. Though there are theoretically a very large number of possible combinations, composers usually confine themselves to groups of instruments that usage has made familiar. These may be groupings of instruments belonging to the same family, such as the string quartet, or those of different families, like flute, cello, and harp. It isn't possible to do more than mention a few customary combinations: trio, made up of violin, cello, and piano; the woodwind quintet, a combination of flute, oboe, clarinet, bassoon, and horn; the clarinet quintet (with strings); the flute, clarinet, and bassoon trio. In recent years, composers have done a considerable amount of experimenting in less usual combinations with varied results. One of the most original and successful is the accompanying orchestra of Stravinsky's ballet *Les Noces*, comprised of four pianos and thirteen percussion instruments.

The most usual of all chamber-music combinations is that of the string quartet, composed of two violins, viola, and cello. If a composer is subjectively inclined, there is no better medium for him than the string quartet. Its very timbre creates a sense of intimacy and personal feeling which finds its best frame in a room where contact with the sonority of the instruments is a close one. The limits of the medium must never be lost sight of; composers are often guilty of trying to make the string quartet sound like a small orchestra. Within its own frame it is an admirably polyphonic medium, by which I mean that it exists in terms of the separate voices of the four instruments. In listening to the string quartet, you must be prepared to listen contrapuntally. What that means will become clearer later on when the chapter on musical texture is reached.

The symphony orchestra is, without doubt, the most interesting combination of instruments composers have yet evolved. It is equally fascinating from the listener's standpoint, for it contains within itself all instrumental combinations, of an endless variety.

In listening to the orchestra, it is wise to keep well in mind the four principal sections and their relative importance. Don't become hypnotized by the antics of the kettledrum player, no matter how absorbing they may be. Don't concentrate on the string section alone, just because they are seated up front nearest you. Try to free yourself of bad orchestral listening habits. The main thing you can do in listening to the orchestra, aside from enjoying the sheer beauty of the sound itself, is to extricate the principal melodic material from its surrounding and supporting elements. The melodic line generally passes from one section to another or from one instrument to another, and you must always be mentally alert if you expect to be able to follow its peregrinations. The composer helps by careful balancing of his instrumental sonorities; the conductor helps by realizing those balances, adjusting individual conditions to the composer's intention. But none can be of any help if you are not prepared to disengage the melodic material from its accompanying web of sound.

The conductor, if rightly looked at, may be of some help in this. He generally will be found giving his primary attention to the instruments who have the main melody. If you watch what he is doing, you will be able to tell, without previous knowledge of a piece, where the center of your interest should be. It goes without saying that a good conductor will confine himself to necessary gestures; otherwise he can be most distracting.

A chapter on tone color, written in America, would be incomplete without some mention of the jazz band, our own original contribution to new orchestral timbres. The jazz band is a real creation in novel tonal effects, whether you like them or not. It is the absence of strings and the resultant dependence on brass and wind as melody instruments that makes the modern dance band sound so different from a Viennese waltz orchestra. If you listen to a jazz band closely, you will discover that certain instruments provide the rhythmic background (piano, banjo, bass, and percussion), others the harmonic texture, with, as a rule, one solo instrument playing the melody. Trumpet, clarinet, saxophone, and trombone are used interchangeably as harmonic or melodic instruments. The real fun begins when the melody is counterpointed by one or more subsidiary ones, making for an intricacy of melodic and rhythmic elements that only the closest listening can unravel. There is no reason why you should not use the jazz band as a way of practising how mentally to disconnect separate musical elements. When the band is at its best, it will set you problems aplenty.

Music and
the Human Spirit (1954)

I have been asked, as part of Columbia University's Bicentennial celebration, to improvise on the theme "Music as an Aspect of the Human Spirit." Most composers would agree, I think, that each new composition constitutes a kind of planned improvisation on a theme. The grander the theme, the more hazardous it is to bring it to fullest fruition. Today's theme is very grand indeed. I very nearly lacked the courage to undertake it, until it struck me that, as a composer, I am occupied each day with this very subject, namely, the expression by way of music of a basic need of the human spirit. To a casual onlooker, I may seem to be doing nothing more when I write my scores than the placing of tiny black marks on ruled paper. But, actually, if I now stop to think about it, I am concerned with one of humanity's truly unique achievements: the creation of an art music. In point of fact, I have been concerned with it for more than thirty years, with no lessening of my sense of humility before the majesty of music's expressive power, before its capacity to make manifest a deeply spiritual resource of mankind.

My subject is so immense that it is hard to know where to take hold of it. To begin at the beginning, can we say what music is? Over and over again this question has been asked. The answers given never seem entirely satisfactory for the reason that the boundaries of music are much too extensive and its effects too manifold to be containable within a single definition. Merely to describe its physical impact upon us is none too easy. How, for instance, would I undertake to describe the art of music to a deaf mute? Even to tell of the effect of a single tone in contradistinction to that of an isolated chord is difficult enough. But how can one adequately encompass the description of an entire symphony? All we know is that for some inscrutable reason most humans vibrate sympathetically to sounds of established pitch when these are coherently organized. These sounds or tones, when produced by instruments or the human voice, singly or in combination, set up sensations that may be deeply moving or merely pleasant or even at times irritating. Whatever the reaction, music that is really attended to rarely leaves the listener indifferent. Musicians react so strongly to musically induced sensations that they become a necessity of daily living.

In saying so much, I have, of course, said very little. One can no more say what music is than one can say what life itself is. But if music is beyond definition, perhaps we can hope to elucidate in what way the art of music is expressive of the human spirit. In a quasi-scientific spirit let me consider, if I may, what I do when I compose. The very idea is a little strange, for one can hardly hope to watch one's self compose. The penalty for so doing is the danger of losing the continuity of one's musical thought. And yet it cannot be claimed that when I compose I am thinking precise thoughts, in the usual meaning of that term. Neither am I mooning over conceptions in the abstract. Instead, I seem to be engrossed in a sphere of essentialized emotions. I stress the word "essentialized," for these emotions are not at all vague. It is important to grasp that fact. They are not vague because they present themselves to the mind of the composer as particularized musical ideas. From the instant of their inception they have specific identity, but it is an identity beyond the power of words to contain or circumscribe. These germinal ideas or essentialized musical thoughts, as I call them, seem to be begging for their own life, asking their creator, the composer, to find the ideal envelope for them, to evolve a shape and color and content that will most fully exploit their creative potential. In this way the profoundest aspirations of man's being are embodied in pellucid fabric of sonorous materials.

Curious, is it not, that so amorphous and intangible a substance as sound can hold such significance for us? The art of music demonstrates man's ability to transmute the substance of his everyday experience into a body of sound that has coherence and direction and flow, unfolding its own life in a meaningful and natural way in time and in space. Like life itself, music never ends, for it can always be recreated. Thus, the greatest moments of the human spirit may be deduced from the greatest moments in music.

It occurs to me to wonder at this point in what way music differs from the other arts in its affirmation of man's spirit. Is it more or less intellectual than literature or the graphic arts? Does it exist merely to melt the human heart or ought our minds to be engaged primarily in grappling with it? I was interested to read a passage in William James' *Principles of Psychology* that indicated the American philosopher feared excessive indulgence in music would have a debilitating effect on the passive listener. He wasn't entirely serious, I suppose, for he suggests the remedy, "never to suffer one's self to have an emotion at a concert without expressing it afterwards in some active way, such as giving up your seat to a lady in the subway." He exempts from this enervating effect of music those who themselves perform or those who, as he puts it, "are musically gifted enough to take it in a purely intellectual way." Here is an idea that has gained much currency. But do the musically gifted take music in a purely intellectual way? They most certainly do not. They take their music as everyone else does, with this difference: their awareness of the music in its own terms is greater, perhaps, than that of the lay listener, but that is all.

Music is designed, like the other arts, to absorb entirely our mental attention. Its emotional charge is embedded in a challenging texture, so that one must be ready at an instant's notice to lend attention wherever it is most required in order not to be lost in a sea of notes. The conscious mind follows joyfully in the wake of the composer's invention, playing with the themes as with a ball, extricating the important from the unimportant detail, changing course with each change of harmonic inflection, sensitively reflecting each new color modulation of the subtlest instrumental palette. Music demands an alert mind of intellectual capacity, but it is far from being an intellectual exercise. Musical cerebration as a game for its own sake may fascinate a small minority of experts or specialists; but it has no true significance unless its rhythmic patterns and melodic designs, its harmonic tensions and expressive timbres penetrate the deepest layer of our subconscious mind. It is, in fact, the immediacy of this marriage of mind and heart, this very fusion of musical cerebration directed toward an emotionally purposeful end that typifies the art of music and makes it different from all other arts.

The power of music is so great and at the same time so direct that people tend to think of it in a static fashion, as if it had always been what we today know it to be. It is scarcely possible to realize how extraordinary the march of Western music has been without considering briefly its historical origins. Musicologists tell us that the music of the early Christian Church was monodic—that is, it was music of a single melodic line. Its finest flower was Gregorian chant. But think what daring it took for composers to attempt the writing of music in more than a single part. This novel conception began to impose itself about a thousand years ago, yet the marvel of it is still a cause for wonder. Our Western music differs from all others mainly in this one aspect: our ability to hear and enjoy a music whose texture is polyphonic, a simultaneous sounding of independent and, at the same time, interdependent contrapuntal melodic lines. It is fascinating to follow the slow growth of musical thinking in the new contrapuntal idiom.

Parenthetically, I might add that we of today, because of our great rhythmic and harmonic freedom, are in a better position than our predecessors to appreciate the unconventionalities of these early composers. From the experimental daring of the early contrapuntists, whose music had mood and character along with a certain stiffness and awkwardness, the musical riches of the Renaissance were born. Musical expressivity developed in depth and variety, in grace and charm. By the year 1600 the peak was reached in the sacred and secular vocal masterpieces of the European continent. Take note that this was a hundred years before Bach took up his pen. Out of this many-voiced music, vocal and instrumental, the science of harmony as we know it gradually evolved. This was a natural phenomenon resulting from the fact that independent melodic lines, when sounding together, produced chords.

Then the unexpected happened. These resultant chords or harmonies, when properly organized, began to lead a self-sufficient life of their own. The skeletal harmonic progression became more and more significant as a generating force, until polyphony itself was forced to share its linear hegemony with the vertical implications of the underlying harmonies. That giant among composers, Johann Sebastian Bach, summarized this great moment in musical history by the perfect wedding of polyphonic device and harmonic drive. The subsequent forward sweep of music's development is too well known to need recounting here. We ought always to remember, however, that the great age of music did not begin with Bach and that after him each new age brought its own particular compositional insight. The Bach summation hastened the coming of a more limpid and moving style in the time of Haydn and Mozart. The Viennese masters were followed in turn by the fervent romantics of the Nineteenth Century, and the past fifty years have brought an anti-romantic reaction and a major broadening of all phases of music's technical resources.

Preoccupation with our own remarkable musical past ought not blind us to the fact that the non-Western world is full of a large variety of musical idioms, most of them in sharp contrast to our own. The exciting rhythms of African drummers; the subtle, melodramatic singing of the Near East; the clangorous ensembles of Indonesia; the incredibly nasal sonority of China and Japan, all these and many others are so different from our own Occidental music as to discourage all hope of a ready understanding. But we realize, nonetheless, that they each in their own way musically mirror cherishable aspects of human consciousness. We needlessly impoverish ourselves in doing so little to make a rapprochement between our own art and theirs.

We needlessly impoverish ourselves also in confining so much of our musical interest to a comparatively restricted period of our own music history. An overwhelming amount of the music we normally hear comes from no more than two hundred years of creative composition, principally the Eighteenth and Nineteenth Centuries. No such situation exists in any of the sister-arts, nor would it be tolerated. Like the other arts, the art of music has a past, a present, and a future; but unlike the other arts, the world of music is suffering from a special ailment of its own, namely, a disproportionate interest in its past, and a very limited past at that. Many listeners nowadays appear to be confused. They seem to think that music's future is its past. This produces as corollary a painful lack of curiosity as to its present and a reckless disregard for its future.

This question of the public's attitude toward the art of music has become crucial in an age when the general interest in music has expanded beyond the expectations of the most optimistic. Since the advent of radio broadcasting of serious music, the expansion of the recording industry, sophisticated film scores, and television opera and ballet, a true revolution in listening habits is taking place. Serious music is no longer the province of a small elite. No one has yet taken the full measure of this gradual transformation of the past thirty years nor calculated its gains and risks for the cause of music. The gains are obvious. The risks come from the fact that millions of listeners are encouraged to consider music solely as a refuge and a consolation from the tensions of everyday living, using the greatest of musical masterpieces as a first line of defense against what are thought to be the inroads of contemporary realism. A pall of conventionalism hangs heavy over today's music horizon. A situation dangerous to music's future is developing in that the natural vigor of present-day musical expression is being jeopardized by this relentless over-emphasis on the music of past centuries.

Every composer functions within the limits of his own time and place and in response to the needs of his audience. But for some curious reason, music lovers persist in believing that music on the highest level ought to be timeless, unaffected by temporal considerations of the here and now. It can easily be shown, however, how far from true that notion is. The music a composer writes makes evident his life experience in a way that is exactly similar to that of any other kind of creative artist, and it is therefore just as closely identified with the esthetic ideals of the period in which it was created. The composer of today must of necessity take into account the world of today, and his music is very likely to reflect it, even if only negatively. He cannot be expected to execute an about-face for the sole purpose of making contact with an audience that has ears only for music of the past. This dilemma shows no sign of abatement. It isolates more and more the new generation of composers from the public that should be theirs.

How paradoxical the situation is! We live in a time that is acutely aware of the medium of sound. The words "sonic" and "supersonic" are familiar to every schoolboy, and talk of frequencies and decibels is a fairly common usage. Instead of composers being looked to for leadership in such a time, they are relegated to a kind of fringe existence on the periphery of the musical world. It is a fair estimate that seven-eighths of the music heard everywhere is music by composers of a past era. Because music needs public performance in order to thrive, the apathetic attitude of the music-loving public to contemporary musical trends has had a depressant effect on present-day composers. Under the circumstances, one must have tenacity and courage to devote one's life to musical composition.

Despite the absence of stimulus and encouragement, composers in Europe and America have continued to push forward the frontiers of musical exploration. Twentieth-Century music has a good record in that respect. It has kept well abreast of the other arts in searching for new expressive resources. The balance sheet would list the following gains: first, a new-found freedom in rhythmic invention. The very modest rhythmic demands of a previous era have been supplanted by the possibilities of a much more challenging rhythmic scheme. The former regularity of an even-measured bar line has given way to a rhythmic propulsion that is more intricate, more vigorous and various, and, certainly, more unpredictable. Most recently, certain composers have essayed a music whose basic constructive principle is founded on a strict control of the work's rhythmic factors. Apparently a new species of purely rhythmic logic is envisaged, but with what success it is too soon to know.

Then the area of harmonic possibilities has also been greatly extended in contemporary writing. Leaving behind textbook conventions, harmonic practice has established the premise that any chord may be considered acceptable, if it is used appropriately and convincingly. Consonance and dissonance are conceded to be merely relative terms, not absolutes. Principles of tonality have been enlarged almost beyond recognition, while the dodecaphonic method of composing has abandoned them altogether. The young composers of today are the inheritors of a tonal freedom that is somewhat dizzying, but out of this turmoil the new textbooks will be written. Along with harmonic experiment there has been a re-examination of the nature of melody, its range, its intervallic complexity, and its character as binding elements in a composition, especially in respect to thematic relationships. Some few composers have posited the unfamiliar conception of an athematic music, that is, a music whose melodic materials are heard but once and never repeated. All this has come about as part of the larger questioning of the architectonic principles of musical form. This is clearly the end result toward which the newer attitudes are leading. Carried to its logical conclusion, it means an abandonment of long-established constructive principles and a new orientation for music.

Sometimes it seems to me that in considering the path that music is likely to take in the future, we forget one controlling factor: the nature of the instruments we use. Isn't it possible that we shall wake up one day to find the familiar groups of stringed instruments—brasses, woodwinds and battery—superseded by the invention of an electronic master instrument with unheard of microtonic divisions of a scale and with totally new sound possibilities, all under the direct control of the composer without benefit of a performing interpreter? Such a machine will emancipate rhythm from the limitations of the performing brain and is likely to make unprecedented demands on the capacity of the human ear. An age that has broken through the sound barrier can hardly be expected to go on producing musical sounds in the time-honored manner of its ancestors. Here, I confess, is a prospect a little frightening to contemplate. For this really may be that music of the future about which Richard Wagner loved to ruminate. All this belongs to the realm of speculation. Only one thing is certain: however arrived at, the process of music and the process of life will always be closely conjoined. So long as the human spirit thrives on this planet, music in some living form will accompany and sustain it and give it expressive meaning.

II
The Life of Music

Identified early in his career as an IYC (Important Young Composer), Copland had little trouble, even in his mid-thirties, assuming a pontifical role that might have been more problematic for anyone else. Given his prodigious memory (before the development of such aids as recordings), he could comment familiarly on many composers and pieces. For all the modesty of his manner and plain style, he could be a brilliant critical historian of modern music.

The American Composer
Gets a Break (1935)

None of the New York newspapers noticed it, nor did the professional music magazines, not even the one which devotes itself expressly to the cause of the native composer. Nevertheless, February 28, 1934 was a red-letter day on the calendar of American music. That night the curtain rose simultaneously, in the nation's music capital, on three modern American operas. Far uptown, at the Juilliard School, George Antheil's *Helen Retires* was having its première; in the Roaring Forties, Virgil Thomson's *Four Saints in Three Acts* was rounding into its second week of successful competition with Broadway hits, cinematic smashes, and the flea circus; while slightly lower on the map, though not on the social ladder, Howard Hanson's *Merry Mount* was being re-performed before the diamond horseshoe of the Metropolitan Opera House. Three American operas on one night! Nobody who remembers the hubbub that formerly accompanied *one*—will fail to appreciate the significance of this event.

But the next few days witnessed several other events, all pointing in the same direction. On March 18, eight Americans were commissioned by the League of Composers to write works which had been pledged *in advance* for performance by eight outstanding organizations: the Philadelphia Symphony Orchestra, the Philharmonic Orchestra of New York, the Chicago Symphony Orchestra, the Cleveland Symphony Orchestra, the Harvard Glee Club, the Adesdi Chorus, the Stradivarius Quartet, and the Pro Arte Quartet. Moreover, on April 1st, the Columbia Phonograph Company issued the first full-length symphony by an American ever to be recorded. And perhaps most remarkable of all, on March 4, the conservative first-line music critic of *The New York Times* ended his regular Sunday article with these extraordinary words: that he is possessed of more than the hope—in fact, he feels an optimistic certainty—that the time is near for some real American achievement in music and some enduring American masterpieces.

Later in the year, the indigenous Werner Janssen was engaged by the Philharmonic Orchestra of New York as guest conductor, with the specific understanding that he was to feature American composition on his programs. What is more, following his successful concerts of last November he has since been re-engaged with the same understanding. And, extending the native triumphs to another realm, the National Broadcasting Company has sponsored a series of six concerts of chamber music, half the programs to be by Americans. In short, our composers have gained victories of late on almost every front.

It was not always thus. I do not have to stretch my memory to recall the time when an American piece of music, particularly of the kind apprehensively called "modern," was the signal for hoots in the concert hall and wisecracks in the press. Only a short time ago, the critic from the *Times* was not throwing bouquets. Indeed, to judge by some of the things written in the last ten years, it would almost have seemed that the American composer was a deliberate nuisance.

Some of the misapprehensions of this earlier period still exist. It is not even now appreciated that a serious and important type of composer functions among us; nor, as a man, is he properly understood. It will be a purpose of this article to correct some of the erroneous impressions that have grown up about him. I have no desire to plead his cause, since in the last analysis his music will have to speak for itself; but I think I may bring to light certain things that will make the situation clearer.

It cannot be doubted that he occupies little or no place even today in the mind of the public at large. We seldom find his name, for instance, on impressive lists of celebrities, though American artists of other kinds are frequently mentioned. He is also subtly high-hatted in the awarding of the Pulitzer Prizes. (This is a typical example of a hangover from an earlier day.) The literary prizes go to those supposed to have written the best novel, the best play, the best biography, etc., during the season; but the single music award is not a prize for something actually done, but a travelling fellowship. Our writers, in other words, are treated as artists who have already arrived; while the composer is regarded as a student who, if encouraged, may possibly do something in the future. One reason for this, perhaps, is that music develops more slowly than the other arts; its entire known history is comparatively recent as compared to the history of literature, painting, or sculpture. In her reluctance to put the composer on a par with other artists, therefore, America is merely mirroring the rest of the world. Another reason, no doubt, for the poor place of the composer in the public's horizon, is his difficulty in being heard. As we all know, the majority of plays produced and books published are new; but seven-eighths of the music performed is old. This allows the contemporary American little room to make himself known, especially since of the remaining eighth the lion's share falls to Europeans.

If the big public is unaware of the composer, the little public, the *cognoscenti*—perhaps through no fault of its own—shows the vaguest acquaintance with him and his work. No informed or thoughtful people still associate him with a flowing necktie or long hair; but our intelligent minority does have other associations with him that are equally incorrect. The gist of these associations is that the American species of composer is without character. This notion was developed in an article which appeared in *The New Republic* in January, 1935, entitled "Wanted—An American Composer." It has also been stated in these very pages [*American Mercury*] by George Jean Nathan, who wrote that the weakness of American music "lies in the circumstance that its hopeful composers are in the aggregate trivial men."

Music Between the Wars
(1918–1939) (1941, 1968)

From the second edition of *The New Music* (1941, 1968), this is a remarkably wide-ranging and yet authoritative essay in cultural history. Copland introduced his later thoughts when the book was reprinted in 1968, prefacing them with the date of the previous year.

Music after the First World War

The music that has been discussed so far was rudely interrupted in its natural growth during the four years of the First World War. The war years isolated composers so that they lost contact with one another. Schoenberg, Stravinsky, and Bartók worked alone, and their compositions had only local circulation.

But once the war was over, an extraordinary period of musical activity set in. It was as if four years of musical starvation had engendered an insatiable hunger to find out what all the composers in the different countries had been doing. By 1920 a whole batch of new composers had appeared on the musical scene—some who were just beginning to be known before the war intervened and were now grown to full musical maturity, others who had been students during the lean war years and were now ready to make their bid for fame. A mere list of these men is impressive: Falla in Spain, Bloch in Switzerland, Szymanowski in Poland, Malipiero in Italy, Kodály in Hungary, Berg and Webern in Austria, Hindemith in Germany, and last, but far from least, the Group of Six in France (Milhaud, Honegger, Poulenc, Auric, Tailleferre, Durey).

It was a period during which composers were frankly out to do original things. A healthy spirit of investigation pervaded all musical activity. Among many other kinds of interests, the ironic and grotesque seemed to exert a particular fascination. No combination of instruments was too outlandish to be tried at least once. There were experiments in jazz, in quarter-tone music, in music for mechanical instruments. Composers vied with one another in damning all conservative music. Each new composition was accompanied by copious explanations as to its newness, as if that alone were justification for its existence. Taken all in all, it was an eventful and lively period, even though the results did not always lead anywhere in particular. The wonder is that so much that is good remains.

After the war the center of musical activity definitely shifted from Germany to France. This gradual swing away from Central Europe had been gaining momentum ever since 1900, and by 1920 Paris was the leading spirit in all new musical things. The bitterness engendered by the war accelerated the pace at which French composers were freeing themselves from the dominance of German music. They became more and more conscious of their own purely Gallic tradition in music, a tradition that antedates the Romantic movement by many years. This fact is of especial significance, of course, in tracing the pull-away from the German hegemony in music.

Whatever happened in France was of importance to the rest of the musical creative world. By the time the war was over, Impressionism was no longer the "latest thing." The musical field was taken over by two factions: one led by Debussy's younger contemporaries Maurice Ravel and Albert Roussel, who were, in effect if not in name, the leaders of a post-Impressionist movement; and the other consisting of still younger men—the anti-Impressionists, one might call them—led by that curious and legendary figure Erik Satie.

Ravel and Roussel

Nowhere can we see the change that had come over the aesthetic ideals of new music better than in comparing the late works of Ravel and Roussel with those of their great predecessor Debussy. Ravel and Roussel were both attacked at first as being mere imitators of the older man. This was true, I suppose, to a limited extent: they borrowed his musical vocabulary, and especially in their youthful works, were attracted by the Impressionist theory. But both Ravel and Roussel were born with distinctive personalities of their own. Their mature music leaves no possibility for confusion; for where Debussy is vague and poetic Ravel and Roussel are precise and *spiritual*. In the end, they both succeeded in adapting Debussy's innovations to their own purposes, and it is only in that sense that they are post-Impressionists.

The essential Classic approach is present in the construction of their music. The musical line is built up carefully, with an unerring instinct for the proportion of the whole. There are no loose ends, no details unaccounted for. The characteristics of reticence, of perceptivity and refinement, of expert craftsmanship—all so typically French—are all there; but combined with them is an open-eyed lucidity about the function and meaning of the music that bespeaks a detachment on the part of the composer that is the antithesis of the Romantic attitude. In certain ways, one might say that the later symphonies of Roussel and the concertos of Ravel owe something to the symphonies and concertos of Saint-Saëns or to the chamber music of Fauré. But whereas these two older men were writing French music within a German framework, Ravel and Roussel were composing their works with a strong sense of relationship to the purely French traditions of a Couperin or a Rameau.

Here the similarities in the music of Ravel and Roussel end. If the young men of the '20s bitterly attacked Ravel on occasion, it was because they saw in his music little reflection of the disabused and hard new postwar world. The sensuousness and sheen of all Ravel's music, the desire to allure and charm, the calculated brilliance and virtuosity, all seemed somehow to be part of the comfortable bourgeois world of prewar days. One ought not to forget also the natural tendency on the part of the young to decry anything so powerfully attractive as the music of Ravel. They intuitively fear its influence. For Ravel certainly had admirers aplenty and imitators, also. Even today, it is not easy to determine exactly where Ravel belongs in the musical cosmos or how viable the future may prove his music to be. Perhaps its very perfection makes us unduly suspicious of the actual musical content. Despite the fact that his music may not cut very deep, no contemporary composer possessed a more integrated style nor a greater passion for the sheer sensuousness of musical sounds. For that we should be thankful.

Roussel fared better at the hands of the young, even though they must have known that he was by nature a less gifted composer than Ravel. But despite his somewhat artificial style, they undoubtedly sensed an inner freshness of spirit. Roussel's is music that does not give up its secret easily. The curiously strained harmonies, the slightly (always slightly) awkward melodies, the brisk but unspontaneous rhythms, the generally acidulous quality that surrounds all his mature work do not gain him easily won friends. But Roussel's work, to the initiated, exerts a fascination of its own. There is an objective and healthy, almost happy, athleticism about his later compositions, such as the Third Symphony, the Suite in F, and the Sinfonietta for strings. In these pieces Roussel left far behind him the nebulous Debussian aesthetic and attached himself to the more advanced tendencies of the day.

Satie and "Les Six"
Only one composer succeeded in attracting to himself the unreserved approval of a small but choice coterie of younger men—Erik Satie. The role

of Satie in French music is not unlike that of [Ferruccio] Busoni in Central Europe. In each case the influence of the man as a leader of the avant garde was perhaps more important than the significance of the music that he himself wrote.

The Satie influence showed itself at first through the work of the Group of Six—particularly in the music of Georges Auric, Francis Poulenc, and Darius Milhaud. The formation of this group had been fortuitous and the association was continued purely as a matter of expediency. The Six decided that they could more easily get a hearing for their work as a unit than as individuals. Erik Satie was their spiritual godfather, and his ideas on music and art were often made manifest through the writings of the young French critic Jean Cocteau.

It is amusing to realize that in his own very French way, Satie was something of a crusader. He set himself against all music that took itself too seriously. He had his own way of crusading—it consisted of poking quiet fun at all officialdom, musical and otherwise. He had the "firmest conviction," as Virgil Thomson puts it, "that the only healthy thing music can do in our century is to stop trying to be impressive." Since almost all music tries for impressiveness in one way or another, we can appreciate how large a crusading job Satie had undertaken.

He indicated the direction he thought new music should take by writing numerous short pieces of a disarming simplicity and an extraordinary rightness of musical feeling. Then he tried to put one off the track by adding whimsical titles (satirizing Debussy's poetic names for pieces), posing as a revolutionist by occasionally leaving out barlines, and imposing idiotic directions for playing in every other measure. "To the uninitiated they [these pieces] sound trifling. To those that love them they are fresh and beautiful and firmly right." I am quoting Thomson again. In an illuminating article on Satie's work he continues: "And that freshness and rightness have long dominated the musical thought of France. Any attempt to penetrate that musical thought without first penetrating that of Satie is fruitless."

Thomson's claim is that Satie invented the only 20th-century musical aesthetic in the Western world. Everything else, by comparison, is old stuff. By eschewing "the impressive, the heroic, the oratorical, everything that is aimed at moving mass audiences" and valuing instead "quietude, precision, acuteness of auditory observation, gentleness, sincerity and directness of statement" Satie showed us how to cut the Gordian knot that ties all music to the shopworn Romanticism of the preceding century. All this is no doubt implicit in the short and unpretentious works of Satie himself. But it might be argued that being simple and direct in one's work might better be set down as a question of temperament and cannot reasonably be blown up to the proportions of a world aesthetic.

However we may judge the connotations of Satie's example, the Six and many younger composers seized upon it as a program for French music. Through it they were going to free themselves not only of the Romantic taint but of the earmarks of Debussy, Ravel, and all their Impressionist confreres.

The Six symbolized a new 20th-century type of composer. They ended forever (we hope) the 19th-century conception of composers as long-haired geniuses who live and starve in garrets. To the Six the creative musician was no longer the high priest of art but a regular fellow who liked to go to night clubs like everybody else. What they wanted to write was "une musique de tous les jours"—a more everyday kind of music. Not the kind that you listen to with your head in your hands, lost in reverie or some sort of emotional fog. All that was ended. We were to listen now with eyes wide open to music that was "down to earth," as Hollywood would say.

All this, whatever else it may have been, proved to be a very effective means for calling attention to a group of unknown composers. The air became charged with musical polemics. The established critics, particularly those who had championed the cause of the Impressionists, became angry and gave the Six even more publicity than they had hoped for. As for the composers themselves, they turned out to be a variegated set of new talents. Francis Poulenc hewed closest to the Satie line, particularly in his first works; Auric wrote a pungent and witty music—somewhat dry and ascetic in quality; Tailleferre could not quite pull herself away from the attractions of Impressionism; and Durey shortly dropped out of sight altogether. It was clear from the start that the two leading members of the group were to be Arthur Honegger and Darius Milhaud.

Of all the group, Honegger was the least affected by the Satie shibboleths. His Swiss origin, and frequent visits to Zurich, left him not untouched with a Teutonic love of the grandiose. He is at his best in large dramatic works—operas and oratorios, like *King David* and *Antigone*—that give his generous gifts full opportunity to spread themselves. For a time, he held the center of the stage as far as new music was concerned. But despite its not inconsiderable qualities, Honegger's music is essentially conventional. He was an important figure in those early postwar years, if only because he made palatable to many listeners a new type of musical language that somehow seemed justified when used to illustrate the pathetic and biblical subject matter of his large choral frescoes. But his music has not worn well. Perhaps it is because he was so well understood then that his music has less attraction for us now.

The Lyricism of Milhaud

Milhaud, on the other hand, had himself partly to blame for the lack of sympathy that enveloped his music when it was new. He quickly gained the reputation of a man who delighted in antagonizing people. His music was more dissonant, his critical reviews were more outspoken, and his general revolutionary tenets were more violent than those of any of the other young radicals who grouped themselves around Satie and Cocteau in 1919. To the majority he seemed a noisy and aggressive upstart; to others more kindly disposed he was an amusing fellow, full of life and verve, but essentially a *blagueur*. It has taken more time than one would have thought necessary to demonstrate a fact that should have been clear from the start, namely, that Milhaud was the most important of the new generation of composers in France.

It was not appreciated at first, either, that Milhaud's musical style is by nature essentially lyric. His music always sings. Whether he composes a five-act opera or a two-page song, this singing quality is paramount. The music flows so naturally that it seems to have been improvised rather than composed. What Milhaud writes comes from the "deep places of the mind"—from a kind of secondary consciousness over which he seems to exert no control.

This utter simplicity of approach has resulted in a style uniquely and unmistakably his own. You can distinguish a page of Milhaud from among a hundred others. Unlike Stravinsky or Schoenberg, who each evolved an individual speech gradually, Milhaud is recognizably himself in his earliest compositions. This did not prevent him from submitting himself to a series of widely differing influences: first Debussy; then, with a two-year stay in Brazil, the popular melodies he heard there; later Stravinsky; then jazz; then Satie. No matter—whatever he touches receives his imprint. Sometimes there is a repetition of certain favorite harmonic and rhythmic formulas. But for the most part his homogeneity of style results from the effortless reflection of a distinct personality.

Three moods are characteristic of much of this composer's music: a violently dramatic and almost brutal mood, a relaxed mood of almost childlike gaiety and brightness, and a tender and nostalgic sensuousness. Perhaps it is this last-named trait, with its naïve and all-pervading charm, that makes Milhaud most understandable. To sense it to the full inevitably means that one has come under the spell of the composer. With a quietly moving diatonic melody and a few thick-sounding harmonies he creates a kind of charmed atmosphere. When darkly colored, it takes on a deeply nostalgic connotation. Since this nostalgia is shared by none of his French confrères, I take it to be a sign of Milhaud's Jewish inheritance. That he is not so racial a composer as Bloch or Mahler seems natural if we remember that his ancestors settled in Provence in the 15th century, so that his Jewishness has long been tempered by the French point of view. Nevertheless his subjectivism, his violence, and his strong sense of logic (as displayed in his strict use of polytonality) are indications that the Jewish spirit is still alive in him.

His music can be quite French when it is gay and alert. In this mood his love for simple folklike tunes and clear-cut rhythms is apparent. It is when the harmonies turn acidulous and the rhythms are oddly accented that his gaiety becomes more brusque and truculent. Very personal, also, is the manner in which the music is put together. The textural buildup is peculiarly his own. (To be more specific on this point would lead us into too many technicalities.) Structurally the music is always under control. One never meets with overdevelopment of an idea in Milhaud. He states the core of the matter and then stops.

This last is surprising in a man who possesses so fertile an imagination. A mere listing of his works in all forms is impressive; they include operas, ballets, oratorios, film scores, theater music, music for orchestra and chamber orchestra, concertos, string quartets, a large number of songs, piano pieces, and choral music. No wonder Milhaud has been accused of writing too much. Naturally some of this is repetitious, and not all is of equal value. The sensible thing to do, as with every other prolific composer, past and present, is to choose the best from among his many productions.

First in importance are perhaps the operas and ballets. There are large, impressive stage works such as *Christophe Colomb* (1928) and *Médée* (1939); shorter lyrical dramas such as *Le pauvre matelot* and *Esther de Carpentras*; and tiny chamber operas lasting no more than eight minutes each: *Thesée, Ariane,* and *L'Enlèvement d'Europe*. The ballets range from the early but striking *L'Homme et son désir* through *Salade, Le Train bleu, Les Songes,* and *The Man from Midian* (1940). Perhaps the most charming of the ballets is *La Création du monde*, composed in 1923. Based on a scenario by Blaise Cendrars, it treats of the creation of the world according to African legends. Much of the musical material is lifted from jazz—there are fugues on a jazz subject, a blues section, and a long melody over a "barbershop" accompaniment. Better than any other European, and before hearing Gershwin's famous *Rhapsody* (first performed in the following year), Milhaud understood how to assimilate the jazz idiom.

1967: The past two decades have shown surprisingly little change in Milhaud's production. Since the end of the Second World War, he has been spending alternate years at his teaching post at Mills College in California and at his apartment in Paris, with an annual summer's stay at the Aspen Music Festival, where he functions as head of the Composition Department. One might reasonably suppose that all this extra-compositional activity would inevitably curtail his productivity, but one would be wrong. He has probably produced a greater quantity of viable music (he is now, in 1967, in his seventy-fifth year) than any other living man. Fifteen years ago he had reached his Opus 320; in the last ten years he has added ten symphonies to

his list of works. No one would or could expect all of this torrential outpouring of notes to be of equal interest. But that is just the point: how are we to
sort out and hear performed a sufficient portion of Milhaud's production to
warrant passing judgment on the totality of the work of the past quarter century? Here is a task for some perceptive investigator that is long overdue.
I venture to say that the investigator would find surprisingly little change in
the composer's style or language or "message." His musical invention has, at
times, turned repetitious, but the general manner is as relaxed and unassum-
ing as ever before. He seems to be approaching closer and closer to Satie's
ideal of the sweetly human composer with no desire to astonish or overawe
his listeners. The cold fact is, nevertheless, that in a time like our own, with
emphasis on new media, new methodologies, and new aesthetics, Milhaud's
late period may quite naturally seem to lack "excitement." No matter. One
can confidently expect that a time will come when a sorting process will reaf-
firm the unique value and range of Milhaud's finest work.

The Jazz Interlude

The interest of Milhaud in jazz was, of course, no isolated phenomenon. In
fact, the preoccupation with the American dance band when first it arrived
in European capitals after the war was widespread. The peak of interest was
reached by about 1925. Nevertheless, ever since that time, jazz phraseology
has continued to seep into contemporary music to such an extent that a
survey of the field would be incomplete without a close examination of the
exact nature of its influence.

There is, of course, plenty of precedent in former times for the borrowing by serious composers from popular dance sources. This may have a
particular piquancy in the present instance because of the "ordinariness"
of jazz by comparison with what is generally thought of as the recondite-
ness of modern music. Still, no one would deny that a parallel does exist
between a composer of the '20s writing a fox-trot and Mozart or Haydn
writing a minuet or Chopin a waltz. Only one step further is taken when
Beethoven transmutes the minuet into a scherzo or Ravel idealizes a dance
form into *La Valse* or the *Bolero*. The serious composer needs freshening
occasionally from the less conscious and more naïve springhead of popular or folk music. Otherwise there is the danger that he may dry up, become
academic and unimaginative. The contemporary composer's use of jazz
had logic and tradition behind it and was more or less to be expected.

It might be added, by way of parenthesis, that the opposite process, in
which jazz borrows from the classics—the so-called "swinging" of the classics that gained temporary currency—is less to be encouraged. Not so
much because of the bastard versions of the classics that it makes known,

though these are tasteless enough, but because it indicates a weakening of invention on the part of our popular composers. It should be discouraged not because it is bad for the classics (they will survive, I imagine), but because it is definitely bad for jazz. It glorifies the arranger at the expense of the tunesmith, whose talents are becoming less and less essential in turning out the Tin Pan Alley product.

When jazz was new a great deal was written about it as an expression of the times we live in. The identification of jazz with the *Zeitgeist* formed the text of many an article during the '20s. What interested composers, however, was not so much the spirit, whatever it symbolized, as the more technical side of jazz—the rhythm, melody, harmony, timbre through which that spirit was expressed.

From the composer's viewpoint, jazz had only two expressions: the well-known "blues" mood, and the wild, abandoned, almost hysterical and grotesque mood so dear to the youth of all ages. These two moods encompassed the whole gamut of jazz emotion. Any serious composer who attempted to work within those two moods sooner or later became aware of their severe limitations. But the technical procedures of jazz had much wider implications, since these were not necessarily restricted to the two moods but might be applied to any number of different musical styles.

By far the most potent influence on the technical side was that of rhythm. No one has been able to trace with any surety the origin of jazz rhythm. It seems safe to suppose that it began long ago on some Negro's dull tom-tom in deepest Africa. In the slave ships of the early traders it came to America, and then, in a new environment, took on different but distinctly related forms in Cuba, in Brazil, and in the United States. In our country we trace jazz rhythm to the minstrel songs of the 1840s and, later, to the spirituals, work songs, and religious "shouts" of the rural Southern Negro. All these related American musical types were crystallized around 1900 into a commercial song-and-dance idiom that went under the name of ragtime.

In 1927 I published an article in the magazine *Modern Music* in which I tried to show the metamorphosis of rhythm in popular music from ragtime to jazz. This analysis has been quoted so often by subsequent writers that I trust I need no further excuse for reprinting it here, at least in part:

"The rhythmic foundation of ragtime is an unchanging *1–2–3–4* bass in quick tempo (stressing the most obvious beats, the first and third). Over the ragtime bass is carried invariably one of two rhythms, sometimes both; either the dotted eighth followed by a sixteenth: ♩ ♫♩ ♩ or this most ordinary syncopation: ♫ ♩ ♫ ♩ . The former of these produced the characteristic ragtime jerk which is perhaps best remembered from *Everybody's Doin' It.*"

Winthrop Sargeant, in his book *Jazz: Hot and Hybrid*, demonstrates that I neglected to point out one further syncopated rhythm that was a late addition to ragtime and became eventually of crucial importance in its transmutation into jazz. In addition to the syncopation already quoted: ♫ ♩ (which Sargeant calls the cake-walk syncopation, familiar as long ago as 1834), we have this less common syncopation: ♩ ♫♩♩ or ♩ ♫♩♫. He concludes, therefore, that from the purely rhythmic angle, jazz is no more interesting than ragtime. This may be true from a strictly analytical viewpoint, but the limited use to which this more complex syncopation was put, plus the relentless insistence of that 1–2–3–4 in the bass, gives to all the early two-steps a honky-tonk quality that makes early jazz, by comparison, seem several paces ahead of ragtime in rhythmic sophistication.

All this is parenthetical to my own analysis, which continues thus:

"Modern jazz began with the fox-trot. For this new dance the four-quarter bass was used as in ragtime but at a considerably slower pace and miraculously improved by accenting the least obvious beats, the second and fourth—1–*2*–3–*4*. With this was combined another rhythmic element, sometimes in the melody but by no means always there, which is generally supposed to be a kind of 1–2–3–4 and is always written: ♩ ♩ ♩ ♩ ♩ ♩ ♩ ♩ ... Don Knowlton was the first to show[1] that this jazz rhythm is in reality much subtler than in its printed form and is properly expressed thus: ♩ ♩ ♩ ♩ ♪ ♫ ♩. Therefore, it contains no syncopation; it is instead a rhythm of four quarters split into eight eighths and is arranged thus: 1–2–3:1–2–3–4–5, or even more precisely: 1–2–3:1–2–3:1–2. Put this over the four-quarter bass:

and you have the play of two independent rhythms within the space of one measure. It is the beginning, it is a molecule of jazz . . .

"The next step infinitely complicated these, in fact it produced polyrhythms. In employing two rhythms within one measure jazz after all merely did something that had been done before, if we remember, for instance, the use by older composers of $\frac{3}{4}$ against $\frac{6}{8}$. But the next era in the

---

[1] "The Anatomy of Jazz," in *Harper's Magazine*, April 1926.

jazz age—typified by Zez Confrey's song *Stumbling*—saw independent rhythms spread over more than one measure, over a series of measures:

That is, while the conventional $\frac{4}{4}$ bass was retained the melody was put into $\frac{3}{4}$ time. . . . Within small limits jazz had achieved a new synthesis in music . . .[2]

"Polyrhythms are, as is known, not in themselves an innovation. They have been highly developed among primitive races and have made intermittent, momentary appearances in the works of recent European composers. They have also occurred abundantly in the English madrigals. The madrigal polyrhythms were the result of the madrigal prosody and therefore an intricate deft interknitting in which no single downbeat was too definitely stressed. In a sense, therefore, the madrigal was arhythmic rather than polyrhythmic. In fact, the madrigalists were charged by later English generations with lacking a proper sense of rhythm.

"But the polyrhythms of jazz are different in quality and effect not only from those of the madrigals but from all others as well. The peculiar excitement they produce by clashing two definitely and regularly marked rhythms is unprecedented in occidental music. Its polyrhythm is the real contribution of jazz."

The serious European composer was influenced to a limited extent by our popular music even before it had any polyrhythmic implications. When jazz was still ragtime Debussy wrote his *Golliwog's Cake Walk* (1908) and later *Minstrels* (1910). During the war years Stravinsky essayed several pieces in the ragtime manner: *Piano Rag-Music, Ragtime* for eleven instruments, and the dance marked "ragtime" in the *Story of a Soldier*. All these pieces make a rather grotesque impression, as if Stravinsky were merely interested in making Cubistic caricatures out of the crudities of jazz. These little compositions have few admirers, but they are interesting as examples

---

[2]It is this three-over-four that Sargeant claims is already present in ragtime. ". . . it is difficult," he says (p. 117), "to lay hands on a rhythmic formula in jazz that was not represented earlier in ragtime. One often hears the theory advanced that polyrhythm is a characteristic of the former and absent from the latter. Both Don Knowlton and Copland subscribed to it. But the facts do not support it." Whatever the facts prove, it is incontrovertible that serious composers became aware of the polyrhythmic nature of Afro-American music only in its jazz phase, so that it is safe to assume a fundamental difference in the effects produced, even though single units of the device look the same on paper.

of the way in which Stravinsky's musical mind works. By extracting and isolating certain typical ragtime features, such as the "cakewalk" syncopated figure and the dotted eighth followed by a sixteenth rhythm, and juxtaposing these and other stock items in unexpected ways, he produces a kind of extract of ragtime that is more characteristic of Stravinsky than it is of Afro-American music. It is interesting to note, however, that in the opening March of the *Story of a Soldier*, and also in the section that follows, *The Soldier's Violin*, there are strongly marked polyrhythmic passages that are not to be found in earlier works of Stravinsky (not even in *The Rite of Spring*, despite its rhythmic complexities) or in those of any other European composer of the same time. It would seem likely that these could have come only by way of jazz influence.

The only other aspect of popular music that has had an influence on the serious composer comparable to that of its rhythm is the special fascination exerted by the timbre of the jazz band. As far as harmony and melody are concerned, it was jazz that did the borrowing. In these two spheres the early jazz composer worked within a strictly limited area. Occasionally the serious composer makes use of typical jazz cadences and "barbershop" harmonies for their humorous effect, and similarly certain characteristic turns of melodic phrase, exploited over and over again in popular music, are introduced into the vocal line, but these are almost always in pieces written frankly "in the manner of" a blues or fox-trot and are seldom found—as jazz-influenced rhythm and tone color might be—in pieces without any jazz connotation.

The jazz band derived its special color partly from the absence of strings (violins, violas, and cellos). Since these have formed the basic tonal body in the symphony orchestra ever since Haydn's day, their mere omission was enough to give the jazz band a sonority of its own. Added to this was the functional way in which jazz instruments were divided into rhythm instruments (piano, banjo, bass, and drums) and melody instruments (clarinets, saxophones, trumpets, and trombones). On the firm basic pulse of the rhythm section the melody instruments were able to weave an independent melodic and rhythmic counterpoint, which had to be carefully listened to if all the subtleties of tone color and rhythmic variety were to be heard. This description applies, of course, only to the performance of the best jazz bands.

The original and effective sonorities produced by what was in reality a small chamber-music combination without strings gave composers an incentive to experiment with timbres outside the well-known groupings of string quartet, woodwind quintet, flute and strings, and so forth. Thus, in 1923 we find Stravinsky writing an Octet scored for flute, clarinet, and two each of bassoon, trumpet, and trombone. His ballet *Les Noces* was rescored in three different versions, the final one being for four pianos and thirteen percussion instruments. One could easily add other similar examples from the literature of new music. Composers everywhere were attracted by the supervirtuosity of the individual jazz performer, by the extraordinary rhythmic attack of the best brass sections, by unusual timbres produced out of thoroughly familiar instruments, and by the general spirit of freedom and unconventionality surrounding a first-rate band.

The preoccupation with the popular idiom in the principal centers of jazz influence—France, Germany, and England—had expended itself by the end of the '20s. The revival of interest in jazz of the "hot" variety, which came into vogue around 1935 under the new name of swing, has thus far, at any rate, had little effect on serious music. This may be due to the fact that swing is really nothing new, or it may also be due in part to the fact that the most interesting feature of swing is its improvisational character, which is the one element of popular music that cannot be notated properly. It is interesting to note, however, that the deliberate use of more and more dissonant chords in recent swing will result in making the public at large more readily accept the unconventional harmonies of the modern composer. A few more years of such harmonic liberties and Stravinsky's boldest flights in that field will sound quite tame to the man in the street.

In France, besides Milhaud, whose ballet La Création du monde has already been mentioned, many composers wrote pieces in the jazz style. Outstanding among these are Ravel in the slow blues of his Violin Sonata, and Honegger in his Concertino for Piano and Small Orchestra. Especially amusing is the final part of the Concertino, with its whiplike cracklings in the brittle piano part over a long and sentimental jazz tune.

In Central Europe the Schoenberg group remained aloof, but the new opera composers like Ernst Krenek and Kurt Weill went in heavily for the music from America. The phenomenal success of Krenek's Jonny spielt auf, with its Negro jazz-band-leader hero, encouraged other Europeans to try their hand at this new style of music. The best composition of them all was Kurt Weill's Three-Penny Opera, not so much because it added anything to jazz—it was, in fact, much inferior as such to the homegrown variety—but because it used the jazz idiom to mirror the depressed and tired Germany of the '20s in an unforgettably poignant way. It should be mentioned, also, that Paul Hindemith, in his early works, was not beyond dabbling in the jazz manner, and the polyrhythmic element may be traced in much of his later work (particularly in his Klavierübung, Opus 37).

To complete the picture, one should add that in the United States serious composers like John Alden Carpenter, Edward B. Hill, and Louis Gruenberg, during the '20s, and Walter Piston, Robert McBride, and Morton Gould, during the '30s, all used jazz with greater or lesser degrees of politeness. (In this list belong several of my own works—especially *Music for the Theatre*, 1925, and the Concerto for Piano and Orchestra, 1926.) While these composers borrowed some of its procedures from Tin Pan Alley, George Gershwin, who began there, brought jazz with him to the concert hall. His works made up in originality and individuality what they lacked in technical finish.

It is safe to say that no living composer has been entirely unaffected by the revitalized rhythmic sense we have all gained through contact with the peoples of the Dark Continent. (Even so Mexican a composer as Carlos Chávez wrote a *Fox* and a *Blues*.) Whether rhythmic counterpoint is to have as profound an effect on Occidental music of the future as melodic counterpoint has had must remain an open question.

1967: In recent times the tables have turned insofar as jazz influence is concerned: jazz has been more influenced by serious music than the other way around. Almost any musical style can be "jazzified"—witness the adaptation of 18th-century Baroque music, Indian ragas, and so on. Performers such as Ornette Coleman and Jimmy Giuffre have abandoned conventional jazz forms and harmonies for the complete freedom of certain kinds of contemporary music. The significance that jazz has assumed, in all its many manifestations, is emphasized by the English critic-composer Wilfrid Mellers in his recent book on American music. He devotes almost half the volume to a discussion of jazz as an independent and essential part of America's musical history.

Serious music, on the other hand, at least in its strictly serial and electronic aspects, has shown little or no interest in making use of jazz-derived elements. Only chance music, with its improvisational and indeterminate factors, has tended to establish a bond, at least of "philosophy," between popular and serious music.

The value of frankly incorporating the present-day progressive type of jazz idiom within the framework of a concert piece has been staunchly defended by Gunther Schuller, an important member of today's middle generation of American composers. Schuller has invented the term "third-stream music" to characterize the marriage of these two musical genres. Moreover, Schuller goes further and claims that the jazz-inspired works of serious composers in the '20s quite missed the point: in his opinion, jazz is synonymous with improvisation. Or, to put it another way, without improvisation there is no jazz. But it seems only fair to point out that during the '20s it would have been out of the question to expect a symphony player to be able to improvise in the jazz manner. Even today, when Schuller wishes to integrate jazz into a symphonic context he must bring into the concert hall or opera house a "jazz combo" to improvise while the orchestra itself plays from the written notes provided by the composer. The California composer Larry Austin has successfully combined serious and jazz idioms in his Improvisations for Orchestra and Jazz Soloists. By 1962, the date of the first performance, it had become practical for Austin to request his symphonic interpreter to "invent rhythmic designs on given pitches within specified spans of time." Composers like Austin and David Reck make one suspect that the last word has not yet been said on the influence of jazz on serious composition, at least in America.

The Neoclassic Movement

The jazz interlude had no permanent effect on contemporary music's trend away from Romanticism. The interest in jazz was temporary, similar to the interest during the same period in the primitive arts and crafts of aboriginal peoples, reflected in contemporary sculpture and painting. In musical terms, it expressed itself primarily in the introduction of complex rhythms, adding to Stravinsky's juxtaposition of different time signatures the new, simultaneous sounding of independent rhythmic units. But few listeners in the early '20s, even among those who considered themselves to be "in the know," were prepared for the final phase of the development we have been following—the conscious adoption of the musical ideals of the early 18th century.

Here again Igor Stravinsky led the way. The French musical world first became aware of this new tendency—referred to in the beginning as "back-to-Bach" movement—with the first performance of the Stravinsky Octet on October 18, 1923. I was in the audience on the night of its premiere at a Koussevitzky concert in Paris and can attest to the general feeling of mystification that followed the initial hearing. Here was Stravinsky, who had created a neoprimitive style all his own, based on native Russian sources—a style that everyone agreed was the most original in modern music—now suddenly, without any seeming explanation, making an about-face and presenting a piece to the public that bore no conceivable resemblance to the individual style with which he had hitherto been identified. Everyone was asking why Stravinsky should have exchanged his Russian heritage for what looked very much like a mess of 18th-century mannerisms. The whole thing seemed like a bad joke that left an unpleasant after-effect and gained Stravinsky the unanimous disapproval of the press. No one could possibly have foreseen, first, that Stravinsky was to persist in this new manner of his, or second, that the Octet was destined to influence composers all over the world in bringing the latent objectivity of modern music to full consciousness by frankly adopting the ideals, forms, and textures of the pre-Romantic era.

From the vantage point of today we can see that this move on the part of Stravinsky was not nearly so arbitrary as it seemed to the audience of 1923. In tracing its origins, one can already detect a certain internationalist aspect in the *Story of a Soldier,* written in Switzerland five years before the Octet. Its march, tango, valse, chorale, and ragtime have a distinctly cosmopolitan flavor in comparison with Stravinsky's early ballets. We must remember, also, that the Bolshevik revolution of the previous year had aroused absolutely no sympathy in the expatriate composer. Perhaps this event contributed to his marked lack of enthusiasm for peasant folk material as a basis for his music from that time forward.

At any rate, his next composition had no Russian tunes. When, in 1919, the impresario of the Ballet Russe, Sergei Diaghilev, suggested that Stravinsky compose a ballet based on fragments of the 18th-century composer Pergolesi, he found him a willing collaborator. For the first time Stravinsky worked with Bach-like materials. All subsequent evidence points to the fact that the ballet that resulted, *Pulcinella,* was a determining factor in the development of his later style—a much more important factor than any of the first spectators of *Pulcinella* could possibly have foreseen.

The years between *Pulcinella* (1919) and the Octet (1923) were marked by a certain indecision. The Symphonies of Wind Instruments (1920) is clearly a transitional work—some of its themes point in the direction of the prewar years, and the exceptionally beautiful coda presages the Neoclassic music to come. As for the one-act stage work *Mavra,* composed a year before the Octet, Stravinsky tells us in his *Autobiography* that he deliberately cultivated "the Europeanized tradition of Russian culture." By this he means, of course, the tradition of Pushkin and Tchaikovsky as opposed to the more militantly nationalist school of the Russian Five.

With the composing of the Octet, Stravinsky established the fundamental outlines of all his subsequent Neoclassic work. He posited a new universalistic ideal for music, based on Classic forms and contrapuntal textures, borrowing his melodic material eclectically from all periods, yet fusing the whole by the indubitable power of his own personality. From this time forward there is a complete unity of aesthetic purpose in all his work. Starting with the colorful realism of *Petrushka* and proceeding through the more impersonal primitivism of *The Rite of Spring* and *Les Noces,* Stravinsky became more and more enamored of the objective element in his creative work until, with the writing of the Octet, he completely abandoned realism and primitivism of all kinds and openly espoused the cause of objectivism in music.

That seems to me to be the fundamental fact. Far from representing a "multitude of aesthetic points of view"—a criticism that has been leveled at Stravinsky over and over again—his work shows a clearly unified purpose. Whatever we may think of the music he wrote during the years

1923–1951, there is no denying its logic. It is the objective attitude that is important and forward-looking, rather than Stravinsky's application of that attitude. For one cannot avoid a certain feeling of dissatisfaction with some facets of Stravinsky's work of this period. Despite the seriousness of tone, the elegance of style, and the brilliance of execution that characterize everything Stravinsky does, it is difficult to understand why he should have felt the need to stay so close to Classic models. There is a reactionary tendency discernible here—in the sudden retreat to more normal musical procedure, in the dependence upon 18th-century melodic contours and forms, and in the general paring down of all the revolutionary elements of his earlier work. These later works constitute what is almost a new phenomenon in music—an "art grafted on art." Only a composer with the personality of a Stravinsky could cope with so many self-imposed limitations. Admirable or not, they make secure Stravinsky's place in the history of the music of our time.

Among the finest works in his Neoclassic manner must be listed the choral *Symphony of Psalms* (1930) and the opera-oratorio *Oedipus Rex* (1927). Both of these bear a definite relation to the pagan feeling of *The Rite of Spring*. In 1928 the ballet *Apollo, Leader of the Muses* added a new suavity and sensuousness to the composer's palette. The crowning work of this period was Stravinsky's opera *The Rake's Progress* (1951), written in collaboration with the poets W. H. Auden and Chester Kallman. It epitomizes the composer's thirty-year fascination with 18th-century ideals.

Now, finally, we have reached the logical end of the movement that began with a small group of obscure Russians in the 1870s—the desire to free music from the stranglehold of German Romanticism. It is as if we have gone all the way around a circle that began with Mussorgsky and ended with Stravinsky—a circle that took some fifty years of the most varied and circuitous efforts to complete itself.

The Neoclassic Influence

One of the least predictable aspects of the Neoclassic movement was the extent of its influence. Very few composers remained entirely untouched by contact with its pre-Romantic ideals. Even composers with firmly established styles of their own found a revitalizing principle in the Neoclassic manner. I am thinking especially of men like Manuel de Falla and his Concerto for harpsichord, flute, oboe, clarinet, violin, and violoncello (1926); Alfredo Casella and his *Scarlattiana* (1926); Albert Roussel and his orchestral Suite in F (1926); Francis Poulenc and his *Aubade* (1931); Ernest Bloch and his Concerto Grosso (1925); Heitor Villa-Lobos and his *Bachianas brasileiras* (1928). Composers who were not directly influenced also found in Neoclassicism an incentive for dropping the mechanistic primitivism of their earlier works. Serge Prokofiev, for example, whose *Scythian Suite* and early ballet *The Age of Steel* had been full of realistic dynamism, struck a brand-new lyrical note in his later stage work *The Prodigal Son* (1928). As for the younger men, they unhesitatingly adopted the classicizing manner. An American composer, Roger Sessions, summed up their new ideals in an article written in 1927, as follows:

"Younger men are dreaming of an entirely different kind of music—a music which derives its power from forms beautiful and significant by virtue of inherent musical weight rather than intensity of utterance; a music whose impersonality and self-sufficiency preclude the exotic; which takes its impulse from the realities of a passionate logic; which, in the authentic freshness of its moods, is the reverse of ironic and, in its very aloofness from the concrete preoccupations of life, strives rather to contribute form, design, a vision of order and harmony."

Of all those who profited by the Neoclassic influence, no one knew better how to develop and reshape it for his own ends than the German composer Paul Hindemith. The appearance of Hindemith on the scene in the early 1920s gave fresh hope to all those who had despaired of finding a man capable of instilling new blood into the exhausted German musical tradition. Beginning his career normally enough under the usual influences of Brahms and Strauss, Hindemith quickly assimilated the latest musical fashions as represented by early Stravinsky and jazz. But his own more characteristic style took shape only when it made contact with the Neoclassic movement.

At this point it is necessary to pause for a moment in order to make clear that the 18th-century ideal had had its own champion in Central Europe even before the war years and certainly before Stravinsky had thought of leading anyone "back to Bach." I am not referring to Max Reger, whose heavy-handed, post-Brahmsian turgidities were mistaken at first for a new form of Classicism. The real leader of the anti-Romantics was the German-Italian composer-pianist Ferruccio Busoni, without doubt one of the most original musical minds of the 20th century. It was the Italian side of his background that made Busoni impatient with Teutonic solutions for all music. Ernst Krenek, who was one of Busoni's best pupils, goes so far as to say that ". . . the concept of neoclassicism originated with Ferruccio Busoni. . . . Busoni's great anathema was nineteenth century romanticism. To him the movement seemed foggy, distorted, pretentious, bombastic, and formless. Against these characteristics he marshalled the crystal clearness, the cool fire, the lucidity, and the wise economy of the classical composers, especially of Mozart."

Busoni produced no final statement of principles in his various writings on music. He preferred to throw out aphoristic suggestions rather than lay down any specific program for the music of the future. Nevertheless, it was clear, as his biographer Edward J. Dent puts it, that ". . . what he sought to achieve was a neoclassicism in which form and expression may find their perfect balance." We can best judge the results of Busoni's theories from his short works, like the *Comedy Overture* or the *Rondo Arlecchinesco*, or from the more ambitious operas *Turandot* and *Doktor Faust*. Opinions differ as to the musical value of these works, but it is impossible to deny their importance as generators of new ideas. The relationship between the *Rondo Arlecchinesco* and some of Hindemith's earlier concert music, for example, is unmistakable. The bounding melodic line, the contrapuntal texture, the absence of any sentimental hubbub—the general buildup of the music on Classic principles—all indicate that the Latin ideals of Busoni had taken hold in the most talented representative of young German music.

The well-known German music critic Alfred Einstein is the authority for the statement that the introduction of new ideas in music was bitterly fought in Germany, "Nowhere else," he says, "was this movement initiated under greater difficulties." Still, Hindemith's talent was such that it impressed all listeners, even those who opposed him bitterly. It is hard to see how they could have avoided being impressed by the forthright quality of the man. From the very start the extraordinary vigor and exuberance of the music, and Hindemith's facility and technical equipment, were generally acknowledged. Whether the mood was healthy and robust or sardonic, boisterous, and full of fun, it was always carried off without the slightest trace of affectation. One would have sworn that these qualities were just what was needed to pull German music out of the doldrums.

Nevertheless, many of these first works suffer from being too eclectic. It wasn't until the Neoclassic trend caught up with him that Hindemith knew best how to exploit his natural gifts. He seemed to have an inborn affinity with the craftsmanlike attitude of the 18th-century composer, with his honest desire to do a job simply and well. He seemed to enjoy attacking many of the old problems, finding his own solutions for them. He wrote a kind of linear counterpoint that infused new life into ancient contrapuntal procedures. He composed long and intricate and pseudo-Bachian melodies, accompanying them with unmistakably 20th-century harmonies. His natural bent for rhythmic energy attached itself to the insistent sixteenth-note motion of a Handelian concerto grosso. He renounced all tonal ambiguity, beginning and ending pieces squarely on the tonic. His forms were sharply defined, each section of each piece having its own clear meaning, as in the works of the 18th-century masters.

Among all the compositions of this period in Hindemith's development, my preference goes to *Das Marienleben*, a cycle of sixteen songs for soprano with piano accompaniment, on poems by Rainer Maria Rilke.

Here, for the first time, one is conscious of the peculiar beauty of the composer's quiet episodes—a searching, wistful, hopeless quality such as can be found nowhere else in contemporary music. The Concerto for Orchestra and the Kammermusik No. 2 for piano solo and twelve instruments should also be mentioned as among Hindemith's best works of this period.

By the time the Third Reich was in the saddle in Germany, Hindemith had lived a very full musical life. He had served as orchestral musician, quartet player, and conductor; he had composed in every known musical form from grand opera and oratorio down to teaching pieces for infants; he could perform passably well on any one of fourteen different musical instruments; and in 1928 he topped off all this by becoming professor of composition at the Hochschule in Berlin.

As it turned out, it was his teaching that most affected his future work. Like all Germans, Hindemith loved orderliness. Sooner or later he was certain to be disturbed by the lack of any logical systematic procedure on the part of the modern composer. How could he correct the compositions of his students with a clear conscience when no one had formulated the laws governing the writing of modern music? Moreover, the time seemed ripe for such an undertaking. The experimental period of contemporary music was definitely on the wane by 1928, and it became possible at least to make a start in the direction of formulating a clear statement of principles underlying all new music.

With characteristic energy Hindemith produced a book, *The Craft of Musical Composition* (*Unterweisung im Tonsatz*), in which he set forth his ideas regarding modern harmony, melody writing, and related subjects. The importance of all this to an understanding of Hindemith's work is that, having put down to his own satisfaction the basic principles governing the composing of music in the new style, he proceeded to correct not only the compositions of his pupils but also his own early compositions (even including *Das Marienleben*) and to make all his subsequent compositions conform to the principles he himself had deduced.

This was a bold step on Hindemith's part: there are very few examples in musical history of the existence of the creator and theorist in one individual. The danger is obvious—given the formula, the creator is likely to underestimate the unconscious part of creation—what André Gide calls "la part de Dieu." Like all very prolific composers, Hindemith had always run the risk of writing music not because he had to but because he was able to. Now it would seem that, whether the works were to have necessity or not, they would at least have logic.

Fortunately, theory or no theory, Hindemith continued to write viable works—at any rate, when he was at his best. Sometimes the formula gets the better of the music, and we are given a series of sonatas for various mediums that present a depressingly homogeneous physiognomy. But in works like the opera *Mathis der Maler*, the four-hand piano sonata, and the *Saint Francis* ballet, we know we are listening to a creative mind that transcends mere methodic formulas.

One might look in vain through all Hindemith's music for any signs of the cruel years through which Germany and all the world passed. On the surface he appears to have continued writing placidly in his accustomed style, indifferent to censure or acclaim. But if one listens more attentively, there seems to be an increasing dependence on what we might call a medievalizing mood—the mood of resignation, of the elegiac tableau—and a corresponding absence of that robust and aggressive manner that was once so typical of Hindemith's work. No doubt it is Hindemith's capacity for ignoring the confusions and cruelties of his day that accounts for his having been able to produce work after work with incredible regularity. And though these compositions often give the impression that he was no longer inventing out of new experience but merely writing from an experience and a formula that had already served him over and over again, we know that at his best he was able to turn out works worthy of one of the finest musical minds of our generation.

1967: It is evident, it seems to me, that in my summary of Hindemith's achievement, written when the composer was forty-six years old, I was not unaware of what one might call the "workhorse" aspect of his nature. The present generation judges him harshly—is, in fact, downright unfriendly. Hindemith is no longer cited among the top men of our time; it is undeniable that a severe downgrading is in process. However, whatever the eventual fate of his more ambitious works, it seems likely that he will continue to live on in the concert hall and the classroom as the composer of many useful and practical compositions written for almost every medium. As years went by, his strongly pedagogic nature gradually preempted the place once held by his more adventurous creative urge. The works he wrote as inspired composer—such as *Das Marienleben* and *Mathis der Maler*—are secure, but they would appear to be fewer than we had once supposed.

The Depression Years

The music of the decade 1930–40 emphasized the apparent decline of the experimental phase of contemporary music. For almost forty years, music had passed through a series of revolutionary crises, as a result of which all the stultifying "rules" of harmony, rhythmic phrase, and melodic construction had been broken down. By 1930, composers everywhere began to sense the necessity for consolidating the gains made for their art through so many years of experimentation. Like Hindemith, they wanted to "cash in" on the discoveries of the pioneers, to take stock of all the new musical resources that were now at their disposal. Moreover, from the aesthetic standpoint, there was no longer anything to fear from Romanticism; it had been firmly established that new music, in whatever style, was to be objective in attitude, clearly conceived, and contained in emotional expression.

All this was the natural swing of the musical pendulum. In the past, every period of experimentation in music had been followed by a summing-up period. This need for a new "order" in contemporary music was intensified by one very important external factor, namely, the reaction—or more exactly, the lack of reaction—on the part of the audience.

Since Wagner's day it had become axiomatic that the lay listener was by nature slow to comprehend innovations in music. During the very critical years of change that followed the death of Wagner, composers had come to take it for granted that their works could be of interest only to the most forward-looking among their audiences. How could the ordinary music lover, comparatively unaware of the separate steps that brought on the gradual changes in musical methods and ideals, be expected to understand music that sounded as if it came from some other planet? Composers, by the end of the '20s, began to have an uneasy feeling that a larger and larger gap was separating them from their listeners. They would have been dull indeed not to have realized that this lack of contact with any real audience was placing them in a critical situation. Moreover, the additional fact that new music was beginning to "normalize" itself made it seem more than ever desirable and even necessary that an effort be made to regain the active interest in contemporary music of the entire music-listening public.

The only new tendency discernible in the music of the decade 1930–40 can be traced to this feeling of dissatisfaction on the part of composers at the lack of any healthy relationship with their potential public. As a result, two steps were taken: first, many composers tried to simplify their musical language as much as possible, and second, they attempted not only to make contact with audiences in the concert hall, but to seek out music listeners and performers wherever they were to be found—in the public schools and colleges, the teaching studios, and the movie houses, over the air waves, through recordings—anywhere, in fact, where music was heard or made.

Historically, we can find the first signs of this new tendency in Central Europe during the middle '20s. It was quite natural that in a country where music was more highly cultivated than anywhere else, composers should be made painfully aware of their lack of contact with the musically educated public. A typically German solution was tried. Composers, with Paul Hindemith at their head, began to write a music especially addressed to the needs of the musical amateur. This kind of music, later called

Gebrauchsmusik—literally, music for use—was designed to familiarize nonprofessional performers with musical devices different from those in the classics they knew so well. This first step was encouraged by the German music publishers, who saw in it the possibility of opening new sales in a hitherto untouched market.[3] But the value of this first step was purely tactical, for the actual musical content of most *Gebrauchsmusik* was weak. Composers continued to reserve their best thoughts for their "serious" music. Nevertheless, the possibility of establishing contact with the ordinary music lover was first tested here.

At the same time, another move toward reaching the public was made in Germany. This time it was the opera public that was sought after. Kurt Weill and Ernst Krenek, already mentioned in connection with the jazz influence, deliberately went in for "popular appeal" in their stage works. Both these men were highly trained composers, capable of writing in the most abstruse style. But the postwar opera goer in Germany was not the comparatively erudite listener of the preceding epoch. He was completely unprepared to appreciate the atonal complexities of Berg and Schoenberg. By introducing songs in a pseudojazz manner in place of the old-fashioned aria, Weill and Krenek gave their public something they could comprehend. Here again it was proved that by changing their objective, composers could make contact with a very broad audience.

But the third and possibly most significant sign of the new tendency came by way of Russia, principally through the works of the Soviet composer Dmitri Shostakovitch. No doubt the example of Shostakovitch could have been multiplied if the works of other Russian contemporaries had been heard as frequently outside the Soviet Union. It is easy to see how a young composer, living in the midst of social revolution, would have uppermost in his mind the problem of his relationship to his audience. Obviously, the new, untutored mass public was totally unprepared to cope with musical subtleties. And yet the Soviet composer must have known that his works could be directed only to that same mass public.

It is curious to note the effect these circumstances also had on the music of Serge Prokofiev, who spent many years abroad but returned to live in the Soviet Union. Prokofiev may not be the greatest of modern composers, but he is certainly one of the most delightful. His style is fresh, clean-cut, articulate, and was so from the very first. It always comes as a surprise to realize

---

[3]In a letter to Nicolas Slonimsky from B. Schott's Sons, Hindemith's publishers (quoted by Mr. Slonimsky in his book *Music Since 1900*), a distinction is made between *Gemeinschaftsmusik*—music for the community—and *Gebrauchsmusik*—music written for some special purpose in contradistinction to concert or art music. In recent times, all music written for some particular purpose or for use by any group outside the concert field has come to be referred to as *Gebrauchsmusik*.

how little the essence of Prokofiev's music changed during two decades, in either emotional scope or technical perfection. Only his orchestration showed an advance over his earlier compositions. One would have guessed that his musical style, so full of melodic invention and *joie de vivre*, would have been just what was needed in the Soviet republics. And one would have guessed right, for as far as can be told from those of his later works that have been heard in the West, his rediscovery of his native land only made him lean more strongly on music of utter simplicity and directness.

But we see the challenge of the unsophisticated audience met most clearly in the music of Shostakovitch. At thirty-five he was the author of operas, ballets, chamber music, numerous film scores, and six symphonies, with more to come. The effectiveness of this music for a large public both inside and outside the Soviet Union has been proved beyond a doubt. Few people would say that this music is first-rate in quality. But if it seems unnecessarily trite and conventional at times, there is no denying the extraordinary "flair" and sheer musical invention displayed. The man certainly can write music. Interesting from a structural standpoint is his individual use of form, in which the music seems to flow easily instead of being tightly knit together with nothing but thematically apposite material, as is the German custom. The emotional intention of the music is always crystal clear—almost too clear, for one tires quickly of movements that are too flatly one thing or the other: satirical or sober, grandiose or sentimental. Whatever his weaknesses, in Shostakovitch the Soviet Union produced a composer with a pronounced personality of his own, who knows how to freshen the tradition of Borodin and Tchaikovsky so that it appeals not only to the proletarian masses of the Soviets but to the musical public everywhere. His influence seems likely to affect other composers with similar ideals.

1967: The balance sheet of Soviet composition for the quarter century that has passed since the above comments were written reads far more dolefully than we had any reason to expect. What happened? As far as can be judged from the admittedly scarce evidence that reaches us, musical creativity in the U.S.S.R. has been stultified. The revolutionary fervor of the war years, exemplified in the Shostakovitch works of that period, degenerated in the compositions of others into a mere conformism. Prokofiev died in 1953, and Shostakovitch is past sixty (in 1967); by now we ought to know the names of half a dozen younger men capable of carrying forward what these two accomplished. Kabalevsky, Khatchaturian, and Shaporin are solid musical citizens working in familiar idioms, but where are the adventurous youngsters who can hold their own with their counterparts in Western Europe or Japan or America? It is hardly possible to believe that in a country so large and so music-conscious the creative urge has petered out.

During a visit to the Soviet Union in 1960 I heard talk in musical circles of certain younger rebels, practitioners of serial methods or chance music. To effectively "forbid" such compositions, it is sufficient merely to make sure that they are not performed. At any rate, if they do exist, they are not being exported.[4] How then are we to gain a complete picture of the state of Soviet composition today? This is a problem for the Russian cultural authorities to take in hand. They cannot hope to have their young composers play a role in contemporary music unless they are willing to encourage them to face up to the musical realities of our day.

Dodecaphonic Developments

Now we must return to the early '20s in order to follow the fascinating progress of Arnold Schoenberg and his disciples toward a new kind of musical organization, which came to be known as the twelve-tone system.

A long period of gestation—approximately eight years—preceded the flowering of the dodecaphonic method devised by Schoenberg. The story is told that during the summer of 1922 the composer said to his student Josef Rufer: "I have made a discovery which will assure the supremacy of German music in the world for the next hundred years." Schoenberg had discovered the ground rules of the twelve-tone technique of composition, which was destined to influence the course of music written since that time.

In this second phase of Schoenberg's revolutionary practice, arrived at after years of experimentation, atonality is no longer chaotic, but is systematized and regulated through the agency of the "basic set of twelve tones."[5] I agree with Willi Reich when he writes that "the recognition of this technique is entirely superfluous to the instinctive understanding of a piece of music so composed." Nevertheless, a brief explanation of Schoenberg's method may be of interest to the general reader, especially since its basic principles are not difficult to grasp.

Schoenberg's method begins with the twelve half tones of the chromatic scale:

---

[4]In recent months some few pieces have been publicly performed in America by younger composers such as Andrei Volkonsky, Edison Denisov, and Valentian Silvestrov.
[5]See the letter from Arnold Schoenberg on the origin of the twelve-tone system in Nicolas Slonimsky's *Music Since 1900*.

These twelve tones are ordered into a specific arrangement of the composer's choice, called a tone-row or tone series (hence the term "serial" for the procedures of the dodecaphonic method). For example:

This is not necessarily a theme consisting of twelve different tones. It is basically a skeletal framework out of which the composer may evolve as many different versions as his fancy dictates. To simplify, instead of using all twelve tones, let us consider just the first six:

Schoenberg suggests three possible arrangements derived from this basic row, all three based on classical procedures. The first is obtained by reading the row backward, as one would read a sentence backward:

The second derivation treats the row by inversion:

In the third derivation, the inversion of the row is itself read backward:

The series can be transposed in the usual way to any other pitch:

And any note can be sounded in any available octave:

In order to avoid the danger of suggesting normal tonality, two further prohibitions are recommended by Schoenberg. One is to avoid repeating any tone (except for immediate repetition), once it has been left, until all the other eleven tones have been sounded. The other is to avoid doubling any tone at the octave, thus:

since doubling also tends to emphasize the importance of that one tone over the other eleven.

Rhythm is to be left free, dependent solely on the composer's choice. Moreover, and this is essential, the twelve-tone series is to be the controlling factor not only melodically, but also harmonically, thus insuring both horizontal and vertical unity. In other words, the notes may be used to form themes, like this:

or they may be used simultaneously, in whole or in part, to produce intervals or chords:

By the early '30s, Schoenberg was master of this new technique, as demonstrated in such works as the Variations for Orchestra, Opus 31, and the opera *Moses und Aron*, begun in 1931.

Roger Sessions once summed up Schoenberg's contribution in terms that seem to me to be eminently true: "The truly immense achievement of Schoenberg lies in the fact that his artistic career embodies and summarizes a fundamental musical crisis. More than any other composer he led the crisis to its culmination. He accomplished this by living it through to its furthest implications. But he also found technical means which could enable composers of his own and later generations to seek and find solutions. He opened up a new vein, toward which music has been tending; and the twelve-tone method is in essence the tool through which this vein can be exploited. Its discovery was an historical necessity; had it not been Schoenberg who formulated it, others would have done so, though possibly in a much slower and more laborious manner."

No one would any longer dispute Schoenberg's key role in the developing story of contemporary music since the second decade of our century. And yet, the music he composed within his new system still arouses strong partisan feelings. Some of the difficulty comes, I believe, from the temperament of the man himself, from the depth of that "Germanness" which is said to have been his special pride. Other contemporary artists have been profoundly German by temperament—Mann, Kokoschka, Brecht. But Schoenberg's case is different: an almost desperate fervor, a sometimes painful intensity, makes for a kind of expressivity that is difficult to empathize with, despite the indisputable sincerity and conviction that lies behind the music. Schoenberg's was an Old World spirit; out of an unbounded reverence for past German masters he felt the need of the revolutionary to bring something new to the art he loved. His classicizing tendencies were at variance with his personal temperament, which leaned toward the deeply tortuous expression of sentiment. No wonder it is difficult to summarize the lifework of such a man in a single paragraph!

And yet, when all is said, there remains something profoundly moving in the contemplation of this fiery creative spirit, burning at full intensity. Despite the contradictions of his complex nature, Schoenberg composed indubitable masterpieces—*Pierrot lunaire*, the Five Orchestral Pieces, the Four Orchestral Songs, the string quartets, and especially the dramatico-musical works, culminating in *Moses und Aron*. For sheer intellectual-emotional command in the dramatic manipulation of musical materials, Schoenberg had no peer. Twentieth-century music is inconceivable without him.

Schoenberg became famous not only as a composer and theoretician, but also as a teacher of younger composers. His two most renowned students, of course, were Alban Berg and Anton Webern, both of whom remained lifelong friends of their master. Despite their very different temperaments, Berg and Webern shared an unbounded enthusiasm for the ideas and personality of their teacher.

Alban Berg, who died in 1935 at the age of fifty, tended to normalize the Schoenberg idiom by relating it more frankly to its Tristanesque origins. In comparison with Schoenberg's complex personality, Berg's seems warm and sweetly human. His operas *Wozzeck* and *Lulu*, his Violin Concerto and *Lyric Suite* for string quartet are among the most appealing creations in the modern repertoire. Certain pages of these works are of a magical inspiration—sensuously lyrical, violently dramatic, and profoundly erotic by turns. Despite Berg's atonality, his spiritual being had closest association with late 19th-century Romanticism.

Berg suffered from a failing, if it can be called that, which Robert Craft once cleverly named "tonal nostalgia." The composer did not hesitate to choose tone-rows whose successions of notes, as in the Violin Concerto, suggest triadic formations. In effect, this practice negates to a certain extent the antitonal basis of the dodecaphonic method. This trait considerably reduces Berg's historical significance, no doubt, but it does not deprive him of an important place within the hierarchy of latter-day Viennese composers.

The case of Webern is much more complex and problematical. Those of us who first heard his compositions in the '20s recognized, without hesitation, his sensitive and rare musical individuality. Like Berg's, his output was small; moreover, all his most characteristic pieces of that period were astonishingly short. No one then had any inkling of the curious fate that lay in store for Webern's *oeuvre* after he died in 1945. Personally, I doubt whether Webern himself could have suspected the widespread influence his work was to have in our time. I cannot hope to do more than touch upon the main features of the "Webern Case"; it is one of the most fascinating in musical history. Hidden beneath the exquisite sensibility of this Viennese musician was the firm and rigorous spirit of an Austrian schoolmaster. The music he wrote demonstrates his purity of motive, his selfless devotion to a cause, and even more important, his ability to think a problem through to the end with clarity and obstinacy, and with utter disregard for worldly success. All these traits were typical of Webern, and as it turned out, had a profound effect on the development of contemporary music.

The clear and logical thinking of Webern freed him, at least in his own compositions, from any lingering attachment he may have had to traditional methods. In comparison, his teacher and his colleague—Schoenberg and Berg—each still had one foot in the 19th century. Pierre Boulez, with characteristic bluntness, puts it this way: "Schoenberg and Berg belong to the twilight years of the great German romantic tradition, whereas Webern reacted against all traditional forms of musical rhetoric."

Boulez was the first, as far as I know, to point out the weak cornerstone in Schoenberg's carefully constructed edifice of the twelve-tone system. Not only did Schoenberg share with Berg a definite tonal nostalgia; he also poured his new wine into the old bottles of the Classic forms—the rondo, the theme and variations, the minuet, and the gigue, to give but a few examples. Boulez accuses him of having been a kind of musical Kerensky, unable to carry through the full implications of the revolution he himself had instigated. "What then was Schoenberg's ambition," Boulez writes, "once the chromatic synthesis had been established by the tone-row? It was to construct works of the same kind as those of the tonal world he had only just abandoned, in which the new technique of composition would prove its possibilities. But, unless some attempt was made to explore the structures specific to twelve-tone composition, how could this new technique yield any satisfactory results? By structure I mean the growth from given material to the form of a composition. On the whole Schoenberg was not much preoccupied with the problem of forms that would derive from a twelve-tone basis. . . . Webern, on the other hand, succeeded in writing works whose form arises inevitably from the given material."

Here, then, was Webern's triumph. It was he who provided the signpost to the future, insofar as the future is bound up with the twelve-tone method. This reproach concerning Schoenberg's lack of daring in regard to his overall formal structures carries with it still wider implications. Because he continued to use themes and rhythms in the usual way, giving them motivic treatment, his works have the kind of continuity and flow associated in our minds with the tonal music of the past. Moreover, he applied the twelve-tone method only to the control of pitches, vertically and horizontally, other elements being left free of control. Therefore Schoenberg has been pictured as a kind of Moses who could see the promised land, but because of his own 19th-century limitations could not lead music into it. This leadership is precisely what Webern was able to provide.

Webern was the first to write music that is athematic and discontinuous and at the same time under rigorous control. Ernst Krenek calls it "the most complete break with tradition in centuries, perhaps in the entire history of occidental music."

It is not certain, of course, that fifty years hence music lovers will share the enthusiasm of today's young generation of composers for Webern's music. Its historical importance is unquestionable, but its longevity as music is still to be fully tested. His influence may turn out to be far greater than the intrinsic value of his own music, which may some day seem too mannered in style and too limited in scope.

Webern worked with a meticulous hand, but his need to be rigorously logical led him to use specially chosen tone-rows which, when broken into segments, seem to exist in space, as tiny microcosms. This treatment produces a music of detachment and impersonality, an effect which is increased by his considerable demands on the technical powers of the players. The musical line becomes "atomized," and each tone is given its own separate color—the famous *Klangfarbenmelodie* treatment.

Stravinsky, who in his seventies adopted a Webernian technique to his own purposes, speaks of Webern as a kind of saint. Something of the asceticism of a saint hangs over the music. Certainly it is written within one of the most self-restrictive techniques ever invented by a composer. It is partly this control which helps to give Webern's later music a Classic impassivity very different from the Romantic afflatus of that of Berg or Schoenberg, thus indicating the path ahead to the younger generation.

Stravinsky's Conversion

It was not only the younger generation that became enamored of the twelve-tone approach. As has just been mentioned, Stravinsky himself became involved in the dodecaphonic method of composition.

It is hard to imagine two creators in any period more different as men and artists than Schoenberg and Stravinsky: not only are the style and content of their music different; the lives they lived also differed, since one was a teacher and theorist and the other a performer and world citizen. It is curious to note that both men found themselves after the Second World War living in southern California. The crowning irony is that Stravinsky, in the end, should have adopted the method developed by Schoenberg.

It is interesting to speculate on why Stravinsky became interested in the music of Schoenberg and his school at precisely the time he did. From our present vantage point it is quite clear that with the writing of *The Rake's Progress* Stravinsky had reached a culminating point in his own Neoclassic style. It is hard to see how he could have continued along that path. Moreover, Schoenberg, last surviving member of the Viennese triumvirate, died in 1951, the same year that saw the opera produced for the first time. Most important of all was the formidably influential presence in the Stravinsky household of Robert Craft, equally adept in the two worlds of the two composers, and a powerful proselytizer for dodecaphony. The winning over of Stravinsky to a serious consideration of twelve-tone composition was a real coup. But it did not happen overnight; Stravinsky's biographer, Eric Walter White, points out that "between 1952 and 1957 his serial essays were cautious experiments carried out within a framework of tonal music."

There are few known examples in musical history of a composer turned seventy readjusting his musical thinking to this extent. But Stravinsky, with all the persistence and originality that is typical of him, did gradually make the transition from expanded tonality to atonality. As it turned out, it was Webern rather than Schoenberg who provided the Russian master with the incentive toward the new line. The new technique does satisfy his pleasure in working things out. The twelve tones, unrelated one to another, provide a schema for the concentration of thought and texture that Stravinsky finds so sympathetic. The single-mindedness with which Stravinsky has pursued his muse in these unfamiliar fields has astonished his admirers, especially since the works themselves, as anyone would agree, have not met with the acceptance of his more "Stravinskian" scores.

It is instructive to follow the composer's progress from the strained and somewhat halting religiosity of the *Canticum Sacrum* of 1955 to the elliptical and original *Movements* for piano and orchestra of 1959. One listens and listens again without being certain of having gotten the message. But something about the short ten-minute work convinces; at any rate one is convinced that a new kind of musical communication is being forged. A more recent work of a similar fascination is the Variations for Orchestra composed in memory of his friend Aldous Huxley. Here the orchestral timbres are uniquely fresh. Most of the compositions Stravinsky has written in his last manner are quite short; an exception is *The Flood*, one of the least successful from a musical and production standpoint of his latter-day works.

It would be foolhardy to attempt a summary of the serial compositions of Stravinsky. They seem to exist in a curious and special ambiance of Stravinsky's own making. They give off a "made" and somewhat awkward quality, but in every measure they bear the mark of the singular individual that is Stravinsky.

Musical Imagination
in the Americas (1952)

Music and Imagination (1952) collects Copland's Charles Eliot Norton lectures presented at Harvard the previous academic year. This lecture shows, among other qualities, his constant awareness of recent developments; Morton Feldman (1926–1967) had published his first graphic score, *Projections I*, in 1950, while Lennie Tristano (1919–1978) began his experiments with shifting improvisation away from a more standard jazz idiom and toward a freer method, in pieces such as "Intuition" and "Digression," in 1949. (S.S.)

An astute fellow musician was responsible for suggesting to me the difficult subject of imagination in the music of the Americas. He put the question to me in this way: The art of music has been practiced for a good many years now in the Western Hemisphere—both north and south; can it be said that we have exercised our own imagination as musicians and not merely reflected what we have absorbed from Europe? And if we have succeeded in bringing a certain inventiveness and imaginativeness of our own to the world of music, what precisely has our contribution been? I protested that to answer such a question satisfactorily was an almost impossible assignment; that perhaps it was in any event too early to ask it; and, moreover, that I myself might be a poor judge of the present situation, because of an over-anxiety to find favorable answers. But my musical friend persisted. He pointed out that everyone agrees that the two Americas are more grown-up musically than they were two generations ago; and besides, he added, you have visited South America and Mexico and Cuba and Canada, and have watched the musical movement in our own country develop for more than thirty years. Aren't you in a better position than most observers to arrive at some conclusion as to how far we have come in making our own special contribution to the world's music? In the end I found myself puzzling over this question. No matter how wrong-headed my reactions may be, it seemed likely that some musicologist fifty years hence might very well be intrigued to discover what answers suggested themselves to a composer in mid-twentieth century America.

If the experience of the Americas proves anything, it indicates that music is a sophisticated art—an art that develops slowly. It is about four hundred years since the first book containing musical notation was published in this hemisphere. That notable event took place in Mexico in the year 1556. In the United States the burgeoning period covers some three hundred years, which is also a considerable time span for the development of an art. Actually it seems to me that in order to create an indigenous music of universal significance three conditions are imperative. First, the composer must be part of a nation that has a profile of its own—that is the most important; second, the composer must have in his background some sense of musical culture and, if possible, a basis in folk or popular art; and third, a superstructure of organized musical activities must exist—that is, to some extent, at least—at the service of the native composer.

In both North and South America it was only natural that from the beginning the musical pattern followed lines which are normal for lands that are colonized by Europeans. In both Americas there was first the wilderness and the struggle merely to keep alive. Our Latin American cousins were more fortunate than we in their musical beginnings. Some of the Catholic missionaries from Spain were cultivated musicians intent upon teaching the rudiments of music to their charges. Pedro de Gante, a Franciscan padre, is credited with having started the first music school in the New World around 1524. He taught the natives to sing hymns and to write musical notation. The Puritan Fathers, on the other hand, were reported as downright unfriendly to the musical muse, although this harsh judgment has been somewhat tempered in recent years. Nevertheless, it is safe to assume that apart from the singing of psalms there exist few if any signs that music as an art was encouraged.

It was during the later years of the colonial period of both North and South America that the first native, primitive composers raised their voices. These were mostly men who wrote their music in their spare time, as an avocation rather than as a profession. They, in turn, were soon aided by the initial influx of a certain number of professional musicians from abroad. In our own country many of these immigrants came at first from England. As Otto Kinkeldey has pointed out, in those days practically all our music came by way of England: Handel, Haydn, Mozart were known to the United States because they were known in England. A later wave came to our shores from Central Europe, especially Germany; and as a result our musical thinking was dominated for a great many years by Teutonic ideals.

In Latin America the immigrant musician came principally from the Iberian Peninsula, as might be expected, while a later wave brought a large number of musical recruits from Italy.

Is there anything imaginative about the music composed in the Americas during the eighteenth and nineteenth centuries? So far as we can tell from the preserved records, very little. A few hardy primitives from the Revolutionary War period, like William Billings, have survived. Billings was a tanner by trade who ended up as a composer of hymn tunes and short patriotic pieces that only recently have been rediscovered and republished. They break harmonic rules occasionally and are sometimes a bit stiff in their contrapuntal joints, but despite that they have a rough honesty about them that keeps them alive for present-day listeners. Mention ought to be made of two other composers of the middle nineteenth century: Louis Moreau Gottschalk of New Orleans and Carlos Gomes of Rio de Janeiro. Both of them achieved fame abroad. Gottschalk led the life of a traveling piano virtuoso in the Lisztian manner. His importance historically comes from the fact that he is the earliest composer we know of who based his compositions on what are loosely called Latin American rhythms. It is only the exceptional piece of Gottschalk's that is of original quality; others are too obviously designed to dazzle the paying public. Nevertheless, he represents the first North American composer who made us aware of the rich source material to be derived from music of Hispanic origins. Carlos Gomes was a very successful opera composer, whose best works were performed at La Scala in Milan. His libretti were based on native Brazilian subject matter, but the musical style in which they were treated was indistinguishable from the Italian models on which they were based. Gomes was, however, the first of his kind and remains to this day a national hero in his own country.

We have our own national hero in Stephen Foster. He was a song writer rather than a composer, but he had a naturalness and sweetness of sentiment that transformed his melodies into the equivalent of folk song. His simplicity and sincerity are not easily imitated, but it is that same simplicity and naturalness that has inspired certain types of our own music in the twentieth century. Billings and Foster have no exact counterparts in the music of the Southern Hemisphere. The closest parallel will be found in the work of two Latin Americans who were active toward the end of the last century—Julián Aguirre in Argentina and Ignacio Cervantes in Cuba. They both composed a type of sensitive, almost Chopinesque, piano piece with a Creole flavor, that was to be followed by so many others in the same manner in Latin America. Aguirre and Cervantes gave us the little piece in its pristine state, with a kind of disingenuous charm, before it was cheapened by the sentimentalities of numerous lesser composers.

If, as you see, the pickings are slim in the field of composed music of serious pretensions during the eighteenth and nineteenth centuries, there is a compensatory richness of invention when we turn to the popular forms of music making. It is not surprising that this should be so. Popular music crystallizes long in advance of composed concert music. After all, it reflects an unpremeditated and spontaneous welling up of musical emotion that requires no training and no musical superstructure. The human voice, with perhaps a drum or a simple folk instrument as accompaniment, is all that is needed to express a wide gamut of feelings. Folk music in the Western Hemisphere awaits some master investigator who can survey what is an immense terrain, and sort out and collate similarities and differences in such a way as to illuminate this whole field for us. I myself am far from being expert in this area, but I do retain vivid impressions of an unbelievably rich and comparatively little known territory of folk expression in Latin America.

I should like, parenthetically, to mention briefly a few examples that come to mind. The Cuban *guajira* is one of these. It is a form of country music of the Cuban farmer. Over the strumming of a few simple guitar chords the singer tells a tale in a singular style of melodious recitative that is drenched in an individuality. It seems to me it could be listened to for hours on end. The same holds true for the deeply nostalgic music of the Peruvian Indian, played on ancient flutes, sometimes in pairs and with a curious heterophony—of an indescribable sadness. The exhilarating rhythm of the *bambuco* as it is danced in Colombia epitomizes the many popular dance patterns that alternate six-eight and three-quarter metrics with delightful effect. And I cannot mention dancing without remembering the incredible *frevo* as I saw it "performed" in the streets of Pernambuco. Musically the *frevo* demonstrates what occurs when the naïve musical mind seizes upon a well-known form—in this case the ordinary street march—and transforms it into a completely Afro-Brazilian manifestation. A similar transformation is worked upon the figurations of a Czerny piano exercise when a Cuban composer of popular music writes a *danzón*. Here pseudo elegance is the keynote—an "elegance" of high life in the Havana of 1905. As a final example I must mention the urban tango as one hears it in Argentina, played in a hard-as-nails manner by several accordions and a few assorted strings. This instrumental combination produces a sonority of knife-edge sharpness, so that even the would-be sentimental sections are played without a glimmer of sentimentality.

These different forms of folk and popular music briefly listed here must stand for many others. Diverting and interesting as they are, however, they are not what my musician friend was referring to when he inquired after signs of imaginativeness in the music of the Western world. Confining ourselves to serious music, there seems to me no doubt that if we are to lay claim to thinking inventively in the music of the Americas our principal stake must be a rhythmic one.

For some years now rhythm has been thought to be a special province of the music of both Americas. Roy Harris pointed this out a long time ago when he wrote: "Our rhythmic sense is less symmetrical than the European rhythmic sense. European musicians are trained to think of rhythm in its largest common denominator, while we are born with a feeling for its smallest units . . . We do not employ unconventional rhythms as a sophistical gesture; we cannot avoid them . . ." Let us see if it is possible to make more precise these remarks of Harris'—whether it is possible to track down the source and nature of these so-called American rhythms.

Most commentators are agreed that the source of our rhythmic habits of mind are partly African and partly Spanish. Since the Iberian Peninsula was itself a melting pot of many races, with a strong admixture of Arab culture from Africa, the Iberian and African influences are most certainly interrelated. In certain countries the aboriginal Indians have contributed something through their own traditional rhythmic patterns, although this remains rather conjectural. As time goes on, it becomes more and more difficult to disengage the African from the Iberian influence. We speak of Afro-Cuban, Afro-Brazilian, Afro-American rhythms in an attempt to circumvent this difficulty. Since Spain and Portugal have, by themselves, produced nothing like the rhythmic developments of the Western countries, it is only natural to conclude that we owe the vitality and interest of our rhythms in large measure to the Negro in his new environment. It is impossible to imagine what American music would have been like if the slave trade had never been instituted in North and South America. The slave ships brought a precious cargo of wonderfully gifted musicians, with an instinctive feeling for the most complex rhythmic pulsations. The strength of that musical impulse is attested to by the fact that it is just as alive today in the back streets of Rio de Janeiro or Havana or New Orleans as it was two hundred years ago. Recent recordings of musical rites among certain African tribes of today make perfectly apparent the direct musical line that connects the Náñigos of today's Cuba or Brazil with their forefathers of the African forest.

What is the nature of this gift? First, a conception of rhythm not as mental exercise but as something basic to the body's rhythmic impulse. This basic impulse is exteriorized with an insistence that knows no measure, ranging from a self-hypnotic monotony to a riotous frenzy of subconsciously controlled pounding. Second, an unparalleled ingenuity in the spinning out of unequal metrical units in the unadorned rhythmic line. And lastly, and most significant, a polyrhythmic structure arrived at through the combining of strongly independent blocks of sound. No European music I ever heard has even approached the rhythmic intensities obtained by five different drummers, each separately hammering out his own pattern of sound, so that they enmesh one with another to produce a most complex metrical design. Oriental musics contain subtle cross-rhythms of polyrhythmic implication, but we of the Americas learned our rhythmic lessons largely from the Negro. Put thus baldly it may be said, with some justice perhaps, that I am oversimplifying. But even if I over-state the case the fact remains that the rhythmic life in the scores of Roy Harris, William Schuman, Marc Blitzstein, and a host of other representa-tive American composers is indubitably linked to Negroid sources of rhythm.

A very different idea of the polymetric organization of pulsations is fa-miliar in European music. How could it be otherwise? Any music which is contrapuntally conceived is likely to have melodic lines that imply differ-ent rhythms, and these would naturally be heard simultaneously. But the point here is one of emphasis and degree. Few musicians would argue that the classical composers wrote music that was polyrhythmically arranged, in the sense in which I am using the term here. Mozart and Brahms were far from being constrained by the bar line, as is made clear by certain re-markable sections of rhythmic ingenuity in their scores, and yet their nor-mal procedure with rhythm implies a regularity and evenness of metrical design that we think of as typical of Western music.

Other examples of Western music, especially in choral literature, demon-strate an unconventional rhythmic organization. But for the purpose I have in mind it will suffice to confine ourselves to two kinds of music, before the twentieth century, which appear to me to be exceptional in this respect, that is, in their concentration on polyrhythmic texture: the recently deciphered scores of French and Italian composers at the end of the thirteen hundreds; and the English madrigals of Shakespeare's day. Exceptional as these are, I hope to show that American rhythms are premised upon a quite different type of polymetrics—a conception that is nowhere else duplicated.

The composers of the late fourteenth century—some of whose music has recently been made available through a publication of the Mediaeval Academy of America—exhibit in their ballades and virelais a most aston-ishing intricacy of rhythmic play. The editor of the volume in question, Willi Apel, suggests that these rhythms may not have been entirely "felt" by their composers, but were perhaps the result of "notational speculation." It is quite possible that their system of notation provided these composers with a new toy by means of which they were enabled to experiment with all manner of unprecedented rhythmic combinations. But even as mere paper rhythms—and it is certainly doubtful whether they are only that—they hold great fascination for the present-day musician.

The rhythmic complexities of the Elizabethan madrigalists, on the other hand, were firmly grounded in English speech rhythms. By retaining these independently in each vocal part a delightful freedom of cross-rhythmic irregularities resulted. And since English is a strongly accented language—with qualitative rather than quantitative values—a rich and supple variety of rhythm was obtained that no other European school of that time could match. Curiously enough, it is only in the twentieth century that the rhythmic skill of the Elizabethans has come to be understood and appreciated. Formerly the very freedom of their metrical designs was thought to be a fault rather than a virtue. Wilfrid Mellers sums this up when he writes: ". . . the sixteenth century, which nineteenth century commentators considered rhythmically 'vague,' actually developed rhythm to the highest point it has reached in European history." And he adds: "Perhaps it is no accident that in England this supreme development of musical rhythm coincides with the development of mature Shakespearean blank verse, which achieves its effect from a delicate tension between speech rhythm and metrical accent."

It is important to point out that the polyrhythmic structures of the Elizabethan composers are different in kind from those that typify American music. They were concerned with the creation of a supple and fluid pulse in which no single strong beat dominated the over-all rhythmic flow. Our polyrhythms are more characteristically the deliberate setting, one against the other, of a steady pulse with a free pulse. Its most familiar manifestation is in the small jazz band combination, where the so-called rhythm section provides the ground metrics around which the melody instruments can freely invent rhythms of their own. Added to this influence from popular sources was the general concentration on rhythmic intensities for which our century is notable. The interest in national musics of different kinds—Russian, Hungarian, Scandinavian—with their unconventional rhythms acted as further stimulus in the breaking down of the tyranny of the bar line. Rhythmic factors became one of the preponderant concerns of serious music in most European countries.

In the Americas, however, the typical feature of our own rhythms was this juxtaposition of steadiness, either implied or actually heard, as against freedom of rhythmic invention. Take, for example, the stylistic device of "swinging" a tune. This simply means that over a steady ground rhythm the singer or instrumentalists toy with the beat, never being exactly *on* it, but either anticipating it or lagging behind it in gradations of metrical units so subtle that our notational system has no way of indicating it. Of course you cannot stay off the beat unless you know where that beat is. Here again freedom is interesting only in relation to regularity. On the other hand, when our better jazz bands wish to be rhythmically exact they come down on the beat with a trip-hammer precision that puts our symphonic musicians to shame. Thus an *ambiance* of playing fast and loose with the rhythm is encouraged which has tended to separate more and more the American and European conception of musical pulse.

The European is taught to think of rhythm as applying always to a phrase of music—as the articulation of that phrase. We, on the contrary, are not averse to thinking of rhythm as disembodied, so to speak, as if it were a frame to which certain tones might be added as an afterthought. This is, of course, not meant to be taken as literally true, but merely indicates a tendency on our part to think of rhythms as separately pulsating quarter or eighth or sixteenth notes—what Roy Harris means when he says we feel at ease with rhythm's "smallest units." Small units, when combined, are likely to add up to musically unconventional totals of five, seven, or eleven by contrast with the more familiar combinations of two plus two or of three plus three. Our European colleagues may protest and claim: "But we too write our music nowadays with the freedom of unequal divisions of the bar lines." Of course they do; but nonetheless it is only necessary to hear a well-trained European musician performing American rhythms to perceive the difference in rhythmic conceptions.

Winthrop Sargeant was making a similar point in terms of the jazz player when he wrote: "The jazz musician has a remarkable sense of subdivided and subordinate accents in what he is playing, even though it be the slowest sort of jazz. This awareness of minute component metrical units shows itself in all sorts of syncopative subtleties that are quite foreign to European music. It is, I think," he adds, "the lack of this awareness in most European 'classical' musicians that explains their well-known inability to play jazz in a convincing manner."

The special concern with rhythm that is characteristic of American music has had, as an offshoot, a rather more than usual interest in percussive sounds, as such. Orchestras, as constituted in the nineteenth century, had only a comparatively few elementary noise-making instruments to draw upon. In recent times the native musics of Cuba, Brazil, and Mexico have greatly enriched our percussive gamut through the addition of an entire battery of noise-making instruments peculiar to those countries. Some of these are slowly finding their way into our more conventional musical organizations. New and distinctive sounds and noises have been added to what was formerly the most neglected department in the symphony orchestra. A departure from routine thinking occurred when contemporary composers began to write for groups of percussion instruments alone. Edgar Varèse was a pioneer in that field in the twenties and his example encouraged other composers to experiment along similar lines. I suppose we may consider Béla Bartók's Sonata for two pianos and two percussion players and Stravinsky's orchestration of his choral ballet Les Noces for four pianos and thirteen percussion players as further proof that an interest in unusual sonorities is typical of our times. But it is the musicians of North and Latin America who come by this interest most naturally, and from whom we may expect a continuing inventiveness and curiosity as to the percussive sound. Villa-Lobos once aroused my envy by showing me his personal collection of native Brazilian percussion instruments. After a visit like that, one asks oneself: how did we ever manage to get along for so long a time with the bare boom of the bass drum and the obvious crash of the cymbals?

Before leaving the subject of rhythm-inspired music something should be said of a specialty of the jazz musician that has been greatly admired, particularly by the European enthusiast. I refer, of course, to the improvisatory powers of the popular performer. If one looks up the word "improvisation" in the music dictionaries, reference will be made to the ability of composers, at certain periods of musical history, to improvise entire compositions in contrapuntal style. The art of improvising an accompaniment from a figured bass line was an ordinary accomplishment for the well-trained keyboard instrumentalist during the baroque period. But the idea of *group* improvisation was reserved for the jazz age. What gives it more than passing interest is the phonograph, for it is the phonograph that makes it possible to reserve and thereby savor the fine flavor of what is necessarily a lucky chance result. It is especially this phase of our popular music that has caused the French *aficionado* to become lyrical about *le jazz hot*.

When you improvise it is axiomatic that you take risk and can't foretell results. When five or six musicians improvise simultaneously the result is even more fortuitous. That is its charm. The improvising performer is the very antithesis of that tendency in contemporary composition that demands absolute exactitude in the execution of the printed page. Perhaps M. Stravinsky and those who support his view of rigorous control for the performer have been trying to sit on the lid too hard. Perhaps the performer should be given more elbow room and a greater freedom of improvisatory choice. A young composer recently conceived the novel idea of writing a "composition" on graph paper which indicated where a chord was to be placed in space and when in time, but left to the performer freedom to choose whatever chords happened to strike his fancy at the moment of execution. Most jazz improvisers are not entirely free either, partly because of the conventionality of jazz harmonic formulas, and partly because of over-used melodic formulas. Recent examples of group improvisations by Lennie Tristano and some few other jazz men are remarkable precisely because they avoid both these pitfalls. When American musicians improvise thus freely, and we are able to rehear their work through recordings, the European musician is the first to agree that something has been developed here that has no duplication abroad.

If Negro and Iberian source materials have exerted a strong hold on the imagination of musicians in the Americas, the influence of the musical culture of the aboriginal Indians seems to have been slight. Tragically little has survived from the music of pre-Columbian civilizations, and what there is comes to us in the form of a few instruments, and the scales that may be deduced from some of them. The Indians of today, when they sing and dance, produce a music that is difficult to authenticate. How much of what they do is the result of oral tradition and how much acquired from the circumstances of their post-Conquest environment is difficult to say. Their influence on serious music has been strongest in those countries where Indian culture was most highly developed and has been best preserved, such as Mexico and Peru. In our own country, where the Indian had not reached the cultural level of the Incas or Aztecs, only a few composers were hopeful of finding stimulus in the thematic materials available to them. Despite the efforts of Arthur Farwell and his group of composer friends, and despite the *Indian Suite* of Edward MacDowell, nothing really fructifying resulted. It is understandable that the first Americans would have a sentimental attraction for our composers, especially at a time when the American composer himself was searching for some indigenous musical expression. But our composers were obviously incapable of identifying themselves sufficiently with such primitive source materials as to make these convincing when heard out of context.

The contemporary Chilean composer, Carlos Isamitt, was more successful in a somewhat analogous situation. The Araucanian Indians of southern Chile are not a highly developed people like the Incas of Peru, and yet Isamitt, by living among them and immersing himself in their culture, was able to draw something of their independent spirit into his own symphonic settings of their songs and dances.

But the principal imprint of the Indian personality—its deepest reflection in the music of our hemisphere—is to be found in the present-day school of Mexican composers, and especially in the work of Carlos Chávez and Silvestre Revueltas. With them it is not so much a question of themes as it is of character. Even without previous knowledge of the Amerindian man, his essential nature may be inferred from their scores. The music of Chávez is strong and deliberate, at times almost fatalistic in tone; it bespeaks the sober and stolid and lithic Amerindian. It is music of persistence—relentless and uncompromising; there is nothing of the humble Mexican peon here. It is music that knows its own mind—stark and clear and, if one may say so, earthy in an abstract way. There are no frills, nothing extraneous, it is like the bare wall of an adobe hut, which can be so expressive by virtue of its inexpressivity. Chávez' music is, above all, profoundly non-European. To me it possesses an Indian quality that is at the same time curiously contemporary in spirit. Sometimes it strikes me as the most truly contemporary music I know, not in the superficial sense, but in the sense that it comes closest to expressing the fundamental reality of modern man after he has been stripped of the accumulations of centuries of aesthetic experiences.

It is illuminating to contrast the work of Chávez with that of his countryman, the late Silvestre Revueltas, whose vibrant, tangy scores sing of a more colorful, perhaps a more mestizo side of the Mexican character. Revueltas was a man of the people with a wonderfully keen ear for the sounds of the people's music. He wrote no large symphonies or sonatas, but many short orchestral sketches with fanciful names such as *Ventanas, Esquinas, Janitzio* (*Windows, Corners, Janitzio*)—the last named after the little island in Lake Pátzcuaro. His list of compositions would be longer than it is were it not for the fact that he died when he was forty years old, in 1940. But the pieces that he left us are crowded with an abundance and vitality—a Mexican abundance and vitality—that make them a pleasure to hear.

In seeking for qualities of the specifically Western imagination it seems to me that there are two composers of South and North America who share many traits in common, and especially a certain richness and floridity of invention that has no exact counterpart in Europe. I am thinking of the Brazilian, Heitor Villa-Lobos, and of the American from Connecticut, Charles Ives.

Leaving aside questions of relative value it seems to me one would have to turn to Herman Melville's biblical prose or the oceanic verse of Walt Whitman to find an analogous largess. Is it illusory to connect this munificence of imagination in both composers with the scope and freedom of a new world? They share also the main drawback of an overabundant imagination: the inability to translate the many images that crowd their minds into scores of a single and unified vision. In the case of Villa-Lobos there is strong temptation to identify his crowded imagination with the luxuriance of a jungle landscape; the very sound of the music suggests it. In Ives we sense the strain of reaching for the transcendental and the universal that was native to his part of America.

Do both Ives and Villa-Lobos suffer from an inflated style? Alexis de Tocqueville, who visited our shores in the eighteen thirties, reported that the "inflated style" was typical for American orators and writers. There must be something about big countries—Brazil, in case you've forgotten, is larger than territorial United States—something that encourages creative artists to expand themselves beyond all normal limits. The lack of restraint made customary by tradition plays a role here. And when lack of restraint is combined with a copious and fertile imagination they together seem to engender a concomitant lack of self-criticism. Is it at all possible to be carefully selective if one possesses no traditional standard of reference? It would hardly seem so. The power in both men comes through in spite of their inability, at times, to exercise critical self-judgment. It is a power of originality of a curiously indigenous kind that makes their music appear to be so profoundly of this hemisphere.

There exist several parallelisms between the work of Ives and of Villa-Lobos. At one point in their careers they both used impressionistic methods to suggest realistic scenes of local life. With this there was the tendency to give their pieces homespun titles: Ives's symphony picture of the *Housatonic at Stockbridge* is matched by Villa-Lobos' *Little Train of Caipira*. Both men have a love for trying to make the "specific richly symbolic of the universal." They both were technically adventurous, experimenting with polytonal and polyrhythmic effects long before they had had contact with European examples of these new resources. (Ives was especially remarkable in this respect.) And they both retain central positions in the history of their country's music because of their willingness to ignore academic European models which for so long had satisfied other composers in their respective lands. And yet, in spite of these many similarities, it is characteristic that their music is utterly personal and distinct, one from the other.

In strong contrast to the floridity and occasional grandiloquence of Ives and Villa-Lobos, but no less representative of another and different aspect of America, is the music of Virgil Thomson and Douglas Moore. There is nothing in serious European music that is quite like it—nothing so downright plain and bare as their commerce with simple tunes and square rhythms and Sunday-school harmonies. Evocative of the homely virtues of rural America, their work may be said to constitute a "midwestern style" in American music. Attracted by the unadorned charm of a revivalist hymn, or a sentimental ditty, or a country dance, they give us the musical counterpart of a regionalism that is familiar in our literature and painting but is seldom found in our symphonies and concertos. Both these men, needless to say, are sophisticated musicians, so that their frank acceptance of so limited a musical vocabulary is a gesture of faith in their own heritage. Both have best exploited this type of midwestern pseudo primitivism in their operas and film scores. Thomson especially, with the aid of Gertrude Stein's texts in *Four Saints in Three Acts* and *The Mother of Us All*, has succeeded in giving a highly original twist to the disarming simplicities of his musical materials. Here, in a new guise, it should be recalled, is an idea of earlier American composers like Gilbert and Farwell who believed that only by emphasizing our own crude musical realities, and resisting the blandishments of the highly developed musical cultures of other peoples, would we ever find our own indigenous musical speech.

I realize that there are undoubtedly among my readers those who disapprove heartily of this searching for "Americanisms" in the works of our contemporaries. Roger Sessions, Walter Piston, and Samuel Barber are composers whose works are not strikingly "American" in the special sense of this chapter, and yet a full summary of the American imagination at work in music—such as this discussion does not pretend to be—would naturally stress the import of their work. There is a universalist ideal, exemplified by their symphonies and chamber music, that belittles the nationalistic note and stresses "predominately musical values." I myself lose patience with the European music lover who wants our music to be all new, brand-new, absolutely different. They forget that we are, as Waldo Frank once put it, the "grave of Europe," by which I suppose he meant to suggest that we have inherited everything they are and know; and we shall have to absorb it and make it completely our own before we can hope for the unadulterated American creation. Nevertheless there is a deep psychological need to look for present signs of that creation. I know this to be true from my own reactions to the music of other nations, especially nations whose music is still unformed, for we inevitably look for the note that makes it characteristically itself. This attitude may be narrow and wrong, but it is an unpremeditated reaction which rightfully should be balanced by the realization that not all the composers of any country are to be limited to an obviously indigenous expression.

In a lecture delivered sometime before 1907, the American composer Edward MacDowell said: "What we must arrive at is the youthful optimistic vitality and the undaunted tenacity of spirit that characterizes the American man. That is what I hope to see echoed in American music." I think MacDowell's hope has been fulfilled—partly, at least—for if there is a school of American composers, optimism is certainly its keynote. But the times have caught up with us, and already mere optimism seems insufficient. If it is not to be mere boyish exuberance it must be tempered, as it is in the work of our best composers, by a reflection of the American man, not as MacDowell knew him at the turn of the century, but as he appears to us with all his complex world about him. Imagination will be needed to echo that man in music.

Jazz Structure and Influence (1927)

Although jazz has been many months now in the hands of professional theorists I have seen nowhere a study of its influence upon non-commercial composers. Its structure, which interests me most as a musician, has received so little attention that it seems to have been avoided. Paul Whiteman admits this in his recent book: "Comparatively little has been written in an analytical way about jazz." And when asked "What is jazz?" he says: "I have been dodging this question for years because I haven't been able to figure out an adequate answer." Speaking exactly, no one else has. In certain quarters it has been suggested that the jazz band created jazz. This is confusing color with substance. Although the jazz band is largely responsible for the present day perfection of the idiom, in the beginning it merely added a distinctive color to what already existed.

One point has been generally made and agreed upon: that the essential character of jazz is its rhythm. Yet no one has carefully analyzed even this. Virgil Thomson has wisely said: "Jazz is a certain way of sounding two rhythms at once . . . a counterpoint of regular against irregular beats." These discerning but epigrammatic investigations have been carried a little though not much farther by Don Knowlton in an article in *Harper's* (April 1926). Henry O. Osgood in his book, *So This is Jazz*, begins by complimenting Mr. Thomson on his definition: "Jazz, in brief, is a compound of (a) the fox trot rhythm . . . and (b) a syncopated melody over this rhythm." But a few pages later he insists: "Jazz is not to be bound by Mr. Thomson's fox trot rhythm, and . . . it is obvious that syncopation, while a frequent characteristic of jazz, is by no means an essential factor." He concludes: "It is the spirit of the music, not the mechanics of its frame . . . that determines whether or not it is jazz."

This seems to me to be far from the truth. I had rather not let jazz pass too easily as indefinable without first inspecting its structure. There may be some connection between Mr. Osgood's attitude and that of most Americans, who believe too confidently that they can tell jazz from what isn't jazz and let it go at that. Such vagueness will do nothing toward a real understanding of it; on the other hand the very first move toward understanding requires precisely what Mr. Osgood by implication advises against, a study of the mechanics of its frame. And this can best be accomplished by considering its origin and development.

It began, I suppose, on some negro's dull tomtom in Africa; it descended through the spirituals, some of which are as much jazz as Gershwin's newest song. Its nearer ancestor is, of course, ragtime. The rhythmic foundation of ragtime is an unchanging *1–2–3–4* bass in quick tempo (stressing the most obvious beats the first and third)—just as *1–2–3* is the rhythmic foundation of the waltz. Over the ragtime bass is carried invariably one of two rhythms, sometimes both: either the dotted eighth followed by a sixteenth:  or this most ordinary syncopation:  . The former of these produced the characteristic ragtime jerk which is perhaps remembered from *Everybody's Doin' It*. Ragtime is much inferior to jazz and musically uninteresting; it consists of old formulas familiar in the classics which were rediscovered one day and overworked.

Modern jazz began with the fox trot. For this new dance the four-quarter bass was used as in ragtime but at a considerably slower pace and miraculously improved by accenting the least obvious beats, the second and fourth—*1–2–3–4*. With this was combined another rhythmic element, sometimes in the melody but by no means always there, which is generally supposed to be a kind of 1–2–3–4 and is always written:

This notation, however, is deceptive, as Mr. Knowlton has pointed out. His article reveals the practice followed by popular music publishers of writing extremely complex jazz compositions very simply so as to sell them more easily to the musically uneducated. He was the first to show that this jazz rhythm is in reality much subtler than in its printed form and is properly expressed thus:

Therefore it contains no syncopation; it is instead a rhythm of four quarters split into eight eighths and is arranged thus: 1–2–3: 1–2–3–4–5, or even more precisely: 1–2–3: 1–2–3: 1–2. Put this over the four-quarter bass:

and you have the play of two independent rhythms within the space of one measure. It is the beginning, it is a molecule of jazz.

Whatever melody is subjected to this procedure comes out jazzed. This explains the widespread facile reincarnation of classic tunes as song and dance hits: It also explains Mr. Whiteman's remark: "Jazz is not as yet the thing said, it is the manner of saying it." And it should make clear to Mr. Osgood how a melody he cites, that of *I'm Always Chasing Rainbows*, can show no signs of jazz and yet be jazz. It is not the melody which determines this point, but the interplay of rhythms around, above, and under it.

The next step infinitely complicated these, in fact it produced poly-rhythms. In employing two rhythms within one measure jazz after all merely did something that had been done before, if we remember, for in-stance, the use by older composers of $\frac{3}{4}$ against $\frac{6}{8}$. But the next era in the jazz age—typified by the song *Stumbling*—saw independent rhythms spread over more than one measure, over a series of measures:

That is, while the conventional $\frac{4}{4}$ bass was retained the melody was put into $\frac{3}{4}$ time. This particular combination of rhythms was probably put to best use by Confrey in his *Kitten on the Keys*:

Within small limits jazz had achieved a new synthesis in music. It was so difficult for ordinary ears and so exhilarating to ordinary sensibilities that the jazz composers, always intent upon their public, dared not use it for more than a few measures at a time. George Gershwin was the composer who took most advantage of the discovery made with *Stumbling*. His *Fascinating Rhythm* is rhythmically not only the most fascinating but the most original jazz song yet composed:

With the introduction of the Charleston the most tyrannical element of our popular music—the evenly rhythmed bass—was eliminated for the space of a few measures at least. The Charleston consists of the upper fox trot rhythm: *1–2–3: 1–2–3–4–5* used below as well as above instead of the formerly unflagging 1–2–3–4 bass:

This old bondage (the unchanging bass) which has probably brought jazz more musical enemies than any other quality, has been broken in another way by Gershwin in his latest dance hit, *Clap Yo' Hands*. Instead of the $\frac{3}{4}$ against $\frac{4}{4}$ polyrhythm which in the brisk competition of Broadway has now become old stuff, he uses this:

That is, he varies a $\frac{4}{4}$ rhythm with two measures of $\frac{3}{4}$ rhythm. Critically, from the standpoint of all music this may be counted a step backward, a return to processes already familiar—in the Russian folk-song for example; but from the standpoint of jazz it means an advance through the relief it offers from the old relentless $\frac{4}{4}$ bass.

Polyrhythms are, as is known, not in themselves an innovation. They have been highly developed among primitive races and have made intermittent, momentary appearances in the works of recent European composers. They have also occurred abundantly in the English madrigals. The madrigal polyrhythms were the result of the madrigal prosody and therefore an intricate deft interknitting in which no single downbeat was too definitely stressed. In a sense, therefore, the madrigal was arhythmic rather than polyrhthmic. In fact, the Madrigalists were charged by later English generations with lacking a proper sense of rhythm.

But the polyrhythms of jazz are different in quality and effect not only from those of the madrigals but from all others as well. The peculiar excitement they produce by clashing two definitely and regularly marked rhythms is unprecedented in occidental music. Its polyrhythm is the real contribution of jazz.

This has not been appreciated by modern European composers although in other ways our American popular music has to some extent influenced them. In the days of ragtime, Debussy and Stravinsky, in the days of jazz, Ravel, Milhaud, Honegger, Hindemith, Jean Wiener exploited it as an exotic novelty. But with most of them it remained a novelty, a monotonous bass, a whining melody, a glissando on a trombone . . . These tricks soon lost their first charm. Meanwhile, however, at least one authentic small masterpiece had been inspired in Europe by America, Darius Milhaud's *La Création du Monde*—little known, strangely, in this country. But according to Milhaud himself, jazz is now distinctly *passé* in Europe and not a young composer there is interested in it any longer.

This is not so in America, nor is it going to be. Since jazz is not exotic here but indigenous, since it is the music an American has heard as a child, it will be traceable more and more frequently in his symphonies and concertos. Possibly the chief influence of jazz will be shown in the development of the polyrhythm. This startling new synthesis has provided the American composer with an instrument he should appreciate and utilize. It should stir his imagination; he should see it freed of its present connotations. It may be the substance not only of his fox trots and Charlestons but of his lullabies and nocturnes. He may express through it not always gaiety but love, tragedy, remorse.

Workers Sing! (1934)

This article from the mid-thirties reflects Copland's Communist sentiments at that time.

The Workers' Music League, a branch of the International Music Bureau, has recently issued the first adequate collection of revolutionary songs for American workers. According to its foreword, the *Workers' Song Book 1934* is made up "exclusively of original revolutionary mass, choral and solo songs with English texts, (the first to be made in America). The composers represented are members of the Composers' Collective of the Pierre Degeyter Club of New York City, an affiliate of the Workers' Music League. With three exceptions the songs were all composed in 1933 as part of the work of the Collective."

Every participant in revolutionary activity knows from his own experience that a good mass song is a powerful weapon in the class struggle. It creates solidarity and inspires action. No other form of collective art activity exerts so far-reaching and all-pervading an influence. The song the mass itself sings is a cultural symbol which helps to give continuity to the day-to-day struggle of the proletariat.

To write a fine mass song is a challenge to every composer. It gives him a first-line position on the cultural front, for in the mass song he possesses a more effective weapon than any in the hands of the novelist, painter, or even playwright. As more and more composers identify themselves with the workers' cause, the challenge of the mass song will more surely be met.

Composers will ask: "What is a good mass song?" In answering this question we must not forget that the opinion of the trained musician will not always coincide with that of the masses. We as musicians will naturally listen to these songs primarily as music, but the workers who sing them will in the first instance decide how they apply to the actualities of the daily struggle. In their eyes the music will not necessarily be of primary importance; if the spirit is right, and the words are right, any music will suffice which does not "get in the way." Composers will want to raise the musical level of the masses, but they must also be ready to learn from them what species of song is most apposite to the revolutionary task.

A good case in point, taken from this first book of American workers' songs, is that of *The Scottsboro Boys Shall Not Die* with words by Abron and music by L. E. Swift. This is the only song in the volume which has already been repeatedly sung by large masses of workers, yet judged from a purely musical standpoint it is certainly not the best song in the collection. The explanation is simple. The issue of the Scottsboro Boys is close to the hearts of class-conscious workers; to these workers the fact that the text of the song does not constitute great poetry, and that the music is effective only in a rather flat-footed and unimaginative fashion is of secondary significance. Nevertheless musicians must continue to insist that the music be of the finest calibre, not for "esthetic" reasons alone, but because a better musical setting will make a song a more thrilling experience and thereby increase its political drive. Swift himself has written better songs musically in the "Three Workers' Rounds": *Poor Mr. Morgan, Red Election*, and *Onward to Battle*, built on an old form of English folk music. Yet these have not taken hold. Our conclusion should be that a first rate mass song must be satisfying in text and music to *both* worker and musician.

On the whole, Carl Sands seems to me to have written the best songs in this present collection. In various ways his work can serve as a model for future proletarian composers. *Mount the Barricades* is an excellent mass song with a simple musical line and unconventional harmonies; *Song of the Builders* for chorus with piano accompaniment has rhythmic variety plus a natural setting of the words; *Who's That Guy* is an amusing kind of "play-song" intended for use with dramatic action. These may not be great songs, but they display a directness of attack and a sure technical grasp which is refreshing.

The songs of Lahn Adohmyan included in this volume are more ambitious. Adohmyan tries for a revolutionary content through use of a revolutionary musical technique. He is not afraid of harsh harmonies and a jagged voice line. These things need careful handling if they are not to result in music which is ungrateful for performers and unrewarding for listeners. Judging from Adohmyan's elaborate *a capella* choral setting of Joseph Freeman's poem *Red Soldiers Singing* and from the mass *Song to the Soldier* one would say that the composer is not always as careful in these matters as he should be. This is the more to be regretted because Adohmyan's music possesses real vitality and a character of its own. It is to be expected, however, that as he matures, the aspect of his music which does not allow it quite to "come off," will be overcome. Already he is out-standing among the younger proletarian composers.

Jacob Schaeffer, the radical movement's veteran choral conductor and composer, presents a different problem in his three songs *Hunger March*, *Strife Song*, and *Lenin, Our Leader*. It is this: can a composer use the musi-cal speech of the nineteenth century to express revolutionary sentiments? One thing is certain: we cannot ask Schaeffer to write in an idiom which is not his own. And it is only natural that, belonging to an older generation, his musical speech will not be as "up-to-date" as that of his younger fellow-composers. But whatever the idiom used, we can demand revolutionary music that is first-rate in quality.

Schaeffer's compositions, however you look at them, seem unnecessarily conventional in spirit. This basic conventionality is sometimes made even more glaring by what would appear to be a conscious attempt on the com-poser's part to be "modern." He is at an added disadvantage in this collec-tion because his songs are translated from the Yiddish. This almost always produces stiff and unnatural prosody. The *Hunger March*, for example, de-serves a better translation, for it is a straight-forward and effective mass song that shows Schaeffer at his best, which is when he is simplest.

Of the fourteen songs in this volume only four are, strictly speaking, mass songs. There should be more. The rest are revolutionary choral com-positions written for performance by trained workers' choruses and solo songs intended for concert performance. (Of the latter group, *God to the Hungry Child* by Janet Barnes is immature and might well have been omit-ted.) These various categories obviously do not belong together, and in later editions, when there are more songs of each type, it would be wise to issue them in separate collections. Also, one would like to see a larger num-ber of composers represented in the collection.

Those of us who wish to see music play its part in the workers' struggle for a new world order, owe a vote of thanks to the Composers' Collective for making an auspicious start in the right direction.

Letter on Varèse and
the League of Composers (1972)

To the Editor:

May I take issue with Joan Peyser's comment on the recently published book about the composer Edgar Varèse by his wife Louise? The book's title is "Varèse: A Looking-Glass Diary." The first volume of the author's recollections, it covers the 1883–1928 era.

In the course of her review, Mrs. Peyser manages to inject a bit of gratuitous musical politics of her own. It is understandable, of course, that Mrs. Varèse should give us a partisan account of the battles of 50 years ago—which resulted in a split between the Varèse led International Composers Guild and the offshoot group led by Mrs. Arthur Reis, which named itself the League of Composers. . . . That Edgar Varèse and Claire Reis (two determined personalities) should have clashed on matters of policy is not at all surprising. The important thing to recall is that this schism profited public and composers alike—for, where there had been one forward-looking group, now there were two.

What seems inexcusable to me is Miss Peyser's ignorant version of what happened. She writes that "Claire Reis broke from the parent group and formed the League of Composers, *which promoted neoclassicism—new works that drew on the tonality of the past at the expense of advanced composition.*" (Italics added.)

How far off the beam can you get? Anyone familiar with the 30-year record of the League knows what that organization accomplished for the propagation of the works of living composers of every possible stripe and complexion. And all composers involved in that history have reason to be grateful for the leadership and devotion to the cause of new music provided by Claire Reis.

Opera and Music Drama (1939)

As *What to Listen for in Music* progresses from the more accessible to the more technical, this chapter appears later in that book.

The question of listening more intelligently has been considered solely in relation to music that comes under the heading of concert music. Strange as it may seem, music that is an end in itself, having no connection with any extramusical idea, is not the natural phenomenon that it seems to be. Music did not begin as concert music, certainly. It was only after century-long historical developments that music, listened to for its own sake, was able to seem self-sufficient.

Theatrical music, on the other hand, is, by comparison, a perfectly natural thing. Its origins go as far back as the primitive ritual music of a savage tribe or the religious chant of a sacred play in the Middle Ages. Even today, music written to accompany a play, film, or ballet seems self-explanatory. The only form of theatrical music that is at all controversial, and therefore in need of some explaining, is the operatic form.

Opera in our own day is an art form with a somewhat tarnished reputation. I speak, naturally, of the opinion of the musical "elite." That wasn't always true. There was a time when opera was thought of as a more advanced form than any other. But until quite recently, it was customary among the elite to speak of the operatic form with a certain amount of condescension.

There were several reasons for the disrepute into which opera fell. Among the first of these was the fact that opera bore the "taint" of Wagner about it. For at least thirty years after his death, the entire musical world made heroic efforts to throw off the terrific impact of Wagner. That is no reflection on his music. It simply means that each new generation must create its own music; and it was a very difficult thing to do, particularly in the opera house, immediately after Wagner had lived.

Moreover, quite aside from Wagnerian music drama, it might truthfully be said that the public that flocked to hear opera did the form little credit. On the one hand, it became associated with what was sometimes called a "barber public"—musical groundlings for whom the real art of music was assumed to be a closed book. On the other hand, there was the "society public," turning the opera into a fashionable playground, with an eye only for its circus aspect.

Moreover, the repertoire currently performed was made up for the most part of old "chestnuts," outmoded show pieces that were fit only to strike awe in the mind of a movie magnate. How could one possibly think of injecting into this situation a new opera written in the more up-to-date manner of the 1920's, despite the fact that this new, revolutionary music was already invading the concert halls? To the musical elite, all music of serious pretentions seemed to be automatically ruled out of the opera house. If by lucky chance a new work did reach the operatic stage, it was more than likely to be found too esoteric for the audience, if it hadn't previously been annihilated by the artificialities of the conventional opera production.

Those are some of the reasons for the low estimate of the opera as a form in the opinion of the people who look upon music seriously. But around 1924 a renewal of interest in opera began, which had its origin in Germany. Every small town in Germany has an opera house. There were said to be, around that time, at least ten first-class and twenty second-class operatic stages that functioned most of the year round. We must not forget that in Germany the opera takes the place of our musical comedy, movie, and theater combined. Every good citizen owns his weekly subscription to the opera, so that there was almost a social obligation for opera to renew itself as a form. Moreover, publishers of music did much to encourage the writing of new operatic works. A really successful opera brought a large financial return to both authors and publishers. There was then plenty of incentive for composers to write operas and publishers to print them, plus the added advantage of a postwar audience interested in experiencing new operatic ventures off the conventional path. Before long, interest spread to other countries, and even our own Metropolitan half-heartedly paid its respects to new opera by an occasional performance of a representative modern work.

If the reader is to be convinced that the life newly imbued in opera has some justification, he must have some understanding of opera as a form. I feel sure that many of my readers are convinced that opera is a dull form and do not ever want to go to an operatic performance if they can possibly avoid it. Let us see what can be said to break down that prejudice.

The first point to be made, and one that cannot be too strongly emphasized, is that opera is bound from head to foot by convention. Of course, opera is not the only form of art that is so bound. The theater, for example, pretends that the fourth wall of a room is there and that we, in some miraculous way, look on while real life is being enacted. Children who visit the theater for the first time imagine that everything that occurs there is really happening; but we grownups have no trouble in accepting the convention of the stage as real, though we very well know that the actors are only making believe. The point is that opera has its conventions, too—and still greater ones than the theater. It is important for you to realize to what an extent you accept convention in the theater if you are to be less reluctant to accept the still greater one of the opera house.

In a sense, an opera is simply a drama sung instead of a drama spoken. That is the first of the conventions and completely at variance with reality. Even so, the drama is not sung continuously (until Wagner's time, at any rate) but, instead, is broken up into regularly contrasted, set musical pieces—which removes it one step farther from any connection with the reality that it is supposedly depicting. Moreover, the story that is being told is often of a fatuity that can hardly be exaggerated. Nothing sensible ever seems to take place on an operatic stage. Nor does the acting of opera singers conspire to aid in making the libretto—as the book of an opera is called—any the less fatuous.

Finally, there is the matter of the recitative—that part of an opera which is neither spoken nor sung but rather is half sung—telling the story part (especially in old operas), without any attempt at stimulating musical interest. When an opera is sung in a language unfamiliar to the listener, as most operas are in English-speaking countries, these recitative sections can be of surpassing boredom. These facts go to prove that the opera is not a realistic form of art; and one must not demand that it be realistic. As a matter of fact, no one is more tiresome than the person who can understand only realism in art. It shows a rather low artistic mentality never to believe anything you see unless it appears to be real. One must be willing to allow that symbolic things also mirror realities and sometimes provide greater esthetic pleasure than the merely realistic. The opera house is a good place in which to find these more symbolic pleasures. In short, what I have been trying to convey is that in order to enjoy what goes on in the opera house you must begin by accepting its conventions.

It is surprising that some people still consider opera a dead form. What makes it so different from any of the other forms of music is its all-inclusiveness. It contains within itself almost every musical medium: the symphony orchestra, the solo voice, the vocal ensemble, the chorus. The character of the music may be either serious or light—and both in the same work. Opera may contain music of a symphonic, or "absolute," nature, or it may be purely descriptive and programmatic. An opera also contains ballet, pantomime, and drama. It passes easily from one to the other. In other words, it is almost impossible to imagine any type of musical or theatrical art that would not be at home in an opera house.

But added to that is the spectacular display which only the opera can give in its own way. It is theater on a grand scale—crowds of people on the stage; magnificence of lights, costumes, and scenery. A composer who isn't attracted by such a medium has very little theatricalism in his soul. Most creators apparently have their share, for opera has fascinated some of the world's finest composers.

The problem of writing an opera is the combination of all these disparate elements to form an artistic whole. It is anything but an easy problem. As a matter of fact, it is practically impossible to choose any one opera and say: "That's the perfect opera! There is the solution of the form that everyone must follow." In a sense, the problem is insoluble, for it is almost impossible to equalize and balance the different elements in an opera in such a way as to achieve a completely satisfying whole. The result has been, practically speaking, that composers have tended to emphasize one element at the expense of another.

That particularly applies to the words of an opera, as the first of the elements with which the composer works. Operatic composers have in practice done one of two things: Either they have given the words a preponderant role, using the music only to serve the drama; or they have frankly sacrificed the words, using them merely as a peg on which to hang their music. So that the entire problem of opera may be reduced to the diametrical pull of words on the one hand and music on the other. It is instructive to look at the history of opera from this standpoint and note the way in which composers solved this problem, each one for himself.

The year 1600 provides a convenient starting point, for it was thereabouts that operatic history began. It was the result—or so the historian tells us—of the meetings of certain composers and poets at the palace of one Count Bardi in Florence. Remember that serious art music up to that time had been almost entirely choral and of a highly contrapuntal and involved nature. In fact, music had become so contrapuntal, so complex, that it was well-nigh impossible to understand a word of what the singers were saying. The "new music" was going to change all that. Note immediately two fundamental qualities of opera at its very inception. First, the emphasis on stressing the words, making the music tell a story. Second, the "high-society" aspect of opera from the very start. (It was forty years before the first public opera house was opened in Venice.)

The ostensible purpose of the men who met at Count Bardi's was the revival of Greek drama. They wished to attempt the recreation of what they thought went on in the Greek theater. Of course, what they accomplished was a completely different thing—the creation of a new form, which was destined to fire the imagination of artists and audiences for generations to come.

The first of the great opera composers was the Italian, Claudio Monteverdi. Unfortunately, his works are rarely given nowadays and would strike our present-day opera lovers as little more than museum pieces if they were performed. From our vantage point, Monteverdi's style is limited in resource—it consists for the most part of what we should call recitative. Nowadays we think of the recitative as of very minor interest in an opera, and we wait always for the aria which follows it to arouse us. In our sense, Monteverdi's operas are innocent of arias, so that they seem to be nothing but one long recitative, with an occasional orchestral interlude. But what is so very extraordinary about the recitative in Monteverdi is its quality. It rings absolutely true; it is amazingly felt. Despite the fact that he comes at almost the very beginning of the new form, no one after Monteverdi was able to put words to music so simply, so movingly, so convincingly. In listening to Monteverdi, it is necessary to understand the meaning of the words, since he puts so much emphasis upon them. That is also true much later in operatic history when certain composers returned to the Monteverdian ideal of opera.

The new art form, which had begun so auspiciously, spread gradually to other countries outside Italy. It went first from Venice to Vienna and from Vienna to Paris, London, and Hamburg. Those were the big operatic centers in the 1700s. By that time, the opera had veered away from the Monteverdi prototype. The words became less and less important, while all emphasis was placed upon the musical side of the opera. The newer form condensed the emotion aroused by the action into what we now think of as arias; and these arias were connected by recitative passages. But these sections are not to be confused with the Monteverdi species of recitative; they were ordinary, workaday recitatives designed merely for the purpose of telling the story as quickly as possible so that the next aria might be reached. The result was a form of opera that consisted of a collection of arias interspersed with recitative. There was no attempt at picturizing in the music events that happened on the stage. That was to come later.

The great opera composer of the seventeenth century was Alessandro Scarlatti, the father of the clavecin composer Domenico, whose works were commented upon in the discussion of two-part form. The model of opera that the elder Scarlatti developed we now connect with the later operas of Handel. In this type of opera, the story is of little import; the drama is static, and the action negligible. All interest is centered on the singer and the vocal part, and opera justifies itself only in terms of its musical appeal. It proved to be a dangerous development, for it wasn't long before the natural desire of singers to hold the center of the stage led to serious abuses which are still by no means entirely eradicated. The rivalry of singers led to the addition of all kinds of roulades and extra furbishings to the melodic line for the sole purpose of demonstrating the prowess of the particular interpreter in question.

What followed was inevitable. Since opera had become so highly formalized and unnatural an art form, someone was bound to come forward as a reformer. The history of opera is sprinkled with reformers. Someone is always trying to make opera more real than it was in the period just before him. The champion of reform who wished to correct the abuses of the Handelian opera was, of course, Christoph Willibald von Gluck.

Gluck himself had written a great many operas in the conventional Italian style of his day before he assumed the role of reformer, so that he knew whereof he spoke when he said that opera was in need of purification. Gluck tried above all to rationalize opera—to have it make more sense. In the older opera, the singer was supreme, and the music served the singer; Gluck made the dramatic idea supreme and wrote music that served the purposes of the text. Each act was to be an entity in itself, not a nondescript collection of more or less effective arias. It was to be balanced and contrasted, with a flow and continuity that would give it coherence as an art form. The ballet, for example, was not to be a mere divertissement introduced for its own sake but an integral part of the dramatic idea of the work.

Gluck's ideas as to operatic reform were sound. Moreover, he was able to incorporate them into actual works. *Orpheus and Eurydice, Armide, Alceste* are the names of some of his most successful achievements. In these operas, he created a massive, stolid kind of music which fitted very well the grandiose subject matter of many of his works. And concomitant with the monumental impression is one of extraordinary calm, a species of calm beauty which is unique in music and utterly removed from the frivolities of the operatic medium of his day. Gluck's works are not to be classed as museum pieces; they are the first operas of which it may be said that time has not impaired their effectiveness.

That is not to say that Gluck was entirely successful in his reform. His operas are undoubtedly more rational than those which preceded him, but much was left to be accomplished by later men. His reform was only a relative one; in many instances, he merely substituted his own conventions for those that were current before him. But he was, nevertheless, a genius of the first rank, and he did succeed in setting up an ideal of opera that showed the way to future reformers.

Mozart, the next great name in operatic history, was not by nature a reformer. What we expect to find in Mozart is perfection in whatever medium he chose to work. Mozart's operas are no exception, for they embody more resourcefulness than can be found in any other opera up to his time. *The Magic Flute* is sometimes spoken of as the most perfect opera ever written. Its subject matter lends itself very well to operatic treatment because of its nonrealistic nature. It is both serious and comic, combining a wealth of musical imagination with a popular style accessible to all.

One contribution that Mozart did make to the form was the operatic finale. This is an effect possible only in opera—that final scene of an act when all the principals sing at the same time, each one singing about something else, only to conclude with a resounding fortissimo to the delight of everyone concerned. Mozart accomplished this typically musical trick in so definitive and perfect a way that all who used it after him—as who has not?—were indebted to him. It appears to be a fundamental effect in operatic writing, since it is just as much alive today as it was in Mozart's time.

Mozart was also in advance of his time in one other respect. He was the first great composer to write a comedy set in the German language. *The Abduction from the Seraglio*, produced in 1782, is the first milestone in the path that leads directly to the future German opera. It set the style for a long list of followers, among whom may be counted the Wagner of the *Meistersinger*.

Richard Wagner was the next great reformer in opera. It was his purpose, as it had been Gluck's, to rationalize operatic form. He visualized the form as a union of all the arts—to include poetry, the drama, music, and the arts of the stage—everything connected with the spectacular opera outlined in the beginning of this chapter. He wished to give a new dignity to the operatic form by naming it music drama. Music drama was to be different from opera in two important respects: In the first place, the set musical number was to be done away with in favor of a continuous musical flow which followed an uninterrupted course from the beginning of an act to its conclusion. The opera of the separate aria connected by recitative was abandoned for the sake of greater realism in the dramatic form. Secondly, the famous conception of the leitmotif was introduced. Through associating a particular musical phrase, or motif, with each character or idea in the music drama, a greater cohesion of musical elements was to be assured.

But most significant in the Wagnerian music drama is the role assigned the orchestra. I had a most pronounced impression of that fact at the Metropolitan one winter on hearing Massenet's *Manon* one night and Wagner's *Die Walküre* the next. With the Frenchman's work one never gave the orchestra any special attention. It played a part not unlike that of a group of theater musicians in a pit; but as soon as Wagner's orchestra sounded, one had the impression that the entire Philharmonic Symphony had moved into the Metropolitan. Wagner brought the symphony orchestra to the opera house, so that the principal interest is often not on the stage but in the orchestra pit. The singers often must be listened to only in a secondary way, while the primary attention is placed on what the orchestra is "saying." Wagner was by nature a symphonist who applied his symphonic gifts to the form of the opera.

The question remains: "Did Wagner achieve reality in the opera house?" The answer must be "No." He achieved it no more than Gluck had. Once again, different conventions were substituted for those current in Wagner's time. Also, we may ask with justice: "Did he achieve the equality of all the arts which he never tired of proclaiming?" There, again, the answer is "No." The honest listener who witnesses a Wagnerian performance is bound to come away with an impression that is primarily a musical, not a dramatic, one. Imagine a Wagner libretto set to different music—none would evince the slightest interest in it. It is only because the music is so extraordinary that Wagner maintains his hold on the public. It is the music that is supreme; by comparison with it, all the other elements of the music drama are weak. Professor Edward Dent of Cambridge has exactly expressed my sentiments in relation to the extramusical considerations of Wagnerian drama. He has said: "A great deal of nonsense has been written, some indeed by Wagner himself, about the philosophical and moral significance of his operas." The final test of music drama, as of opera, must be the opera house itself. It is only the overpowering command of musical resources represented by Wagner's work that makes it bearable in the opera house.

Only two or three contemporaries were able to compete with Wagner on his own ground. Verdi was the principal of these. Like Gluck, he wrote a large number of conventional Italian operas, which were wildly acclaimed by the public but found little favor with the nineteenth-century admirers of music drama. But there has been a tendency in recent years on the part of the cognoscenti to reestimate the contribution made by Verdi. Somewhat chastened, not to say bored, by the static and "philosophical" music-drama stage, they are now in a position better to appreciate the virtuoso theatrical gifts of a man like Verdi. His operas were no doubt too traditional, too facile, and at times even too vulgar; but they *moved*. Verdi was a born man of the theater—the sheer effectiveness of works like *Aïda*, *Rigoletto*, *Traviata* assure them a permanent place in the operatic repertoire.

Verdi himself was somewhat influenced by the example of Wagner in the composition of his last two works, *Otello* and *Falstaff*, both written when the composer was past seventy. He put aside the separate operatic aria, used the orchestra in a more sophisticated manner, concentrated more directly on the dramatic implications of the plot. But he did not relinquish his instinctive feeling for the stage. That is why these two works—amazing examples of the powers of an old man—are on the whole better models for the edification of the young opera composer than the more theoretical music drama of Wagner.

Moussorgsky and Bizet were both able to create operas that are worthy of comparison with the best of Verdi or Wagner. Of the two, the Russian's operas have had the more fruitful progeny. His *Boris Godounoff* was the first of the nationalist operas, written outside Germany, which showed a way out of the Wagnerian impasse. *Boris* is operatic in the best sense of the word. Its main protagonist is the chorus rather than the individual; it derives its color from Russian locale; its musical background is freshened by the use of typically Russian folk-song material. The scene of the second tableau, which pictures the court of the Kremlin backed by the Czar's apartments, with the coronation procession crossing the stage, is one of the most spectacular ever conceived in the operatic medium.

The influence of *Boris* was only slowly felt, for it was not performed in Western Europe until the present century. But Debussy must have known of its existence during the visits that he made to Russia in early manhood. In any case, the influence of Moussorgsky is patent in Debussy's only opera, *Pelléas et Mélisande*, which is the next great landmark in operatic history. In *Pelléas*, Debussy returned to the Monteverdian ideal of opera; the words of Maeterlinck's poetic drama were given their full rights. The music was intended only to serve as a frame about the words, so as to heighten their poetic meaning.

In method and feeling, Debussy's opera was the antithesis of Wagnerian music drama. This is immediately seen if we compare the big scene in *Tristan* with the analogous one in *Pelléas*. In Wagner's opera, when the lovers declare themselves for the first time, there is a wonderful outpouring of the emotions in music; but when Pelléas and Mélisande first declare their love for each other, there is complete silence. Everyone—singers, orchestra, and composer—is overcome with emotion. That scene is typical of the whole opera—it is a triumph of understatement. There are very few forte passages in *Pelléas*; the entire work is bathed in an atmosphere of mystery and poignancy. Debussy's music added a new dimension to Maeterlinck's little play. It is impossible any longer to imagine the play apart from the music.

Perhaps it is just because of this complete identity of play and music that *Pelléas et Mélisande* has remained something of a special case. It provided no new program for the production of further operas in the same tradition. (Few other plays are so well designed for musical setting.) Moreover, the appeal of *Pelléas* was largely confined to those who understand French, since so much of the quality of the work is dependent on an understanding of the words. Because *Pelléas* had almost no offspring, the leaders of musical opinion lost interest in the operatic form altogether and turned instead to the symphony or the ballet as the principal musical form.

Reasons have already been given for the revival of interest in opera around 1924. All the operas written since then are in full reaction against Wagnerian ideals. Opera composers of today are agreed on at least one point: They are ready to accept frankly the conventions of the operatic stage. Since there is no possible hope of making opera "real," they have willingly renounced all attempt at reform. They bravely start from the premise that opera is a nonrealistic form, and, instead of deploring that fact, they are determined to make use of it. They are convinced that opera is, first of all, theater and that, as such, it demands a composer who is capable of writing stage music.

The most significant modern opera since *Pelléas* is, in the opinion of most critics, Alban Berg's *Wozzeck*. Berg's opera is striking on several counts. He, like Debussy, began with a stage play. *Wozzeck* was the work of a precocious nineteenth-century playwright, George Büchner. He tells the story, in 26 short scenes, of a poor devil of a soldier, at the bottom of the social scale, who through no fault of his own lives in misery and leaves nothing but a trail of misery behind him. This is a realistic theme, with social implications; but as Berg treated it, it became realism with a difference. The impression that we get is one of a heightened, what is sometimes called an expressionistic, realism. Everything in the opera is extremely condensed. One swift scene follows another, each relating some essential dramatic moment, and all connected and focused through Berg's intensely expressive music.

One of the reasons for the slow acceptance in musical circles of this original work is the language of the music itself. Berg, as a devoted pupil of Arnold Schoenberg, made use of the atonal harmonic scheme of his teacher. *Wozzeck* was the first atonal opera to reach the stage. It is indicative of the dramatic power of the music that despite the fact of its being difficult to perform and almost as difficult to understand, it has made its way in both Europe and America. One other curious feature should be mentioned, which is found in *Wozzeck* and in the last work that Berg finished before his death, his second opera *Lulu*. Berg had the somewhat strange notion of introducing strict concert-hall forms, such as the passacaglia or rondo, into the body of his operas. This innovation in operatic form has no more than a technical interest, since the public hears the work with no idea of the presence of these underlying forms, this, according to the composer's own admission, being exactly his intention. Like every other opera, Berg's work holds the stage by virtue of its dramatic power.

A few modern operas have taken hold of the public imagination because of their treatment of some contemporary subject. The first of these was Krenek's *Jonny spielt auf*, which enjoyed an enormous vogue for a time. It seemed quite piquant to the provincial public of Germany that the hero of an opera should be a Negro jazz-band leader and that the composer should dare to introduce a few jazz tunes into his score.

Kurt Weill developed that popularizing tendency in a series that made opera history in pre-Hitler Germany. His most characteristic work of that period was the *Three Penny Opera*, with a telling libretto by Bert Brecht. Weill openly substituted "songs" for arias and a pseudo-jazz band for the usual opera orchestra and wrote a music so ordinary and trite that before long every German newsboy was whistling it. But what gives his work a distinction that *Jonny spielt auf* did not have was the fact that he wrote music of real character. It is a searing expression in musical terms of the German spirit of the 1920s, the hopelessly disintegrated and degenerated postwar Germany that George Grosz painted with brutal frankness. Do not be fooled by Weill's banality. It is a purposeful and meaningful banality if one can read between the lines, as it were, and sense the deep tragedy hidden in its seemingly carefree quality.

Opera as a comment on the social scene was once more demonstrated by the Italian-American composer Gian-Carlo Menotti in his *The Consul*. How long this tendency will continue is difficult to prophesy. But unless composers are able to universalize their comment and present it in terms of effective stage drama, no good will have come from bringing opera closer to everyday life.

This discussion of modern opera would be incomplete without some mention of one of the most prolific of contemporary opera composers, the Frenchman Darius Milhaud. Milhaud's most ambitious effort in this field has been his opera *Christopher Columbus*, a grandiose and spectacular affair which has had several productions abroad but none in this country. Milhaud can be violent and lyrical by turns, and he has used both qualities to good effect in *The Poor Sailor, Esther of Carpentras, Juarez and Maximilian*, and other stage works. A good idea of his dramatic power may be had from listening to an excerpt available on records, from his *Les Choephores*, called *Invocation*. Singer and chorus rhythmically declaim to the accompaniment of a whole battery of percussion instruments. The effect is quite overwhelming and points to new, unplumbed possibilities for the opera of the future.

If any of my readers still doubt the viability of modern opera or, for that matter, theatrical music in general, I ask them to consider this final fact. Three of the works that proved to be milestones in the development of new music were works designed for the stage. Moussorgsky's *Boris*, Debussy's *Pelléas*, and Stravinsky's *Rites of Spring* have all contributed to the advance of music. It may very well be that the next step forward will be made in the theater rather than the concert hall.

There still remains the question of opera in America or, to be more exact, American opera. Some of our writers have advanced the theory, with a good deal of reason, that the movies legitimately take the place of opera in the American scene. To them, opera is a typically European manifestation of art, not to be transplanted to American soil. But from the composer's standpoint, the opera is still a fascinating form, no matter how one looks at it. If it is to be transplanted with any chance of real success, two things must happen: Composers must be able to set English to a melodic line that does not falsify the natural rhythm of the language; and opera performances will have to be more numerous than they are at present in our country. As a matter of fact, some of the healthiest of native operatic ventures, such as the Thomson-Stein *Four Saints in Three Acts* or Marc Blitzstein's *The Cradle Will Rock*, found their way on to the stage without benefit of an established opera organization. Perhaps the future of American opera lies *outside* the opera house. But in any event, I feel sure we have not heard the last of the form, either here or abroad.

Tip to Moviegoers:
Take Off Those Ear-Muffs (1949)

This essay, along with the example of Copland's scores for films, made film composing more credible for later serious American composers. Copland reworked the "Film Music" chapter from What to Listen for in Music *into this article for* The New York Times Magazine.

The next time you settle yourself comfortably into a seat at the neighborhood picture house don't forget to take off your ear-muffs. Most people don't realize they are wearing any—at any rate, that is the impression of composers who write for the movies. Millions of moviegoers take the musical accompaniment to a dramatic film so much for granted that five minutes after the termination of a picture they couldn't tell you whether they had heard music or not.

To ask whether they thought the score exciting or merely adequate or downright awful would be to give them a musical inferiority complex. But, on second thought, and possibly in self-protection, comes the query: "Isn't it true that one isn't supposed to be listening to the music? Isn't it supposed to work on you unconsciously without being listened to directly as you would listen at a concert?"

No discussion of movie music ever gets very far without having to face this problem: Should one hear a movie score? If you are a musician there is no problem because the chances are you can't help but listen. More than once I've had a good picture ruined for me by an inferior score. Have you had the same experience? Yes? Then you may congratulate yourself: you're definitely musical.

But it's the spectator, so absorbed in the dramatic action that he fails to take in the background music, who wants to know whether he is missing anything. The answer is bound up with the degree of your general musical perception. It is the degree to which you are aurally minded that will determine how much pleasure you may derive by absorbing the background musical accompaniment as an integral part of the combined impression made by the film.

One's appreciation of a work of art is partly determined by the amount of preparation one brings to it. The head of the family will probably be less sensitive to the beauty and appropriateness of the gowns worn by the feminine star than his wife will be. It's hopeless to expect the tone-deaf to listen to a musical score. But since the great majority of movie patrons are undoubtedly musical to some degree, they should be encouraged not to ignore the music; on the contrary, I would hope to convince them that by taking it in they will be enriching both their musical and their cinema experience.

Recently I was asked rather timorously whether I liked to write movie music—the implication being that it was possibly degrading for a composer of symphonies to trifle with a commercial product. "Would you do it anyhow, even if it were less well paid?" I think I would, and, moreover, I think most composers would, principally because film music constitutes a new musical medium that exerts a fascination of its own. Actually, it is a new form of dramatic music—related to opera, ballet, incidental theatre music—in contradistinction to concert music of the symphonic or chamber music kind. As a new form it opens up unexplored possibilities, or should.

The main complaint about film music as written today in Hollywood is that so much of it is cut and dried, rigidly governed by conventions that have grown up with surprising rapidity in the short period of twenty-odd years since the talkies began. But, leaving the hack composer aside, there is no reason why a serious composer, cooperating with an intelligent producer on a picture of serious artistic pretensions, should not be able to have his movie scores judged by the same standards applied to his concert music. That is certainly the way William Walton in *Henry V*, Serge Prokofieff in *Alexander Nevsky*, or Virgil Thomson in *Louisiana Story* would want to be judged. They did not have to lower their standards because they were writing for a mass audience. Some day the term "movie music" will clearly define a specific musical genre and will not have, as it does have nowadays, a pejorative meaning.

Most people are curious as to just how one goes about putting music to a film. Fortunately, the process is not so complex that it cannot be outlined here.

The first thing one must do, of course, is to see the picture. Almost all musical scores are composed *after* the film itself is completed. The only exception to this is when the script calls for realistic music—that is, music which is visually sung or played or danced to on the screen. In that case the music must be composed before the scene is photographed. It will then be recorded and the scene in question shot to a playback of the recording. Thus, when you see an actor singing or playing or dancing, he is only making believe as far as the sound goes, for the music had previously been put down on film.

The first run-through of the film for the composer is usually a solemn moment. After all, he must live with it for several weeks. The solemnity of the occasion is emphasized by the exclusive audience that views it with him: the producer, the director, the musical head of the studio, the picture editor, the music cutter, the conductor, the orchestrator—in fact, anyone involved in scoring the picture. At that showing it is difficult for the composer to view the photoplay coldly. There is an understandable compulsion to like everything, for he is looking at what must necessarily constitute the source of his future inspiration.

The purpose of the run-through is to decide how much music is needed and where it should be. (In technical jargon this is called "to spot" the picture.) Since no background score is continuous throughout the full length of a film (that would constitute a motion-picture opera, an unexploited cinema form), the score will normally consist of separate sequences, each lasting from a few seconds to several minutes in duration. A sequence as long as seven minutes would be exceptional. The entire score, made up of perhaps thirty or more such sequences, may add up to from forty to ninety minutes of music.

Much discussion, much give and take, may be necessary before final decisions are reached regarding the "spotting" of the picture. In general my impression has been that composers are better able to gauge the over-all effect of a musical accompaniment than the average non-musician. Personally I like to make use of music's power sparingly, saving it for absolutely essential points. A composer knows how to play with silences; knows that to take music out can at times be more effective than any use of it might be.

The producer-director, on the other hand, is more prone to think of music in terms of its immediate functional usage. Sometimes he has ulterior motives: anything wrong with a scene—a poor bit of acting, a badly read line, an embarrassing pause—he secretly hopes will be covered up by a clever composer. Producers have been known to hope that an entire picture would be saved by a good score. But the composer is not a magician; he can hardly be expected to do more than to make potent through music the film's dramatic and emotional values.

When well contrived there is no question but that a musical score can be of enormous help to a picture. One can prove that point, laboratory fashion, by showing an audience a climactic scene with the sound turned off and then once again with the sound track turned on. Here briefly is listed a number of ways in which music serves the screen:

(1) *Creating a more convincing atmosphere of time and place.* Not all Hollywood composers bother about this nicety. Too often, their scores are interchangeable; a thirteenth century Gothic drama and a hard-boiled modern battle of the sexes get similar treatment. The lush symphonic texture of late nineteenth century music remains the dominating influence. But there are exceptions. Recently, the higher grade horse-opera has begun to have its own musical flavor, mostly a folksong derivative.

(2) *Underlining psychological refinements—the unspoken thoughts of a character or the unseen implications of a situation.* Music can play upon the emotions of the spectator, sometimes counterpointing the thing seen with an aural image that implies the contrary of the thing seen. This is not as subtle as it sounds. A well-placed dissonant chord can stop an audience cold in the middle of a sentimental scene, or a calculated wood-wind passage can turn what appears to be a solemn moment into a belly-laugh.

(3) *Serving as a kind of neutral background filler.* This is really the music one isn't supposed to hear, the sort that helps to fill the empty spots between pauses in a conversation. It's the movie composer's most ungrateful task. But at times, though no one else may notice, he will get private satisfaction from the thought that music of little intrinsic value, through professional manipulation, has enlivened and made more human the deathly pallor of a screen shadow. This is hardest to do, as any film composer will attest, when the neutral filler type of music must weave its way underneath dialogue.

(4) *Building a sense of continuity.* The picture editor knows better than anyone how serviceable music can be in tieing together a visual medium which is, by its very nature, continually in danger of falling apart. One sees this most obviously in montage scenes where the use of a unifying musical idea may save the quick flashes of disconnected scenes from seeming merely chaotic.

(5) *Underpinning the theatrical build-up of a scene, and rounding it off with a sense of finality.* The first instance that comes to mind is the music that blares out at the end of a film. Certain producers have boasted their picture's lack of a musical score, but I never saw or heard of a picture that ended in silence.

We have merely skimmed the surface, without mentioning the innumerable examples of utilitarian music—offstage street bands, the barn dance, merry-go-rounds, circus music, cafe music, the neighbor's girl practicing her piano, etc. All these, and many others, introduced with apparent naturalistic intent, serve to vary subtly the aural interest of the sound track.

Perhaps it is only fair to mention that several of these uses come to the screen by way of the long tradition of incidental music in the legitimate theatre. Most workers in the theatre, and especially our playwrights, would agree that music enhances the glamour and atmosphere of a stage production, any stage production. Formerly it was considered indispensable. But nowadays only musical comedy can afford a considerable-sized orchestra in the pit.

With mounting costs of production it looks as if the serious drama would have to get along with a union minimum of four musicians for some time to come. If there is to be any combining of music and the spoken drama in any but the barest terms, it will have to happen in Hollywood, for the Broadway theatre is practically out of the running.

But now perhaps we had better return to our hypothetical composer. Having determined where the separate musical sequences will begin and end he turns the film over to the music cutter who prepares a so-called cue sheet. The cue sheet provides the composer with a detailed description of the physical action in each sequence, plus the exact timings in thirds of seconds of that action, thereby making it possible for a practiced composer to write an entire score without ever again referring to the picture. Personally I prefer to remain in daily contact with the picture itself, viewing again and again the sequence I happen to be working on.

The layman usually imagines that the most difficult part of the job in composing for the films has to do with the precise "fitting" of the music to the action. Doesn't that kind of timing strait-jacket the composer? The answer is, No, for two reasons: first, having to compose music to accompany specific action is a help rather than a hindrance, since the action itself induces music in a composer of theatrical imagination, whereas he has no such visual stimulus in writing absolute music. Secondly, the timing is mostly a matter of minor adjustments, since the over-all musical fabric is there.

For the composer of concert music, changing to the medium of celluloid does bring certain special pitfalls. For example, melodic invention, highly prized in the concert hall, may at times be distracting in certain film situations. Even phrasing in the concert manner, which would normally emphasize the independence of separate contrapuntal lines, may be distracting when applied to screen accompaniments. In orchestration there are many subtleties of timbre—distinctions meant to be listened to for their own expressive quality in an auditorium—which are completely wasted on sound track.

As compensation for these losses, the composer has other possibilities, some of them tricks, which are unobtainable in Carnegie Hall. In scoring one section of *The Heiress*, for example, I was able to superimpose two orchestras, one upon another. Both recorded the same music at different times, one orchestra consisting of strings alone, the other constituted normally. Later these were combined by simultaneously re-recording the original tracks, thereby producing a highly expressive orchestral texture. Bernard Herrmann, one of the most ingenious of screen composers, called for (and got) eight celestas—an unheard-of combination on Fifty-seventh Street—to suggest a winter's sleigh ride. Miklos Rozsa's use of the "echo chamber"—a device to give normal tone a ghost-like aura—was widely remarked, and subsequently done to death.

Unusual effects are obtainable through overlapping incoming and outgoing music tracks. Like two trains passing one another, it is possible to bring in and take out at the same time two different musics. The *Red Pony* gave me an opportunity to use this cinema specialty. When the daydreaming imagination of a little boy turns white chickens into white circus horses the visual image is mirrored in an aural image by having the chicken music transform itself into circus music, a device only obtainable by means of the overlap.

Let us now assume that the musical score has been completed and is ready for recording. The scoring stage is a happy-making place for the composer. Hollywood has gathered to itself some of America's finest performers; the music will be beautifully played and recorded with a technical perfection not to be matched anywhere else.

Most composers like to invite their friends to be present at the recording session of important sequences. The reason is that neither the composer nor his friends are ever again likely to hear the music sound out in concert style. For when it is combined with the picture most of the dynamic levels will be changed. Otherwise the finished product might sound like a concert with pictures. In lowering dynamic levels niceties of shading, some inner voices and bass parts may be lost. Erich Korngold, one of Hollywood's top men, put it well when he said: "A movie composer's immortality lasts from the recording stage to the dubbing room."

The dubbing room is where all the tracks involving sound of any kind, including dialogue, are put through the machines to obtain one master sound track. This is a delicate process as far as the music is concerned, for it is only a hair's breadth that separates the "too loud" from the "too soft." Sound engineers, working the dials that control volume, are not always as musically sensitive as composers would like them to be. What is called for is a new species, a sound mixer who is half musician and half engineer; and even then, the mixing of dialogue, music and realistic sounds of all kinds must always remain problematical.

In view of these drawbacks to the full sounding out of his music, it is only natural that the composer often hopes to be able to extract a viable concert suite from his film score. There is a current tendency to believe that movie scores are not proper material for concert music. The argument is that separated from its visual justification the music falls flat.

Personally, I doubt very much that any hard and fast rule can be made that will cover all cases. Each score will have to be judged on its merits and, no doubt, stories that require a more continuous type of musical development in a unified atmosphere will lend themselves better than others to re-working for concert purposes. Rarely is it conceivable that the music of a film might be extracted without much re-working. But I fail to see why, if successful suites like Grieg's *Peer Gynt* can be made from nineteenth century incidental stage music, a twentieth century composer can't be expected to do as well with a film score.

As for the picture score, it is only in the motion picture theatre that the composer for the first time gets the full impact of what he has accomplished, tests the dramatic punch of his favorite musical spot, appreciates the curious importance and unimportance of detail, wishes that he had done certain things differently and is surprised that others came off better than he had hoped. For when all is said and done the art of combining moving pictures with musical tones is still a mysterious art. Not the least mysterious element is the theatregoers' reaction: Millions will be listening but one never knows how many will be really hearing, so the next time you go to the movies remember to be on the composer's side. Remove those ear-muffs.

Second Thoughts
on Hollywood (1940)

As perhaps the best American composer to work intensively in Hollywood, Copland knew well the possibilities and limitations offered by movie-land to the serious artist.

Everyone is so prepared to hear the worst about Hollywood that it is a pleasure to be able to start these observations on a cheerful note. The best one can say about Hollywood is that it is a place where composers are actually needed. The accent is entirely on the living composer. Day after day and year after year there are copyists, instrumentalists, and conductors who do nothing but copy, perform, and conduct the music of contemporary composers. Theoretically, at any rate, the town is a composer's Eldorado.

For the movies do need music, and need it badly. By itself the screen *is* a pretty cold proposition. In Hollywood I looked at long stretches of film before the music had been added, and I got the impression that music is like a small flame put under the screen to help warm it.

It is this very function, however, which so often gives the composer a minor role. There is no sense in denying the subordinate position the composer fills. After all, film music makes sense only if it helps the film; no matter how good, distinguished, or successful, the music must be secondary in importance to the story being told on the screen. Essentially there is nothing about the movie medium to rule out any composer with a dramatic imagination. But the man who insists on complete self-expression had better stay home and write symphonies. He will never be happy in Hollywood.

Whether you are happy or not largely depends on two factors: the producer you work for, and the amount of time allotted for completing the score. (I am assuming that the film itself is an intelligent one.) The producer is a kind of dictator, responsible only to the studio executives for every phase of the picture's production. This naturally includes the musical score. The trouble is not so much that these producers consider themselves musical connoisseurs, but that they claim to be accurate barometers of public taste. "If I can't understand it, the public won't." As a result of this the typical Hollywood composer is concerned not with the reaction of the public, as you might think, but with that of the producer. It isn't surprising therefore, that all film music originating in Hollywood tends to be very much the same. The score of one picture adds up to about the score of any other. You seldom hear anything fresh or distinctive partly because everyone is so intent on playing safe. A pleased producer means more jobs. That alone is sufficient to explain the Hollywood stereotype of music.

The demand for speed from the composer is familiar to anyone who has ever worked "in pictures." The composer may sit around no end of time, waiting for the picture to be done; as soon as it's finished the director, the producer, the script writer—everybody is in a frightful hurry; valuable time is passing and the studio has visions of the money it is losing each day that the film is not in a theatre. It is difficult to make studio executives realize that no one has yet discovered how to write notes any faster than it was done circa 400 A.D. The average movie score is approximately forty minutes long. The usual time allotted for composing it is about two weeks. For *Of Mice and Men* I had about six weeks, and I believe that other composers insist on that much time for writing an elaborate score.

The purpose of the film score is to make the film more effective, that's clear enough. But I don't think anyone has as yet formulated the perfect solution for this problem. In fact I came away with a sense of the mysterious nature of all film music. In retrospect, I can see three important ways in which music helps a picture. The first is by intensifying the emotional impact of any given scene, the second by creating an illusion of continuity, and the third by providing a kind of neutral background music. Of these three, the last presents the most mysterious problem—how to supply the right sort of music behind dialogue.

Intensification of emotion at crucial moments is, of course, an old tradition of theatre music. True, it is no more than the Hearts and Flowers tradition, but still, perfectly legitimate. The one difficulty here is to get the music started without suddenly making the audience aware of its entrance. To use a favorite Hollywood term, you must "steal the music in."

Obvious too is the continuity function of music. Pictures, jumping from episode to episode, from exterior to interior, have a tendency to fall apart. Music, an art which exists in time, can subtly hold disparate scenes together. In exciting montage sequences where the film moves violently from shot to shot, music by developing one particular theme, or one type of rhythmical material, or some other unifying musical element, supplies the necessary continuous understructure.

But "background" music is something very special. It is also the most ungrateful kind of music for a composer to write. Since it's music behind, or underneath the word, the audience is really not going to hear it, possibly won't even be aware of its existence; yet it undoubtedly works on the sub-conscious mind. The need here is for a kind of music which will give off a "neutral" color or atmosphere. (This is what creates the indefinable warmth that the screen itself lacks.) To write music which must be inex-pressive is not easy for composers who normally tend to be as expressive as possible. To add to the difficulty, there's the impossibility of knowing in advance just what will work in any given scene. If one could only test the music by adding it to the scene before it is shot, or have the music per-formed while the actors speak their lines! But this is utopian. Once the scene is done and the music is added, the result is fairly problematical. Even dubbing it down almost below the listening level will not always prove satisfactory.

If Hollywood has its problems it has also its well-known solutions. Most scores, as everybody knows, are written in the late nineteenth century sym-phonic style, a style now so generally accepted as to be considered inevita-ble. But why need movie music be symphonic? And why, oh why, the nineteenth century? Should the rich harmonies of Tchaikovsky, Franck, and Strauss be spread over every type of story, regardless of time, place, or treatment? For *Wuthering Heights*, perhaps yes. But why for *Golden Boy*, a hard-boiled, modern piece? What screen music badly needs is more differ-entiation, more feeling for the exact quality of each picture. That does not necessarily mean a more literal musical description of time and place. Cer-tainly very few Hollywood films give a realistic impression of period. Still, it should be possible, without learned displays of historical research and without the hack conventions of symphonic music, for a composer to re-flect the emotion and reality of the individual picture he is scoring.

Another pet Hollywood formula, this one borrowed from nineteenth century opera, is the use of the leit-motif. I haven't made up my mind whether the public is conscious of this device or completely oblivious to it, but I can't see how it is appropriate to the movies. It may help the spectator sitting in the last row of the opera house to identify the singer who appears from the wings, if the orchestra announces her motif. But that's hardly necessary on the screen. No doubt the leit-motif system is a help to the composer in a hurry, perhaps doing two or three scores simultaneously. It is always an easy solution to mechanically pin a motif on every character. In *Drums Along the Mohawk* this method was reduced to its final absurdity.

One theme announced the Indians, another the hero. In the inevitable chase, every time the scene switched from Indians to hero the themes did too, sometimes so fast that the music seemed to hop back and forth before any part of it had time to breathe. If there must be thematic description I think it would serve better if it were connected with the underlying ideas of a picture. If, for example, a film has to do with loneliness, a theme might be developed to induce sympathy with the idea of being lonely, something broader in feeling than the mere tagging of characters.

A third device, and one very peculiar to Hollywood, is known as "Mickey-Mousing" a film. In this system the music, wherever possible, is made to mimic everything that happens on the screen. An actor can't lift an eyebrow without the music helping him do it. What is amusing when applied to a Disney fantasy becomes disastrous in its effect upon a straight or serious drama. Max Steiner has a special weakness for this device. In *Of Human Bondage* he had the unfortunate idea of making his music limp whenever the club-footed hero walked across the scene, with a very obvious and it seemed to me vulgarizing effect. Recently Mr. Steiner has shown a fondness for a new device. This is the mixing of realistic music with background music. Joe may be walking around the room quietly humming a tune to himself (realistic use of music). Watch for the moment when Joe steps out into the storm, for it is then that Mr. Steiner pounces upon Joe's little tune and gives us the works with an orchestra of seventy. The trouble with this procedure is that it stresses not so much the dramatic moment as the ingenuity of the composer. All narrative illusion is lost the instant we are conscious of the music as such.

It may not be without interest to retrace some of the steps by which music is added to a film. After the picture is completed it is shown in the studio projection room before the producer, the director, the studio's musical director (if any), the composer and his various henchmen, the conductor, the orchestrator, the cue-sheet assistants, the copyists—anybody in fact who has anything to do with the preparation of the score. At this showing the decision is reached as to where to add music, where it should start in each separate sequence and where it should end. The film is then turned over to a cue-sheet assistant whose job it is to prepare a listing of every separate moment in each musical sequence. These listings, with the accompanying timing in film footage and in seconds, is all that the composer needs for complete security in synchronising his music with the film. The practised Hollywood composer is said never to look at a picture more than once. With a good memory, a stop-watch, and a cue-sheet he is ready to go to work. Others prefer to work in the music projection room where there is a piano, a screen, and an operator who can turn the film on and off. I myself used a movieola, which permits every composer to be his own operator. This is a small machine which shows the film negative through a magnifying glass. Using the movieola I could see the picture whenever and as often as I pleased.

While the music is being written the film itself is prepared for recording. Each important musical cue must be marked on the film by some pre-arranged signal system that varies in every studio. These "signals" show the conductor where he is. If he wants to hit a certain musical cue which, according to the cue-sheet, occurs at the forty-ninth second, the negative must be marked in such a way as to indicate that spot (always with sufficient warning signals) and if the conductor is competent he can nearly always "hit it on the nose." In Hollywood this knack for hitting cues properly is considered even more important in a conductor than his ability to read an orchestral score. Another method, much more mechanical, but used a good deal for Westerns and quickies is to synchronize by means of a so-called click-track. In this case, the film is measured off not according to seconds, but according to regular musical beats. There is no surer method for hitting cues "on the nose." But only the experienced composer can ignore the regularity of the beat and write his music freely within and around it.

For the composer the day of recording is perhaps the high point. He has worked hard and long and is anxious to test his work. He hears his music sounded for the first time while the film is being shown. Everything comes off just as it would in a concert hall. But if he wishes to remain happy he had better stay away from the sound-recording booth. For here all the music is being recorded at about the same medium dynamic level so that later on the loudness and softness may be regulated when the moment comes for re-recording.

Re-recording takes place in the dubbing room. This is a kind of composer's purgatory. It is here that the music track is mixed with other sound tracks—the dialogue, the "effects" track, etc. It is at this point that the composer sees his music begin to disappear. A passage once so clear and satisfying seems now to move farther and farther off. The instant a character opens his mouth, the music must recede to the near vanishing point. This is the place that calls out all a composer's self-control; it's a moment for philosophy.

From the composer's standpoint, the important person in the dubbing room is the man who sits at the controls. It is he who decides how loud or soft the music will be at any given moment, and therefore it is he who can make or ruin everything, by the merest touch of the dials. But surprisingly, in every studio these controls are in the hands of a sound engineer. What I don't understand is why a musician has not been called in for this purpose. It would never occur to me to call in an engineer to tune my piano. Surely only a musician can be sensitive to the subtle effects of musical sound, particularly when mixed with other sounds. A Toscanini would be none too good for such a job—certainly a sound expert is not qualified.

While on the subject of sound levels I might as well mention the unsatisfactory way in which sound is controlled in the picture theatre. The tonal volume of a picture is not set for all time; no mechanical contraption permanently fixes the loudness or softness of the music. The person who decides on the sound levels is not even the film-operator but the individual theatre manager who is of course susceptible to advice from Tom, Dick, and Harry sitting anywhere in the house. People who love music tend to prefer it played loudly. Those who don't care for it especially want to hear it only at a low level. So no matter how much care is taken in the dubbing room to fix proper tonal levels, the situation will remain unsatisfactory until a method is found to control the casual and arbitrary way in which dials are set in the theatre operator's booth.

Hollywood, like Vienna, can boast its own star roster of composers. Alfred Newman, Max Steiner, Victor Young, Anthony Collins are composers created by the film industry. While it is easy enough to poke fun at the movie music they turn out as so much yardage, it would at the same time be foolish not to profit by their great experience in writing for the films. Newman, for example, has discovered the value of the string orchestra as a background for emotional scenes. Better than the full orchestra, the strings can be de-personalized. This is important in a medium where the sound of a single instrument may sometimes be disturbing. Another secret of movie music which Steiner has exploited, is the writing of atmosphere music almost without melodic content of any kind. A melody is by its nature distracting since it calls attention to itself. For certain types of neutral music, a kind of melody-less music is needed. Steiner does not supply mere chords, but superimposes a certain amount of melodic motion, just enough to make the music sound normal, and yet not enough to compel attention.

Composers who come to Hollywood from the big world outside generally take some time to become expert in using the idiom. Erich Korngold still tends to get over-complex in the development of a musical idea. This is not always true, however. When successful, he gives a sense of firm technic, a continuity not only of feeling but structure. Werner Janssen, whose score for *The General Died at Dawn* made movie history, is still looked upon as something of an outsider. He shows his pre-Hollywood training in the sophistication of his musical idiom, and in his tendency to be over-fussy in the treatment of even the simplest sequence. Ernst Toch, who belongs in the category with Korngold and Janssen, wrote an important score for *Peter Ibbetson* several years ago. On the strength of this job, Toch should be today one of the best-known film composers. But unfortunately there aren't enough people in Hollywood who can tell a good score when they hear one. Today Toch is generally assigned to do "screwy music." (In Hollywood music is either "screwy" or "down to earth"—and most of it is down to earth.) Toch deserves better.

The men who write Hollywood's music seem strangely oblivious of their reputations outside the West Coast. I have often wondered, for instance, why no concerted effort has ever been made to draw the attention of music critics to their more ambitious scores. Why shouldn't the music critic cover important film premieres? True, the audience that goes to the films doesn't think about the music, and possibly shouldn't think about the music. Nevertheless, a large part of music heard by the American public is heard in the film theatre. Unconsciously, the cultural level of music is certain to be raised if better music is written for films. This will come about more quickly, I think, if producers and directors know that scores are being heard and criticized. One of the ways they will find out what's good and what's bad is to read it in the papers. Let the press now take this important business in hand.

Composer's Report on Music in South America (1947)

Copland's journals from his travels, included with his personal writings later in the book, display his blunt and balanced assessments of his experiences. When writing for the large public, as here, Copland tended to focus on positives. The text below omits subheads that seem to have been editorially added to the original published text. (S. S.)

As far as I know, no one had ever before seen an American composer in Pernambuco's capital city of Recife. The same was true for colonial Bahia, and the more "modern" Fortaleza in the state of Ceara. These north coastal towns of Brazil—themselves separated by many hundreds of miles—don't very often get to see American musicians of any kind. But a composer of symphonic music is indeed a rare bird.

The Department of State sponsored my tour through these provincial capitals under its program of exchanging professors in various fields with Latin American countries. My itinerary also included the more usual big towns like Montevideo, Buenos Aires, Rio de Janeiro, São Paulo, and Porto Alegre.

In all these places our government cooperates with local persons to maintain cultural centers for the teaching of English and the spreading of comprehensive ideas about our civilization. The cultural centers lend books, phonograph recordings, printed music, organize lectures and concerts, and in general help to give the local citizen a truer picture of the United States than can be obtained from a Hollywood movie.

Bahia and Recife were just as anxious to tell me about their native songs and dances as I was to tell them about American music. When I was in Rio I caused a minor flurry by complaining that it was difficult to hear a real samba in that city. The Broadway version of the samba was obviously exerting a baleful influence on Rio's samba composers. In Bahia they claim to have preserved the real thing. Perhaps it should be explained that Bahia is the Alabam' of Brazilian popular music. Everybody always seems to want to go there.

As a matter of fact, Brazil's finest composer in the popular style, Dorival Cayme, actually does come from there. When I heard him sing, accompanying himself on the guitar, I discovered that it is not the rhythmic element that gives the samba interest. What gives it character and originality is the wealth of melodic invention—the large curve of the line, the unequal and unexpected phrase lengths, the rapidity of execution, and the amusement of the words cascading into a frenzy of cross accents against the basic rhythm. All this makes a real samba very indigenous and very hard to sing, copy or remember. I was told that they have to be simplified for ordinary carnival use, and I don't wonder.

And in Bahia I heard for the first time a new (for me) instrument called the berimbau. (A musician rarely has the pleasure of hearing an instrument with a really new sound.) No one seemed able to tell me its origins, though the theory was advanced that Moorish influence was paramount. The berimbau looks like the bow of a bow and arrow. It has a single string and produces only two notes a whole tone apart. These are struck by a small wooden stick. The trick that gives it fascination is a wooden shell, open at one end, which is held against the string and reflects the sound in the manner of an echo chamber. At the same time the hand that wields the wooden stick jiggles a kind of rattle. When several berimbau players are heard together they set up a sweetly jangled tinkle. I've never heard anything quite like it.

In Recife I was honored by a full evening's demonstration of their popular arts. Most interesting was the frevo, danced in the street outside the cultural center. To dance the frevo is no cinch. You dance it alone, and it seems to consist of a continual turning to the rear and an almost falling backwards. To the hazard of falling is added the hazard of violently bumping your neighbor, for the frevo is danced in a deliberately restricted space.

The accompanying music derives from street marches like our New Orleans jazz. As played today, the music of the frevo has terrific bounce. For my benefit an Army band of twenty-eight men was rounded up and played frevos in a very fine way. The brass were particularly amusing in the way they interjected upward thrusting phrases and sudden isolated chords. The precision and energy displayed were remarkable, particularly when it is remembered that the music was being produced at night in a hot country by a group of men with dead-pan faces on Army rations and Army pay.

These side tours into Brazilian popular music were highly diverting. My main concern, however, was with concert life as it exists today in Rio, São Paulo, Montevedeo, and Buenos Aires, particularly as it relates to American music. The situation as regards our music seemed somewhat better than it was six years ago, when I first visited Latin America. People in the know are familiar, at least with the names, if not the music, of our composers.

Live performances of American music are still a comparative rarity. Chamber music, piano pieces, and songs are occasionally heard at the concerts of the smaller avant-garde groups, such as the Argentine League of Composers or the Brazilian Chamber Music Society. Orchestral performances are still greatly hindered by the lack of available orchestral materials.

The "big" public gets its contact with American music solely through recordings. Most recordings of serious American music are practically unobtainable in phonograph shops, but the radio stations seem to have them and perform them. Gershwin's music is universally known and liked. Among living Americans the names of Samuel Barber, Roy Harris, Walter Piston, and William Schuman are most familiar. On the other hand, no one seemed ever to have heard of Leonard Bernstein!

In each city visited I made certain to inquire about the younger composers. Buenos Aires has produced an impressive batch of youngsters, thanks to an active concert life and several competent teachers. Brazil has fine composers but few good teachers. The pickings in Rio at the present time are therefore disturbingly thin. Speaking generally, music of the French school no longer exerts so exclusive and pervasive an influence on the younger generation as was true of their elders. That's a step in advance.

Music-lovers who imagine that South America is still a musical desert, creatively considered, simply don't know what is going on. Composers like Camargo Guarnieri, Luis Gianneo, José María Castro, and Alberto Ginastera are worth anybody's time.

Festival in Caracas (1954)

Caracas, unlike Paris, is a newcomer in the field of present-day music. Nevertheless it recently succeeded in putting itself on the contemporary musical map—and with a bang. Nobody, not even Paris, had ever before thought of organizing a festival of orchestral works by contemporary Latin-American composers.

This happened for the first time anywhere in Caracas, which, incidentally, is full of vitality at the moment, thanks to an oil-engendered prosperity. The town boasts a good orchestra, a brand-new open-air amphitheatre seating 6,000 persons, and a lively cultural organization, the Institucion José Angel Lamas, headed by Dr. Inocente Palacios.

Within the space of two and a half weeks, forty symphonic compositions originating in seven Latin-American countries were performed in a series of eight concerts. This was a major effort for all concerned, especially for the courageous musicians of the Orquesta Sinfonica Venezuela and the festival's principal conductors: Heitor Villa-Lobos, Carlos Chávez, Juan José Castro, and Rios Reyna.

The event was planned with typical present-day Venezuelan largesse. Three prizes totaling $20,000 were offered for symphonic pieces by composers of Latin America. An international jury awarded the first prize of $10,000 to the *Corales Criollos* by Señor Castro, Argentine composer now resident in Italy. Two $5,000 prizes were won by Señor Chávez, for his Sinfonía No. 3, and by the 28-year-old Cuban composer Julian Orbón for his Three Symphonic Versions.

It is safe to say that none of those present had ever before had the opportunity of hearing so complete a cross section of Latin-American orchestral output. It came as no surprise that Villa-Lobos and Chávez confirmed their reputation as the two leaders of Latin-American composition. But the program planners seemed to me to over-emphasize the folklore-inspired side of South American music. Such works, heard in rapid succession, do not sit well together. When heard thus it is difficult to judge them on their separate merits. Villa-Lobos chose to present three such colorful works of his own, all sprawling in form and luxuriant in manner. They leave one astonished, but also quite confused. It is works like these that make Villa-Lobos the pride and despair of his Latin-American colleagues.

Chávez balanced the vibrant Indianism of his popular *Sinfonía India* with the austerities of the *Sinfonía de Antigona*. His new Sinfonía No. 3 belongs to the *Antigona* category and is entirely characteristic—very personal and very uncompromising. Its four brief and connected movements have an almost sadistic force that compels attention. The sinfonía is powerful music, but not music that can be easily loved, or even absorbed, in a single hearing.

The other two prize works were much more ingratiating. Castro's *Corales Criollos* is undoubtedly his finest work thus far. I much preferred it to his rather showy Piano Concerto that was also heard, in a knockout performance by Jesús Maria Sanromá. The new work is just as elegantly written as the concerto but it seems to come from a deeper source within the composer.

Julián Orbón, Spanish-born composer who lives in Havana, proved to be one of the finds of the festival. Everything he writes for the orchestra "sounds." His prize-winning *Three Symphonic Versions* has a naturalness and spontaneity that makes it immediately attractive. Another discovery of the festival was 38-year-old Antonio Esteves of Caracas. Eight thousand persons turned out to see him conduct his *Cantata Criolla* for soloists, chorus, and orchestra, and shouted their approbation. He has written a flavorsome work, with felicitous touches of local color. It has its weak moments, but the talent is undeniably there, shining through the faults, leaving one hopeful for the composer's future.

A few gripes are in order at this point. Chile was inadequately represented, except for a single work by Domingo Santa Cruz: his Sinfonía Concertante. Glaringly conspicuous by their absence from the programs were the Brazilian Camargo Guarnieri, and the young Chilean Juan Orrego-Salas. Two overtures by the Mexican [Rodolfo] Halffter and the Argentine Ginastera were neither truly representative. Most of all, one missed an experimental note. Of dodecaphonic music there was not a trace. The most problematical piece programmed was *Triptico de Santiago* by Cuba's José Ardevol. He strangely mixes theory and instinct in such a way that striking moments exist alongside inexplicably ineffective ones.

Caracas promises another festival in two years—this time including los Americanos del Norte. Ojalá!

III
The Musician's Life

A Note on Young Composers (1935)

As a music politician concerned about restricted possibilities for both himself and his colleagues, Copland had a continuing concern with the social circumstances impinging on his profession. In the 1930s, he commended incidentally the Soviet ways of supporting composers.

The problem of the young composer is perennially with us. When I arrived in France in 1921 the *Groupe des Six* was then in its heyday. Anyone would have predicted that the young composers who came after Milhaud, Honegger, Auric, etc. would be destined to carry on the sense of excitement and brilliance that came into French music with these new personalities. I suppose the same was true in Germany around the 1900s when Strauss and Mahler were in the full flush of their artistic careers. In both these cases one would seem to have been justified in predicting a brilliant succession of new and talented young men. But, strangely enough, in the German case, a hiatus of twenty to thirty years occurred between Mahler and Strauss on the one hand and Hindemith on the other; and in the case of France, it is difficult to point to a single outstanding French composer in his young twenties of whom one can say that he is continuing the renaissance that began with Debussy and Fauré.

We in America have our own special problem of seeing to it that the sense of new life that came into American music soon after the War be continued in a fresh batch of younger "lights."

In the first place, young composers should try to help by seeing themselves clearly. Any young composer who is really aware must realize that he faces a completely new set of facts. Those who were young composers in America in the 1920s, we understand now, had comparatively easy going. Their career was more or less mapped out for them. One studied in America, after which one went to Europe for a finishing. But nowadays, not only does the young composer not go to Europe, but he is lucky if he has enough money with which to complete his studies in America. Again, in the old days, one returned from Europe to find a new group of societies devoted to the sole purpose of introducing modern works for a small but eager public. Nowadays the young composer has no one society solely devoted to his needs, and it becomes increasingly difficult for him to "break into" the programs of the older organizations. Moreover, the whole field of modern music no longer carries with it a sense of novelty or even of experimentation. The audiences that used to expect to find a new genius with each new composer are tired. Perhaps rightly so.

How do these new conditions affect our younger composers? I have recently met composers of the younger generation who seemed to have a full realization of the times they live in. These young people are generally either pessimistic or optimistic. The pessimistic ones say, "What's the use, since music seems to mean so little in the modern world, why bother?" The optimistic ones are trying more or less successfully to connect themselves and their music in a more direct way with the social problems of the world today. But in either case, these young composers are faced with a question which we older men did not have to face in any so direct a manner, namely: "Whom are you writing your music for?"

This is something which every young composer should, and eventually will, have to face. It has larger implications than might at first appear. For it is obvious that those young people who just a few years ago were writing pieces filled with the *weltschmerz* of a Schoenberg now realize that they were merely picturing their own discontent and that the small audience which existed for Schoenberg's music could never be stretched to include their own. Let these young people say to themselves once and for all, "No more Schoenberg. The music I write must have more pertinence than Schoenberg's had even to his own Vienna."

Those who have taken the early Stravinsky as their model probably find themselves unable to follow the Russian master into the Elysian fields of his neo-classical manner. Likewise, it is equally obvious that the magnificent life of such works as *Petrouchka* and *Les Noces* cannot be recreated in 1935. But if there is to be no more Schoenberg, and no more Stravinsky, where are we?

It is no secret that many of the young composers who had taken one or the other of these two older men as their models have now thrown in their lot with that of the working class. These young people, at any rate, have settled the problem of their audience. But at the same time they have taken on other problems, new ones, which result directly from the kind of audience they now wish to reach. These new problems have to do with such broad questions as the style and content of their music, practical possibilities (usually limitations) in performance, sectarian dangers, etc., which do not obtain in the same way in the ordinary bourgeois field of music.

Hence, the young composer who allies himself with the proletarian movement must do so not with the feeling that he has found an easy solution, but with a full realization of what such a step means, if his work is to be of permanent value to the workers and their cause.

Yes, the problem of the young composer is perennially with us. Of course, it is true that the creative artist's life has never been an easy one in any epoch. (Undoubtedly, in the Soviet Union they order these things better.) Still, I look about me and wonder why I see no young composer in America with a "First Symphony" under his arm. Inevitably, one wonders where the fault lies. Does our young composer lack the necessary craftsmanship, or the sense of economic stability, or an ideological basis for his work, or what? Each young composer must examine his own conscience, and draw his own conclusions.

But as for myself, I admit to a certain uneasiness of feeling until that "First Symphony" (or "Quintet" or proletarian oratorio) is forthcoming.

Effect of the Cold War
on the Artist in the U.S. (1949)

Copland delivered this previously unpublished speech at the World Peace Conference at the Worldorf-Astoria Hotel, in New York, spring 1949. In retrospect, that occasion seems the last gasp of pro-Soviet "popular front" sentiments among prominent American cultural figures.

I am going to start by saying that I wrote this paper myself. Nobody told me what to say, and if anybody had tried to tell me what to say, I wouldn't be here. I feel I have to put it that bluntly because the press has quoted the Governor of this State and a spokesman of the State Department as stating that this Conference and all its panels are mere fronts for the spreading of Communist propaganda. Communism and the countries that have Communist regimes are facts—major facts—and they must be dealt with as such, but they are not the reason for my being here today. I am here this morning as a democratic American artist, with no political affiliations of any kind, not at all interested in doctrinaire Communism, but very much interested in the United States—in the policies of the United States, and in how those policies will affect artists in the United States. I came here this morning because I am convinced that the present policies of our government, if relentlessly pursued, will lead us inevitably into a third World War. I came here this morning because I wish to protest an attitude that has turned the very word "Peace" into a dirty word.

There is a concerted effort on the part of the press and radio to convince the American people that nothing remains for us to do but to make a choice between two diametrically opposed systems of thought. We are being taught to think in neat little categories—in terms of blacks and whites, East and West, Communism and the Profit System. In historical perspective, one can find plenty of precedent for that kind of schematized thinking, wrong as it may be. During the religious wars of the 16th century it certainly must have seemed inconceivable that Catholicism and Protestantism could ever peacefully co-exist in the same world. Later the libertarian ideas of the French Revolution and English traditionalism seemed hopelessly incompatible. In the field of music there was a time when you were supposed to make up your mind as between Richard Wagner and Johannes Brahms. To find some virtues in both was considered impossible. Nowadays a similar cleavage is supposed to exist between the mass-appeal music of Shostakovitch and the musical radicalism of Schoenberg.

All the dichotomies of the past were in some measure resolved, just as we shall have, in some way, to resolve our own. I do not wish to minimize the difficulties of the present world situation. But I am convinced that it is the duty of every citizen—artist and non-artist alike—to insist and insist that every possible effort be made toward a peaceful solution of world problems. Wars can be manufactured whenever war-makers are ready. But to find a way to a peaceful solution of our very real differences may be the patient work of years by men of good-will.

I agreed to talk today specifically on the subject of the Effect of the Cold War on the Artist in the United States. I have spent some thirty years as a practicing composer in America and I have lived through two great wars. Artists, by definition, hate all wars—hot or cold. But lately I've been thinking that the Cold War is almost worse for art than the real thing—for it permeates the atmosphere with fear and anxiety. An artist can function at his best only in a vital and healthy environment for the simple reason that the very act of creation is an affirmative gesture. An artist fighting in a war for a cause he holds just has something affirmative he can believe in. That artist, if he can stay alive, can create art. But, throw him into a mood of suspicion, ill-will and dread that typifies the Cold War attitude and he'll create nothing.

Artistic creation is a life-giving force—it says a great 'Yes' to the business of living. Convince an artist that the human race is incapable of finding a way of living together and you take away his very desire to create. An artist is moved by a need to communicate his deepest emotions to his own people and to people everywhere. Tell that artist that nothing but a world conflagration lies ahead and you'll effectively choke off his basic need to communicate.

To create a symphony or novel or a large canvas in today's world takes real faith. The Cold War is the invention of men who have lost faith—men who are intent upon stirring up fears and hatreds that can only breed destruction. No art can thrive for long in that kind of a world.

How different it might be! All of us are aware of how powerful an agent art can be in giving all humanity a sense of togetherness. How unfortunate it is that our lawmakers have so little conception of the way in which the work of our composers, painters, and writers might be used in order to draw closer bonds between our own people and those of other nations.

Some attempts have of course been made in that direction. Your moderator this morning, Mr. [Olin] Downes, and myself were invited with other musicians to sit on a Committee organized by our own State Department for the purpose of bringing closer cultural ties with the Soviet Union. It is rather ironic to remember that that happened only a few years ago. The Department of State in a recent press release claims that it still would like to foster closer cultural ties with the Soviet Union but that they have been repeatedly rebuffed by the Russians. Naturally a private citizen has no way of knowing to what extent the Russians have or have not been willing to cooperate. But I am in a position to relate an incident which took place three years ago, and which I believe to be very a propos.

For several seasons an organization existed called the American-Soviet Music Society. Its purpose was to further musical interchange between these two countries. Serge Koussevitzky, conductor of the Boston Symphony, was Chairman of the Society. Concerts were given, a journal was published, and greetings exchanged between the musicians and composers of this country with those of Russia. As a first step toward an interchange of personalities the Ukrainian government sent us two of their best singers, members of the State Opera House at Kiev, for whom we arranged an elaborate tour. The tour had hardly begun, when without previous warning, the Department of Justice ruled that the two singers would be obliged to register as agents of a foreign power. To vigorous protests from prominent musicians the Justice Department replied that since the two singers had arrived as members of a group of visiting Ukrainians whose purpose was judged political in nature they would have to register or leave the country. Of course the two singers left the United States almost immediately, abandoning their good will tour almost before it had begun. Such an incident naturally threw cold water on future projects for musical interchange. The Soviet Union has been understandably reluctant to send artists to this country who would be in danger of being treated like undercover spies. You can imagine that with the stepping up of the Cold War the American-Soviet Music Society ceased to exist. It was a minor casualty, perhaps, but it was indicative of events to come.

From my vantage point it would seem that the determinedly unfriendly attitude of the Western Powers to the Soviet Union has produced a kind of Cold War in reverse. By that I mean that the Soviet Union itself has now officially adopted a disapproving attitude toward much contemporary art, and especially in the field of music. I have no wish to embarrass our distinguished composer-guest from the Soviet Union but I see no reason why we should not point out in a friendly way that all cultural interchange becomes difficult, if not impossible, when all foreign music from the West is condemned in advance. At any rate that is the impression that has been given us. As a composer from the West myself I naturally find that attitude extreme. It makes no more sense to reject the artistic findings of a foreign composer than it would to reject the scientific investigations of a foreigner. One can never tell in advance what will stimulate the imagination of an artist. If a brilliant new composing talent emerges from Tadjikistan we all want to hear what his music is like. If a bright new composing star rises out of the Kentucky Mountain area we think the Russian people should know what his music is like.

No doubt it seems naïve to explain what must appear to be self-evident. But actually the Cold War has only intensified a situation that has never been too good. Our former allies are poorly informed as to present-day American music. After all, when the Russian Revolution took place in 1917, we had very little music that was worth exportation. The last thirty years have changed that. We have earned the right to have American music heard throughout the world. The Soviet Union is impoverishing itself in the cultural sphere by not encouraging every possible musical exchange with our country.

What is the alternative? To cut ourselves off from each other is exactly what the proponents of the Cold War would like. To prove to them that friendly relations are possible in the cultural sphere would be a first step toward resuming friendly talks in the political sphere. The presence of Dmitri Schostakovitch at this Conference is proof that the Soviet Union and other neighboring countries are anxious to further the cause of peaceful relations. Of course such relations via the arts only symbolize what should be taking place on the plane of international politics.

Introducing Shostakovitch
at Dinner (1949)

It is one of the marvels of the art of music that it makes us all forget ideological differences—at least for as long as the music sounds. America does not often take to its heart the serious music of a living composer. There have been exceptions—George Gershwin was one—and our next speaker is another. His symphonies and operas, his film scores and chamber music are known throughout the world. The urgency and sincerity of his music, its lyrical drive, its power to move great mass audiences everywhere has been one of the major factors in the music of our time. On this occasion I think we owe him a simple 'thank you' for the musical pleasure he has given countless audiences in our country. As an American composer I am indeed glad to welcome to our democracy one of the world's outstanding creators, the distinguished Soviet composer and our next speaker: Dmitri Shostakovitch.

When Private and Public Worlds Meet (1968)

Twenty years later, the sentiments expressed in Copland's writings were more appreciative of American entrepreneurial effort.

Some 20 years ago during the course of a memorable evening at the Stravinskys' home in Los Angeles, the venerable maestro turned to me and said, in no uncertain terms: "My dear, you should conduct your own music. All composers should conduct their own music!"

Most composers would, of course, very much like to be able to conduct their own music, yet only a comparatively few do so. To the layman it would seem only natural that a man who was capable of writing an orchestral score, with its manifold complexities, would certainly be able to indicate to an orchestra how to carry out his musical intentions. Strangely enough, it doesn't necessarily work that way, for the composer who can do just that is exceptional. In most cases these two musical functions—composing and conducting—are quite distinct one from the other. There are few more pitiable sights than to watch a gifted composer trying to lead an orchestra through his own composition with only the foggiest notion of how to get what he so desperately wants from the massed musicians before him. What makes it worse is the knowledge that any professionally competent conductor with an inkling of the composer's intentions could be relied upon to make some musical sense out of the piece.

As a composer who took Stravinsky's advice to heart, I think I have a just awareness of the wide gap that separates these two careers. A composer's life is a private one, very different from the public exposure demanded of the conductor. A composer in the process of creation is a being removed. Absorbed in the private world of his own imaginings, he is intent on putting down his innermost thoughts with a coherence that makes

133

them communicable to the world outside. Intuition, instinct, inborn musicality provide the spark; acquired knowledge, experience, and stick-at-it-ness are essential ingredients. In the end, the sounds he hears in his head gradually form themselves into a completely realized composition. The conductor, on the other hand, starts with the finished pages. He must reconstruct what it was the composer had in mind when shaping the work; what human "message" it conveys, as we used to say. It is easy to understand, therefore, what an advantage it is for the composer himself to be able to communicate his conception to both orchestra and audience without the intermediary of an interpreter.

Take Stravinsky himself, for example. By now music lovers around the world have had the good fortune to observe him in the role of conductor. It would be inconceivable, with the maestro on the podium, for an orchestra to sentimentalize a tender passage or to perform a Stravinskian *allegro barbaro* in a rhythmically ragged fashion. Some listeners may complain that Stravinsky's beat results in too dry, too precise, too clipped a sonority. But even such an exaggeration, if exaggeration it be, points to a basic and significant personality trait.

One can learn surprising things about a composer's idea of his own style by attentive listening to the sounds he elicits from a group of musicians. I still recall with some astonishment a performance heard many years ago of *Pierrot Lunaire* under Schoenberg's direction. It was fascinating to note to what a degree the composer underplayed the latent hysteria of his revolutionary work.

Richard Strauss was said to have retained a markedly cool detachment when conducting his own compositions. I should like to have seen him whipping up a typical Straussian orchestral storm with this same cool approach. On one occasion he is reported to have advised a young conducting aspirant, anxious to give his all for a Strauss performance: "Never, under any circumstances, *ever* look at the brass!"

Paul Hindemith was known to be exacting with his composition students. Yet whenever I observed him on the conductor's podium he seemed to take a comparatively business-like approach to the job of conducting. No *Schwarmerei* and no textural muddiness anywhere; straightforward and unadorned music-making appeared to be the extent of his conducting ambition.

By contrast, Benjamin Britten, with the simplest of gestures, evokes a certain poetic aura from his players. He is especially persuasive with the natural unfolding of a long lyrical line as it arises out of the surrounding Brittenish harmonies. One knows for a certainty that he is in absolute control of everything that transpires. Carlos Chávez, with a very different temperament, produces an incisive and commanding beat that brooks no nonsense from his performers. A personal and tensile strength is the result so much so that his music never sounds quite the same under anyone else's direction.

Most of the composer-conductors mentioned above have conducted works other than their own. What happens then? Well, for one thing, it is safe to say they no longer enjoy the same degree of confidence and authority granted them by orchestra and audience when leading their own works. That is only to be expected. Yet, from one point of view, a composer conducting the works of others has a certain advantage: he tends to relive them, "feeling" them as if he himself had composed them. It is a kind of insight that presupposes an empathy with the work in hand, a supposition that might tend to limit the composer-conductor's repertoire. (No wonder we were all astonished when composer Boulez agreed to conduct *Parsifal* at Bayreuth!) In this connection, Leonard Bernstein and Lukas Foss are in a category of their own, since both were, from the inception of their careers, equally adept as performers and composers. It is not surprising in such a case that a gift as composer should be so well balanced by an executant ability.

Nothing I have written here is meant to imply that the composer who conducts has nothing to learn from the noncomposer conductor who performs his work. On the contrary. It is not easy, especially when a work is new, for a creator to have sufficient perspective to know in every respect how his composition should be interpreted. A conductor of instinct can suggest tempi adjustments, especially in transitional passages; better balances in orchestral textures; more precision in metronome markings—always a major hazard for the composer—and even, at times, changes in the emotional inflection of a work. Conductors may play a role somewhat similar to that of a stage director with a playwright or a sympathetic editor with the author of a book. Obviously there is more than one way to read the lines of a play and more than one way to interpret a musical composition. A conductor, whoever he may be, understands a work through his own temperament, background and training. Any composer would do well to keep an open mind when listening to a gifted performer "reading" his work.

Serge Koussevitzky, a lifelong sponsor and conductor of the composers of his day, spoke to me more than once of the value he attached to watching a composer conduct—even badly conduct—his own work. Despite technical limitations, he claimed that something could be learned concerning the basic character of the work. Character is a key word in my mind. Above all, the experienced composer-conductor should be able to draw from an orchestra and make evident to an audience the essential character of his music.

Musical notation is severely limited—notes by themselves tell you not nearly enough. This applies as well to the rhythmic life of a piece despite the fact that rhythms are able to be notated with a fair degree of precision. Yet each time that I have conducted abroad, either a work of my own or a work by a fellow-American, European musicians seem particularly intrigued by what they take to be our American rhythmic sense. American rhythms have their own brand of liveliness, of vigor and vitality, with a derivation from jazz, no doubt. This indigenous quality is also sensed by the foreign musician in relation to our expression of sentiment, which tends to be discreet and rather reserved by European standards. To paraphrase Dr. Koussevitzky again: "You will never 'sell' American music in the larger sense and never convince listeners of its value until you develop American conductors to conduct it." Something of the same thought must have been in Virgil Thomson's mind when he wrote: "Nobody, literally nobody, who has not passed his formative adolescent life in this country ever conducts American music with complete intelligibility."

These, I realize, are concerns of an older generation. The new wave of composer-conductors of the fifties and sixties has other preoccupations. Music that is international in style and hair-raising in complexity is the order of the day. You have to be a very daring young man to risk picking up a baton to conduct your own music nowadays. If you take the risk you had better be as sure of your conducting technique as you are of your composing know-how. In which case, watch out, or you may end up as a conductor—period.

Is the University
Too Much With Us? (1970)

As a successful composer who never accepted a permanent university position,
Copland could regard classical music's other world with a certain objectivity.

A remarkable phenomenon has been taking place during the past dozen
years or so, namely, the extent to which, in America at least, the new music
movement has moved onto the university campus. Nowadays one rarely
reads the biographical data of a native composer born after 1930 without
finding mention of the academic institution where he studied composition, or where he now teaches, or at the very least, where his music has
been performed. Even without reference to statistics, we know that a large
proportion of contemporary music-making takes place at university centers. The institution supplies the hall, the performers, and the audience,
and sometimes even a paying job for the composer. What more can a creative musician ask?

In the old days a college music department was likely to be a citadel of
musical conservatism, concerning itself primarily with the history of
music and studies in musicology, and headed by some old dodo intent on
preserving intact the musical ideals of a past era. How changed all that is
now! The university has become a center for musical radicalism, with experimental composers as members of the teaching staff, and concerts of
far-out music an ordinary occurrence.

As long ago as 1952, Columbia University began the trend by research-
ing the possibilities of electronically produced sound materials. By 1959,
Princeton had joined forces with Columbia to establish a joint Electronic
Music Center with the assistance of the Rockefeller Foundation, while en-
gaging in its own exploratory investigation into the latest twelve-tone developments. At about the same time, U.C.L.A. encouraged Lukas Foss to

137

organize his Improvisation Chamber Ensemble for "reviving the art of improvisation in modern terms." The movement spread: Wesleyan University housed John Cage for a time and published his original notions concerning chance operations, the University of Michigan furthered the ONCE Group, and the University of Chicago co-sponsored the Fromm Concerts. Many smaller colleges, such as Dartmouth, Brandeis, and Oberlin, sponsored lively festivals of present-day composition, providing a forum for new composers while enhancing the musical life of the college community.

One should also point out that a large number of noncomposing performers have found a haven for their musical activities within the academic community. These performers are not content merely to remain on campus; more often than not, the university performing group finds a way to give their concerts of advanced music in metropolitan centers, thereby providing much needed variety in the musical life of our bigger cities.

One wonders how the musical scene, and especially our composers, are affected by these new developments. Is it advisable for so many of our younger men to take refuge with in college walls? Clearly there is a positive and a negative side to their situation. By comparison with the relative isolation of the typical prewar composer, the university creator can take courage in numbers. College music departments, as a rule, foster group action, which certainly should be a stimulus to the lone composer. And the presence on the staff of fine performers and performing groups must be a boon to the ambitious younger men.

This proximity and possible cooperation of live performers have put unusual emphasis on the writing of music for small groups of performers and have resulted in an apparent falling off of interest in composing works for large symphony orchestras. It would be a great pity if this tendency were to become a permanent feature of our musical life. One can easily appreciate that a composer who writes a highly complex chamber music score for a few performers of special expertise in the new idioms may have a problem in trying to adapt his style to the more limited technical capabilities of run-of-the-mill orchestral musicians. As a member of the American generation that produced a considerable symphonic repertoire—I'm thinking of Sessions, Harris, Piston, Schuman, et al.—I'm naturally anxious that we have some progeny in the orchestral field, and not only for the sake of the composers but for the artistic health of our symphonic organizations as well.

Another ever-present hazard of the academic environment for the practicing composer is the tendency to over-emphasize compositional analysis as a teaching discipline. The danger here is not so much to the student as to the teacher himself. Ten years ago Igor Stravinsky warned young composers, especially Americans, against the dangers of university teaching.

"However pleasant and profitable to teach composition at a rich American Gymnasium like Smith or Vassar," he said. "I am not sure that that is the right background for a composer." Harold Rosenberg, the art critic, had something similar in mind when he wrote: "In the classroom . . . it is normal to formulate consciously what one is doing and to be able to explain it to others. Creation is taken to be synonymous with productive *processes*" (my italics) "and is broken down into sets of problems and solutions."

Note for note analysis on the way a piece of music functions had its heyday when fascination with the Webernian twelve-tone structures was at its height. That's fine for the scholarly approach; but what about the composer who hits upon a musical idea spontaneous-fashion and manages to develop it on the basis of his own musical instinct? Virgil Thomson warns that such a composer would be headed for downgrading in an American university where, as he puts it, "the apparatus of scientific research and application of mathematics seem so much safer an expenditure of money and time than unpredictable adventures with talent or with inspiration." As I myself once told an interviewer, it bothers me that "one doesn't meet up more often with the kind of composer we used to think of as being 'musical.' Nowadays, to stress the 'musicality' of a composer would seem to be somehow pinning a bad name on him or making him seem lesser or limited or not so interesting." This is true even though everyone knows that composing in an advanced musical idiom guarantees nothing in respect to quality.

Some years ago, Milton Babbitt published an article in a popular record magazine with the alarming title: "Who cares if you listen?" In it he argues for the self-imposed withdrawal of the serious young composer within a university environment where he would be free to pursue a private life of professional achievement, in a manner somewhat similar to that of the dedicated scholar and scientist. This monklike role may be what some composers thrive on, but most of the species that I have met are neither scientific nor scholarly by nature and badly need contact with a live audience. Actually, *they* care very much if no one is listening. No, at some point the new music must invade our normal concert life. Any other solution is unacceptable.

Whatever one concludes from these observations, there is no denying that the university is where the action is. Fortunately, a fair amount of new music produced there is available through recordings—mostly from smaller record companies. In that way, a broad public, if interested, has the possibility of staying abreast of the latest serial, chance, electronic or what-have-you manifestations. In view of the amount of effort expended, it seems surprising that more single works have not come through as permanent additions to current repertoire. In any event, we're waiting, and we're interested.

Tanglewood's Future (1952)

Copland was a major force in the establishment of Tanglewood as a center of American music-teaching and performance. This "report" gives a sense of his involvement in all levels of its success, as well as his skills as a promoter. Subheads, likely added later by an editor, have been removed.

The summer of 1952 will mark the tenth anniversary session of the Berkshire Music Center. No one will find it strange, I suppose, if those of us who have been with the school from the start feel that this is a moment for rejoicing. This by now well-known school of music was established in 1940 because Serge Koussevitzky persuaded the trustees of the Boston Symphony Orchestra to undertake an unprecedented step: the formation of a summer school under the aegis of a symphony orchestra.

Before long the plan was enlarged to include the departments of opera production, composition, and the study of the art of conducting. Beyond this—and here was a special love of Dr. Koussevitzky—a division of the school was to be set up for the musical enthusiast who wanted to spend a summer of "living and working in music."

Dr. Koussevitzky had the profound satisfaction of seeing his dream brought to reality. Everyone knows what Tanglewood came to mean in the mind of this great leader. Upon his death last spring there arose considerable speculation as to the course the school would take. It is indeed a pleasure to be able to announce in no uncertain terms that Tanglewood will go on! The trustees of the Boston Symphony Orchestra, who have maintained the school at considerable sacrifice, have shown a sympathetic understanding of what is being accomplished in the Berkshire hills.

Last summer, to fill the gap caused by the death of Dr. Koussevitzky, the group of musicians who head the school's departments formed an administrative committee to carry out the projects he had planned. This board consisted of Richard Burgin, the concert-master of the Boston Symphony, Leonard Bernstein, Hugh Ross, Gregor Piatigorsky, William Kroll, Boris Goldovsky, and myself.

It has always been the hope of the sponsors of the school that no talented student would be prevented from attending the center for lack of money to pay tuition fees. This year for the first time certain sections of the school are being placed frankly on an all-scholarship basis. This means that any student accepted for active work in the advanced departments will receive tuition grants from the Tanglewood Revolving Fund.

Unfortunately, no funds are available for living expenses. But, with the burden of present tuition fees removed and the basis of admission entirely that of aptitude and talent, the center expects to have an even more brilliant group of students than in the past.

One point I should like to emphasize most strongly. Tanglewood has become so identified in the public mind with advanced work on a pre-professional level that we have not succeeded in making clear to the public at large that a quite different kind of music lover is equally welcome. This year a significant development is planned in this direction. For the first time a section of the school will be called the Tanglewood Study Group, and will work under its own supervisor.

We have secured the services of a remarkable musician from California, Ingolf Dahl—composer, conductor, pianist, and musical historian—who will head this division. It will be his job to see to it that the intelligent amateur and music enthusiast, also the general music student and music educator, will combine forces for the exploration, discovery, and performance-for-the-joy-of-performing such music as seems appropriate for their needs.

Another innovation for this group: Tanglewood has never before accepted students for less than the full six-week summer session. This year, however, in order to make the study group available to those who cannot attend the full school term, students in that division will be accepted for shorter enrollments of two and four weeks as well as six. It goes without saying that members of the study group are encouraged to take part in the varied activities of the school.

A final new development is the opening of the chamber music and song repertoire divisions to students who wish to concentrate in these alone, without the requirement to take part in the orchestra or opera department as has formerly been the case. There has been an increasing demand for just such training from students who wish to concentrate in these special fields. These students, however, are not to be included in the all-scholarship policy mentioned above.

From the '20s to the '40s
and Beyond (1945)

Looking back, certain facets of our present musical life appear to have become visible for the first time during the last twenty years. Of course, if one mulls over old magazines or books on American music published around 1900, the impression is strong that things were beginning to happen as far back as the turn of the century. It wasn't all pure imagination either. The earlier years helped to build toward today. Still, without losing our sense of orientation completely, I think we are justified in saying that we have come a particularly long way in the last two decades.

Aside from the general advance conceded by almost everybody, there are certain ideas and events which are definitely the progeny of the '20s and '30s. They should be known as such. Looking backward, they appear to be brand new phenomena. Looking a little forward, they seem certain to influence our future musical life.

One of these phenomena might be described as composer economics. During the past ten years, the serious composer's economic education may be said to have begun. No courses were given and no accredited teachers were found, but the idea gradually took hold that a composer ought to be able to draw his major income from composition. Suddenly it seemed clear that it makes no sense for at least two-thirds of our composers to spend two-thirds of their time busy at occupations other than the creation of music. The feeling grew that something ought to be done about it.

Composers have now learned not to expect any considerable return from the sale of their music, but to demand instead the income due them from their performance rights. (I shall always remember the amazement on the face of old Henry F. Gilbert in 1925 on hearing that one of our

143

major symphony orchestras had paid an American composer for the performance rights to his first composition—"just like Richard Strauss!")

As they themselves absorbed some of these basic facts, composers came to realize that the public at large also needs education on this economic problem. Everyone knows that authors live on their royalties, and painters on the sale of their paintings. Few people, however, have ever asked how composers live. Even interpretive musicians, who ought to know better, believe that they flatter composers by the casual proposal: "Why don't you write me something?" Interpreters, too, still need to learn that there is a simple parallel between getting pay for their services and paying composers for theirs.

The next twenty years will undoubtedly see a more rigid enforcement of this principle which is already clear enough. First, however, lawmakers must come to realize the necessity for a change in the obsolete copyright laws. Record makers, too, need thoroughly to revise their estimate of a composer's rightful share in the profits of his composition. And the American Society of Composers, Authors and Publishers, yes, ASCAP itself, must be educated to enforce the copyright provisions for the protection of serious music in exactly the way it enforces protection of popular music. And finally it devolves upon music-users in general to understand that if they use the music of living composers in any way, they share a responsibility toward the support of those composers. Perhaps here we are looking a little beyond the immediate future.

Another entirely new chapter of recent musical history might properly be headed "government in music." The title is doubtless still rather optimistic. If you had the temerity to suggest that official Washington was "interested" in music, more than one Congressman would suspiciously ask if you were discussing an accompaniment to fan dancing. However, we have the depression of 1929 to thank for the government's involvement in music. So far the only frank sponsorship of a music program has been that of the Works Progress Administration. All other aid has been surreptitiously introduced via riders tagged on to bills relating to "national defense," "inter-American relations," and such items. No one in a responsible position has yet dared make the forthright statement that our government should have a fine arts policy. Nevertheless, all signs point to an increasing commitment of government in the arts.

The dangers of state sponsorship have been too well exploited to need much discussion here. Art should be free, yet under government all activity tends to stem from one restricted source; policy is likely to be safe, sound, and dull. Moreover, government aid has the effect of discouraging private support, particularly in this country. But right or wrong, for better or worse, our post-war future seems certain to witness an increased participation of government in the creative arts.

As a matter of fact, composers are more needed by government today than they realize. On the home front, for instance, they can stimulate and inspire love of country. To Latin-America they can demonstrate that not all U.S. energy and talent go into manufacturing and the selling trades. To meet these demands why should Washington have to beg, borrow, or cajole compositions from composers? If the government needs music it should, in all its official dignity, help the composers produce it.

IV
Precursors

Defends the Music of Mahler (1925)

Like all artists who are also verbally articulate, Copland needed to steer among his predecessors. Much that the young composer appreciates in Gustav Mahler he wishes for himself.

To the Editor of *The New York Times:*

The music critics of New York City are agreed upon at least one point—Gustav Mahler, as a composer, is hopeless. Year in and year out, the performance of one of Mahler's works is invariably accompanied by the same disparaging reviews. Yet no critic has been able to explain just what it is that [the Dutch conductor Wilhelm] Mengelberg—and for that matter all Germany, Austria, and Holland—finds so admirable in Mahler's music.

If I write in defense of Mahler it is not merely for the pleasure of contradicting the critics. As a matter of fact. I also realize that Mahler has at times written music which is bombastic, long-winded, banal. What our critics say regarding his music is, as a rule, quite justified, but it is what they leave unsaid that seems to me unfair.

If one discounts for the moment the banal themes, the old-fashioned romantico-philosophical conceptions so dear to Mahler—if one looks at the music qua music—then it is undeniable that Mahler is a composer of today. The Second Symphony, which dates from 1894, is thirty years ahead of its time. From the standpoint of orchestration, Mahler is head and shoulders above Strauss, whose orchestral methods have already dated so perceptibly. Mahler orchestrates on big, simple lines, in which each note is of importance. He manages his enormous number of instruments with extraordinary economy, there are no useless doublings, instrument is pitted against instrument, group against group. So recent a score as Honegger's *Pacific 231* is proof of Mahler's living influence.

The present-day renewed interest in polyphonic writing cannot fail to reflect glory on Mahler's consummate mastery of that delicate art. The contrapuntal weaving of voices in the Eighth symphony—especially in the first part—is one side of Mahler's genius which I believe the critics have not sufficiently appreciated.

As for the banality of Mahler's thematic material, I have found that generally no matter how ordinary the melody may be, there is always somewhere, either in the beginning or end, one note, one harmony, one slight change which gives the Mahler touch. (Every page he wrote has that individual quality that we demand from every great composer—he was never more Mahler than when he was copying Mozart.) In any case, even when his musical ideas prove barren, I am fascinated by what he does with them and how he clothes them.

That Mahler has on occasion been grandiloquent is undeniable, but I fail to find any bombast whatsoever in *Das Lied von der Erde*. Most critics, I believe, would agree with that statement. Yet they are so prone to discussing Mahler's music in generalities that anyone unfamiliar with that composition would be led to suppose that it, too, was full of sound and fury signifying nothing.

Mahler has possibly never written a perfect masterpiece, yet, in my opinion, such things as the first movement of the Seventh Symphony, the scherzo of the Ninth, the last movement of the Fourth, and the entire *Das Lied von der Erde* have in them the stuff of living music.

The Ives Case (1933, 1941, 1967)

For American composers of Copland's generation, Charles Ives was at once
an inspiration, a puzzle, and an obstacle.

It will be a long time before we take the full measure of Charles Ives. His career as composer has already taken on a legendary character. The story of
Ives is the story of genius in a wasteland. His small-town background, his
revolutionary work as composer while heading an insurance firm in downtown New York, his discovery in the early '30s by the younger men, his sudden acclaim by the press in 1940 after the successful performances of his
piano sonata *Concord, Mass., 1840–1860*—all this, like the man himself,
forms a unique picture in the short history of creative music in America.

It is far from easy to get a rounded view of Ives's gift as composer. For
one thing, the man has written much that no one has ever heard. (None of
his major works, aside from the Sonata, has been given adequate hearing.)
For another, the music that we have seen is so full of technical complexities
as to be almost unreadable, let alone playable. But even with our smattering of information concerning his extensive list of works, it seems safe to
say that Ives was far more originally gifted than any other member of his
generation. At the same time, it seems equally certain that, as Elliott Carter
says, ". . . his work . . . falls short of its intentions." Ives had the vision of a
true pioneer, but he could not organize his material, particularly in his
larger works, so that we come away with a unified impression.

All this, however, must necessarily remain on a conjectural plane until
such time as we are vouchsafed first-rate performances of his best work. In
the meantime, it is possible to study closely at least one aspect of the composer's many-sided activities—his career as a writer of songs. In that way
we may gain some idea of his gift as a whole and the curious position of the
composer in the American scene.

In 1922 Charles Ives issued a privately printed collection of one hundred and fourteen songs that he had composed over a period of thirty years. During the first ten years of its existence this unusual volume aroused little or no comment. But apparently this neglect was of only temporary significance, since it is no longer unusual to find the songs on an occasional concert program. To make them available to a larger public many have been reprinted, seven by the Cos Cob Press and thirty-five others (including some new ones) by New Music [Edition].

Besides these one hundred and fourteen songs—an achievement in sheer output of which any man might be proud—the original edition contains an essay or, more exactly, a series of loosely connected paragraphs in Ives's characteristically animated, though diffident, style. Here one comes upon several surprising statements. In the first place, we find Mr. Ives apologizing for having published the volume at all. His excuse is that by so doing "a few clear copies could be sent to friends." But later he gives a different reason; ". . . this volume," he says, "is now thrown, so to speak, at the music fraternity, who for this reason will feel free to dodge it on its way— perhaps to the waste basket." At any rate he assures us that from his own standpoint the publication of this stout book containing "plenty of songs which have not been and will not be asked for" is merely a kind of housecleaning. "Various authors have various reasons for bringing out a book . . . Some have written a book for money; I have not. Some for fame; I have not. Some for love; I have not. Some for kindlings; I have not. I have not written a book for any of these reasons or for all of them together. In fact, gentle borrower, I have not written a book at all—I have merely cleaned house. All that is left is out on the clothes-line. . . ."

Obviously Ives is a modest human being. But he carries modesty to an exaggerated degree, for after having apologized for presenting his fellow citizens with a unique volume of American songs he very nearly manages to apologize for being a composer in the first place—a composer, that is, in the usual sense of the term. Whereas it is true that he did compose these songs, and admits having composed them, he wrote them only "on the side," as it were. Composing to him constitutes only one part of a busy life; as everybody knows, Mr. Ives is a successful man of business. But if we are to believe him, the fact that he composes music does not make him different from other businessmen, for, he says, "every normal man . . . has, in some degree, creative insight, and a . . . desire . . . to express it." This leads him to picture for us a time when every man will be encouraged to be his own Beethoven.

But Mr. Ives is not content to pause there. It is generally assumed among us that the composer who can dedicate his life to the single purpose of musical creation without distraction of any kind is a particularly fortunate creature. Ives has little sympathy for this attitude. He holds that to devote oneself to the business of life is serious, and to devote oneself to writing music while one is in business is serious, but to devote oneself solely to the business of writing music is somehow not serious. It tends to impoverish the artist in the man instead of developing a spiritual sturdiness—a "sturdiness which . . . shows itself in a close union between spiritual life and the ordinary business of life." As one remedy for bringing the merely "professional" composer back into actual contact with reality he suggests that "for every thousand dollar prize a potato field be substituted so that these candidates of Clio can dig a little in real life. . . ."

It would serve little purpose to argue this last point with Mr. Ives. But the question that is of interest is this: why did Ives take so timid an attitude in presenting his songs to the public (since he is certainly not a timid soul either in his music or in his prose style) and why did he choose to glorify the businessman composer as opposed to the so-called professional composer? Let us put off attempting an answer for the moment and examine the songs instead, both for their own sake and for whatever light they may bring to bear on these two questions.

The first impression, on turning to the one hundred and fourteen songs themselves, is bound to be one of confusion. For there is no order here— either of chronology, style, or quality. Almost every kind of song imaginable can be found—delicate lyrics; dramatic poems; sentimental ballads; German, French, and Italian songs; war songs; songs of religious sentiment; street songs; humorous songs; hymn tunes; folk tunes; encore songs; songs adapted from orchestral scores; piano works; and violin sonatas; intimate songs, cowboy songs, and mass songs. Songs of every character and description, songs bristling with dissonances, tone clusters, and "elbow chords" next to songs of the most elementary harmonic simplicity. All thrown together helter-skelter, displaying an amazing variety and fecundity of imagination, but without the slightest key or guide for the benefit of the unsuspecting recipient of this original edition.

It is self-evident, then, that this publication was not designed to give the musical public a clear conception of Ives's gifts as composer. In fact—and this seems to me to be crucial—Ives apparently not only had no public in mind when printing this book but hardly had even the few friends of whom he speaks in mind. The truth is he had only *himself* in mind. For after gathering together the fruits of thirty years' work (which, in effect, literally was a kind of "housecleaning") Ives found himself alone with his songs.

No artist creates for himself alone. To be cut off from the vitalizing contact of an audience, to compose in a vacuum as it were, will of necessity profoundly influence the character of a man's work. Do these songs, then, examined individually, show signs of just such an isolation?

To take the least representative group first: how otherwise can we explain the publication of songs that the composer himself says "have little or no value." He specifically names eight of these; at least fifteen more might easily be added to the list. Most of them were composed in the 1890s and belong to the sentimental, silver-threads-among-the-gold variety. To these may safely be joined about fifteen others, written about the same time, which, if they are not quite worthless, are nevertheless hardly better or worse than hundreds of songs in the same genre by other composers. The songs to French and German texts belong in this group, closely patterned as they are after foreign models. Nevertheless, here in the shadow of Schumann, Massenet, and Brahms, one catches a first glimpse of the later Ives. A somewhat daring middle section, an unexpected close or sharply tinted chord betray the future pioneer.

The first songs of importance date from around 1900. *Where the Eagle* is an excellent example of this group, which includes *Berceuse, I Travelled among Unknown Men,* and *The Children's Hour.* It is only one page in length, but it is remarkable for its depth of feeling, its concision, its originality. Certainly no other American composer at the turn of the century was capable of producing a song of this worth. It is not that these songs reflect no outside influence (that of Hugo Wolf, in particular, is evident), but that the emotional content is authentic; in the rich harmonies and sensuous line of the *Berceuse* or in the charming flow and imagination of *The Children's Hour* one knows oneself to be in the presence of a composer of imagination, a real creator.

The historical significance of Ives as an innovator has been stressed many times. Although the above-named songs are "modern" for their time, they are by no means revolutionary. But what, if not revolutionary, can one call a song like *Walking* (dated 1902)? In imitation of the village church bells heard on a Sunday morning walk, Ives essayed harmonies that are as daring as, if not more daring than, any written by Debussy and Strauss in the same period. This song plainly demonstrates the origin of much of Ives's venturesomeness; he is a musical realist, a copier of nature. This is further illustrated in songs like *Rough Wind* (1902) and *The Cage* (1906). The latter, with its curious melodic line and its omission of barlines, is obviously meant to suggest the turning about of an animal in its cage. It should be noted, however, that these songs are more successful as experiments than they are as finished artistic productions.

In so brief a summary, one can hardly do more than mention the songs composed around 1908–10 (comparatively undistinguished) or those adapted by the composer from his orchestral and chamber music. To judge these adaptations as songs would be unfair. However, *The Housatonic at Stockbridge* (which originally was a movement in a set of pieces for orchestra) and *At the River* (from the Fourth Violin Sonata) are admirable arrangements of what in the first place must have been cherishable music and remains so in its new garb.

Ives, like no other serious American composer before him, was fascinated by the kind of music that any village band plays. The three "war songs" and the five "street songs" are attempts to incorporate popular material into a serious musical style. His method in several of these songs is to evoke the mood of the past at the beginning with the aid of rather complex harmonies and then to give the popular music in unadulterated form. This mixture of styles is not a happy one; it results in making these the least successful of the songs thus far considered.

But the works on which Ives's reputation as a song composer must eventually rest are the remaining forty or more, that are dated 1919–21.[1] Taken as a whole, despite many and serious shortcomings, these songs are a unique and memorable contribution to the art of song writing in America, an art that is still in its first youth among us; a contribution that, for richness and depth of emotional content, for broad range and strength of expression, for harmonic and rhythmic originality, will remain a challenge and an inspiration to future generations of American composers.

Where else in American music will you find more sensitiveness or quietude than in a song like *Serenity*, with its subtle syncopations and its instinctive melodic line; where more delicate tone painting than the setting of lines from *Paradise Lost* called *Evening*; where a more rousing or amusing knockout of a song than *Charlie Rutlage*, with its exciting cowboy quotations; where songs to compare with *The Indians* or *Ann Street* or *Maple Leaves* or *The See'r* or *The New River* (this last containing remarkable Hindemithian premonitions)? There are others, of course, almost as good— *The Swimmers*, *Two Little Flowers*, *Like a Sick Eagle*, *The Greatest Man*. All these are characterized by an essential simplicity—no matter how complex the harmonic or rhythmical materials may be, there is always a directness of emotional appeal and always an unadorned, almost naïve melodic line for the voice.

These qualities are present even in songs that are not successful as a whole. *Walt Whitman*, despite the unforgettably apt setting of the phrase "How is it I extract strength from the beef I eat," remains an unsatisfying fragment, and the deeply moving last page of *Grantchester* does not compensate for the fact that the song as a whole is not sustained. One could add other examples of songs that are mere fragments or are overcomplicated in harmonic texture or deficient in consistency of style.

---

[1] Many of these songs were composed at an earlier period but were either rewritten or rearranged at the time of publication, which explains the large number bearing the date 1921.

Weaknesses such as these and others—and it would be foolish to gloss them over—arise from a lack of that kind of self-criticism that only actual performance and public reaction can bring. This indispensable check on the artist Ives never had. A careful examination of these songs will convince the open-minded reader that he lacked neither the talent nor the ability nor the métier nor the integrity of the true artist—but what he most shamefully and tragically lacked was an audience. "Why do you write so much—which no one ever sees?" his friends asked. And we can only echo, "Why, indeed?" and admire the courage and perseverance of the man and the artist.

Little wonder, then, if we find Ives overtimid in presenting the songs to the public for the first time; and little wonder if we find him rationalizing his position of businessman composer until he made it appear to be the only natural role for the artist to assume in America. For Ives had every reason to be timid and to rationalize in a world that had no need for him as an artist.

The small drama that I have pictured here is by no means the drama of Ives alone, but in a larger sense is that of every American composer of serious pretensions. The problem of the audience—not a passive audience but an active one—an audience that *demands* and *rejects* music, that acts as a stimulus and a brake, has never been solved. Not every composer deserves such an audience, of course. But for men of the stature of Ives that audience must be found, or American music will never be born.

1967: A gathering crescendo of interest has finally become all-pervasive: the audience has most decidedly discovered the music of Charles Ives. And that audience is more than national; it includes music lovers everywhere. Ives has preempted the place once held by Edward MacDowell as the first truly significant composer of serious music in our country.

I trust no one will object if I give myself a slight pat on the back for having gauged the stature of Ives in 1933. Actually, any interested musician might have perceived it if he had had access to the music itself. But the Ives works were hard to come by during those years. It was Henry Cowell's New Music Edition that issued the first regularly published work of the composer, in 1929, the second movement of the Fourth Symphony. My own impressions of his music at that time were based partly on that complex second movement, but mostly on an acquaintance with the *114 Songs*, which Ives himself had sent me.

The upsurge of interest on the part of the general music public has come about largely because of the increased number of performances and recordings—especially recordings—of the composer's orchestral and chamber works. In a recent conversation which I had with Nicolas Slonimsky, an early Ives enthusiast and the first conductor of his works abroad, we both puzzled over the reluctance of musicians to cope with the performance difficulties of Ives's scores in earlier days. The consensus at that period was that his music undoubtedly showed the mark of genius, but that it was texturally confused, inextricably complex, and hopelessly impractical for public presentation. How ironic it is to realize that nowadays it is this very "confusion" that makes the Ives music so absorbing to listeners.

I myself was guilty of a similar misapprehension in my 1933 article when I said that Ives "could not organize his material, particularly in his larger works, so that we come away with a unified impression." His complexities don't always add up, but when they do, a richness of experience is suggested that is unobtainable in any other way. For Ives it was a triumph of daring, a gamble with the future that he has miraculously won.

Among the best of the orchestral works recently brought to performance, one must name first the Fourth Symphony, an astonishing conception in every way. But shorter works, such as *Decoration Day* (from *Holidays*), the *Harvest Home Chorales*, and the too-little-played First Piano Sonata are unquestionably among the finest works ever created by an American artist.

Schoenberg's Expressionism
(1941, 1967)

If it was difficult for composers everywhere to extricate themselves from the Wagnerian cul-de-sac, it must have been doubly so for men like Schoenberg, who were born and grew up in the midst of German music. Schoenberg inherited the full weight of the German tradition; he was the spiritual son of Bruckner, Strauss, and Mahler. He paid them homage in early works like the first songs, the string sextet *Verklärte Nacht*, and the choral symphony *Gurre-Lieder*.

These were the works of a greatly gifted young musician whose mastery of his medium was evident to all. His compositions expanded the language of his predecessors; they contained daring harmonic progressions and an unusual handling of cyclic forms. But they also embodied his own profound attachment to the language and spirit of German music. In the light of his later career, it is ironic to realize how truly conservative Schoenberg was in his instincts and personality. Even the revolution he engendered was made in the name of tradition. Schoenberg himself once wrote: "I claim the distinction of having written a truly new music which, based on tradition as it is, is itself destined to become tradition." Those were prophetic words. Hanns Eisler used to say: "Schoenberg is the true conservative, he even created a revolution so that he could become a reactionary."

Let us see if we can trace the line of his development after the writing of works like *Gurre-Lieder* and *Verklärte Nacht*. Why was he not content to continue writing more such works? The answer can be found in Schoenberg's realization that the tonal system as he knew it was in the process of disintegration. What happened in this composer's harmonic imagination around 1911 was truly unprecedented. With extraordinary boldness, he proposed nothing less than the complete reorientation of our tonal sense.

The basic premise of Schoenberg's harmonic revolution was his denial of our hitherto unquestioned need for the sense of a central tonality. It is difficult, if not impossible, to explain the principle of tonality in nontechnical language, without benefit of live musical illustration. Still, the most untutored musical ear can distinguish something radically "wrong" with Schoenberg's post-Wagnerian harmonies. This sense of "wrongness" comes principally from the lack of any central key feeling.

During the course of the 19th century, music's harmonic language had become richer through more and more chordal complexity. Just think of the difference in sound between the harmonies of Mozart and those of Wagner. It is not a question of whose harmonies are "better," but of a natural historical process based on the physical fact that our ears became attuned gradually to more and more complicated chordal progressions. Thus, starting from a music based on a strong tonal center, with modest modulations, the 19th-century composer moved on to more recondite modulations, until all sense of tonality became ambiguous. Tonal centers in Wagner's music are in such a state of continual flux that even today theorists find much to argue about in analyzing the harmonic structure of his operas.

Up to this point, we can divide Schoenberg's work into two phases: first, the gradual breakdown of tonality as an organizing principle, and second, the frank adoption of an atonal harmonic language.

It took only one logical step forward to achieve a music without tonal center of any recognizable kind. It was a small step—but a crucial one. Only a daring and self-convinced composer could take it, and Schoenberg accepted the role with all its consequences. To other composers it meant that now each tone of the chromatic scale was to be considered of equal importance. It meant, further, the end of consonance and dissonance in the old sense or, as Schoenberg himself put it, "the emancipation of the dissonance." But most important of all, it meant the end of musical structure as we had known it, since structure had as a fundamental basis the orderly progression of harmonies belonging to a recognizable tonal system.

It is not clear to what extent Schoenberg realized at first the full implication of the course he had taken. Trusting his musical instinct, he wrote a series of works between 1907 and 1913 which are strikingly original and inspired: the Second String Quartet (with voice); the piano pieces, Opus 11 and Opus 19; the Five Orchestral Pieces, Opus 16; the *Book of the Hanging Gardens,* a setting of poems by Stefan George, for voice and piano; and especially *Pierrot lunaire.*

Aesthetically these works belong with the hyperexpressive paintings of Kandinsky and Kokoschka, the tense and tortured world of Franz Kafka, and *The Cabinet of Dr. Caligari.* The movement these artists represented became known as Expressionism; an exaggerated and almost hysterical

Romanticism characterizes their work, with prophetic presentiments of the Age of Anxiety that was to follow. These strong works of Schoenberg's second period have, with one exception—the Second String Quartet—one characteristic in common: they are all made up of a series of brief movements. It is as if the composer, at that time, equated extreme emotionality with brevity, sometimes even extreme brevity. The reason is clear: without benefit of the underpinning of a clarified harmonic structure, an atonal work of any length is in danger of falling apart. (Incidentally, Schoenberg objected to the word "atonal" on semantic grounds, but rightly or wrongly, the word has continued in general use to describe this period of his music.) Ernst Krenek speaks of "the unbridled, expressive, and often terrifying outburst of pent-up energy in the early days of atonality."

The most striking and influential work of this period is without doubt *Pierrot lunaire*. It holds a position in Schoenberg's output analogous to that of the *Rite of Spring* in the work of Stravinsky. Both were written at about the same time, around 1912. *Pierrot lunaire* is a series of twenty-one songs for a "speaking voice" and a chamber ensemble of five performers. James [Gibbons] Huneker, who was present at its first performance, tells us of the strange impression this composition made on its first listeners in 1913. One wonders what astonished them most—the curious vocal line, half spoken and half sung, the total lack of any recognizable tonal bearings, the thinly stretched and strained sonorities, the complexities of texture, or the almost neurotic atmosphere engendered by the music itself.

Whatever else may be said about it, *Pierrot lunaire* is without question original music. The harmonic daring of the work has no precise precedent in any other music; it bespeaks an extraordinarily keen aural imagination. Out of the few instruments called for, Schoenberg extracts an incredible variety of instrumental imagery—and with the greatest economy of means. It marks the beginning of a subsequent development: the writing by other composers of works for a varied assortment of instruments in small ensemble groups. Texturally, there is strong emphasis on the independence of contrapuntal lines. The complex web of sound is firmly based on known strict forms such as passacaglia, fugue, and canon. The *Sprechstimme*, a curious elecutionary use of the voice, here occurring for the first time, was employed again by Schoenberg in later works and by many younger composers. Perhaps one should add that, as sometimes happened with Schoenberg, he was none too happy in his choice of texts, in this instance by the Belgian poet Albert Giraud. The poems, concerning a moondrunk Pierrot, have faded; nevertheless, with these poems as pretext, Schoenberg created a phantasmagoria that has retained its freshness. (A work such as Pierre Boulez' *Le Marteau sans maître* is unthinkable without *Pierrot lunaire*.)

A lesser composer than Schoenberg would have been content to write more such works. But as a good German, with the German passion for order and systematic thinking, Schoenberg was faced with the necessity of bringing logic and control to the disconcerting freedom of atonality. That this was not easy to do we can deduce from Schoenberg's subsequent silence of eight years. During this period he brought to the problem his gift as theoretician and thinker, and evolved, as he called it, "a method of composition with twelve tones."

Stravinsky's Dynamism
(1941, 1967)

Around 1910, the only other practically unknown musical figure comparable in importance to Arnold Schoenberg was Igor Stravinsky, then a recent
arrival in the French capital. To appreciate fully the originality of Stravinsky's contribution, one must keep in mind a picture of musical life in Paris
at that time. Impressionism was the order of the day. Debussy and his self-
appointed Impressionist disciples were the unquestioned musical leaders
of the period. They had engulfed all new music in a kind of luminous fog.
Most foreign composers who visited the French capital were soon lost in
the exquisitely shimmering half lights of the Impressionist school. But apparently the diminutive Igor was too thoroughly Russian to adapt himself
to French ways. And so, before many years had passed, it was the Frenchmen who were aping the musical practices of this lone Russian.

Heading the list of Stravinsky's original gifts was his rhythmic virtuosity. Nothing like it had ever been heard in Paris. It has already been pointed
out in connection with Mussorgsky that rhythm was not the forte of the
Romantic school. With few exceptions (notably Schumann and Brahms),
19th-century composers were thinking principally about harmony or
melody or form, least of all about rhythm. And so their rhythmic schemes
were generally of the square-cut, unimaginative kind, like those used in a
march. Once the rhythmic pattern was started it tended to remain the
same. Even Debussy did little more than make his rhythms less rigid. It was
Stravinsky who first revitalized our rhythmic sense. He gave European
music what amounted to a rhythmic hypodermic. It has never been the
same since.

Stravinsky's rhythmic innovations were principally of two kinds: either
he played on the repetition of certain definite rhythms with all the insis-

tence of a wild-eyed Tartar, producing in the listener a kind of intoxicated rhythmic trance, or instead of confining himself to the more conventional metrical units of 2, 4, or 6, he exploited unusual rhythms of 5, 7, or 11. Even when retaining the normal 2, 4, or 6 units, he alternated these abruptly. "Such a procedure looks something like this: ONE-two, ONE-two-three, ONE-two-three, ONE-two, ONE-two-three-four, ONE-two-three, ONE-two, etc. Now read that in strict tempo as fast as you can. You will see why musicians found Stravinsky so difficult to perform when he was new. Also, why many people found these new rhythms so disconcerting merely to listen to. Without them, however, it is hard to see how Stravinsky could have achieved those jagged and uncouth rhythmic effects that first brought him fame."[1] Thus, something of the barbaric and unspoiled vigor of primitive rhythms found their way into European music during this period.

This extraordinary rhythmic puissance Stravinsky owes to his Russian heritage—to the folk songs of his country, the music of Mussorgsky and Borodin and of his teacher Rimsky-Korsakov. Later on he was to add still another potent device to his rhythmic scheme, a device borrowed from or suggested by American jazz—the combination of two or more simultaneous and independent rhythms. But of this more later.

In the ballets written about this time—*The Firebird, Petrushka, The Rite of Spring*—the musical world of 1910 became aware of a new type of harmony. Here for the first time we find that bold use of dissonance that is characteristic of so much later modern music. One can only marvel at the rightness of Stravinsky's instinct in handling these new and unprecedented chordal conglomerations. His deliberate choice of shrilly dissonant tonal mixtures shocked and delighted a new generation of music lovers, at the same time revolutionizing the composer's harmonic stock in trade.

Stravinsky's dissonances have very little relationship, of course, to the atonal writing of Schoenberg, except that both composers immeasurably widened our conception of harmonic possibilities. In the Russian's work the tonal texture is much more closely akin to that of our normal harmonic system. What he did was merely to extend that system. This extension brought with it only one new harmonic device, namely, the combining of two or more independent tonalities at the same time. This came to be known as polytonal harmony.

Unlike Schoenberg's atonal system, which attempts to break down our ideas of tonality, polytonality is in a real sense a reaffirmation of the old principles of harmony, but in a new guise. No one has tried to set up any

---

[1] Quotation from the chapter on Rhythm in my book *What to Listen for in Music*, New York, 1939.

logical system based on polytonal writing. For the most part, composers have used it in an incidental way, rather than trying to apply the principle consistently in large works.

One other important facet of Stravinsky's new style—one admired even by his early detractors—is the masterly way in which the modern orchestra is handled. The Italian composer Malipiero pointed out that even an old orchestra would sound transformed into a modern one if it were given Stravinskian harmonies and rhythms to play. But there is more than these to the clean brilliance of Stravinsky's instrumentation. His stunning effects are mostly arrived at through a careful choice of unhackneyed instrumental combinations, balanced and juxtaposed in such a way as to keep their separate tonal values clearly distinguishable in the orchestral mass. In these early works Stravinsky chooses sharply defined colors not unlike the strong reds and browns of a modern painter. His new orchestral sonorities have little affinity with either the overlush orchestra of Strauss or the over-refined Debussian orchestra. Once again, as in Mahler, the orchestra plays "without pedal." It produces a hard, dry, crackling sonority unlike anything to be heard in previous music.[2]

Stravinsky borrowed his melodies liberally, during this first period of his career, from Russian folk song. Short, simple folk phrases are put through a Stravinskian formula that has them turning about themselves in a manner peculiar to the composer. It is these plain tunes that make Stravinsky's music sound so very Russian. They are also responsible for the accusation, heard repeatedly, that Stravinsky seriously lacks any real melodic invention. In line with this reproach, which is not without foundation, it is curious to see how, in later works, Stravinsky managed to supply himself with melodic material, even after he had abandoned the use of native Russian folk melodies.

All these startling innovations in rhythms, harmonies, and orchestral timbres were obvious even to a casual listener. What was less obvious at the time was the historic role Stravinsky's ballets were to play in the reorientation of music away from the German tradition. True enough, anyone could see that there was something brutally unsentimental that separated this music from music of the Romantic era. By comparison, this new music

---

[2] It is interesting to compare Stravinsky's orchestral methods with those of Arnold Schoenberg, who achieved an orchestral style of his own, ideally suited to the hypersensitive quality of his music. This he accomplished by applying the chamber-music technique to the large orchestra. Instead of dividing the seven notes of a given chord among seven instruments of the same group, he carefully distributed them among instruments of different groups, thereby gaining the richest possible texture for each chord. Characteristic of one small corner of his orchestration is the love of a magical, bell-like sonority that is somehow extracted from harp, celesta, glockenspiel, mandolin, and so forth. Alban Berg took full advantage of that hint in his last orchestral works.

seemed blunt, direct, and nonerotic. People were right in calling the young Stravinsky a sophisticated primitive. Even the relationship of Stravinsky to the Russian world of Mussorgsky and his colleagues was clear enough. But only today are we able to see the connection between this music of Stravinsky's and the eventual goal of objectivism that was to dominate a large segment of the contemporary musical movement.

It is not necessary to be a profound student of music to realize that a close parallel exists between the realistic approach of Mussorgsky in the creation of his protagonist Boris Godunov and the attitude of Stravinsky in the creation of his puppet Petrushka. There is a clear distinction between their approach and that of Wagner, for instance, in the creation of his Tristan. When we listen to Wagner's opera we seem to be hearing the voice of Wagner himself speaking through the stage character of Tristan, but when we listen to Mussorgsky's Boris we seem to be hearing the voice of an entire people. In a similar way, although on a lesser plane, one never for a moment can imagine Petrushka as a mouthpiece for an expression of Stravinsky's personal emotions. The composer in this case cannot possibly be identified with his puppet hero. He seems to feel for and sympathize with Petrushka, standing on one side of the stage and contemplating, as it were, the pitiful antics of the puppet, much in the way that the audience itself is moved by the little tragedy. In other words there is an objective quality in the composer's attitude that separates it completely from the 19th-century Romantic attitude. This desire for objectivity developed later, as we shall see, into the conscious adoption of a Neoclassic style.

The key work of this period is, by common consent, Stravinsky's ballet of pagan Russia, *The Rite of Spring*, composed for Sergei Diaghilev's Ballet Russe in 1913. This is not the composer's most perfect work, but it is certainly his most strikingly original composition. An almost hieratic atmosphere is evoked—coldly mystic and calculatingly savage by turns. Here again the detached spirit I speak of is clearly discernible. The formal structure is the least successful aspect of the work, which, because of its explosive nature, tends to be disjointed. Stravinsky was consciously avoiding, no doubt, the usual German procedures for developing a piece of music, but he had as yet no clear plan of his own to substitute for them.

The Rite of Spring is the last of Stravinsky's large works that has its roots partly in the Romantic movement. Despite the generally detached spirit, there are certain Romantic traits: the lushness of texture in the opening sequence, the tonal painting in the seduction scene, the sense of the enactment of elemental emotions, and the overpowering climaxes of sound—all these are not unrelated to the sonorous magnificences of Strauss or the early Ravel. The works that were fully emancipated from the Romantic strain were to come later.

Béla Bartók (1941, 1967)

In a review of this important prewar period, the name of the Hungarian composer Béla Bartók must figure prominently. He belongs with Stravinsky and Schoenberg as one of the leading spirits of the new musical movement. Bartók was both lucky and unlucky in his background. He was lucky in his inheritance of an untouched native source material. He and his compatriot Kodály spent years in searching out, collating, and utilizing native Hungarian melodies. Bartók was the best of the folklorists, using his indigenous material as the basis for a music that is both high in quality and very characteristic of the modern musical school.

But Bartók was far from lucky in gaining recognition for his pioneering efforts in the contemporary idiom. He, too, wrote polytonal harmonies, as early as 1908; he, too, was expressive in the tortured manner of Schoenberg, and felt at least as much at home in rhythmic intricacies as Stravinsky. But for some reason these other men were more successful in enlisting the public's attention and in gaining credit with critics and commentators for the introduction of new musical methods.

Perhaps one reason why Bartók did not figure more prominently during this time is the lack of one or more imposing works to dramatize and summarize his achievements. The list of his compositions includes an opera, a ballet, several orchestral works, six string quartets, and much piano music, but does not include any one work such as *Pierrot lunaire* or *The Rite of Spring* to symbolize his output for the public at large. But there are other reasons, also, reasons inherent in the man himself. Bartók's very individual style turned out to be a kind of stumbling block to his full development. I agree with Paul Rosenfeld when he writes: "His [Bartók's] mind has gone into subtlety and intricacy more than range and scope of experience." This tendency toward self-repetition, both of mood and of technical device, made some of his work less inventive and exciting than it should have been.

Bartók's musical style lends itself well to literary description, not because of any programmatic content but because of its highly graphic nature. His music is of a dry, unsentimental facture, full of incisive rhythms and sharp harmonic dissonances. Quite special to Bartók are his slow movements. These have a certain shell-shocked atmosphere, profoundly pessimistic in tone. The Second String Quartet, written during the darkest years of the First World War, is characteristic of this mood, with its bitter harmonies and cheerless melodies. It is deeply expressive music, making no concession to mere prettiness. In his last years, Bartók became an indefatigable explorer in clangorous sonorities. When these are applied to music in slow tempo, a highly personal, rock-like quality results, relentless and uncompromising from the standpoint of audiences brought up on Romantic music.

All his music is intelligently made, almost diagrammatic in conception. Sometimes this proves a pitfall for the composer—when his interest in the formal plan and its realization on paper seem to outweigh the purely musical interest. This danger is also inherent in Bartók's love of tonal effects. A work such as the Fifth String Quartet, remarkable as it is in technical handling of the musical materials, sometimes gives us ingenious manipulation of notes in lieu of spontaneously conceived music. But when he is at his best, as in the Music for Strings, Percussion, and Celesta, Bartók takes his place in the front rank of contemporary musicians.

1967: In retrospect I was right to have been mystified as to why Béla Bartók did not reach a larger public during his lifetime. His public image has entirely changed. For reasons difficult to fathom, his death in 1945 set off a chain reaction that gave him, within a few years, his rightful place in the forefront of contemporary music everywhere. Works that had long been admired by forward-looking musicians, but infrequently played, have become firm repertory items. I am thinking of the six string quartets, the Violin Concerto, and especially the 1943 Concerto for Orchestra. These works have not changed, but public acceptance has mellowed. It is an all too familiar phenomenon: the disappearance of the creator coincides with the resurrection of his work.

V
Contemporaries

Having become prominent early in his career, Copland was frequently invited to write about his contemporaries. These surveys initially served to introduce unfamiliar names to a larger public. Behind these articles about his contemporaries is a generosity served by a prodigious memory. Indicatively, no composer does such essays today—none has the authority or the broad range of contacts. Indeed, no one prominent in any art does anything comparable. The last to try was Norman Mailer, four decades ago, in his acerbic comments on the "talent in the room." Notwithstanding their tone of casual simplicity, the Copland surveys provide cunning insight and remain curious not only for their inclusions but their omissions, such as the essentially tonal composers Ruth Crawford, Alan Hovhaness, or Lou Harrison.

The Younger Generation
of American Composers:
1926–59 (1960)

[A.C.'s] Prefatory Note [1960]: A reading of these three articles in chronological sequence should provide some perspective on the unfolding of America's creative talent during the past thirty years. Through no fault of my own several late-comers are not named: Walter Piston in the twenties, William Schuman in the thirties, and Leon Kirchner in the forties. They are missing because their music was little known until a later time. George Gershwin, on the other hand, was famous in 1926, but was down in everyone's book as a composer of popular music with only two concert pieces to his credit. Most significant, it seems to me, is the fact that the writing of articles such as these has become increasingly hazardous due to the variety and complexity of our present-day musical scene.

1926: America's Young Men of Promise

To discover the important composers of tomorrow among the young men of today has always proved a fascinating diversion. Franz Liszt, in his time, concerned himself with every rising young talent in Europe who happened to cross the path of his meteoric career. More recently Erik Satie played godfather to a whole brood of young Frenchmen. Braving ridicule, he even sought among the high-school boys for young genius. Others beside Satie have gathered about them the significant young men—Busoni and Schönberg in Central Europe, Casella in Italy.

In America our new composers have been left to shift for themselves. When, as occasionally happens, a young talent does emerge from obscurity, this can almost always be attributed to the sensational element in his

171

work, never to its purely musical merits. The public wants only a name. But there are other composers, less fortunate, who must be content to add opus to opus with little or no hope of being performed. If these cannot be heard, they can at least be heard about. Perhaps hearing about them may induce someone to let us really hear them.

This is not intended to be a complete presentation of the youngest generation of composers in America. I have simply chosen seventeen names among those men, born here, whose ages lie between twenty-three and thirty-three, whose music has seemed to me to be worthy of special note. Not that this is, in any sense, a critical estimate of their work. It is too soon for that. But it does indicate a promising group of young men whose compositions deserve consideration. For convenience, these seventeen names might be grouped as follows:

Four Prix de Rome men: Leo Sowerby, Howard Hanson, Randall Thompson, G. Herbert Elwell.

Three revolutionaries: George Antheil, Henry Cowell, Roger Sessions.

Five freelances: Roy Harris, Avery Claflin, Edmund Pendleton, Richard Hammond, Alexander Steinert.

Three pupils of Ernest Bloch: Bernard Rogers, W. Quincy Porter, Douglas Moore.

Two pupils of Nadia Boulanger: Virgil Thomson, Quinto Maganini.[1]

Of the first four, recipients of the American Prix de Rome, at least two, Leo Sowerby and Howard Hanson, are too well known to need introduction. The same cannot be said, unfortunately, of either Randall Thompson or G. Herbert Elwell.

Randall Thompson, after three full years in Rome, has but recently returned to this country. His preliminary training at Harvard and a year under Bloch have given him a firm grasp of the materials of composition. He writes with ease in all forms. His most mature works, written in Rome, include choral settings for *Seven Odes of Horace* (three with orchestral accompaniment), *Piper at the Gates of Dawn* for orchestra, a piano sonata and suite, and a string quartet.

Each one of Thompson's compositions is finished with a most meticulous pen—not an eighth note that does not receive full consideration before it is put on paper. For the moment this very excellence of workmanship seems to be offered in lieu of a more personal style. While Thompson never borrows outright from any one composer, it is not difficult to detect the influence of certain Europeans, Pizzetti, Bloch, Stravinsky, in the several movements of a single work. Thus far Thompson's *Ode*

---

[1]It is interesting to note that the subsequent importance of Mademoiselle Boulanger as teacher of American composers was not yet apparent.

to Venice, for chorus and orchestra, and especially his string quartet are the works in which he seems nearest to the achievement of a personal idiom.

In G. Herbert Elwell, now residing at the Academy in Rome, we have a young composer who will not long remain the unknown quantity he is in American music. Elwell is no conventional winner of prizes. He has spent the last five years in Europe—London, Paris, Rome—living life his own way. In 1919 he came to New York from Minneapolis to study composition with Ernest Bloch and continued later in Paris under Nadia Boulanger during the years 1922–24.

Even Elwell's earliest student work had stamped upon it the distinct mark of his own individuality. That individuality is most easily recognized in his scherzo movements, an elflike quality, not of delicacy and charm, but of sharp quips and puckish fancies. His music is dynamic, muscular, alive—weakest, perhaps, in its lyrical moments. There have been passing influences of Rimsky-Korsakoff, Dukas, Bloch, but these need cause us no great concern. With every new work his art becomes more ripe.

Elwell has written much for the piano—a sonatina, a sonata, nine short pieces. His *Quintet* for piano and strings is being presented in Paris this spring. The *Centaur* for orchestra (1924) and his most recent work, a ballet based on Max Beerbohm's *Happy Hypocrite*, complete the list of his compositions.

It is a sign of health that we in America also have our radicals in the persons of George Antheil, Roger Sessions, Henry Cowell. For one reason or another their names have been bruited about, though their music has remained more or less inaccessible here.

George Antheil, the most notorious of the trio, must by now be weary of hearing himself called the *enfant terrible* of American music. Antheil's fame first spread among his literary fellow-countrymen in Berlin and Paris. These expatriates were none too careful of their superlatives. Potentially speaking, Antheil is all they claim and more; one needn't be particularly astute to realize that he possesses the greatest gifts of any young American now writing. No one can venture to dictate just how he may make the best use of his great talents; one can simply remark that so far the very violence of his own sincere desire to write original music has hindered rather than helped the attainment of his own ends.

Antheil's latest work, with its use of numerous mechanical pianos and electrical appliances, takes on the aspect of visionary experiment. This is probably a passing phase. He is still under twenty-five; the next few years will give the true measure of his importance.

Of Roger Huntington Sessions I can speak only from hearsay. No example of his work has been given publicly in the larger music centers, yet the high opinions of his music held by Ernest Bloch and Paul Rosenfeld command respect. Up to the spring of 1925 he acted as Bloch's assistant in Cleveland, which in part explains his very small output. A work that has aroused much comment is his incidental music to Andreyev's play, *The Black Maskers*. He is at present in Florence, devoting his entire time to composition.

Henry Cowell has hardly suffered from lack of publicity. He has presented programs of his music from coast to coast and throughout the Continent, even in districts as remote as Poland. He has written much for the piano and for small groups of instruments. Like Schönberg, Cowell is a self-taught musician, with the autodidact's keen mind and all-inclusive knowledge.

But Cowell is essentially an inventor, not a composer. He has discovered "tone clusters," playing piano with the forearm, and the string piano. Yet from a purely musical standpoint his melodies are banal, his dissonances do not "sound," his rhythms are uninteresting. Cowell must steel himself for the fate of the pioneer—opposition and ridicule on the one hand, exploitation and ingratitude on the other. His most interesting experiments have been those utilizing the strings of the piano. *The Banshee*, when performed in a small room, is musical noise of a most fascinating kind. Perhaps if Cowell develops along these lines he may even make a distinctive path for himself as composer.

Something of the variety of American life and its effect upon musicians as compared with the usual conservatory product of Europe can be seen in the destinies of three young men of twenty-seven—Avery Claflin, Roy Harris, and Edmund Pendleton. They have but little music to their credit, yet each one writes from an absolute inner necessity that forces its way out in spite of material obstacles.

Avery Claflin, a New Englander by birth, had most of his musical training in Boston and at Harvard. The war brought him to France, where he remained for a year after the armistice, during which time he had contact with the Cocteau-Satie group. He is at present connected with a bank, so that his time for composition is strictly limited. His works are quickly listed: a one-act opera on an adaptation of Edgar Allan Poe's *Fall of the House of Usher*, a trio, a chorus for male voices, and several songs. Claflin does not write with great freedom; he seems somewhat hampered by a lack of facility in composing. This does not detract, however, from the simple charm of certain episodes and the inherent musical quality in all his work.

Roy Harris, a Californian, possesses a talent that should be carefully nurtured. Until a few years ago he was engaged in one form or another of manual labor so that he is seriously handicapped by his late start in music. But on the other hand he was born with a full-fledged style of his own.

Harris is a child of nature with a child's love for his native hills and a child-like belief in the moral purpose of music. His music reflects these things faithfully—it owes nothing to city influences, but seems always full-blooded and spiritually pure. His melodies and, even more particularly, his harmonies are in no way revolutionary, yet they have a strangely personal flavor. Harris has written very little, his most ambitious undertaking being six movements for string quartet and two movements of an incomplete Symphony for large orchestra.

It is difficult to supply much information concerning Edmund Pendleton. In the spring of 1924 I heard an orchestral work by this young composer at the Salle Gaveau in Paris. In spite of the apparent influence of Stravinsky this one work placed Pendleton among the promising young men of today. He has lived abroad for more than five years now, studying at one time under Eugene Cools, the French composer. A more recent orchestral composition, *When the Circus Comes to Town,* had its première in Paris in the fall of 1925.

Richard Hammond is a composer who cannot be easily classified. Except for short pieces his works are rarely performed in public. He studied for several years with Mortimer Wilson and his major compositions comprise a *Suite of Six Chinese Fairy Tales* for orchestra, a sonata for oboe and piano, several song cycles with the accompaniment of orchestra or piano, and numerous piano pieces.

Due to insufficient information about the work of Alexander Steinert, a talented young composer of Boston, I have been unable to do more than include his name here.

It is surprising, to say the least, to note the number of these young men who have profited by the teachings of Ernest Bloch or Nadia Boulanger or both. Bernard Rogers has the distinction of being Bloch's first pupil in America. He is not unknown in these parts, several of his compositions, *To the Fallen,* a *Prelude to The Faithful, Soliloquy* for flute and string orchestra, have been presented by major organizations. America possesses few composers with Rogers' seriousness of purpose. He is an idealist, a dreamer—New York, his native city, repels him with its crass materialism. His music is sensitive, poetic, carefully made, even though for the present it lacks the imprint of a pointedly individual style. He has recently completed a new score, *Japanese Impressions,* and is now at work on a symphony.

Both Douglas Moore and W. Quincy Porter have emerged from the same background, the Yale School of Music and, later, Bloch. At present Moore is in Paris on a Pulitzer scholarship. I can speak of his work only from hearsay. His two suites for orchestra, *Museum Pieces* and *P. T. Barnum,* are said to contain pages of rare humor.

Since 1922, W. Quincy Porter has been teacher of theory at the Cleveland Institute of Music. Like Hindemith, Porter is a first-class viola player and has accordingly written much for strings. A *Ukrainian Suite*, for string orchestra, and two string quartets comprise his major works. All these are characterized by an especially fine mastery of contrapuntal technique and an easy handling of the problems of form. But unfortunately they are largely derivative in inspiration—Stravinsky and Bloch in the quartets; Russian masters in the *Suite*. Porter is not yet thirty, he has chosen fine models, we can confidently await his more mature development.

Of Nadia Boulanger's pupils two should be singled out for special mention—Virgil Thomson and Quinto Maganini. Virgil Thomson, besides composing, writes uncommonly well about music. His academic training was at the Harvard School of Music, from which he was graduated in 1922. There is much that is paradoxical in his music. It is generally of two kinds, diametrically opposed to each other: sacred vocal music like the *Mass* for men's voices, *Three Antiphonal Psalms* for women's voices, songs for voices and piano on biblical texts; and on the other hand, tangos for orchestra and light pieces for piano. At its best his work displays a melodic invention of no mean order and a most subtle rhythmic sense growing out of a fine feeling for prosody. Certainly Thomson has not entirely found himself as yet. One waits with more than usual curiosity to see what he will do in the future.

Quinto Maganini, despite the Italianate sound of his name, is a native American, brought up in California. A large part of his knowledge of composition has been gained in a practical way as flautist in symphonic orchestras. Though not yet thirty, Maganini has a considerable list of works to his credit. He has traveled extensively and is strongly attracted by local color, so that one finds him writing a *Fantasy Japonaise*; *La Rumba de Monteagudo*, based on Cuban popular music; *Tuolumna*, for orchestra, with a suggestion of Indian themes. A symphonic nocturne, *Night on an Island of Fantasy*, is perhaps his most successful effort in the larger forms. With a more critical pen Maganini should make one of our promising composers.

The day of the neglected American composer is over. That is to say, he is neglected only if he remains unknown. These seventeen young men are presented as proof of the fact that there is a new generation of composers whose efforts are worthy of encouragement.

1936: America's Young Men—Ten Years Later

"America's Young Men of Promise" was the title of an article that may be remembered as having appeared just ten years ago. Seventeen composers were boldly chosen—all of them born here, ranging in age from twenty-three to thirty-three—as most likely to accomplish important things in American music. With bated breath let me relist the composers I named, leaving it to the reader to decide whether they were wisely chosen. Among those present were George Antheil, Avery Claflin, Henry Cowell, Herbert Elwell, Howard Hanson, Roy Harris, Richard Hammond, Quinto Maganini, Douglas Moore, Edmund Pendleton, Quincy Porter, Bernard Rogers, Roger Sessions, Alexander Steinert, Leo Sowerby, Randall Thompson, and Virgil Thomson.

My purpose in bringing out this list again is twofold: first, to reconsider these composers in the light of a decade of activity on their part, and, second, to juxtapose a new list of "America's Young Men of Promise," since discovering the "important composers of tomorrow among the young men of today" is still as fascinating a diversion as it was in 1926.

The first question that suggests itself is whether that original band of seventeen did represent a real generation of American composers. I think that it did. Perhaps it is not too much to say that they represented the most important generation of composers America had yet produced. Originating in all parts of the country, they nevertheless shared many experiences in common: student days before and during the war years, European contacts made soon after 1919, followed by a busy period of creative activity during the healthy, hectic years of the twenties. By 1926 their main characteristics as composers were already discernible.

In general they were technically better equipped and more aware of the idiom of their contemporaries than any preceding generation of Americans. None of them suffered from the folkloristic preoccupation of their elders with Indian and Negro thematic material. Still, the idea of expressing America in tone was uppermost. Yet they seemed no more able than their predecessors to forge a typically indigenous American style in music.

For purposes of identification these seventeen men can now be described as roughly falling into four different categories: Those who have made a more or less sudden rise to prominence since 1926; those who have continued to compose along the same lines in a steady, unwavering fashion; those who have remained in comparative obscurity; and those who have abandoned composing altogether.

I make no claim to being familiar with every piece of music written by each of these men since 1926. Nor is it my purpose to criticize the single work of any individual composer. What appears interesting is to examine their present status in the light of a decade of experience and activity; to check up, as it were, on their progress during the past ten years.

In the first category mentioned above belong Roy Harris, Virgil Thomson, and, in a lesser degree, Roger Sessions. The case of Roy Harris is probably most striking. His admirers and detractors are already legion. I do not belong among those who seem satisfied with continually pointing out his weaknesses. Without in any way wishing to condone them, I believe that the work he has already done, stamped as it is with the mark of a big personality, is something to build on, something we can ill afford to treat slightingly. Harris's music shows promise of being able to reach a very wide audience, wider probably than that of any other American. His name is already almost analogous with "Americanism" in music. This is a rather remarkable record for one who was not only completely unknown ten years ago, but who was, musically speaking, practically inarticulate. For Harris the problem of being fully articulate still remains. When he solves that, all barriers will be down between himself and his audience.

Virgil Thomson needs no introduction to my readers. The success of *Four Saints* came as a surprise certainly, but on second thought seems quite natural. For Thomson is a composer who knows exactly what he wants. *Four Saints* is thoroughly characteristic of his work as a whole. In it he proves himself to be essentially a vocal composer. As I have pointed out on other occasions, Thomson is the first American whose sense of the English language seems really acute. His vocal line is based on the rhythmic flexibility and natural inflection of human speech, and may well serve as a model for future composers.

In contrast with Harris and Thomson, Roger Sessions has achieved slowly but surely a wide reputation both as a composer of serious works and as a musician of solid culture. In 1926 we took it on the word of Bloch and Paul Rosenfeld that Sessions was a musical radical. But now it is clear that Sessions is really the classicist par excellence. The small number of his works make up in quality what they lack in quantity. Sessions' music cannot be expected to appeal to large audiences—in a certain sense he writes a musician's music, intent as he is upon achieving a plastic and formal perfection, with little regard for audience psychology. His influence as composer and pedagogue will surely be felt increasingly.

Randall Thompson and Bernard Rogers have both gradually been making their mark on American music. Thompson, particularly, enjoys a well-deserved reputation as an expert craftsman. It is curious to observe how a man of Thompson's scholarly interest and academic background has come to make a definite bid for popular appeal, as in his Symphony No. 2. Thompson has the audience very much in mind when he composes. This attitude is not without its dangers, particularly when the composer gives us the impression, as Thompson sometimes does, that he has been concentrating on the sonorous effect rather than the musical thought behind it.

Bernard Rogers has composed much in the past few years. But since none of his major works has been performed outside of Rochester, where he makes his home, I cannot speak authoritatively about them.

Recently Quincy Porter's name has come to the fore through his string quartets and his sonata for viola alone. Porter has turned out a considerable number of works, especially for stringed instruments, since my first article appeared. These are so gratefully written for the strings that it would be strange if they did not become better known. But Porter's essential problem still remains—to create a music entirely his own.

In speaking of the second category—composers who have continued more or less along the same lines they had adopted before 1926—I had in mind such varied personalities as Hanson, Sowerby, Cowell, and Moore.

Hanson and Sowerby were well launched even ten years ago. Their sympathies and natural proclivities make them the heirs of older men such as Hadley and Shepherd. Their facility in writing and their eclectic style produce a kind of palatable music that cannot be expected to arouse the enthusiasm of the "elite," but does serve to fill the role of "American music" for broad masses of people.

Cowell remains the incorrigible "experimenter" of the twenties. In 1926 I wrote: "Cowell is essentially an inventor, not a composer."[1] I must regretfully still subscribe to that opinion, despite the ingenuity of such inventions as his *Synchrony* for orchestra.

Douglas Moore early showed a predilection for making use of an American subject matter as a basis for his work. After *P. T. Barnum* we got *Moby Dick* and *Babbitt*. Unfortunately these works have been too infrequently played for us to know whether the music is as American as the titles.

Four of the original seventeen composers—Hammond, Claflin, Maganini, and Steinert—have receded into comparative obscurity.[2] This is possibly less true of Steinert, whose works are performed from time to time. He has with difficulty extricated himself from a definitely impressionistic bias. Hammond, Claflin, and Maganini have written much music during the past ten years but very little of it has been played. Can this be simply a matter of neglect or is it the fault of the music itself?

Two composers have apparently stopped composing altogether: Herbert Elwell and Edmund Pendleton. Both, however, lead active lives as musicians and writers on music: Pendleton in Paris and Elwell in Cleveland as critic of the Cleveland *Plain Dealer*.[3]

George Antheil, as always, belongs in a category of his own. In 1926 Antheil seemed to have "the greatest gifts of any young American." But something always seems to prevent their full fruition. Whether this is due to a lack of artistic integrity, or an unusual susceptibility to influences, or a lack of any conscious direction, is not clear. All we know is that Antheil is

---

[1]This opinion needs revision in view of Cowell's eleven symphonies and other recent works.
[2]"Obscurity" cannot in justice describe the busy musical lives of Steinert, Claflin, and Maganini.
[3]Both Elwell and Pendleton have resumed their composing careers along with their profession of music criticism.

now thirty-five, and we have a right to expect definitive works from him by this time.

Two or three composers should be mentioned who, because of their age, rightfully belong with the original group, but were omitted because they were unperformed before 1926.

First of these, and most important, is Walter Piston. His preparation for composing was obviously an arduous one. His earliest listed music, a Piano Sonata, is dated 1926, when Piston was thirty-two. Since then a steadily mounting number of works has been matched by a steadily increasing and well-merited reputation. Piston belongs with Sessions as one of the most expert craftsmen American music can boast.

A second and almost parallel case as far as dates are concerned is that of Robert Russell Bennett. His "first" work, written at the same date and age as Piston's, is a *Charleston Rhapsody* for orchestra. He is well known now as the composer of music that is light in touch and deftly made, with a particular eye on orchestral timbre, of which he is a past master.

William Grant Still began about twelve years ago as the composer of a somewhat esoteric music for voice and a few instruments. Since that time he has completely changed his musical speech, which has become almost popular in tone. He has a certain natural musicality and charm, but there is a marked leaning toward the sweetly saccharine that one should like to see eliminated.

Turning to the youngest composers of today one is immediately conscious that they find themselves in a quite different situation from that of the preceding generation. In a sense they form a "depression generation," for they live in a moral climate that is none too good for the nurturing of new talent. While opportunities for getting their work before the public have definitely increased, the public itself is apathetic to new music as a whole, showing a lack of interest toward the new men.

There seems to be no other explanation for the general impression that no especially outstanding personalities are to be found among the new men who are comparable in stature to the outstanding members of the preceding generation.

They can be conveniently divided according to age: Those who are just about twenty-five, and those who are either older or younger than twenty-five. The first group, which includes some of the most gifted men, is made up of Robert McBride, Jerome Moross, Paul Bowles, Hunter Johnson, and Samuel Barber.

The older men, including some of the more mature talents, are Marc Blitzstein, Israel Citkowitz, Gerald Strang, Ross Lee Finney, Elie Siegmeister, Irwin Heilner, Lehman Engel, Paul Creston, and Edwin Gershefski.

The youngest are: Henry Brant, David Diamond, and Norman Cazden.

A larger number of names will be familar than would have been true ten years ago. Marc Blitzstein's is probably best known. Blitzstein shows a definite "flair" for composition, although his early works were largely derivative (Stravinsky was the all-absorbing influence). Later, when he managed to throw off these influences, his music took on an exaggeratedly laconic and abstract quality, which militated against its even achieving performance. Recently, however, he has returned to a simpler style more nearly approaching the best parts of his early ballet *Cain*, or some of his film music for *Surf and Seaweed*. This new simplicity may be attributed to Blitzstein's sympathy for leftist ideology, with its emphasis on music for the masses.

The identification of one's musical aims with the needs of the working class is a brand-new phenomenon in American music. Young men like Siegmeister, Heilner, Moross, and Cazden have felt irresistibly drawn toward the movement to the left, which has influenced all other arts before reaching music. Unfortunately it cannot be said that their works show the salutary influence of a collectivist ideal. (This is not so strange when we consider that to compose a music of "socialist realism" has stumped even so naturally gifted a man as Shostakovitch.)

Siegmeister has had difficulty in adopting a real simplicity in his more serious works. Too often, as in his *Strange Funeral at Braddock*, we get a kind of crude effectiveness, quite undistinguished in style. What is needed here is more honest self-criticism. Heilner is a naturally gifted composer, though he is given to extremes. He recently abandoned a highly complex tonal fabric, inspired no doubt by the examples of Ives, in order consciously to embrace banality. That idea for reaching the masses is literary and certainly will not satisfy a musician like Heilner for long.

Moross is probably the most talented of these men. He writes music that has a quality of sheer physicalness, music "without a mind," as it were. It is regrettable that we cannot yet point to any finished, extended work. What he seems to lack is a sense of artistic discipline and integrity, which his talent needs for development.

Norman Cazden, an excellent pianist, has recently been brought to our attention as the composer of a Piano Sonatina and a String Quartet that augur well for his future as a creative artist.

Of a completely different inspiration is the music of Citkowitz and Bowles. Both these men are lyricists and write an unmistakably personal music. Citkowitz, who is certainly one of the most sensitive and cultured musicians we have, has produced but little in the past few years. It is to be fervently hoped that the composer of such delicate and admirable pieces as the *Joyce Songs* and the Movements for String Quartet will soon get his second wind, and present us with works we have a right to expect from him.

Paul Bowles is the exceptional case among our young composers. There are those who refuse to see in Bowles anything more than a dilettante. Bowles himself persists in adopting a militantly non-professional air in relation to all music, including his own. If you take this attitude at its face value, you will lose sight of the considerable merit of a large amount of music Bowles has already written. It is music that comes from a fresh personality, music full of charm and melodic invention, at times surprisingly well made in an instinctive and non-academic fashion. Personally I much prefer an "amateur" like Bowles to your "well-trained" conservatory product.

If it is careful workmanship that is desired, turn to the music of Ross Lee Finney and Samuel Barber. Finney's music becomes more interesting with each new work. He composes largely in the neoclassic model, which produces a certain sameness that should be avoided in the future. Barber writes in a somewhat outmoded fashion, making up in technical finish what he lacks in musical substance. So excellent a craftsman should not content himself forever with the emotionally conventional context of his present manner.[4]

Three composers—Engel, Brant, and Diamond—are extremely prolific and facile. Facility brings it own pitfalls, of course. To compose easily is admirable, but the music must always spring from a deep need. Neither Engel nor Brant, despite self-evident musicality, has yet completely convinced us that each is "hopelessly" a composer. David Diamond is a new name on the roster of young composers. It is a name to remember. Not yet twenty-one, Diamond has a musical speech that is, of course, only in the process of formation. But already one can recognize an individual note in his last-movement rondos with their perky, nervous themes and quick, impulsive motion.

Robert McBride has also but recently made his metropolitan bow. Those who heard his *Prelude to a Tragedy*, performed by Hans Lange and the Philharmonic, were greatly impressed. McBride's orchestral sense is both keen and original. Being himself a performer on several orchestral instruments, he approaches the whole problem of composing from a more practical standpoint than is general among our young men, who too often find themselves divorced from direct contact with the materia musica. McBride has yet to learn how to purify his style of extraneous elements, and how to create a feeling of inevitability in the musical thought. Still, no composer during the past few years has made so fresh an impression on first acquaintance.

Finally there are the young men whose names are little known: Strang of California, Johnson of the Middle West, Gershefski of Connecticut, and

---

[4]Written when Mr. Barber was twenty-six. He must have arrived at a similar conclusion, if one can judge by the sophisticated style of his more mature music.

Creston, a native New Yorker. It is a characteristic sign that they are all composers of excellent training. In general, however, their work has a disturbing tendency toward overcomplexity of texture and a somewhat abstract musical thought. There is a certain unreality about their music, which probably comes from their lack of contact with a real audience. Perhaps it is wrong to generalize about four such different personalities. Strang's music has been little played outside his native state. All the others have recently had evenings of their work at the WPA Forum Laboratory Concerts and will undoubtedly profit by their experiences there.

In 1946 we shall know more about all these men.

1949: The New "School" of American Composers

When I was in my twenties I had a consuming interest in what the other composers of my generation were producing. Even before I was acquainted with the names of Roy Harris, Roger Sessions, Walter Piston, and the two Thom(p)sons, I instinctively thought of myself as part of a "school" of composers. Without the combined effort of a group of men it seemed hardly possible to give the United States a music of its own.

Now—and how soon, alas—my contemporaries and I must count ourselves among the spiritual papas of a new generation of composers. But personally I find that my interest in what the young composers are up to is just as keen as it ever was. For it is obvious that you cannot set up a continuing tradition of creative music in any country without a constant freshening of source material as each decade brings forth a new batch of composers.

It seems to me that one of the most important functions of those who consider themselves guardians of musical tradition, particularly in our Western Hemisphere, where the creative musical movement is still so young, is to watch carefully and nurture well the delicate roots of the youngest generation; to see to it that they get a sound musical training, that their first successful efforts are heard, and that they feel themselves part of the musical movement of their country.

In the United States young composers appear to be sprouting everywhere. My impression is that we are just beginning to tap our creative potentialities. The generation of the 1930s—Marc Blitzstein, William Schuman, Samuel Barber, David Diamond, and Paul Bowles—is now well established. The generation of the 1940s—with which this article is concerned—is being encouraged with prizes, commissions, fellowships, money grants, and, more often than not, performances of their works. Nowadays, in this country at any rate, a young composer with exceptional talent would have a hard time escaping detection.

Unlike the composers of my own generation, most of these younger men have not (as yet) been to Europe. In a very real sense Europe has come to them, for many of them have had personal contact with Stravinsky, Hindemith, Schönberg, Milhaud, and Martinů, all of whom are living and composing in the United States [in 1949]. It would be strange indeed if the presence of these contemporary masters had no effect whatever on our younger generation.

But added to this influence by way of Europe there is a new note: our young composers follow closely the work of their older American colleagues. My own generation found very little of interest in the work of their elders: [Edward] MacDowell, [George W.] Chadwick, or [Charles Martin] Loeffler; and their influence on our music was nil. (We had only an inkling of the existence of the music of Charles Ives in the twenties.) Nowadays a young American composer is just as likely to be influenced by Harris or Schuman as he is by Stravinsky or Hindemith. (Perhaps, to fill out the picture, I should add that numbers of them have been accused of writing like me!)

In general, the works of the youngest generation reflect a wide variety of compositional interests rather than any one unified tendency. In the United States you can pick and choose your influence. Of course, we also have our twelve-tone composers, most of them pupils of Krenek or Schönberg, even though they have not yet played much of a role. All this would seem healthy and natural, given the particular environment of our musical life and the comparatively recent development of our composing potential.

But enough of generalities. I have chosen seven names as representative of some of the best we have to offer among the new generation: Robert Palmer, Alexei Haieff, Harold Shapero, Lukas Foss, Leonard Bernstein, William Bergsma, John Cage. Most of these composers either are just approaching thirty or have just passed thirty. (Foss is the youngest of the group, having only recently turned twenty-four.) They are all native-born Americans, with the exception of Haieff and Foss, both of whom came to the United States at the age of fifteen and were musically formed here. All of them are composers of serious works that have been publicly performed and, occasionally, published and recorded.

Robert Palmer is perhaps the least well known of this group. He is also one of the oldest—thirty-two. His music is seldom heard in ordinary concert life; most of it found its way to public performance on special modern-music programs or at annual festivals of American music. Palmer happens to be one of my own particular enthusiasms. I remember being astonished ten years ago when I first saw him, and tried to make some connection in my mind between the man and his music. His outward appearance simply did not jibe with the complexities of the metaphysical music he was writing at that time.

Ives and Harris were his early admirations, to which he added his own brand of amorphous transcendentalism. Later he came under the sway of Bartók's rhythmic drive. Two string quartets represent him at his best.

They are lengthy works, not easy to perform, and not easy for the listener to digest.

But both quartets contain separate movements of true originality and depth of feeling. Palmer is not always as critical as he should be, especially in the outlining of the general proportions of a movement, but always his music has urgency—it seems to come from some inner need for expression.

In two recent works, an orchestral *Elegy for Thomas Wolfe* and a sonata for two pianos, he has managed to discipline the natural ebullience of his writing, though sometimes at the expense of a too rigid polyrhythmic or melodic scheme. Palmer may never achieve the perfect work, but at least he tries for big things. In recent years too much of his energy has gone into his teaching at Cornell University, but teaching is a familiar disease of the American composer. Thus far in his career Palmer has enjoyed little public acclaim; nevertheless, if he has the capacity to endure and to develop, his future seems to me assured.

Alexei Haieff was born in Russia and brought up in China, but had his musical education under Rubin Goldmark in the United States. Later he studied in Paris under Nadia Boulanger. His background and training give him a strong affinity with the music of Stravinsky, and, in fact, Haieff is a close personal friend of that master. Stravinsky's shadow was pervasive in his earlier works, but gradually Haieff has emerged with a sharply defined personality of his own. He combines a sensitive and refined musical nature with an alert musical mind that often gives off sparks of mordant humor. He delights in playful manipulation of his musical materials, and has a special fondness for sudden interruptions of the musical flow with abrupt silences or unexpected leaps or brief backtrackings.

Thus far Haieff has composed few large and imposing works. Although he has written a First Symphony, he seems most at home in his shorter pieces such as his *Divertimento* for chamber orchestra, Sonata for two pianos, Five Pieces for Piano, and other short works for violin and piano or cello and piano. Almost all of these pieces are a musical pleasure—they have personality, sensibility, and wit. They divert and delight the listener, not in a superficial sense but in the sense that such terms might be applied to a Couperin or a Scarlatti. Haieff is at present engaged in the composition of a long ballet based on *Beauty and the Beast*, to be choreographed by George Balanchine for the Ballet Society of New York. It will be interesting to see how he handles a large canvas.

Harold Shapero, it is safe to say, is at the same time the most gifted and the most baffling composer of his generation. This young Bostonian, now twenty-seven, has a phenomenal "ear" and a brilliant (though sometimes erratic) mind. The ear and the mind were subjected to a methodical training under Krenek, Piston, Hindemith, and Boulanger. These teachers left their mark; Shapero now possesses an absolutely perfected technical equipment.

To examine one of his scores closely is a fascinating experience. Few musicians of our time put their pieces together with greater security either in the skeletal harmonic framework, in the modeling of the melodic phrases, or in the careful shaping of the whole. Shapero knows what he's doing, but that is the least of it: the exciting thing is to note how this technical adroitness is put at the service of a wonderfully spontaneous musical gift. Despite this there is, as I say, something baffling about what he has produced thus far.

Stylistically Shapero seems to feel a compulsion to fashion his music after some great model. Thus his five-movement Serenade for String Orchestra (a remarkable work in many ways) is founded upon neoclassic Stravinskian principles, his Three Sonatas for Piano on Haydnesque principles, and his recent long symphony is modeled after Beethoven. For the present he seems to be suffering from a hero-worship complex—or perhaps it is a freakish attack of false modesty, as if he thought to hide the brilliance of his own gifts behind the cloak of the great masters. No one can say how long this strange attitude will last. But when Shapero decides to make a direct attack on the composing problem, to throw away all models, and to strike out unconcernedly on his own, I predict the whole musical world will sit up and take notice.

Lukas Foss is, in a way, the *Wunderkind* of this group of composers, and something of the aura of the *Wunderkind* still hangs about him. Born in Berlin, where he had his first music lessons, he continued his studies at the Conservatoire in Paris during the Hitler years, and finally arrived in New York with his parents at the age of fifteen. At thirteen he had already composed piano pieces (subsequently published by G. Schirmer) that are almost indistinguishable from those of his later master, Hindemith.

The contact with America was crucial. In Europe he had acquired a kind of impersonal cocksureness that was not at all sympathetic. In America, as he grew up, he became more human and more anxious to reflect the atmosphere of his newly adopted country. His first large work of "American" inspiration was an oratorio, *The Prairie*, for soloists, chorus, and orchestra, with a text chosen from Carl Sandburg's indigenous poems. It was a striking work to come from the pen of a nineteen-year-old boy. Since then he has composed two long works for solo voice and orchestra—*Song of Protest* for baritone, and *Song of Songs* for soprano, both based on texts from the Bible.

I cannot honestly say that I always admire his treatment of the English language. But it is impossible not to admire the spontaneity and naturalness of his musical flow, the absolute clarity in texture, and the clean and easy handling of large formal problems. That Foss is a born composer is obvious.

William Bergsma is a native of California and a musical product of the Eastman School of Music in Rochester, New York. Hardly out of school himself, he already is one of the teachers of composition at the Juilliard School. (William Schuman, head of the school, was quick to recognize Bergsma's sure craftsmanship.)

Bergsma is, by temperament, a sober and serious workman. I realize that this is not a very exact description of his particular talent, but it is difficult to say more at the present time, for the specific quality of his personality is not yet clear. He possesses a poetic and critical mind, and one is certain that his compositions are put together slowly, after mature reflection. Thus far he has composed orchestral and chamber music, songs, piano pieces, and a ballet. At this writing he is engaged upon a first symphony. How truly original or how broad in scope his music may turn out to be is a question for the future. But already it is clear from works like his two string quartets that Bergsma represents one of the solid values of the younger generation.

Leonard Bernstein's composing gift has been overshadowed by his brilliance as conductor and pianist. In a sense it would be strange if he could not compose, for his ability in that direction is only one of the various facets of an extraordinarily versatile musical personality. For us Bernstein represents a new type of musician—one who is equally at home in the world of jazz and in the world of serious music. George Gershwin made something of an attempt to fill that role, but Bernstein really fills it—and with ease.

Although his composing time is severely restricted by his activities as conductor, Bernstein has to his credit a symphony, *Jeremiah*; two ballets, *Fancy Free* and *Facsimile*; a clarinet and piano Sonata, songs, and piano pieces.

The most striking feature of Bernstein's music is its immediacy of emotional appeal. Melodically and harmonically it has a spontaneity and warmth that speak directly to an audience. (After so much dissonant counterpoint and neoclassic severity this was a new note for a young composer to strike.) At its worst Bernstein's music is conductor's music—eclectic in style and facile in inspiration. But at its best it is music of vibrant rhythmic invention, of irresistible élan, often carrying with it a terrific dramatic punch. It is possible that some form of stage music will prove to be Bernstein's finest achievement. In general it is difficult to foretell the durability of music like Bernstein's, which is so enormously effective on first hearing.

I have saved for the last one of the curiosities of the younger generation: the music of John Cage. During the late twenties the experimental percussion music of Edgar Varèse and Henry Cowell made much noise among the musical *avant-garde*. Cage stems from there, much to the surprise of many of us who thought that the percussion period in modern music was definitely over.

Cage began in California with a percussion music of his own, obviously derived from that of his elders. But gradually he devolved the use of the so-called "prepared" piano as a percussive medium. A piano is "prepared" by inserting various metal and non-metal materials between the strings of the instrument. This produces a muted tone of delicately clangorous variety with no resemblance whatever to piano tone. It must be heard to be appreciated—and it must be heard close by, for the tone is tiny and of little duration, somewhat like that of the harpsichord. But even music for prepared pianos must, in the end, be judged like other music.

Fascinating as it is, I fear that Cage's music has more originality of sound than of substance. Stylistically it stems from Balinese and Hindu musics, and more recently from Arnold Schönberg.

Serious music is thriving in the United States. One factor not often noted is the way our music schools and colleges are turning out composers in numbers unparalleled in our musical past. If we can gauge the musical future of a nation by the healthy activity of its younger generation of composers, then America is likely to do well.

The seven composers discussed in this article are near the top of the heap, but in many ways they are typical of their generation. They are all well-trained musicians and, what is more, American-trained. Their works show influences, of course. But it is a sign of the times that those influences are no longer solely European, for the older generation of American composers has helped to orient them.

It is also typical that they can knock out all sorts of music: a successful ballet like Leonard Bernstein's *Fancy Free*; a big oratorio like Lukas Foss's *Prairie*; a real symphony like Harold Shapero's; expert string quartets like those of William Bergsma or Robert Palmer; unusual forms like the piano music of John Cage; delightful shorter pieces like those of Alexei Haieff.

These young men don't form a "school" in a stylistic sense. But they all write music that is rhythmically alive, richly melodic, and clearly conceived. I believe that, taken altogether, these representative seven men and their colleagues throughout the country form an impressive group—one that need not fear comparison with the younger generation of any other country. That is something new for America.

1959: Postscript for the Generation of the Fifties

In my prefatory note to the three preceding articles on American composers I mentioned the variety and complexity of our creative musical scene of today. It is a question whether anyone can hope to summarize the work of the generation of the fifties. One would have to live simultaneously in the four corners of the U.S.A. to know what is going on. There are so many composers active in so many parts of the country that no one observer can pretend to know them all. To take one instance: for every one opera written during the twenties there must be twenty being composed nowadays; and comparable figures are true for other musical media.

Nevertheless, if we leave aside the large mass of competent and average music that is always being produced, and concentrate on the ambitious compositions of our more adventurous composers, certain tendencies are discernible. The most striking one is the return, since 1950, to a preoccupation with the latest trends of European composition. This comes as a surprise, for, from the standpoint of their elders, it is retrogression of a sort. It is retrogression because it places us in a provincial position *vis-à-vis* our European confreres. The older generation fought hard to free American composition from the dominance of European models because that struggle was basic to the establishment of an American music. The young composer of today, on the other hand, seems to be fighting hard to stay abreast of a fast-moving post-World War II European musical scene. The new continental composer of the fifties began by re-examining the twelve-note theories of Arnold Schönberg in the light of their more logical application by Anton von Webern. From there he proceeded to a music of total control and its opposite, the music of chance and the music of non-simultaneity, with side forays into the fascinating world of electronically produced sounds, their mixture with normal music, and so forth. All this stirred things up considerably, especially since these young leaders of musical thought abroad—Pierre Boulez in France, Karlheinz Stockhausen in Germany, and Luigi Nono in Italy—have found sponsors and publishers to back them, instrumentalists—and this is important—willing to struggle with their pyrotechnical difficulties, and audiences willing to take them on faith. They created what we in America would call a workable setup.

Our own youngsters have been less successful in that regard. They have not managed thus far to create a world in which they can fully function as composers. They have been encouraged by awards and fellowships, but their music has not been furthered by conductors on the lookout for new things, and only an occasional performer has ventured to perform their music in public. Such circumstances can be frustrating in the extreme, and it is hard to see where they can possibly lead. That such a cul-de-sac is far from inevitable is proven by the fact that John Cage and his followers have developed audience support and press interest with music that is no less experimental in nature.

One might point also to the example of Elliott Carter, who has shaped a music of his own out of a wide knowledge of the music of our time. His theories concerning metrical modulation and structural logic have engaged the attention of our younger composers. Their own music, however, lacks similar directional drive. I detect in it no note of deep conviction: they seem to be exploring *possible* ways of writing music suggested to them by the example of composers abroad rather than creating out of their own experience and need a music that only they could write.

I am, of course, generalizing, which is always a dangerous thing to do. Already some youngster may be giving the lie to my reasonings. Even within the area I have outlined we have young talents whose music commands attention: Billy Jim Layton, Salvatore Martirano, Seymour Shifrin, Edward Miller, Yehudi Wyner, Kenneth Gaburo, and the young Robert Lombardo. A composer like Gunther Schuller has asserted his independence by calling for a cross-fertilization of improvised jazz with contemporary serious music. His own music seems born out of a striking instrumental imagination; later on he may fill it out with a musical substance that matches the fascination of his sonorities. Easley Blackwood, who was a musical rebel in his teens, has developed along conservative lines a music that is arresting. Surprisingly few younger composers belong in that category, but one might add the names of Noël Lee and Mordechai Sheinkman.

Many of the questions that puzzled the generation of the twenties are still being asked today. What kind of music ought we to visualize for a future America? What form should it take? To whom shall it be addressed? Obviously our younger men will work out their own solutions without asking our advice. But it is only natural that we should hope that they will be able to find sustenance in the answers we found for the music of our own time.

America's Young Men
of Music (1960)

You probably want to know something about our younger American composers, and about their position in our American music world today.

One of these, not really a "young" man but one who has come to notice only in the last five or ten years, is Elliott Carter.

Carter began as a Neo-Classicist, very much under the influence of Stravinsky, and we could not have prophesied this rather late development—he has just turned 50—and his interest for the younger people. He is a very intellectual sort of fellow; for a composer I would say *very* intellectual. He is interested in all sorts of things other than music, and his music shows the intellectual strain in his temperament.

Sensational Quartet

For instance, his First String Quartet caused something of a sensation, both at home and abroad. It was conceived rather differently from any other string quartet ever written before. It did not sound like a proper string quartet: the four instruments did not seem to be making harmonies together; they seemed to be working rather on their own; each separate instrument seemed to be playing a separate sonata for himself, and somehow, it all did add up into a string quartet.

He did that partly through the use of something that has come to be called "rhythmic modulation." He devised a method of moving gradually from one rhythm to another. It was mathematically calculated, and yet not obvious; so that the four instruments might move at a slightly different pace all at the same time. They were like four racehorses, one of which passed the others and you could not tell which was going to get ahead. It gave the rhythmic life a great fluidity and made it sound rather different from anything one had heard before.

I believe from reading about the new quartet that he has again continued seeking out rather independent voice-writing. Sometimes it creates rather strong clashes—rather difficult to take—but at any rate it gives the music a sound that no other composer's string quartet has, which is already something. Carter wrote a series of Variations for Orchestra for the Louisville Symphony Orchestra which are very original in sound. One has the feeling that his mind is very alert and one cannot guess in advance just what he is going to come up with next. So he is a very live figure in the minds of our younger men.

One might talk about the younger people a little bit as from the places they hail from. There is a kind of "Boston School"—at any rate they began in and around Boston: I am thinking of men like Harold Shapero, Lukas Foss, Irving Fine, Arthur Berger; and of course Leonard Bernstein himself was born near Boston and grew up there. They grew up at a time when Stravinsky's Neo-Classicism was very important in their lives. Now that has rather been dissipated and they all are busily writing music.

Shapero created the most interest for a considerable time. I am sorry to say he has not written many works in the last few years. He has been teaching at Brandeis University, and maybe has been lazy. I do not know what the reason is, but we regret it. But he wrote a symphony, a long 40-minute symphony, which despite its Stravinskian influences has some lovely things in it: some beautifully written inner voices, a lovely sense of orchestration. A really fine piece.

Men from Juilliard

Foss was with me in the Soviet Union. He has written a considerable amount of orchestral music. He likes to write for the voice and orchestra. And a recent work of his called *Symphony of Chorales* should certainly be heard here. It has a very original sound. It is the best thing he has done so far. If you do not know it—I do not see how you could because it is not recorded—you do not know what he can do at his best.

There is another group of composers who are active—or were until very recently—the Juilliard School, men like Peter Mennin, William Bergsma, Vincent Persichetti. There is a group of composers active out on the West Coast, in California. I am thinking of men like Leon Kirchner and Andrew Imbrie.

Kirchner, especially, has had much attention in the last few years. He was a pupil both of Schoenberg and Sessions, and has a definite tendency toward the chromatic style.

His earlier pieces might be connected with Berg and Bartók. There is a kind of "dishevelled" quality in the earlier pieces that makes them exciting to listen to. You cannot quite guess them in advance. They seem always on the verge of being chaotic but not quite. They are a little like Bartók, except that Bartók always has such a firm control of materials, while Kirchner almost dares to let them get the better of him. When it does not come off, of course, it is not at all successful. But when it does it creates very exciting music.

Among the still-younger men there has been a strong Twelve-Tone tendency. Schoenberg, after all, taught in California for about 12 years. Everyone says he taught no Twelve-Tone writing—he taught you how to analyse a Beethoven quartet. Even so, there he was writing it himself and so obviously he had influence on the people he taught, and in general.

Then, when the wave of interest in Webern hit Europe, it had its reflection in the United States. Milton Babbitt, who teaches music at Princeton University, has been a strong influence in that direction. The fact that Luigi Dallapiccola has taught in the States, and that Stefan Wolpe lives and teaches there, have also been strong influences on younger people trying to find a new way to construct their music and to make new sounds.

Classics and Jazz

Unfortunately there has not yet been any outstanding figure among the younger Twelve-Tone writers. Perhaps the name of Gunther Schuller would come to mind first. He might resent my putting him in with these Twelve-Tonists—he is not that strict about it, and he also has other ideas that I think may bring forth some interesting things.

One of Schuller's main ideas is the combination of classical music and jazz. He wants them to infiltrate one another—rather different from the way we did in the 1920s. He knows a lot about recent progressive jazz, and he is very anxious to get serious musicians to improvise. He says we were really fooling ourselves by imagining in the 1920s that we were treating jazz materials, because you cannot have jazz materials unless you have people improvising.

Well, perhaps so. At any rate that is *his* problem right now; because it is very hard to get a serious musician to improvise—he gets nervous when he does not have the notes in front of him!

George Antheil (1925)

A great deal of nonsense has been written about George Antheil. The real personality of this extremely talented young American composer has been cleverly concealed by a welter of words from the most varied sources.

First we have the Antheil concocted by the musical journals,—a godless, red-as-they-come Bolshevik, whose concerts have resembled riots and whose final pleasure and purpose is to turn all Europe topsy-turvy with his astounding musical noises. Then there is the Antheil of the high-brow, literary magazines—Mr. Ezra Pound's Antheil,—the young "genius" who has invented the "new propulsion of time-spaces," "new mechanisms," the fourth dimension of music, etc., etc. Finally, there is Mr. George Antheil's Antheil who, strangely enough, is hardly less a figment of the imagination. Mr. Antheil sees himself as a modern Mozart, experimenting in disjointed rhythms and ear-splitting dissonances, hopelessly misunderstood by the music critics of Berlin, Paris, and London.

For those interested in the future of American music, some attempt should be made to present George Antheil as he really is.

It must be clear from the outset that Antheil is no mere upstart. There was a time, perhaps, when he used rather questionable methods of calling attention to himself—touring Germany as a self-styled futurist composer and publishing wild manifestoes in the *avant-garde* magazines. In the last analysis, this was not charlatanism but simply the naïveté of a very youthful person carried away by the mode of the day. Certainly he was awarded a greater *réclame* than was good for him and it did, in some measure, turn his head. But Antheil is essentially a very sincere musician, absorbed in his work and oblivious to the opinions of everybody.

It is not sufficient, however, to be merely sincere. Antheil is more than that—a born musician if ever there was one. He is of Polish extraction although Trenton is his native town. From the age of four to thirteen he lived in Poland and those nine impressionable years have left their mark on his music. He possesses a gift of melody-making and a keen feeling for striking rhythmic agglomerations that are uncommon in so young a composer. It is difficult to remain coldly critical before his perfect musicianship. Hear him play the accompaniment of a Mozart concerto and you will understand what is meant; when he plays his own compositions the effect is electrifying.

Although Antheil has a considerable list of works to his credit, few of them withstand close examination. The Symphony for Five Wind Instruments has no backbone, no structural significance; the Sonatas for Violin and Piano lack a sense of climax; the Jazz Sonata is simply a poor restatement of the Stravinsky *Piano Rag-Music*. And if Antheil's music did not make us suspect his lack of a natural feeling for form, the various articles he has written on musical subjects would convey that impression. Occasionally they are a mere "mass of verbiage" and "must be taken rather as evidence of mental activity than as exposition of ideas." In the same way it is to be feared that, so far, Antheil's compositions have been signs of musical activity rather than finished art-contributions with a life of their own.

All this points to the inference that Antheil's teachers, Von Sternberg and Ernest Bloch, had very little influence upon him. "Counterpoint," he says, "can be learned by any idiot in a couple of years." Bloch, the teacher, hardly interested him, but Bloch, the composer, fascinated him. Before that, Antheil had undoubtedly been fascinated by many another contemporaneous master; his early piano pieces sound for all the world like pure Debussy and others make excellent use of the Scriabinic technique. Antheil, himself, would be the last to blush because of all this unconscious plagiarism. "Every Beethoven," he says, "must have his Mozart."

In 1921, when Antheil returned to Europe for a second time, he met his Mozart in Igor Stravinsky. Ever since, he has been struggling to shake off the powerful influence of that Russian giant. Antheil was not simply content to write four-hand piano duets in the manner of the *Cinq Pièces Faciles*, but he must note them down on manuscript paper of the same shape and size used by the Swiss publishers. Because Stravinsky utilized dynamic effects with consummate mastery Antheil became convinced that "all music is rhythm" and that anyone who composed solely in a $\frac{3}{4}$, $\frac{2}{4}$, $\frac{6}{8}$, or $\frac{4}{4}$ bar for an entire piece, was writing nothing but "doggerel." It must be admitted that the lot of the young composer who comes after Stravinsky is truly a hard one. He cannot even react from Stravinsky as Debussy reacted from Wagner, for the simple reason that Stravinsky has already reacted from himself.

Fortunately, Antheil now realizes the part Stravinsky has played in his musical development. That means that he is one step nearer to finding his own personal idiom. Exactly what kind of music he will write in the future would be impossible to prophesy. But certain passages in the Piano Concerto, in the two Sonatas for Violin and Piano, and especially in the Symphony for Five Wind Instruments make us confident that an enviable future is before him.

Darius Milhaud (1929)

Enthusiasm for the music of Darius Milhaud is almost non-existent in America. There has been no lack of opportunity to hear his work—Milhaud himself has twice toured the country as conductor and pianist, playing his own compositions—but the public and the journalists remain uninterested, when they are not openly antagonistic. Even those who specifically concern themselves with new music invariably show marked surprise when I voice admiration for the composer of *La Création du Monde*. They seem completely mystified when I add that in my estimation no other living composer is less well understood (at any rate, none whose work has gained recognition and performance to the same extent) and that Milhaud has proved himself the most important figure among the younger Frenchmen.

A simple and unprejudiced approach to Milhaud's music was made difficult from the start by the peculiar circumstances surrounding his early years of activity as a composer. Almost immediately the real Milhaud was obscured by a legend which sprang up around his name. He gained the reputation of a man who delighted in antagonizing people. As has been said, when others were thinking "Down with Wagner" it was Milhaud who cried "Down with Wagner." His music was more dissonant, his critical reviews more outspoken and his general revolutionary tenets more violent than those of any of the other young radicals who grouped themselves about Satie and Cocteau in 1919. To the majority he seemed a noisy and aggressive upstart; to others more kindly disposed he was an amusing fellow, full of life and verve, but essentially a "blagueur." Milhaud did nothing to correct this impression—possibly he enjoyed encouraging it. Sympathetic commentators strengthened the misunderstanding by placing the greatest stress on the "crude, highly colored, noisy" aspect of the composer.

Even today something of this original legend hangs about Milhaud. How false it is has been pointed out by the astute Boris de Schloezer whose article on Milhaud in *La Revue Musicale* of April 1925 is the only just appraisal of his work known to this writer.

One fact is incontrovertible: above every other consideration Milhaud's gift is clearly that of a lyricist. His musical nature impels him toward one end: a spontaneous outpouring of the emotions in terms of pure music. Schloezer considers Milhaud closer to the romantic Schönberg than to the classic Stravinsky. I cannot follow him in this. Milhaud's art is certainly more subjective than that of Stravinsky but it is romantic only in the sense that all lyricism in the modern age is associated with the romantic spirit; in emotional content it is much nearer the classic lyricism of a Fauré than the expressionism of the Viennese school. Milhaud's subjectivism is calm, detached—it sounds what one might call a humanistic note and when, as sometimes happens, it turns violent, it never can be confused with the exasperated violence belonging to the heart-on-the-sleeve school of the last century.

Springing from a native lyricism, his music always sings. Whether he composes a five-act opera or a two-page song this singing quality is paramount. The music flows so naturally that it seems to have been improvised rather than composed. What Milhaud writes comes from the "deep places of the mind"—from a kind of secondary consciousness over which he seems to assert no control.

This utter simplicity of approach has endowed him with a style uniquely and unmistakably his own. You can distinguish a page of Milhaud from among a hundred others. Unlike Stravinsky or Schönberg, who both evolved an individual speech gradually, Milhaud is recognizably himself in his earliest compositions: witness, for example, certain sections of his first opera, *La Brebis Egarée*, begun at the age of eighteen, or the song, *Paper Boats*, from *Child Poems*, written at twenty-four. At the same time he has been able to enrich his own style by submitting to a series of widely differing influences: first Debussy, then, with his two year stay in Brazil, the popular melodies he heard there, later Stravinsky, then jazz, then Satie. Whatever he touches becomes pure Milhaud. The *Poèmes Juifs*, the *Rag-Caprices*, the ballet *Salade* (derived respectively from Jewish melodies, jazz, and Satie) have all received his imprint. Milhaud is, it is true, sometimes guilty of repeating certain harmonic and rhythmic formulas. But for the most part his homogeneity of style results from the effortless reflection of a distinct personality.

Milhaud's most characteristic trait is a tender, naïve, and all-pervading charm. To sense it to the full inevitably means that one has come under the spell of the composer. With a quietly moving diatonic melody and a few thick-sounding harmonies he creates a kind of charmed atmosphere entirely without impressionistic connotation. When it is darkly colored it becomes the expression of profound nostalgia—a nostalgia which has nothing of pessimism in it and almost no yearning, but a deep sense of the tragedy of all life. Since this nostalgia is shared by none of his French confrères, I take it to be a sign of Milhaud's Jewish blood. That he is not so racial a composer as Bloch or Mahler seems natural if we remember that his ancestors settled in Provence in the fifteenth century so that his Jewishness has been long tempered by the French point of view. Nevertheless, his subjectivism, his violence, and his strong sense of logic (as displayed in his use of polytonality) are indications that the Jewish spirit is still alive in him.

His music can be quite French when it is gay and alert. In this mood his love for simple folk-like melodies and clear-cut rhythms is apparent. When the harmonies turn acidulous and the rhythms are oddly accented his gaiety becomes more brusque and truculent. Structurally, the music is always under complete control. One never meets with over-development in Milhaud—he states the core of the matter and then stops. Thus a long work is often built up on a series of short, highly condensed forms. Very characteristic also is the personal manner in which the music is put together. In this respect it is curious to compare Milhaud with a composer like Hindemith who uses his phenomenal technical equipment in an almost impersonal way. With Milhaud even the musical materials are fashioned by an entirely individual hand. (To specify exactly how this is done would lead us into too many technicalities.)

This young Frenchman possesses an amazing facility. A short three-act opera is composed in a period of less than two weeks. Few men of thirty-six can boast so large and varied an output. The musical presses of several countries have been busy issuing his work and still a great deal remains unpublished. A list of his compositions includes operas, ballets, oratorios, incidental music for several dramas, music for orchestra and chamber orchestra, a large number of songs, piano pieces, and choral music. Little wonder that Milhaud has often been reproached with writing too much. Naturally all this music cannot be of equal value. Moreover he sometimes repeats himself. But I do not join those who demand that Milhaud compose more carefully; his productiveness is too essential a part of his musical gift. As with every other prolific composer, past and present, we must be content to choose the best from among his productions.

Let me point to a few lyrical examples of his work for which I hold a special brief.

In the first rank I should place his ballets. The third one particularly, *La Création du Monde*, is a little masterpiece. Composed in 1923 on a scenario of Blaise Cendrars, it treats the creation of the world according to African legends. Much of the musical material is based, appropriately enough, on jazz—there is a fugue on a jazz theme, a fascinating blues section, and then a long breathed melody over a barbershop chord accompaniment. Milhaud has understood better than any other European how to assimilate the jazz idiom. In *La Création du Monde* he has completely transformed the jazz spirit. When jazz is long forgotten this work will live. As a stage picture it is less striking than *L'Homme et Son Désir* but from a purely musical standpoint—melodic invention, form, orchestration—it is one of Milhaud's most perfected pieces of work.

Since 1924 Milhaud has turned his attention to the operatic stage and has produced in quick succession *Les Malheurs d'Orphée; Esther de Carpentras; Le Pauvre Matelot;* three one-act chamber operas: *L'Enlèvement d'Europe; Thésée, Ariane;* and, most recently, a large opera-oratorio, *Christophe Colomb.* Ten years ago Milhaud had a deserved reputation as experimenter: in *Protée* he tried his hand at unaccompanied groups of percussion, in the Fifth String Quartet his polytonality was more logical and strict than any yet attempted, in the Sixth Symphony he wrote for novel instrumental combinations. But in these recent works he has renounced all interest in technical innovations; he seems content merely to give to the stage the purest expression of his lyricism.

Le Pauvre Matelot will serve as example. It was performed for the first time in December 1927 at the Opéra-Comique and according to first-night reports was a notorious failure. The libretto by Jean Cocteau relates the banal story of a long-lost sailor who returns disguised as a stranger to a faithful, waiting wife. At the end an unconventional twist is given to the simple plot when the wife kills the disguised stranger, not recognizing her husband. This story is set to music of the utmost simplicity, music which is without relation to what we usually consider operatic. Simple characters sing a succession of simple songs, some in a folk vein, others like popular romances. At a first hearing the work seems trite and ordinary. Later its quiet charm and naturalness grow on one. It cannot be counted among Milhaud's best works, but it is easy to understand why the unsophisticated audiences that form the regular public of the Opéra-Comique, faithful as ever to their *Manon* and Puccini, have accepted *Le Pauvre Matelot* more readily than the first-nighters, thereby making it one of the successful operas of the repertoire. Milhaud, the revolutionist, must smile at this strange fate.

A word should be accorded the three little one-act chamber operas. They last about eight minutes each—Milhaud calls them "opéra-minute"—and deserve to be classed as miniature master-works. It is difficult to choose a favorite among them. They are delightfully fresh in melody and rhythm and perfectly adapted to the new medium of chamber opera. The final scene of *L'Enlèvement d'Europe* is one of the most personal and sensuously beautiful that Milhaud has yet written.

In his earlier work also, many arresting examples of Milhaud's lyricism can be found. A detailed analysis of each one is not possible here, but a few should be named: the Sonata for two violins and piano, the Fourth and Seventh String Quartets, the *Poèmes Juifs* and the *Catalogue des Fleurs* for voice and piano, the *Saudades do Brazil* for piano, *Le Printemps* for violin and piano.

Little of this music has been given an adequate number of hearings in America. Milhaud is a good example of the modern composer who suffers from the inevitable superficiality of most of our professional criticism and public opinion regarding new music, based as it usually is on a single and often imperfect performance of a new work. It is true that few new works demand more than a single hearing. But it is no less true that the personality of a new and worthwhile composer is no different from the personality of a new and worthwhile acquaintance; they both impose upon us the necessity for longer familiarity than can be obtained in the quick exchange of the concert hall if we are to judge of their significance. The mere fact of being able to follow each strand of melody or even the structure of a new work is often only comparable to knowing that the new acquaintance has delicate fingers and a well built body. To think that you know Milhaud because you have heard a few of his works is an illusion. He is eminently the kind of composer whose art must be understood as a whole. When we have been given the opportunity for more than a glance at occasional examples of his work, when his major compositions have been played and replayed and we are able to coordinate our impressions, a basis will have been found for an appreciation of the true value of Darius Milhaud.

Virgil Thomson and Marc Blitzstein
(1940, 1968)

No country's musical life appears to be entirely mature until its composers succeed in creating an indigenous operatic theater. I am not quite sure why this should be so, but I do know that all the history books give it as a special triumph that the English, the French, and the Germans—after the "invention" of opera in Italy—should each, in turn, have developed their own kind of opera. This attitude is no doubt partly to be explained by the fact that you can't very well create a truly national opera without combining the words with a melodic line that really fits—and to have done so properly inevitably means that you have written a kind of music suited to the particular language. In short, there is a close connection between language and tone that makes their successful marriage in dramatic form, with stage incidentals, seem like one of the necessities—and when accomplished, one of the triumphs—of any native musical art.

America is no exception to this general rule. For a long time there existed a strong desire for somebody to write a real American opera. The dozen or more native stage works produced by the Metropolitan Opera Company in as many years left us just about where we were. They all made English sound like "translationese." But now at last we have had two composers—Virgil Thomson and Marc Blitzstein—who seem to have set us on our way toward having our own kind of operatic piece. I am not sure that what they have written is to be called opera, but it certainly is a form of musical drama that is thoroughly absorbing and attacks the primary operatic problem of the natural setting of English to music.

Except for their common interest in the operatic theater, Thomson and Blitzstein were poles apart. Virgil Thomson, the older of the two men, is about as original a personality as America can boast, in or out of the musical field. He comes from the Middle West—Kansas City, Missouri, to be exact; but long residence at Harvard and many years spent in Paris have made a thorough cosmopolite of him. As everyone knows, he leaped into sudden fame in 1934 with the success of his opera *Four Saints in Three Acts*, for which Gertrude Stein supplied the libretto. Since that time his talent as a writer has brought him into national prominence through his musical reviews, devastatingly clever and urbane, which appeared in the *New York Herald Tribune* for a period of fourteen years.

I have always found it difficult to convince my fellow musicians that Thomson is a man to be taken seriously as a composer. They usually adopt the attitude that what he writes may be amusing, but essentially that is all it is. Judged by the standards of the usual type of composer, with his imposing double fugues and triple concertos, I suppose Thomson's work may seem lacking in weightiness. But one must evaluate it not by conventional standards, but in terms of what he himself is trying to accomplish.

Thomson is a man with a thesis. Whether or not his own compositions really come off, his theory about music has validity for all of us. For a long time now, ever since the middle '20s, Thomson has maintained that so-called modern music is much too involved and pretentious in every way. While most composers of the musical left are busily engaged in inventing all sorts of new rhythmic and harmonic devices, intent upon being as original and different as possible, Thomson goes to the opposite extreme and deliberately writes music as ordinary as possible—so ordinary, in fact, that at first hearing it often strikes one as being merely foolish. But even if we agree that the music is sometimes foolish, the idea behind it is not so foolish. This idea is derived from the conviction that modern music has forgotten its audience almost completely, that the purpose of music is not to impress and overwhelm the listener but to entertain and charm him. Thomson seems determined to win adherents through music of an absolute simplicity and directness.

The relationship of this attitude to the Erik Satie aesthetic is, of course, immediately apparent. Thomson would be the first to admit it. But that does not render worthless the point of view or the music written from that point of view. As a matter of fact, Thomson's music does not particularly remind one of Satie's. Aside from an elementary simplicity, it is rather noncommittal in style. It impresses one principally with a feeling of thorough relaxation, with an apparent unconcern about any musical banalities that such relaxation may engender. It is essentially plain and simple music making, in which half the pleasure is derived from the natural, easy flow of the musical line. Thomson has little patience with the Teutonic idea of music as a tightly packed, neatly tied package. He likes a music less relentless in its logic, more free and unpredictable and easy.

There is no doubt that the Thomson theory works best—in his case at any rate—when applied to vocal composition. His chamber works, such as the Violin Sonata and the Second String Quartet, are not quite free from a certain artful sophistication. One can never entirely forget the *parti pris*. And in his relaxed manner he sometimes admits such utterly trifling material—old waltz tunes or *romances sans paroles*—as to make an entire movement seem like a stale joke. Thomson has made use of a great many different types of thematic materials—old hymn tunes, vocal exercises, Gregorian chants, Mozartean phrases, French chansons. Everything goes. When carried off with real flair, the general flow of the music makes one willing to overlook any momentary reminiscences. But by all odds they disturb one least in the vocal works.

This success is due, I feel sure, to Thomson's extraordinary felicity in the handling of the vocal text. His gift for allowing English to sound natural when sung is almost unique among American composers. We can all learn from him in this respect. His uncommonly acute sensitivity to the inner rhythm of English is evident, from the early *Five Phrases from the Song of Solomon* to the later Gertrude Stein songs. That he is no less sensitive to French is evident in his settings of that language, such as Max Jacob's *Stabat mater* and Bossuet's *Funeral Oration*. In all these settings of varied texts, Thomson maintains a remarkably high level of seriousness and rightness of musical feeling. There is never too much music in these songs. It is as if Thomson merely wished to draw a musical frame around the words. This very simplicity of the underlying musical urge is what permits the composer to put all stress on the exact setting of the rhythm of the language. Too much music would seem like an intrusion. Within these comparatively narrow limits in the musical background, one obtains a sense of freedom and variety and naturalness such as is rarely found in vocal settings, particularly in English.

The success of *Four Saints* was due partly to this kind of subtle and natural setting for Miss Stein's by no means simple text. Any other composer would have found the absence of literal meaning in the text a serious stumbling block. But Thomson employed an ingenious device in the handling of this problem: he gave the words their true speech inflections just as if their literal meaning were continuously understandable, while at the same time creating a musical scene that was crystal clear in its emotional intention. The trick lay in making his musical emotion entirely serious and entirely unambiguous in its purpose—practically without regard to the thing said. That is what gave the opera its amusement and charm. One must add also the inverted shock provided by Thomson's antimodernism. Swinging away from whatever might jar or confuse the ear, he wrote with a simplicity unprecedented among contemporary composers, often confining himself to the most rudimentary scales and harmonic progressions. There may be only a minimum of music in *Four Saints*, but out of this music, in combination with the unique costumes and stage setting (by Miss Florine Stettheimer), the all-Negro cast, the melodious prose of the libretto, and the fresh scenic action, an original theater work was created that made all other American musical stage pieces seem dull by comparison.

1967: In recent years Thomson has poured forth an impressive collection of works. Of different sizes and shapes, they are written for all sorts of occasions and combinations of performers. The mere listing of them in the Thomson biography covers twenty-three pages of small print. Among his best-known compositions are the second Stein-Thomson opera, *The Mother of Us All*, and the film scores for *Louisiana Story*, *The River*, and *The Plow That Broke the Plains*. Choral and orchestral works and dozens of songs and *pièces diverses* for solo piano and assorted instruments have also been added to his list of compositions. The production of such a cornucopia-full of music clearly implies a bountiful and purposeful and various gift. I like John Cage's comment: "[Thomson] expresses only those feelings he really has; at the same time"—Cage adds—"his attention does incline to move by means of joy and energy away from an inner emphasis to the outer world of nature, events, and people." One does get the impression that each work is written in a direct and "artless" way, without puzzlement or *arrière-pensée*—almost, I might add, without pretensions. In the end the evidence is conclusive: Virgil Thomson is a unique personality in the recent history of our music.

1941: Marc Blitzstein's talent as a writer for the stage developed slowly. In the very early part of his career he was something of a problem child. He seemed to have all the requisites for composing—talent, ability, technique—but somehow he had more difficulty than most composers in finding out exactly what he wanted to do. From time to time he wrote works destined for the stage, such as the unproduced ballet *Cain*, an unusually promising piece, and the light one-acter *Triple Sec*, which found production in a musical revue. But these were only incidental in a fairly long list of concert pieces, few of which actually reached the concert hall. The reason was that not many of them really came off in a way that one could thoroughly approve. Either a composition was too obviously derivative, or it tried too hard to be astonishing, or the style adopted was too rigidly abstract. It wasn't until Blitzstein began writing primarily for the stage that he really found himself.

His stage works belong to a category that is better called musical theater than opera. They are meant to be performed not by singers with trained voices, but by actors who can sing after a fashion. Consequently they have a reality as stage drama that opera usually lacks. At the same time there is a loss of the emotional range made possible in opera by the complete exploitation of that most expressive of all instruments, the human voice. As much as Blitzstein sacrificed in giving up the fullness and amplitude of the operatically trained voice he gained in the naturalness and charm of the singing actor. There is little likelihood that one will ever replace the other. I myself should not like to see the musical theater accepted as a substitute for opera. But it certainly brings us closer to a realization of that dream of an American grand opera.

Blitzstein's success as theatrical composer rests on three works: *The Cradle Will Rock*; *No for an Answer*; and *Regina*, based on Lillian Hellman's play *The Little Foxes*. He wrote, besides, an effective score for a half-hour radio opera called *I've Got the Tune*, scores for some documentary films, and incidental music for several straight dramas. In his work for the musical theater he had the inestimable advantage of being able to write his own texts. (You have to know how very rare good librettos are to appreciate what that means.) Most commentators are agreed that Blitzstein had an unusual flair for dialogue and lyrics but did less well in the construction of a tightly knit dramatic plot.

In his first full-length work for the stage, *The Cradle Will Rock*, Blitzstein was clearly influenced by Kurt Weill and Hanns Eisler. *The Three-Penny Opera* of Weill set the model: spoken dialogue interspersed with recitative and with more formal numbers such as solos, trios, and choruses. There is nothing new in the formula itself, for it is mostly a reversion to a pre-Wagnerian kind of opera—with these differences, however: the subject matter is entirely contemporaneous, the solos and concerted numbers are in the manner of popular songs rather than operatic arias and choruses, and the spoken dialogue and music are more evenly balanced. The whole is something of a cross between social drama, musical revue, and opera. Blitzstein was the first to apply this formula to an American stage work. Some of the tunes that he wrote still show the Weill or Eisler derivation, but they all have their own character—satirical, tender, bitter, or pessimistic. The prosody, which is subtle and complex, nevertheless has all the naturalness of hard-boiled English as sung in a jazz song—an accomplishment in itself. One innovation peculiar to Blitzstein was introduced: the musical sections, instead of being formally set with definite beginnings and endings, seem to start and finish casually, so that one is rarely conscious of where the music begins and the dialogue leaves off, or vice versa. Thus the general flow of the stage action is less likely to be cut up mechanically through the separation of speech and song.

Blitzstein brought with him from his experience as a concert composer all the formal discipline of the trained musician. He possessed a passionate love of design. One of the most striking characteristics of *The Cradle* is the extent to which every moment in the piece seems controlled. Nothing is left to chance. Every word in the text appears to have its set place in the dramatic web, just as in music a theme has its set place in the contrapuntal web. I mention this concern with structure with some emphasis because it was obviously one of Blitzstein's principal preoccupations and played a large part in any work he undertook.

No for an Answer is an advance on the first work in every way. For one thing it is closer to straight opera than *The Cradle*—there is more continuous singing. Then, too, the choral sections are enormously exciting. Here the lack of trained voices is least apparent. For once, the chorus seems to know what it is singing about, and this, combined with a directness and surety in the thing said, makes for a completely infectious enthusiasm. But perhaps Blitzstein's outstanding achievement is the fact that for the first time in a serious stage work he gives musical characterization to the typical American tough guy. Just imagine what it means to make a taxi driver sing so that the result sounds natural. In *No for an Answer* the composer has one of the little guys, in this case a panhandler, sing a song in accents so true as to make us feel that no one has ever before even attempted the problem of finding a voice for all those American regular fellows that seem so much at home everywhere except on the operatic stage. If the opera had nothing more than this to recommend it, its historical importance would be considerable.

With *No for an Answer* Blitzstein finally found his own musical style. You can recognize it in the short, clipped musical sentences, the uneven phrase lengths, the nervous energy, the unerring sense of design. There is subtle use of a talky prose rhythm over a musical background that is very personal to the composer. His melodic line as a rule, is straightforward, but the accompaniments may be exceedingly complex, though almost never obtrusive. Thus, the man in the gallery has a tune to hang onto, and the more erudite listener has added musical interest with which to occupy himself. His style, as musical theater, is always enormously effective, whether the mood is one of heart-sick yearning or punch-line sarcasm, social uplift or the dregs of dejection. It is a thoroughly malleable style that can be applied in the future to almost any subject matter.

This is important in view of the criticism leveled at *The Cradle Will Rock* and *No for an Answer* because they both are obviously works with a social message. The old cry of "propaganda" has been raised. I have purposely avoided a discussion of the so-called propaganda angle of Blitzstein's pieces, because it in no way invalidates their musical effectiveness, and this is primarily a book about music. But there is this to be said: every artist has the right to make his art out of an emotion that really moves him. If Blitzstein, like many other artists in every field, was moved to expression by the plight of the less privileged in their struggle for a fuller life, that was entirely his right. If these works fail in a certain sense, it is not because they are a form of propaganda art but because the propaganda is not couched in terms that make the pieces valid for audiences everywhere. They are not without a certain sectarianism that makes them come off best before a public that doesn't need to be won over to the author's point of view. This limits their circulation as works of art and therefore their effectiveness as propaganda. No doubt, it is not an easy matter to find a satisfactory solution for this knotty problem.

1967: Marc Blitzstein died in 1964. It is saddening to think that he is no longer working at his appointed task. And it is disheartening to realize how little the present generation knows who he was or what he accomplished. Ironically, his present-day fame rests largely on his talent as the translator of the Brecht-Weill *Three-Penny Opera*.

Anyone who followed the course of his career was bound to admire his courage. One must be almost doggedly foolish to mess with the musical theater in our world. This is especially true of a man like Blitzstein, who began as a child prodigy in Philadelphia, wrote much concert music in his teens and early twenties, and studied with teachers like Scalero, Boulanger, and Schoenberg—only to turn his attention to that most resistant of all media, the musical stage.

In the last two decades of his life, Blitzstein created only one work that held the boards for any length of time, his opera *Regina*. In the choral-orchestral field he composed the text and music for two longish works, *Symphony: The Airborne* (composed in London during the war years) and *This Is the Garden*, subtitled *A Cantata of New York*, 1956. Although the Symphony is the more successful of the two, both works are charged with a telling immediacy of musical effect, dissipated on occasion by banalities in the texts. Blitzstein could not resist a certain pleasure in needling his audiences, in telling unpleasant truths straight to their faces. To sing these truths, he thought, gave them even greater point. The moral fervor of these works, when they come off, is irresistible but when they don't, the effect is merely embarrassing. Nevertheless, despite weaknesses, both these cantatas deserve to be heard more often for the qualities they indubitably have.

In retrospect *Regina* must be rated one of Blitzstein's best works and one of the significant 20th-century American operas. Unlike *The Cradle Will Rock*, *Regina* is a real opera, composed for opera singers, not for singing actors. It has lyrical verve and convincing dramatic impact. The Hubbard family, with whom the story concerns itself, are an unsavory lot, but they provide the composer with an opportunity to demonstrate his gift for musical characterization—sarcastic, parodistic, even derisive if necessary; however, he could also be gentle, touching, and tragic. The work, to my mind, has two main drawbacks. First, although the composer fashioned his own libretto from Lillian Hellman's play, he was unable to overcome entirely the handicap of setting to music what is basically a spoken drama. Second, the injection into the music from time to time of a style derived from musical comedy has a jarring effect in scenes of high seriousness. In short, *Regina* is not without its blemishes, but on the stage the work retains a dramatic force that would seem to guarantee its future, at least in the realm of native opera.

Marc Blitzstein's life exemplifies a truism that bears restatement today: Every artist has the right to make his art out of an emotion that really moves him. Those of our composers who are moved by the immense terrain of new techniques now seemingly within their grasp would do well to remember that humanity's struggle for a fuller life may be equally valid as a moving force in the history of music.

Carlos Chávez (1928, 1968)

One of the strangest consequences of the Second World War has been the belated discovery that there is music to the south of us. Why it should have taken a war in Europe to arouse our curiosity concerning the serious composers of Latin America is hard to say. An active nucleus of composers has been functioning for some time in Brazil, Argentina, Mexico, Chile, and Uruguay. There are signs of nascent groups in Peru, Colombia, and Cuba. All portents seem to indicate that we are going to be busy for the next few years familiarizing ourselves with a host of strange-sounding names of composers and their compositions. But already two names stand out as neither strange nor unfamiliar: Heitor Villa-Lobos, of Brazil, and Carlos Chávez, of Mexico.

The music of Chávez has been known to some of us for more than a decade. He spent several years during the late '20s living and working in New York, and his earliest compositions were performed there at concerts of the International Composers' Guild. In a sense he belongs with the composers of the United States, for he owes much to our country, just as Thomson and Piston owe something to France. The efficacy of the good-neighbor policy needs no better proof than the music of this Mexican.

Carlos Chávez is one of the best examples I know of a thoroughly contemporary composer. His music embodies almost all the major traits of modern music: the rejection of Germanic ideals, the objectification of sentiment, the use of folk material in its relation to nationalism, the intricate rhythms, linear as opposed to vertical writing, the specifically "modern" sound images. It is music that belongs entirely to our own age. It propounds no problems, no metaphysics. Chávez's music is extraordinarily healthy. It is music created not as a substitute for living but as a manifestation of life. It is clear and clean-sounding, without shadows or softness. Here is contemporary music if ever there was any.

Chávez has always manifested an independent spirit in everything that he has done. It is characteristic that from the first he was unwilling to accept a teacher in harmony or counterpoint. He read the theory books for himself, compared them critically, re-examined the truth or falsity of their rules. With the autodidact's instinct he accepted nothing on hearsay. As a young man he invented his own simplified version of the conventional sign for the treble clef—a small point certainly, but indicative of his independent nature.

Chávez himself feels that he learned to compose principally by analyzing the works of the classic masters. Using these as models, he had already, before the age of twenty-one, produced a considerable number of works. Fully to appreciate his subsequent development, one must keep in mind the provincial Mexican musical background from which he emerged. Mexico, when he was a student, was a country virtually without serious composers of any importance, without organized orchestras, without even a musical season. No indigenous tradition of art music existed there—instead the Mexican musician of serious intentions was submerged in a German-conservatory atmosphere that was completely devoid of contact with any modern musical currents. Coming from this unpromising milieu, Chávez succeeded in forging a music that not only is his own but is recognizably Mexican. (Later he was to found and direct the only permanently functioning symphonic orchestra that Mexico ever had, and when for a short time he was head of the Mexican Conservatory, he gave that musty institution a thorough overhauling. More recently he was head of the National Institute of Fine Arts.)

One of the most interesting facets of Chávez's work is its Mexican-ness. There was every incentive in modern musical practice to encourage him to use the native tunes as the folklorist composer usually does. Mexico possesses a rich fund of indigenous material in the ritualistic music of the Mexican Indian. Little known even in Mexico, it was difficult to hear and had never been taken seriously by the professional musicians of the country. Chávez had visited the Indians each year, and knew and admired their music even before he himself had consciously thought of it as a possible basis for a typically Mexican music.

In 1921, however, Chávez composed his first Mexican ballet—*The New Fire*. For the first time he had looked away from Europe, turning to sources in his own country for inspiration. In this initial try, Chávez used his Indian themes literally, in much the same way that Falla had used Spanish themes in his ballets. After a three-year period of gestation, he wrote a series of three sonatinas—for violin and piano, cello and piano, and piano solo. The curious thing is that although no Indian melodies are quoted in these sonatinas, they possess a distinctly Mexican flavor. Chávez had managed to digest and rethink the material so that only its essence remained. The piano sonatina is the most characteristic of the group. It is refreshing, original music with a kind of hard charm and distinctive Indo-American doggedness. Here and there perhaps a recognizably native turn of phrase can be discerned, but as a whole the folk element has been replaced by a more subtle sense of national characteristics.

This is an important point in understanding the more mature works of this composer. As Debussy and Ravel reflected the clarity, the delicacy, and the wit of the French spirit without recourse to French folklore, so Chávez had learned to write music that caught the spirit of Mexico—its naïve, stolid, *mestizo* soul. It is a curious fact that he should have been able in his more recent work to alternate and combine the two kinds of nationalism represented, respectively, by the French and Russian schools. Thus, with keen intuition, singlehandedly he has created a tradition that no future Mexican composer can afford to ignore. If I stress this point it is because I feel that no other composer—not even Béla Bartók or Falla—has succeeded so well in using folk material in its pure form while also solving the problem of its complete amalgamation into an art form.

It is easy to see the difference between these two kinds of treatment by comparing two of the composer's best-known orchestral works, the *Sinfonía India* and the *Sinfonía de Antigona*. Both are unmistakably Chávez, and both are unmistakably Mexican, yet the Indian symphony is a medley of delightful native tunes, whereas the *Antigona* suite is entirely free of any Mexican source material. This same double-barreled trait is characteristic of other pieces that bear the indelible mark of the composer yet at the same time reflect many of the usual modern trends. I am thinking of the symbolic machine-age music at the end of his ballet *HP* (*Horse Power*), of the piano pieces *Blues* and *Fox*, of the urban popular music in the *Huapango* section of *HP*, and of the re-creations of an imagined Aztec music in the *Xochipilli-Macuilxochitl*. All this music veritably breathes personality, leaving the listener with an impression of absolute clarity and sharpness of outline.

Certain of the Chávez works are perhaps almost too personal. At first or even second hearing, they are likely to seem hermetic and inaccessible to anyone but a Chávez adept like myself. The Piano Sonata (1928), for example, which I have always considered a fine work, thoroughly characteristic of the composer, has rarely been performed. Its four movements are no doubt too continuously taut, too highly condensed for common consumption. It contains a profusion of short melodic germs, none of which is developed in the conventional manner. The piano writing is thin and hard, without lushness of timbre. The general style is contrapuntal, with sudden unexpected mixtures of acid dissonances and bright, clear unisons. There is a certain down-rightness about the whole work that seems to imply, "This is how it is, and you can either like it or leave it."

Something of the same quality occurs also in a later work, the Sonata for Four Horns. It is impossible to imagine a more personal piece of music. There is that same obstinacy of purpose, the same will to write down music exactly as he hears it, without compromising one iota with the public taste. They are superbly Mexican in quality, these pieces, but Mexican-Indian—stoic, stark, and somber, like an Orozco drawing.

It is paradoxical but true that in his own country Chávez is sometimes reproached for not being Mexican enough. This is usually said when his music is contrasted with that of Silvestre Revueltas, whose untimely death robbed Mexico of a very gifted composer. It was Chávez who induced his colleague Revueltas to write his earliest orchestral works, and it was Chávez who gave their premières with his orchestra. Revueltas was the spontaneously inspired type of composer, whose music is colorful, picturesque, and gay. Unfortunately, he never was able to break away from a certain dilettantism that makes even his best compositions suffer from sketchy workmanship. Certain circles in Mexico are anxious to prove that in comparison with the music of Revueltas, with its natural spontaneity, that of Chávez is essentially cold and cerebral. But I see absolutely no need to choose here. It is not a question of Chávez *or* Revueltas, as at one time it was thought to be a question of Wagner *or* Brahms. We can have both men and their music for exactly what each is worth to us. In my own mind there is no doubt whatever that Chávez is the more mature musician in every way.

In recent years, Chávez's activities as conductor and animator of musical life in Mexico have seriously limited his output as composer. A newly completed piano concerto, a long and serious work, would indicate, however, that the composer has no intention of allowing these interruptions to be anything more than temporary. Whatever the future holds in the way of new and unexpected works from his pen, he has already written enough to place him among the very few musicians in the Western Hemisphere who can be described as more than a reflection of Europe. We in the United States, who have long desired musical autonomy, know best what that means. We cannot borrow from so rich a melodic source as Chávez has at hand, perhaps, or lose ourselves in an ancient civilization, but we have been stimulated and instructed, nonetheless, by his example. As for Chávez's work itself, it is becoming more and more generally recognized that here we have one of the first authentic signs of a New World with its own new music.

1967: Now entering his late sixties, Carlos Chávez has discontinued his former activities as animator of Mexico's musical life. He divides his time between composition and guest appearances as conductor and teacher in various parts of the world. His style of composition has changed comparatively little, except that specific national references no longer occur in his music. Their absence makes surprisingly little difference in the overall effect, since the *ambiente* remains pure Chávez, nonetheless. One detects an increasingly didactic strain, which takes on two opposing aspects. In certain works he remains what he was—a bold and lucid inventor of new sonorities. His recent *Resonancias*, for example, composed on commission for the opening of the National Archeological Museum in Chapultepec, has nothing of the *pièce d'occasion* about it. Instead, Chávez assaults the ear with sonorities that exploit the extremes of high and low in all the instruments. He is not showing off, he is rather testing his imagination in regard to the sonic possibilities of unusual instrumental combinations and deliberately chosen harmonic tensions. On the other hand, in his symphonies, of which there are four additions (his Third, Fourth, Fifth, and Sixth), a marked classicizing tendency is evident. Long, firmly-shaped, tonal melodies propulsively sing themselves out against counterpointed melodies in bass and inner voices. Chávez writes generously; sometimes the sheer welter of notes thrown at the listener without letup or pause (in the Piano Concerto, for example) is simply overwhelming. But then, Chávez has never been a "comfortable" composer; his music has often been strewn with *inconvenientes* for both the listener and the executant. Whatever the style, harsh or mellifluous, it is the music of a personality, one of the most striking of our time.

Stefan Wolpe (1948)

In the welter of musical activity in America the publication of two more songs would seem to make little difference one way or another. But these songs (Two Songs for Alto and Piano from the *Song of Songs*) are exceptional. They draw attention to the work of Stefan Wolpe, one of the most remarkable of living composers. And they draw attention also to the venturesome Hargail Music Press, to whom we are indebted for more than one unlikely publication.

America doesn't seem to know what to do with strong talents like Wolpe. If his music were less grimly serious, less stark, less uncompromising, it would undoubtedly fare better in the musical market place. Although Wolpe has been composing and teaching among us for the past decade (he arrived here from Germany via Palestine about 1939), only a small group of professionals and pupils have come to know his value. To me Wolpe's music is strikingly original, with a kind of fiery inner logic that makes for fascinated listening. Some pounding natural force brings it forth and gives it reality. It is a sad commentary on the state of our musical house that this man must create in comparative isolation. Wolpe is definitely someone to be discovered.

These two compositions for alto and piano, with text from the *Song of Songs*, are part of a larger series of Palestinian songs. Wolpe has put the essence of himself in these songs in something of the same way that *Das Marienleben* contains in microcosm the essence of Hindemith. They are intensely alive, deeply Jewish, and very personal. The first of the two alto songs is especially characteristic: the curiously restless rhythmic structure, the bareness and severity of the two-part piano accompaniment, the fresh flavorsome quality of the folklike melodic line. By comparison, the second song is less arresting, though it is by ordinary standards nobly expressive. Both songs demand superior interpreters. They make one keenly anticipate the publication of the remainder of Wolpe's Palestinian songs.

Benjamin Britten (1963)

One thing that growing old denies one is the kind of camaraderie that creative youngsters share at the start of their careers. This is particularly true in music where the line between young and old is often sharply drawn. Young composers need one another for they learn more from the attentive eye and sensitive ear of a fellow-craftsman than from almost any other source. Long before one is afforded the luxury of hearing one's own orchestration in actual sound there is the possibility that a young colleague will "hear" it for you. Peering at the same four measures of orchestral score for fifteen minutes, carefully weighing the pros and cons of instrumental balance while you wait with bated breath, your composer friend is likely to come up with some completely unexpected judgement such as you never would have thought of yourself.

It is this kind of composer rapport that I connect with a visit to Snape a quarter of a century ago. Despite my usually stumbling memory, I can still recall the weekend I spent there and the excitement of exchanging ideas with a new-found composer friend, twenty-four year old Benjamin Britten.

We had only recently come to know one another at a concert of the International Society for Contemporary Music. The 1938 International Festival was being held in London that year and I had come from America to hear Sir Adrian Boult give the European premiere of my *El Salón México*. A few days before that performance, I had heard my first Britten piece, the *Variations on a Theme of Frank Bridge*. My delight at the technical adroitness and instrumental wizardry of that early composition is still vivid in my memory. Perhaps the fact that we were both represented by the lighter side of our wares drew us together. In any event, our chance meeting had the happy result for me of an invitation to Snape where the young composer was living at that time.

The address I was given had an air of quaint charm, at least, for an American it had: The Old Hill – Snape – Saxmundham – Suffolk. And the places themselves, both old mill and village, were no less charming and quaint. I hadn't realized before my arrival that we were in East Anglia, nor had I any idea of Britten's strong attachment to his home territory. His studio in a converted tower of the old mill was in strong contrast to the loft studio I had in my own home territory of New York. Our backgrounds and circumstances were clearly different, but the affinity of our musical interests was soon apparent.

Taking advantage of a sunny spell, we spent a day with some family and friends on the nearby shingle. (Why have we no shingle in America?) Before long it became clear that the assembled group was in danger of becoming "roasted." When I politely pointed out the obvious result to be expected from lying unprotected on the shingle, I was told: "But we see the sun so rarely."

What I remember best, of course, was the exchange of musical impressions of all sorts. I had with me the proofs of my school opera, *The Second Hurricane*, composed for young people of 14 to 17. It had been performed the previous year for the first time by a group of talented students at a Lower East Side settlement school in New York. It didn't take much persuasion to get me to play it from start to finish, singing all the parts of principals and chorus in the usual composer fashion. Britten seemed pleased. Sometimes I flatter myself that his subsequent preoccupation with young voices may have been in part an offshoot of his pleasure in *The Second Hurricane*. Occasionally I've even had the illusion of hearing an echo of one of the choruses of the opera ("What's happened, Where are they?") in a fleeting moment of a Britten work. Illusion or no, I like to think of it as a souvenir of Snape.

In return for the playing of the opera, Britten played me his recently completed Piano Concerto No. 1. I was immediately struck by the obvious flair for idiomatic piano writing in the Concerto, but had some reservations as to the substance of the musical materials being used. Here was a delicate moment: I felt my enthusiasm was half-hearted by comparison with his own. As it turned out, I had no need for concern; if anything, my frankly expressed opinion helped to cement our growing friendship. (For the record, it should be added that what I heard was a first version of the Piano Concerto; it was revised by the composer seven years later.)

Less than a year after this visit, Britten was on his way to North America. Perhaps our meeting in Snape had some part in his decision to try his luck abroad. In any case, it is certain that the few years he spent in America were deeply formative ones. They will have to be studied in depth by anyone who wishes to follow the steady growth in stature of this greatly gifted composer and warm friend.

Elliott Carter (1971)

Long a member of the American Academy of Arts and Letters, Copland was frequently enlisted to present AAAL awards to his colleagues.

Fifty-two years ago, in 1919, the Institute awarded its first Gold Medal for musical composition to Charles Martin Loeffler. In all that time only seven other composers have been so honored. Elliott Carter richly deserves having his name added to that choice roster.

Most composers hit their stride fairly early. Elliott Carter was an exceptional case. He had reached the age of forty before he began producing music that aroused special attention. Since then, during the past twenty years, he has gradually produced a body of work so original in conception and so imaginative in execution that we can proudly point to it as among the finest examples of musical creation that we in America have—or that any other country has.

How did he do it? That's his secret. All I can tell you is that he writes a music that is unlike that of any other composer on the contemporary scene. It reflects a rare combination of heart and brain: the man of feeling and the man of intellect. Its inventive ingenuity and its complexity of musical thought are something very special. Other composers may create a polyphony of musical lines, but Carter creates a polyphony of musical thoughts. He has a remarkable gift for interlacing a multiplicity of musical ideas for expressive purposes that are peculiarly his own.

His virtuoso handling of the rhythmic aspects of music has often been pointed out. Here again there is nothing quite like it in other men's music. Carter's way with rhythms has come to be known as "metrical modulation," by which is meant a simultaneity of rhythms, each one moving ahead at its own pace without in any way encroaching on the rhythmic independence of its neighbor. To conceive such a notion is one thing; to carry it out with the clarity and imagination of Carter's rhythmic sensibility is a major achievement.

But perhaps I am overstressing Carter's always conscious control of his musical materials. The curious fact is that despite the element of conscious control, the overall impression his music makes is often delightfully improvisatory in effect. He himself has described his music, and rightfully so I think, as dealing with "the poetry of change, transformation, reorientation of feelings and thoughts, and gradual shifts of emphases." In accomplishing this aim, he has kept himself free from the restraints of the fashions of contemporary music. Moreover, in so doing, he has developed a musical language that has served as a liberating force for the younger composers of today, opening up for them whole new areas of musical exploration.

As you see, there is good reason to hold Elliott Carter in highest regard. He is without question a leading force in the music of the seventies. It is, therefore, a great pleasure and honor for me, as colleague and friend, to present to him, in the name of the Institute, its highest award, The Gold Medal for Musical Composition.

William Kapell[1] (1954)

Dear Anna Lou: When a dear friend is lost to us we try to bring some solace to the nearest of kin by writing a letter. Many thousands of music-lovers in many parts of the world must have felt that impulse when they learned of your husband's tragic end on October 29. I too had that impulse, and writing you this letter my hope is that I may possibly express some of the things that are certainly in the hearts of William Kapell's many admirers.

When I think of Willie I think of him as having been above all else the personification of the artist. Except for yourself and the children, I never recall discussing anything but music with him. The singleness of his passion for the art we both loved was almost frightening, even to a composer like myself. It was as if the sound of music created a hypnotic spell about him—and whether it was sound made by himself or sound listened to made little essential difference. When music was heard nothing else mattered. I know that this is said to be true for most musicians, but for the most part that is a pleasant fiction; in Willie's case it was quite literally true. As you well know, to him a house without a piano was no better than an empty shell; to find himself in a situation where no piano was within easy reach was physically intolerable. In that connection he more than once reminded me of George Gershwin—seeing either of them in a room where there was a piano meant that sooner or later the man and the instrument would meet.

All this has little significance compared with the way in which William was profoundly the artist, both in his very nature and in the symbolic role he was fated to play in the concert world. The artist in him was startlingly evident in his person and in his performing gift: he was passionate, intense,

---

[1]William Kapell died in an airplane accident in 1953.

restless, devoted, in love with perfection as a goal, forever striving toward that goal—straining toward it, even. At times his friends must have seemed inadequate and distant to him, for the force and drive of his temperament were such as necessarily to make him dissatisfied when confronted with the signs of sweet reasonableness. His questioning and demanding spirit gave off sparks of a youthfulness that never left him. Willie, if he had lived, would always have remained a youthful artist, in the best sense of that term. The search for artistic growth, the ideal of maturity was a central and continuing preoccupation with him. Emerson once wrote that the artist is "pitiful." He meant, I suppose, that the true artist can never be entirely satisfied with the work he does. William Kapell was that kind of true artist.

And yet he was among the few top pianists of our time. Why? What qualities were particularly his? There were brilliance and drama in his playing, songfulness and excitement. On the platform he had the fire and abandon that alone can arouse audiences to fever pitch. He knew his power, and I have no doubt was sometimes frightened by it. The big public can be a potential menace, after all; it can elicit the best and the worst from the artist. Characteristically, when playing on the stage, Willie often turned his head away from the auditorium, the better to forget us, I imagine. Nevertheless, even when most lost within himself, he instinctively projected his playing into the hall, for he was indubitably the performer. I cannot conceive of his ever having given a dull performance—an erratic one perhaps, a misguided or stylistically incongruous one maybe, but invariably one that was electric and alive.

We both know that he was, at times, an easy target for the reviewers of the daily press. He exaggerated their importance, ignored the good things said, and remembered only the bad. I always took this to be a measure of his own seriousness. The successful performer of today cannot plead ignorance of his own playing. He has the recorded disc for mirror. Willie knew better than anyone when he was in top form; to be unjustly evaluated after such performances pained and tortured him. Unlike the composer in a similar position, he could not expect justification from posterity. No wonder he was unusually nervous before stepping on the platform. Like every basically romantic artist, he never could predict what was about to happen on the stage, but on the other hand the satisfaction of an outstanding performance must have been enormous.

I shall always treasure the thought of William's deep attachment to my own music. He never tired of telling me what my music meant to him, and I, on my part, never ceased being surprised at the intensity of his feeling for it. What was most surprising was his fondness for the most forbidding aspects of my music; he repeatedly played precisely those pieces that his audiences were least likely to fathom. He played them with a verve and grandeur and authority that only a front-rank pianist is able to bring to unfamiliar music. He played them, I often felt, in a spirit of defiance: defiance of managers with their cautious notions of what was right and fitting for a Kapell program; defiance of the audience that had come to hear him in works from the regular repertoire; played them, one might almost say, in defiance of his own best interests. In actuality I believe he played them in order to satisfy a deep need—the need every artist has to make connection with the music of his own time. I am touched and moved at the thought of the high regard in which he held them. His programming of new music was an act of faith; it was Willie's contribution toward a solution of one of the most disturbing factors in our musical life: namely, the loss of connection between the performer and the contemporary composer of his own time.

When William died he was expecting a new piano work from my pen. It was a promise I had gladly given him. It is a promise I intend to keep, and when the work is written I can only hope that it will be worthy of the best in William Kapell.

My love and sympathy are with you.

Ralph Hawkes (1950)

Copland's obituary for Ralph Hawkes, of his long-time publisher Boosey &
Hawkes, reflects his warm appreciation for people in every aspect of his life,
even in the most thankless roles. (S.S.)

Ralph Hawkes, of London and New York, for many years an outstanding
figure in the world of music, died suddenly on Friday morning, September
8th, at his home in Westport, Connecticut, at the age of 52.

Born in London on August 18, 1898, the son of Oliver and Amelia Hay-
man Hawkes, he has spent a major portion of the past five years in the United
States. Mr. Hawkes, whose career was closely identified with both New York
and London, was the Senior Director of Boosey & Hawkes, Ltd., international
music publishers with head offices in London, and has been an active member of the Board of Directors of each of the firm's branches throughout the
world—Toronto, Buenos Aires, Capetown, Paris, Bonn, Sydney, New York,
and London. At the time of his death he was president of the American firm,
Boosey & Hawkes, Inc., in New York with offices in Chicago and Los Angeles.

He has also been prominent in the field of musical instrument manu-
facture from an early age and was on the Board of Directors of Hawkes &
Son (London) Ltd., founded by William Henry Hawkes, prior to 1850.
Ralph Hawkes, with Leslie Boosey, of Boosey & Co., was a major force in
the amalgamation of these two internationally known family businesses,
prominent among England's musical firms—thus forming in the early
1930s, Boosey & Hawkes, Ltd.

For many years a member of the Board of Directors of the Performing
Right Society Ltd. of England, Mr. Hawkes was appointed their personal
representative for the United States and Canada.

Mr. Hawkes has been a leading pioneer in the field of contemporary
music and a strong force not only in publishing the works of contemporary composers, but also in organized movements for the protection of the

composers' interests. Perhaps the most outstanding example of his recognition and support of creative talent is Benjamin Britten, who at the age of 21 first came to the attention of Mr. Hawkes. Since that time Britten's career has been closely allied with that of Mr. Hawkes and his publishing houses. Among the many outstanding composers represented by his firm are Béla Bartók, Arthur Benjamin, Aaron Copland, Frederick Delius, Zoltán Kodály, Gustav Mahler, Bohuslav Martinů, Walter Piston, Serge Prokofieff, Serge Rachmaninoff, Igor Stravinsky, and Richard Strauss; for during the last decade he has built, from a number of sources, one of the world's greatest symphonic and operatic catalogues. Under his aegis have been brought together the musical properties of Edition Russe de Musique and Edition Gutheil (originally formed by Serge and Natalie Koussevitzky), Furstner Ltd., and several of the leading composers from the Universal Editions, Vienna catalogue.

Through the efforts of Ralph Hawkes and his brother, Geoffrey, the scope of instrument manufacturing activities of the firm has been steadily enlarged until today it is the biggest manufacturer of musical instruments outside of the United States.

In 1945, Mr. Hawkes, with his partner, Leslie Boosey, secured on behalf of Boosey & Hawkes, Ltd., the lease for the Royal Opera House, Covent Garden in London, so that it might be available once again, and restored to its international position in the world of Opera and Ballet. Covent Garden was thus spared from the fate of continued use as the public dance hall for which it had been leased during the war.

The ballet-loving public will forever be indebted to Mr. Hawkes for his initiative which is responsible for the presence of the Sadler's Wells Company for their first tour in the United States and Canada last year, and their five-month tour which is now opening at the Metropolitan Opera House.

He was known as a keen sportsman and yachtsman, winning many of the International Ocean Races with his yacht, the *Firebird*. Other famous boats he raced were the *Crests* and *Blue Marlin*. In his younger days he was active in winter sports and was several times a member of the winning bobsled team on the famous Crests Run at St. Moritz.

VI
His Own Works

Over the years, Copland frequently wrote short notes on his own pieces—sometimes for concert programs; other times for the score's publication; yet other times for record sleeves. Notes initially written for one purpose were often used on other occasions. Since the original source and date of some of the following notes is hard to identify securely, the credit lines refer to the texts published here. In cases where more than one set of comments exist for a piece, both sets are included, slight repetitions notwithstanding. The notes appear in the order that Copland composed the pieces, with an alphabetical index appended below. The absence of dates for some notes indicates a lack of information about when Copland initially wrote each of his comments. (S.S.)

Alphabetical List of Compositions

Appalachian Spring (1944)
Billy the Kid (1938)
Concerto for Clarinet and String Orchestra with Harp and Piano (1948)
Concerto for Piano and Orchestra (1926)
Connotations (1962)
Dance Panels (1959, rev. 1962)
Dance Symphony (1925)
Danzón Cubano I & II (1942)
Emblems (1964)
Fanfare for the Common Man (1942)
Inscape (1967)
Lincoln Portrait (1942)
Midday Thoughts (1944, finished 1982)
Music for a Great City (1964)
Music for Movies (1942)

Music for the Theatre I & II (1925)
Orchestral Variations (1957)
An Outdoor Overture (1938)
Piano Fantasy I & II (1957)
Proclamation (1973–1982, arranged 1985)
The Red Pony (1948)
El Salón México (1936)
Sextet (1937)
Something Wild (1961)
Statements (1934)
Symphony for Organ and Orchestra (1924)
Third Symphony (1946)
Three Latin American Sketches (1959–1972)
12 Poems of Emily Dickinson (1950)
Two Pieces for String Orchestra (1928)
Variations on a Shaker Melody (1956)

Symphony for Organ and Orchestra

These notes about Symphony for Organ and Orchestra appear on the sleeve of an LP on CBS. (S.S.)

The organ is treated as an integral part of the orchestra rather than as a solo instrument with orchestral accompaniment; yet, it always remains very much in the foreground.

The three movements of the Symphony are loosely connected by a recurrent motto based on tones of the minor triad. Unlike most musical mottoes, however, it is not immediately recognizable as such. At first it plays a seemingly inconsequential part as mere accompaniment, but as the work progresses its real significance is made clear.

(I. *Prelude: Andante* $\frac{6}{8}$) The first movement, or *Prelude*, is quite short and bears no relation to the traditional first movement of a symphony. It is rather an introductory reverie for the organ, with some incidental material for solo instruments of the orchestra. Its formal structure is very simple: there is but one theme, announced by the organ, which recurs several times after slight episodic digressions.

(II. *Scherzo: Allegro molto* $\frac{3}{4}$; *Moderato* $\frac{4}{4}$) In the first section of the *Scherzo* two themes are exposed, the first by the oboe, the second—of a more sustained character—by the organ, with imitations by the strings. A climax of the full orchestra is gradually effected, giving free play to what was originally the oboe theme. This is suddenly interrupted by the motto announced by a solo horn and imitated by a trumpet. A repetition by bassoon and flute leads to the middle section. (*Moderato* $\frac{4}{4}$) This is a solo for the organ except for the occasional references by the clarinet to the first theme of the movement. Suddenly, without warning, all the brass bursts in, and the repetition of the first section is engendered in slightly modified form. A short coda brings the movement to a close, *fortissimo*.

(III. *Finale: Lento; Allegro moderato* $\frac{4}{4}$) The *Finale* corresponds to the usual first movement of a symphony, being cast approximately in sonata form. Without any introduction, the first theme is given out in unison by the violas. The first three notes of this theme are the first three notes of the motto. This motive is immediately worked up into a *stretto* by all the strings, then by the trumpets and trombones, and, finally, the organ, *con tutta forza*. The entrance of the kettledrum (*Allegro moderato*) brings with it the second, more vigorous, theme, played by violins and violas on the G string over a double-bass pizzicato accompaniment, which is nothing more than the motto used as a *basso ostinato*. There follows an episode, *fortissimo*, for organ and orchestra, based on a fragment of the second theme. This brings a sudden quieting down, when, over the same relentless *basso ostinato*, there is a contrapuntal interweaving of themes by oboe, English horn, and violas. In the midst of this passage, the organ enters unobserved, but with a gradual crescendo assumes increasing importance, until, at the climax of the exposition section, it chants the second theme *fortissimo*, against the motto, in augmentation, in trumpets and trombones.

What might be termed the development section begins with a solo for the organ. As counterpoint, the solo violin evolves from the motto a new, vivacious theme which later plays an important part. The development is not very long. It merges imperceptibly into the recapitulation, which in this case is merely a final simultaneous announcement of the four main elements of the *Finale*. The Symphony ends with a brief coda.

Music for the Theatre I

Copland's notes about *Music for the Theatre* appear on the sleeve of an LP on Columbia. (S.S.)

The composer had no play or literary idea in mind. The title simply implies that, at times, this music has a quality which is suggestive of the theater.

I. Prologue (*Molto moderato*, $\frac{2}{4}$). The first theme is announced almost immediately by the solo trumpet. Shortly, this gives way to the entrance of the strings, who gradually form a background for the oboe singing the second theme. A short development follows (allegro molto), built upon a transformation of the first trumpet theme. After a quickly attained climax, there is a return to the first part and a quiet close.

II. Dance (*Allegro molto*, $\frac{5}{8}$). This is a short, nervous dance, with form and thematic material so simple as to make analysis superfluous.

III. Interlude (*Lento*, $\frac{4}{4}$). The Interlude is a kind of "song without words," built on a lyric theme which is repeated three times, with slight alterations. The English horn solo plays an introductory phrase, and then to an accompaniment of strings, piano, and glockenspiel, the main theme is sung by a clarinet.

IV. Burlesque (*Allegro vivo*, $\frac{3}{8}$). The form of this movement is best expressed by the formula A-B-A-B. For the rest, this Burlesque is best explained by its title.

V. Epilogue (*Molto moderato*, $\frac{4}{4}$). No new themes are introduced here. Material from the first and third parts only is used. The quiet mood of the Prologue is recaptured and the work ends *pianissimo*.

II

Certain pieces have careers of their own, independent or the lives of their authors. The *Valse Triste* of Sibelius or the *Andante Cantabile* of Tchaikovsky are cases in point. It would be interesting to know what sent these two pieces on their phenomenal way. Invidious comparisons aside, I have sometimes wondered what made conductors choose *Music for the Theatre* more frequently than any other piece of mine.

I strongly suspect that it may partly be explained by the jazz content in several of the movements. When this work was written Gershwin's *Rhapsody in Blue* was a mere infant two years old, and Darius Milhaud's ballet, *The Creation of the World*, was practically unknown in this country. Jazz in the concert hall, in those pre-Benny [Goodman] days, was frowned upon as plain sacrilege. Any piece based on the jazz idiom was assured of a mild *succes de scandale*, and *Music for the Theatre* was no exception.

The composition was written in 1925 at the behest of the League of Composers, and Serge Koussevitzky introduced it at a special League concert in Town Hall, New York. The critics of the local press were less than pleased. Mr. Olin Downes of the *Times*, gave a conservative estimate of the critical reaction when he wrote: "we do not care if a long time elapses before we listen again to *Music for the Theatre*." Mr. Koussevitzky promptly decided that the piece had been misunderstood, and braving the wrath of the critical fraternity, brought it back to town for a second hearing two months later—this time as a regular part of a Boston Symphony program at Carnegie Hall. The reaction, I am happy to say, this time was better; and Mr. Koussevitzky continued to program *Music for the Theatre* from time to time in places as far apart as Brooklyn, New York and Paris, France. In 1933 he conducted it at one of Mrs. Elizabeth Sprague Coolidge's annual festivals in Washington, and in 1938 he chose it as the first American piece to be played at the Berkshire Symphonic Festival.

In fairness to Mr. Downes, and as proof that he isn't afraid to change his mind, I think I should quote from his review of the Washington performance: "In 1925 or 1926, when first heard, this music impressed the writer as ultra modern to the point of affectation. Today he feels that this is music of genuine inspiration and feeling, music composed and not merely invented, that it has personal color, fancy and, in the best moments, emotion . . ." etc.

The Paris performance stands out in my mind because of an incident that involved the well known French composer, Florent Schmitt, who was equally well known for his sharp-tongued wit. After the concert was over he came to me and said reproachfully. "See here, Monsieur Copland, what is the meaning of this? If you Americans begin now to export music instead of merely importing it, where will we poor French composers be?"

The following year *Music for the Theatre* was one of two works chosen to represent the United States at the International Festival of Contemporary Music which was held in Frankfort. It was cruel to watch these honest German musicians confronted with jazz rhythms for the first time in their lives. I played the piano part myself in that performance, and during the intermission periods at rehearsals the men used to gather round the piano to get first-hand advice on how to manage these new American rhythms.

Another rehearsal of *Music for the Theatre* left a distinctive impression. This time the scene was New York, and Walter Damrosch was at the conductor's desk. Since Dr. Damrosch had never made any secret of his antipathy to so-called modern music, I was surprised and rather flattered at the programming of my work, fancying that perhaps, unknown to myself, I had made a convert. But this illusion was short-lived. One day, when the good doctor spied me at a rehearsal, he stopped the orchestra abruptly on an astringent chord that obviously disturbed him, and turning to me said: "Must that chord be that way?" I stood my ground with all the temerity of youth and firmly replied: "Yes, Dr. Damrosch, that's the way that chord must be." But the conductor had his revenge in the end, for when the concert was announced the advance sheets read: New York Symphony Orchestra, Walter Damrosch conductor, presents a Program of Modern Music—Pleasant and Unpleasant.

The term modern music no longer holds the same terrors it ones did: most people nowadays think of music as good or bad and let it go at that. Personally, I like to think of *Music for the Theatre* as a *jugend-werk*, with all that that implies of youthful enthusiasm and unhackneyed ideas. No doubt this is the fond illusion of a doting parent. At any rate, now that the work is available on wax, record buyers can judge for themselves.

Dance Symphony

The *Dance Symphony* is divided into three distinct units. However, a thin wisp of transitional material connects them, and the movements must be played without any separating pauses. There is no thematic relationship between the movements.

There is a short, slow introduction, whereupon the first movement (Allegro) breaks out softly with a light, precise little motive on the bassoon, accompanied by plucked violins. The oboe continues the motive, slightly altered, as more fiddles pluck. The harp comes in to help with the plucking, then the clarinet continues a derivative of the little motive. There are further derivatives; presently the flute sings a flowing strain which might be regarded as a new motive. The plucking keeps up in some form, on fiddles or harp, throughout the entire movement, except for a few spots where the piano is substituted. A climax is worked up, at the summit of which the movement ends.

The second movement begins, with a gentle melody prominently limned by the English horn over a bass in which the bass clarinet swings persistently from one of two notes to the other. Other woodwinds help develop the melody. Another melody ensues which violins and violas announce softly in canon to harp accompaniment. The first melody is developed into a great climax in which the second melody joins.

If the first movement is thin, dainty, and pointed, the second movement is songful and sustained. The third movement is characterized by violence and syncopation. Its initial jazzy motive can be heard *fortissimo* on the woodwinds, percussively reinforced by the piano, while violins, English horn, and xylophone execute a sustained trill. A second motive soon starts *fortissimo* on the low strings and trombones. A figure of reiterated notes also assumes prominence. There is an extended development of all the material. An amusing interruption occurs: the notes of the initial motive appear masquerading as an exaggeratedly languishing waltz. At the very end, all the motives are blazoned forth at once.

Concerto for Piano and Orchestra

Though played without interruption, the Concerto [for Piano and Orchestra] is really divided into two contrasted parts, which are linked thematically. The first is a slow, lyric section, the second a fast rhythmic one.

A short orchestral introduction announces the principal thematic material. The piano enters quietly and improvises around this for a short space, then the principal theme is sung by a flute and clarinet in unison over an accompaniment of muted strings. This main idea recurs twice during the course of the movement—once in the piano with imitations by the woodwind and French horns, and later in triple canon in the strings, mounting to a sonorous climax.

A few transitional measures lead directly to the second part which, roughly speaking, is in sonata form without recapitulation. The first theme, announced immediately by the solo piano, is considerably extended and developed before the second idea is introduced by a soprano saxophone. The development, based entirely on these two themes, contains a short piano cadenza presenting difficulties of a rhythmic nature. Before the end, a part of the first movement is recalled. This is followed by a brief coda.

Two Pieces for String Orchestra

The sleeve of a Columbia LP with Copland conducting contains notes for Two Pieces for String Orchestra (below) and *An Outdoor Overture*. (S.S.)

These Two Pieces were originally composed for string quartet. In that form they were first performed by the Lenox String Quartet on May 6, 1928, at the second of the Copland-Sessions Concerts of Contemporary Modern Music, in New York. I transcribed them for string orchestra during the summer of 1928 at the MacDowell Colony, and this version was first performed by the Boston Symphony Orchestra, Serge Koussevitzky conducting, at Symphony Hall, Boston, on December 14, 1928. A five-year interval separated the composition of these Two Pieces. The first (Lento molto) was completed in New York in April 1928, while the second (Rondino) was written in Paris in 1923. The form of both pieces is too simple to require analysis. The notes of the principal theme of the Rondino were designed to spell the name of Gabriel Fauré.

These Two Pieces are dedicated to Roy Harris.

Statements

The London Symphony Orchestra performs *Statements* and *Music for a Great City* on a CBS LP, which contains notes on its sleeve about both of these pieces. (S.S.)

Statements was commissioned by the League of Composers for performance by the Minneapolis Symphony Orchestra. I spent the summer of 1934 vacationing at Lake Bemidji in northern Minnesota, where I sketched in several of the movements. The orchestration was completed in New York City in June 1935. Two movements (the fifth and sixth) were first played by the Minneapolis Symphony Orchestra under Eugene Ormandy's direction in an NBC broadcast on January 9, 1936. The first complete performance took place at Carnegie Hall, New York, on January 7, 1942, with Dmitri Mitropoulos conducting the New York Philharmonic.

The word "statement" was chosen to indicate a short, terse orchestral movement of a well-defined character, lasting about three minutes. The separate movements were given evocative titles as an aid to the understanding of what I had in mind when writing these pieces.

The statement called "Militant" is based on a single theme, announced in unison at the beginning by three flutes, two oboes, bassoon, and strings. The "Cryptic" statement is scored for brass and flute, with an occasional use of bass clarinet and bassoon. The "Dogmatic" statement is in tri-partite form; the middle section quotes the theme of my "Piano Variations." The "Subjective" statement is orchestrated for strings alone, without double basses. "Jingo" utilizes the full orchestra. It is built in rondo form on a chromatic melody, with episodic bows to a well-known tune. The final section, a "Prophetic" statement, is rhapsodic in form and centers around a chorale-like melody sung by the solo trumpet.

El Salón México

These notes about *El Salón México* (1936) come from the sleeve of a 1975 CBS LP with Copland conducting, as do the notes from *Danzón Cubano*, *Dance Panels*, and *Three Latin American Sketches*. (S.S.)

During my first visit to Mexico, in the fall of 1932, I conceived the idea of writing a piece based on Mexican themes. I suppose there is nothing strange in such an idea. Any composer who goes outside his native land wants to return bearing musical souvenirs. In this case my musical souvenirs must have been very memorable, since it wasn't until 1933 that I began to assemble them into the form of an orchestral work.

From the very beginning, the idea of writing a work based on popular Mexican melodies was connected in my mind with a popular dance hall in Mexico City called "Salón México." No doubt I realized, then, that it would be foolish for me to attempt to translate into musical sounds the more profound side of Mexico, the Mexico of the ancient civilization or the revolutionary Mexico of today. In order to do that, one must really know a country. All that I could hope to do was to reflect the Mexico of the tourists, and that is why I thought of the "Salón México." Because in that 'hot spot' one felt, in a very natural and unaffected way, a close contact with the Mexican people. It wasn't the music I heard, but the spirit that I felt there, which attracted me. Something of that spirit is what I hope to have put into my music.

I followed no general rule in the use of the themes I treated. Almost all of them come from the *Cancionero Mexicano* by Frances Toor, or from the erudite work of Rubén M. Campos, *El Folk-lore y la Música Mexicana*. Probably the most direct quotation of a complete melody is that of *El Mosco* (No. 84 in the book by Campos), which is presented twice, immediately after the introductory measures (in which may be found fragments of *El Palo Verde* and *La Jesusita*).

Sextet

Copland plays piano on the 1970 CBS LP of his chamber music that contains these notes about Sextet (1937) on its sleeve. (S.S.)

The work [Sextet] is in three movements (fast, slow, fast) played without pause. The first movement is scherzo-like in character. Once, I toyed with the idea of naming the entire piece *The Bounding Line* because of the nature of the first section. The second movement is in three brief sections—the first rises to a dissonant climax, is sharply contrasted with a song-like middle part, and returns to the beginning. The finale is once again bright in color and rhythmically intricate.

Billy the Kid

Notes on a Cowboy Ballet (1938)

When Lincoln Kirstein, director of the Ballet Caravan, asks you to write a ballet for him it is a foregone conclusion that you are going to tackle an American subject. Still, when he suggested Billy the Kid as a proper hero for a native ballet, I had certain misgivings. Not about Billy the Kid, of course—for where could one find a better protagonist for an American work—but about my own capabilities as a "cowboy composer." Lincoln Kirstein, however, thought differently—and since he is a very enthusiastic young man, it wasn't long before I was convinced that fate had chosen me and none other to compose this folk-ballet about a young desperado of the wild West.

I don't know how other composers feel, but as for myself, I divide all music into two parts—that which is meant to be self-sufficient and that which is meant to serve one of the sister arts—theatre, film, or ballet. I have never liked music which gets in the way of the thing it is supposedly aiding. That is why I began with one single idea in writing Billy—a firm resolve to write simply. If it is a question of expressing one's soul, you can always write a symphony. But if you are involved in a stage presentation, then the eye is the thing, and music should play a modest role, helping when help is needed, but never injecting itself as if it were the main business of the evening.

There was one other reason for being simple—namely, our hero, Billy. No matter how complex a character he may have been from the psychological standpoint, he makes a simple enough stage figure, this boy bandit who bragged that he had killed twenty-one men, "not counting Indians." Therefore my problem resolved itself into finding the correct musical style to express the peculiar character of Billy the Kid.

To use or not to use cowboy songs as the basis for my ballet became a major issue. Mr. Kirstein said he didn't care—and quietly tucked two slim collections of Western tunes under my arm. I have never been particularly

239

impressed with the musical beauties of the cowboy song as such. The words are usually delightful and the moment of singing needs no praise from me. But neither the words nor the delivery are of much use in a purely orchestral ballet score, so I was left with the tunes themselves, which I repeat, are often less than exciting. As far as I was concerned, this ballet could be written without benefit of the poverty-stricken tunes Billy himself must have known.

Nevertheless, in order to humor Mr. Kirstein, who said he didn't really care whether I used actual cowboy material or not, I decided to take his two little collections with me when I left for Paris in the summer 1938. It was there that I began working on the scenario as it had been outlined for me. Perhaps there is something different about a cowboy song in Paris. But whatever the reason may have been, it wasn't very long before I found myself hopelessly involved in expanding, contracting, rearranging, and superimposing cowboy tunes on the rue de Rennes in Paris. If you listen closely you can hear in full or in part (in the order of their appearance) "Great Grandad," "Whoopee Ti Yi Yo, Git Along Little Dogies," "The Old Chisolm Trail," "Old Paint," "The Dying Cowboy," "Trouble for the Range Cook," and so forth. I can guarantee that I did not use "Home on the Range." (You see I had decided to draw the line someplace.)

"In rounding up this bunch of western songs from the plains and hills, we aren't aiming to educate you any." That's one way the editors of one of my sources books introduce their collection. "We have only one object," they continue, "to be entertaining, and we hope that our efforts will be considered from that angle." That is just about the way I would have put it myself. Except that I had the added difficulty of humanizing these simple tunes without benefit of the usual accompanying chords. It is a rather delicate operation—to put fresh and unconventional harmonies to well known melodies without spoiling their naturalness. It's a moment for the composer to throw caution aside and to depend wholly on his instinct for knowing what to do. Courage and instinct are the only things that can be of help at that point.

Before leaving New York I had seen Jared French's lovely costume designs. The story around which the choreography was to be designed had been supplied to me after discussions with our choreographer Eugene Loring. In the finished script, the action begins and closes on the open prairie. The events which take place between the introduction and coda are merely typical of many such episodes on the long trek to the Pacific.

The central portion of the ballet concerns itself with significant moments in the life of Billy the Kid. The first scene is a street in a frontier town. Familiar figures amble by. Cowboys saunter into town, some on horseback, others with their lassoes. Some Mexican women do a *jarabe*, which is interrupted by a fight between two drunks. Attracted by the gathering crowd, Billy is seen for the first time, as a boy of twelve, with his mother. The brawl turns ugly, guns are drawn, and in some unaccountable way, Billy's mother is killed. Without an instant's hesitation, in cold fury, Billy draws a knife from a cow-hand's sheath and stabs his mother's slayers. His short but famous career begins.

In swift succesion we see episodes in Billy's later life. At night, under the stars, in a quiet card game with his outlaw friends. Hunted by a posse led by his former friend Pat Garrett, Billy is pursued. A running gun battle ensues. Billy is captured, a drunken celebration takes place. Billy in prison is, of course, followed by one of Billy's legendary escapes. Tired and worn in the desert, Billy rests with his girl. (Pas de deux.) Starting from a deep sleep, he senses movement in the shadows. The posse has finally caught up with him. It is the end.

If we are ever to have a fully developed ballet company in America—the ballet company in the tradition of the Russians—it will come by way of just such companies as the Ballet Caravan, and just such subject matter as Billy the Kid. Speaking of the work of the Ballet Caravan in the pages of *Modern Music*, Edwin Denby, has this to say: . . . "they show that an American kind of ballet is growing up, different from the nervous France-Russian style . . . Our own ballet had an easier, simpler character, a kind of American straightforwardness, that is the roughly agreeable . . . I think this is the highest kind of praise, because it shows the ballet has taken root and is from now on a part of our life."

An Outdoor Overture

An Outdoor Overture was composed especially for the 1938 mid-winter concert given by the school orchestra of the High School of Music and Art in New York City. The first performances took place in the school auditorium on December 16 and 17, 1938, under the direction of Alexander Richter. The *Overture* owes its existence to the persuasive powers of Mr. Richter [who] had witnessed a performance of my high school opera, *The Second Hurricane*, in the spring of 1937. He made up his mind that I was the man who was to write a work especially for his school orchestra. Mr. Richter explained to me that my work was to be the opening gun in a long-term campaign that the High School of Music and Art planned to undertake with the slogan "American music for American youth." This last argument I found irresistible . . . here was an opportunity too good to be missed. As it turned out, the composition was an overture, definitely optimistic in tone. When Mr. Richter first heard me play it from the piano sketch, he pointed out that it had an open-air quality. Together we hit upon the title.

One of Mr. Richter's admonishments was "Don't forget the percussion section." The percussion section was, therefore, not forgotten.

Lincoln Portrait

Artur Rodzinski conducts *Lincoln Portrait* on the Columbia LP with a sleeve containing these notes. (S.S.)

It was in January, 1942, that Andre Kostelanetz suggested the idea of my writing a musical portrait of a great American. He put teeth into the proposal by offering to commission such a piece and to play it extensively. My first thought was to do a portrait of Walt Whitman, the patron poet of all American composers. But when Mr. Kostelanetz explained that the series of portraits he was planning already included a literary figure, I was persuaded to change to a statesman. From that moment on the choice of Lincoln as my subject seemed inevitable.

On discussing my choice with Virgil Thomson he amiably pointed out that no composer could possibly hope to match in musical terms the stature of so eminent a figure as that of Lincoln. Of course he was quite right. But secretly I was hoping to avoid the difficulty by doing a portrait in which the sitter himself might speak. With the voice of Lincoln to help me I was ready to risk the impossible.

The letters and speeches of Lincoln supplied the text. It was a comparatively simple matter to choose a few excerpts that seemed particularly apposite to our own situation today. I avoided the temptation to use only well-known passages permitting myself the luxury of quoting only once from a world speech. The order and arrangement of the selections are my own.

The first sketches were made in February and the portrait finished on April 16. The orchestration was completed a few weeks later. I worked with musical materials of my own, with the exception of two songs of the period: the famous *Camptown Races* and a ballad that was first published in 1840 under the title of *The Pesky Sarpent*, but is better known today as *Springfield Mountain.* In neither case is the treatment a literal one. The tunes are used freely, in the manner of my use of cowboy songs in *Billy the Kid.*

The composition is roughly divided into three main sections. In the opening section I wanted to suggest something of the mysterious sense of fatality that surrounds Lincoln's personality. Also, near the end of that section, something of his gentleness and simplicity of spirit. The quick middle section briefly sketches in the background of the times he lived in. This merges into the concluding section where my sole purpose was to draw a simple but impressive frame about the words of Lincoln himself.

Music for Movies

Music for Movies is a five-part suite for small orchestra drawn from material used in three film scores: *The City, Of Mice and Men,* and *Our Town.* The originals were composed in 1939 and 1940, and the rearrangement was completed in 1942. *Music for Movies* was first performed by the Saidenberg Little Symphony, Daniel Saidenberg conducting, at an all-Copland concert in Town Hall, New York, on February 19, 1943. The score is dedicated to the French composer Darius Milhaud.

The first and third sections—"New England Countryside" and "Sunday Traffic"—derive from the documentary film *The City.* "New England Countryside" depicts the quiet and peaceful living of a typical small town in that section of the United States. "Sunday Traffic," which supplies the scherzo of the suite, originally accompanied scenes that ironically pictured problems that beset the Sunday driver in urban America.

"Barley Wagons"—the second movement—was lifted intact from the soundtrack of *Of Mice and Men.* It evokes the broad vistas of a California landscape, with distant wagons slowly bringing produce back to the barns. The fourth section—"Story of Grovers Corners"—was used as a kind of leit-motif in *Our Town.*

The final movement—"Threshing Machines"—was also taken from *Of Mice and Men.* Here the composer attempted to combine the mechanical noises of the machines with passing reference to the dramatic action. The rather grandiose coda of this movement draws upon material from the title music of the film.

Music for Movies represents one of the infrequent examples of Hollywood background film music being made available in concert form.

Fanfare for the Common Man

Like many other American composers during World War II, I was eager to contribute to the war effort, so when Eugene Goossens, the conductor of the Cincinnati Symphony Orchestra, asked me along with several other composers for a fanfare, I immediately agreed. Those fanfares were intended to be a kind of patriotic gesture, so I thought I would try for a certain nobility of tone, which suggested slow rather than fast music.

As can be seen by this sketch, the final title did not come easily. First, I considered *Fanfare to the Spirit of Democracy*; then *Fanfare for the Rebirth of Lidice* (Lidice, in Czechoslovakia, was the scene of a 1942 Nazi massacre); and even the unlikely-sounding *Fanfare for Paratroops*. In the long run, I think I was inspired by the title which my colleague Walter Piston chose for his piece, *Fanfare for the Fighting French*. It seemed to me that if the fighting French got a fanfare, so should the common man, since, after all, it was he who was doing the dirty work in the war.

Danzón Cubano I

Boosey & Hawkes's score for *Danzón Cubano* includes these notes. (S.S.)

The danzón is a well-known dance form in Cuba and other Latin American countries. It is not a fast dance, however, and should not be confused with the rhumba or conga. It fulfills a function rather similar to the waltz in our own dance, providing contrast for the more animated numbers. Its special charm is a certain naïve sophistication, alternating in mood between passages of rhythmic precision and a kind of non-sentimental sweetness.

The *Danzón Cubano* is based on melodic and rhythmic fragments heard by the composer during several visits to Cuba. The danzón is normally constructed in two halves, which are thematically independent. This is in no sense intended to be an authentic danzón, but only an American tourist's impression of an absorbing Cuban dance form.

II

Danzón is not the familiar hectic, flashy, and rhythmically complicated type of Cuban dance. It is more elegant and curt and is very precise as dance music goes. The dance hall itself seemed especially amusing to me because it had a touch of unconscious grotesquerie, as if it were an impression of "high-life" as seen through the eyes of the populace—elegance perceived by the inelegant. . . . I didn't actually intend the piece to be grotesque, but, of course, there is that element in the original dance itself. Similar to that style, *Danzón Cubano* is very *secco*, very precise and elegant. It contrasts strong, rhythmically marked sections with a rather sentimental tune following immediately after but not quite mixing with the dryness of the preceding part.

Appalachian Spring

Letters Regarding (1944)

This series of letters to the head of the Library of Congress's Music Division, Harold Spivacke, gives details on the development of this famous composition, commissioned by the Library through the patron Elizabeth Coolidge.

Stockbridge, Mass.
Aug. 21, 1942
Dear Harold [Spivacke]:

Thanks a lot for the prompt action re the enclosed material. I am returning it to you, and if it seems properly filled out, would you kindly send it to Doris Goss.

As I told you on the phone, I contemplate the giving up of my composing activities with the greatest reluctance, but if I must be used in the war effort, I wish to be as useful as possible. I hope you won't mind if I come rushing at you for further advice if and when the moment comes.

Until this matter takes on clearer shape, perhaps we had better let the question of Mrs. Coolidge's commission ride. Whether or not I can fulfill such a commission depends entirely on how my future pans out.

With best regards, and again—thanks.

Stockbridge, Mass.
Sept. 3, 1942
Dear Harold:

Your letter cheered me up considerably—I mean the part about composers in the Army being given "time for composing." You can't imagine how right I hope you are. But I should warn you that "composing" to me means a private room with a piano and some consecutive time for writing.

(Unlike Beethoven and Hindemith I don't work in the fields.) If the Army can provide that, its set-up is even more intricate than I thought. Well anyway, I'm only too happy to take your word for it that army life and composing are not incompatible.

I am returning to New York next week (after Tuesday my address is the Hotel Empire.) I'll be seeing Martha Graham in N.Y., and as soon as I get a clearer picture of what she plans to do for you I'll write you an "official" letter to settle up the matter of the Coolidge Commission. I'm quite willing to go through the making of arrangements for the commission, always assuming that it can be carried out—army life permitting.

In the meantime I hope you will do whatever you can to press for action in the matter of my personnel questionnaire for a commission of another sort.

Yours cordially

Sept. 17, 1942
Dear Harold:

I wanted you to know that I have had my army physical examination and came through with flying colors. Of course my eyes would limit me to what the doctor calls "limited service," but I assume that that only improves my case with the Army Specialist Corps.

I had a letter from Charlie Thomson in which he said the two of you had been "exploring possibilities" in relation to me. If there is anything more you can tell me without breaking confidences, of course I'd like to know it.

Thanks a lot for expediting matters in regard to the commission. You would help me enormously if you could tell me what your guess is as to the earliest possible date for my relinquishment of civilian life. In other words, in making plans for the immediate future I badly need to know up to what date I can safely promise to be around. Naturally I know your answer can only be approximate and only a guess, but even that would be a help.

I am seeing Martha Graham to-morrow and will communicate with you again.

Best regards to you.

[Hollywood, California]
April 13, 1943
Dear Harold:

Your letter, sent to Stockbridge, just reached me out here. Since I hadn't heard from Martha Graham in several months, I was going on the assumption that the idea of a ballet was in abeyance. Your letter now brings the whole thing to life again.

When I last saw her in New York, she promised to send me a scenario which we could discuss. That was around Christmas time and I haven't heard from her since. We also agreed that when the rights to the ballet are released after the first year, she would be willing to pay me a royalty performance fee on a per performance basis. Therefore, as far as Miss Graham goes, everything is set, except that I have nothing to work with, until she prepares a scenario suitable to us both.

Because of the job I have out here, doing the score for a picture called *The North Star*, my time will be pretty much taken up until the middle of June. However, I can probably sneak in some work on the ballet nevertheless. I assume that the performance date is still planned for late September.

As far as the terms of the commission go, I think the Foundation should take into account the fact that this is a stage work, and therefore ought to be handled somewhat differently from the commissions given for chamber music. I think that the $500 fee should cover three points: 1) the writing of the work especially for the Foundation, 2) the premiere performance, and 3) exclusivity for a year from the premiere performance. I believe however, that in fairness to the composer, a small royalty fee of $15 per performance should be paid the composer each time the work is given after the premiere. That is the customary procedure with the ballet companies, though of course the rates are about double that for regular commercial outfits. Such an arrangement also provides more incentive for a publisher who might be interested in bringing the work out immediately.

My suggestion is that you write to Miss Graham, finding out the present status of her scenario, and then let me know how the whole matter stands.

Best greetings to you!

May 10, 1943
Dear Harold:

I'll be waiting with much curiosity to see Miss Graham's scenario. It hasn't arrived as yet, however. I'm also glad to see that the date of the premiere is as late as Oct. 30 now. Don't be concerned about the number of musicians. There is no difficulty on that point since it's being taken into account as early as this. The type of musical instruments needed will depend on the nature of Miss Graham's scenario. I'll try to stick to Chávez' choice of instruments as far as practicable.

Your letter of April 15th was illuminating on the subject of performance fees. Since you state that "the likelihood of the Coolidge Foundation sending the ballet on tour . . . is practically nil" and that only a few performances are contemplated during the year of exclusivity, I assume you would have no objection if I ask that the number of "free" performances included in the commission fee be limited to five.

Best greetings to you,

June 8, 1943.
Dear Harold:

Thanks for your letter of the 2nd. I received the script from Martha Graham and like it very much, on the whole. I've written to her, suggesting a few changes.

I assume we are now all set, since your letter clears up our "business" arrangements, and is satisfactory to me. If you have occasion to write Miss Graham, please tell her that I have no intention of holding her to a minimum or maximum of ten performances during the first year, but only to the "usual" $15 performance fee whenever she performs the ballet on her own.

I shall assume that the premiere date is October 30th unless I hear to the contrary. Please be sure to let me know if there is any change, as the more time I have the better. Also, if you can find out from Chávez what instruments he intends using, that would be a help.

I think I have my first theme!

Best greetings to you.

July 21, 1943
Dear Harold:

Two days ago I sent a long letter to Martha Graham, and was just about to write to you when your wire arrived. I can easily understand your anxiety about the score, but the situation was too complex to be taken care of in a wire.

I wrote to Martha because I had just received the final version of the scenario. As I think I pointed out to you, I had suggested certain changes in the first version she sent me, and she promised to make them. Then there elapsed about a six-week interval. She realized, of course, that the delay was serious because of the pressure of time, but apparently couldn't make the revisions any sooner. The new scenario is an improvement, and I wrote her my acceptance.

In the meantime I was at work on the score, and have perhaps a third done. If I had nothing to do between now and Sept. 1st but write the ballet, I wouldn't hesitate to promise it for that date. But through a series of unforseen incidents the picture score I am contracted to do is just now getting under way. In another week I shall be in the midst of it—and there are a lot of notes to write!

Martha wrote that the Chávez score is still not in her hands. Knowing him well, and the heavy season he has in Mexico at this time, I can hardly hope that his score will arrive soon[,] giving Martha something to work on until I am ready. As you probably know, he is famous for getting things done at the last possible moment.

In view of all this, I told Martha I thought she ought to write to you with the idea of finding out whether there was any chance of postponing the performances until Spring. I was very reluctant to make the suggestion, and only did so because I thought we could all do ourselves greater justice if we took a few more months time.

As I see it, if the postponement is out of the question, I can let Martha have about half the ballet to work on during the first weeks of September, and will finish up by Oct. 1st. This is on the assumption that the movie score will be out of the way by Aug. 31st. By "score" I mean piano reduction, from which I later make the instrumentation. In my case the instrumentation comes last, and all I can say is that it will be ready in time for orchestra rehearsals.

There is one other detail that hasn't worked out as I had hoped. Because of the nature of the scenario I have decided that the best possible instrumentation for my ballet would be piano and strings. In the case of the premiere that could mean piano and double string quartet. Since you have a flute and clarinet for the Chávez anyway, I may decide to add those two instruments. This means an addition of five players to the Chávez group, and I hope won't cause too much upset in the finances.

I hope this gives you a clear picture of the set-up. Let me know what is decided as soon as you conveniently can.

Greetings,

Aug. 30, 1943
Dear Harold:
Your letter announcing the decision to postpone the Graham performance reached me while I was up to my neck in notes for *The North Star.* I'll be out of the woods in another week or so, and can then turn to the ballet score with a free mind. So the postponement is something of a godsend as far as I am concerned. Also I plan to be back in New York by October first, so can keep in close touch with Martha Graham, which ought to produce better results than long distance correspondence.

I have about a third of the work completed so far. I am going on the assumption that the scoring for double string quartet and piano will be satisfactory.

All best wishes—and I hope to see you during the course of the winter.

January 31, 1944
Dear Harold:

Thanks for the encouraging words about the part of the ballet you received from me. Martha Graham tells me you are planning for a premiere around October. I really think you don't need wait to get the score completely orchestrated in order to make definite plans. As far as I am concerned, I think that it is quite safe to go ahead as soon as you get the completed piano sketch. The orchestration is a mere detail.

I have revised my scheme a bit in regard to the instruments for which the ballet will be scored. I told Martha the other day that the ideal combination now seems to me to be the double string quartet with double bass, one piano, and three woodwinds (probably flute, clarinet, and bassoon). That adds up to thirteen men which is one more than your original letter called for if I remember correctly. I hope that's OK with you.

Best regards,

June 9, 1944
Dear Harold:

The instrumentation is as follows:
Double String Quartet, with one doublebass, piano, flute, clarinet, bassoon. Total of 13 players.

I have about two more minutes of music to write on the ballet, and am one-third through the instrumentation. Hope to be done by July first.

I'm doing the score on thin sheets so that both Martha and myself can have a copy. Subsequently, I hope I can purchase as many copies as I may happen to need. In the same way, I hope you will be able to copy the parts on thin sheets so that we get independent sets for ourselves if they are needed at some later time.

Best regards,

July 8, 1944
Dear Harold:

At last I am able to write you that the complete score of the ballet has been mailed to you. Since I put the score on thin master sheets I hope you will send a copy to Martha Graham soon, so that she may have some idea of the sonorities. I am also planning to make some piano records for her, so that she will know my tempi. Unfortunately, she had left for Bennington before I had arrived back here, so I had no opportunity to play the completed score for her. Also I hope you are planning to send me a photostat of the score for my "collection."

I hope also that you will be able to send her a copy of the piano version of the ballet made from master sheets that I am about to send you. (I have had to hold on to them for a few more days so as to make the recording.) Martha has the ballet complete already,—but since sending it to her there have been some minor changes made, so that she ought to have this final version for comparison. Please return the originals of the piano version to me with the orchestral score copy, as I never know when I may need further copies.

I am about to leave for Mexico for the summer, so hold everything until you get an address from me. That goes for the check also!

I hope the ballet all turns out well, and that you and Mrs. Coolidge will feel properly rewarded for all your pains!

Yours,

P.S. I wrote Martha that if the orchestration for 13 players is too much for her on the road, the score could be played (with slight rearrangements) with only a single string quartet for the string section, instead of the double string quartet and bass now called for. That would reduce the number of players to 8.

Tepoztlan,
Morelos,
Mexico.
Sept. 7, 1944
Dear Harold:

I am planning to fly up to Washington for the sole purpose of attending the Festival. Therefore, if anything should happen to change plans for the event at the end of October, please make me the first person to be told about it.

However, on the assumption that all is to go ahead on schedule, would you let me know as soon as possible, what date Martha Graham will be having her first rehearsals in the Library Hall? That's the day I should like to arrive. Also, it would be nice if your secretary could make me a reservation in the likeliest hotel for the period of the Festival.

One more request: would you have an invitation sent to Dr. Hans Heinsheimer of Boosey & Hawkes, 43 West 23 St., NYC. Since he is the eventual publisher of the ballet, he naturally wants to be there for the premiere. The other day I visited the library of the National Conservatory in Mexico. The librarian assured me that no books had ever been received from the USA from the (Cowell) Distribution Project, or any other source. Could you tell me where in Mexico such grants, if any, were made? The day I was at the Conservatory the library was filled with students. They have an excellent collection of the classics (or so it seemed to me), but no funds available for contemporary music. Since the Conservatory is one of the prime centers of musical activity in Mexico, and an ideal depository for American music, I very much hope that you will use your influence to see to it that they get an allotment of material whenever it starts going out.

That's all for now!

Tepoztlan,
Morelos,
Mexico
Sept. 25, 1944
Dear Harold:

Thanks for the prompt reply to my last letter. Also for the check that came through safely.

I had no idea Martha would be coming for rehearsals as early as five days before the event. Naturally I don't intend to make a nuisance of myself during all that time!

My present plan is to fly up from here on the 25th, reaching Washington the following day. So please reserve a room for me from Thursday the 26th. (Even if I'm put off the plane for a day through lack of priorities I can still make the dress rehearsal.) My budget will stand $4 or $5 a day for a room—but the main thing is to put me where "everybody" will be. Half the fun of going to festivals is bumping into people in your hotel lobby.

If anything happens to make me change my plans I'll wire you. I hope you'll do the same. Please ask your secretary to write me the name of the hotel I'm to go to, in the event that I reach Washington at some ungodly hour, not knowing where to go. I'd like it if she could include some sort of announcement of the Festival, so that I can mull over the events to come in quiet contemplation.

Best greetings to you!

Nov 13, 1944
Dear Harold:

Thanks a lot for sending the voucher covering the price of records. It's doubly appreciated since it wasn't part of our "agreement."

There's little likelihood of the ballet going to press before next eason, but if and when it does of course I'll add the note about the commissioning.

Sorry the Met idea fell thru — but it would have been a miracle if it hadn't. If I get any bright ideas, I'll write you. The only one I have to date is to ask Hurok to have the Ballet Theatre invite Martha (as guest artist) to present it in their Spring season at the Met. (The precedent for this is Argentinita and her company.) It would cause much talk, and perhaps end an old battle between the balletomanes and the modern dance enthusiasts—or at any rate, set up a truce.

I'll be looking forward to receiving the orchestral records.

Yours always

P.S. That was an awful nice "appreciation" letter you sent. Many thanks!

Box 294
Bernardsville, N.J.
Sept. 28, 1945
Dear Harold:

I thought you might be interested to know that Mr. Heinsheimer of Boosey & Hawkes tells me that four orchestras have announced *Appalachian Spring* on their opening programs—NY Philharmonic, Boston, Cleveland, Pittsburgh. Later on performances are scheduled for Los Angeles, San Francisco, Kansas City. Koussevitzky plans to record it for RCA Victor at the end of October. Perhaps you can listen in to the Philharmonic broadcast on Sunday the 7th.

Martha Graham is trying to negotiate a satisfactory contract with Hurok for a tour lasting two seasons, and later Europe. If it comes off, the ballet will be widely seen. I think you have the right to feel just a bit triumphant about your brain child.

Greetings to you!

Aaron

PS. Perhaps Mrs. Coolidge would like to know about the above.

Third Symphony

A 1979 CBS LP with Third Symphony contains these notes on its sleeve. (S.S.)

Regarding my Third Symphony, one aspect ought to be pointed out: It contains no folk or popular material. During the late twenties, it was customary to pigeon-hole me as a composer of symphonic jazz, with emphasis on the jazz. I have also been catalogued as a folk-lorist and purveyor of Americana. Any reference to jazz or folk material in this work was purely unconscious.

For the sake of those who like a purely musical guide through unfamiliar terrain, I add a breakdown by movements of the technical outlines of the work:

I. *Molto moderato*. The opening movement which is broad and expressive in character opens and closes in the key of E major. (Formally it bears no relation to the sonata-allegro with which symphonies usually begin.) The themes—three in number—are plainly stated: the first is in the strings, at the very start without introduction; the second in related mood in violas and oboes; the third, of a bolder nature, in the trombones and horns. The general form is that of an arch, in which the central portion is more animated, and the final section an extended coda, presenting a broadened version of the opening material. Both first and third themes are referred to again in later movements of the Symphony.

II. *Allegro molto*: The form of this movement stays closer to normal Symphonic procedure. It is the usual scherzo, with first part, trio, and return. A brass introduction leads to the main theme, which is stated three times in Part I: at first in horns and violas with continuation in clarinets, then in unison strings, and finally in augmentation in the lower brass. The three statements of theme are separated by the usual episodes. After the climax is reached, the trio follows without a pause. Solo woodwinds sing the new trio melody in lyrical and canonical style. The strings take it up, and add a new section of their own. The recapitulation of part I is not literal. The principal theme of the scherzo returns in a somewhat disguised form in the solo piano, leading through previous episodic material to a full restatement in the *tutti* orchestra. This is climaxed by a return to the lyrical trio theme, this time sung in canon and in *fortissimo* by the entire orchestra.

III. *Andantino quasi allegretto:* The third movement is freest of all in formal structure. Although it is built up sectionally, the various sections are intended to emerge one from the other in continuous flow, somewhat in the manner of a closely-knit series of variations. The opening section, however, plays no role other than that of introducing the main body of the movement.

High up in the unaccompanied first violins is heard a rhythmically transformed version of the third (trombone) theme of the first movement of the Symphony. It is briefly developed in contrapuntal style, and comes to a full close, once again in the key of E major. A new and more tonal theme is introduced in the solo flute. This is the melody that supplies the thematic substance for the sectional metamorphoses that follow: at first with quiet singing nostalgia, then faster and heavier—almost dance-like, then more child-like and naïve, and finally vigorous and forthright. Imperceptibly the whole movement drifts off into the higher regions of the strings, out of which floats the single line of the beginning, sung by a solo violin and piccolo, accompanied this time by harps and celesta. The third movement calls for no brass, with the exception of a single horn and trumpet.

IV. *Molto deliberato* (Fanfare)—*Allegro risoluto:* The final movement follows without pause. It is the longest movement of the Symphony, and closest in structure to the customary sonata-allegro form. The opening fanfare is based on *Fanfare for the Common Man,* which I composed in 1942 at the invitation of Eugene Goossens for a series of wartime fanfares introduced under his direction by the Cincinnati Symphony. In the present version it is first played *pianissimo* by flutes and clarinets, and then suddenly given out by brass and percussion. The fanfare serves as preparation for the main body of the movement which follows. The components of the usual form are there: a first theme in animated sixteenth-note motion; a second theme—broader and more song-like in character; a full-blown development and a re-fashioned return to the earlier material of the movement, leading to a peroration. One curious feature of the movement consists in the fact that the second theme is to be found embedded in the development section instead of being in its customary place. The development, as such, concerns itself with the fanfare and first theme fragments. A shrill *tutti* chord, with flutter-tongued brass and piccolos, brings the development to a close. What follows is not a recapitulation in the ordinary sense. Instead, a delicate interweaving of the first theme in the higher solo woodwinds is combined with a quiet version of the fanfare in the two bassoons. Combined with this, the opening theme of the first movement of the Symphony is quoted, first in the violins, and later in the solo trombone. Near the end a full-voiced chanting of the second song-like theme is heard in horns and trombones. The Symphony concludes on a massive restatement of the opening phrase with which the entire work began.

The Red Pony

André Previn conducts *The Red Pony* on the Columbia LP that contains these notes on its sleeve. (S.S.)

Steinbeck's tale is a series of vignettes concerning a 10-year-old boy called Jody and his life in a California ranch setting. There is a minimum of action of a dramatic or startling kind. The story gets its warmth and sensitive quality from the character studies of the boy Jody; Jody's grandfather; the cowhand Billy Buck; and Jody's parents, the Tiflins. The kind of emotions that Steinbeck evokes in his story are basically musical ones, since they deal so much with the unexpressed feelings of daily living. It seems to me that Lewis Milestone, in directing the picture, realized that fact and, therefore, left plenty of room for musical treatment—which, in turn, made the writing of the score a grateful task.

In shaping the suite, I recast much of the musical material so that, although all the music may be heard in the film, it has been reorganized as to continuity for concert purposes.

I. *Morning on the Ranch*. Sounds of daybreak. The daily chores begin. A folk-like melody suggests the atmosphere of simple country living.

II. *The Gift*. Jody's father surprises him with the gift of a red pony. Jody shows off his new acquisition to his school chums, who cause quite a commotion about it. "Jody was glad when they had gone."

III. *Dream March and Circus Music*. Jody has a way of going off into daydreams. Two of them are pictured here. In the first, Jody imagines himself with Billy Buck at the head of an army of knights in silver armor; in the second, he is a whip-cracking ringmaster at the circus.

IV. *Walk to the Bunkhouse.* Billy Buck was "a fine hand with horses," and Jody's admiration knew no bounds. This is a scene of the two pals on their walk to the bunkhouse.

V. *Grandfather's Story.* Jody's grandfather retells the story of how he led a wagon train "clear across the plains to the coast." But he can't hide his bitterness from the boy. In his opinion, "Westering has died out of the people. Westering isn't a hunger any more."

VI. *Happy Ending.* Some of the title music is incorporated into the final movement. There is a return to the folk-like melody of the beginning, this time played with boldness and conviction.

Although some of the melodies in *The Red Pony* may sound rather folk-like, they are actually mine. There are no quotations of folklore anywhere in the work.

Concerto for Clarinet and String Orchestra with Harp and Piano

The first movement is simple in structure, based upon the usual A-B-A song form. The general character of this movement is lyric and expressive. The cadenza that follows provides the soloist with considerable opportunity to demonstrate his prowess, at the same time introducing fragments of the melodic material heard in the second movement. Some of this material represents an unconscious fusion of elements obviously related to North and South American popular music. (For example, a phrase from a currently popular Brazilian tune, heard by me in Rio, became imbedded in the secondary material in F major.) The overall form of the final movement is that of a free rondo, with several side issues developed at some length. It ends with a fairly elaborate coda in C major.

12 Poems of Emily Dickinson

Copland's program notes for *Twelve Poems of Emily Dickinson* appear both in Boosey & Hawkes's score and on the sleeve of a 1956 Columbia LP. (S.S.)

The poems center about no single theme, but they treat of subject matter particularly close to Miss Dickinson: nature, death, life, eternity. Only two of the songs are related thematically, the sixth and eighth. Nevertheless, it is my hope that, in seeking a musical counterpart for the unique personality of the poet, I have given the songs, taken together, the aspect of a song cycle.

Variations on a Shaker Melody

Boosey & Hawkes's score of *Variations on a Shaker Melody* includes these notes. (S.S.)

Variations on a Shaker Melody is an excerpt from *Appalachian Spring* which was composed in 1943–44 as a ballet for Miss Martha Graham on a commission from the Elizabeth Sprague Coolidge Foundation. The ballet was first performed by Miss Graham and her company at the Coolidge Festival in the Library of Congress, Washington, D.C., on October 30th, 1944. The original scoring called for a chamber ensemble of thirteen instruments. The present arrangement for symphony orchestra was made by the composer especially for performance by school and community orchestras.

The Shaker Melody on which the *Variations* are based is entitled "Simple Gifts." It was a favorite song of the Shaker sect, from the period 1837–1847. The melody and words were quoted by Edward D. Andrews in his book of Shaker rituals, songs, and dances, entitled *The Gift to Be Simple*. The words of the song are as follows:

'Tis the gift to be simple, 'tis the gift to be free,
'Tis the gift to come down where we ought to be,
And when we find ourselves in the place just right,
'Twill be in the valley of love and delight.
When true simplicity is gain'd,
To bow and to bend we shan't be asham'd,
To turn, turn will be our delight
'Till by turning, turning we come round right.

Piano Fantasy I

Copland's notes on *Piano Fantasy* appeared before the piece's premiere in both the *New York Times* and *Tempo* magazine. We have omitted the sub-headings that were likely added by an editor to Copland's original notes. (S.S.)

My *Piano Fantasy*, completed in January of this year, is a large-scale work in one movement, lasting half an hour in performance. A long and continuous one-movement form has always seemed to me one of the most taxing assignments a composer can undertake. The word assignment is perhaps ill-chosen, since this particular task was self-imposed. My idea was to attempt a composition that would suggest the quality of fantasy, that is, a spontaneous and unpremeditated sequence of "events" that would carry the listener irresistibly (if possible) from first note to last, while at the same time exemplifying clear if somewhat unconventional structural principles.

"The spontaneous," says Paul Valéry, "is the fruit of conquest." It implies a creator who can "keep the unity of a work's ensemble while realizing the separate parts and without losing its spirit or nature on the way." To give free rein to the imagination without loss of coherence—to be "fantastic" without losing one's hearings, is venturesome, to say the least. And yet a work of art seems to me the ideal proving ground for just such a venture. At any rate, my Piano Fantasy *is* such a venture.

Like my two previous extended works for solo piano, the Piano Variations (1930) and the Piano Sonata (1939–41), the new work belongs in the category of absolute music. It makes no use whatever of folk or popular musical materials. I stress this point because of a tendency in recent years to typecast me as primarily a purveyor of Americana in music. Commentators have remarked upon my "simplicity of style" and my "audience appeal" in such a way as to suggest that that is the whole story, and the best of the story.

As a matter of fact a composer in our time is comparatively helpless as to the picture of himself that will be presented to the listening public. Commercial exploitation of serious music, even contemporary serious music, is by definition plugging the "well known." By and large, performances are restricted to a narrow list of one's more accessible works, and this restriction often obtains in concert and broadcast performances. I do not mean to belittle the value of accessibility, nor the value for native music of a certain Americanism in our musical language. But neither do I wish to be limited to that frame of reference. In my own case a rounded picture would have to take into account works like my *Piano Quartet* and *Piano Fantasy*.

The musical framework of the entire *Piano Fantasy* derives from a sequence of ten different tones of the chromatic scale. To these are subsequently joined the unused two tones of the scale, treated throughout as a kind of cadential interval. (In fact, a good case could be made for the view that the over-all tonal orientation is that of E major.) Thus, inherent in the materials are elements able to be associated with the twelve-tone method and with music tonally conceived.

To describe a composer as a twelve-toner these days is much too vague. Too many composers in too many countries have been making too varied a use of dodecaphonic techniques to justify so simple a label. My own *Fantasy*, for example, is by no means rigorously controlled twelve-tone music, but it does make liberal use of devices associated with that technique.

As I see it, twelve-tonism is nothing more than an angle of vision. Like fugal treatment, it is a stimulus that enlivens musical thinking, especially when applied to a series of tones that lend themselves to that treatment. It is a method, not a style; and therefore it solves no problems of musical expressivity.

As a method, it seems nowadays to be pointing in two opposite directions: toward the extreme of "total organization" with its concomitant electronic applications, and toward a gradual absorption into what has become a very freely interpreted tonalism. But, these are preoccupations of the musical kitchen; audiences have other things to think of things that are more fundamental to the expressive content of a piece. Is the *Fantasy* a large and free utterance, serious and thought-provoking? From my standpoint, that is the more absorbing question.

The *Piano Fantasy* was commissioned by the Juilliard School of Music as part of its fiftieth anniversary celebration. Because the work was not ready in time for performance, as originally planned, at the special series of concerts held in February, 1956, to memorialize that event, the Juilliard administration has arranged a special concert for its presentation on Friday.

II

A Columbia LP with *Piano Fantasy* contains these comments in its liner notes. (S.S.)

The *Piano Fantasy* was commissioned by the Juilliard School of Music on the occasion of its fiftieth anniversary and was completed on January 19, 1957. It is dedicated to the memory of the American pianist William Kapell. The work was given its première at the Juilliard Concert Hall by William Masselos on October 25, 1957. The composer supplied the following note on the work:

Sketches for an extended piano solo work are to be found in my notebooks as far back as the early fifties. Consecutive work on the *Fantasy* was carried on during 1955 and 1956 in southern France, at the MacDowell Colony in New Hampshire and at my home in the Hudson Valley. Like my two previous extended works for solo piano, the Piano Variations (1930) and the Piano Sonata (1939–40), the new *Fantasy* belongs in the category of absolute music. It makes no use whatever of folk or popular music materials. My purpose was to attempt a composition that would suggest the quality of fantasy, that is, a spontaneous and unpremeditated sequence of 'events' that would carry the listener (if possible) from the first note to the last, while at the same time exemplifying clear if somewhat unconventional structural principles.

The musical framework of the entire piece is based upon a sequence of ten different tones of the chromatic scale. To these are joined, subsequently, the two unused tones of the scale, treated throughout as a kind of cadential interval. Thus, inherent in the materials are elements able to be associated with the twelve-tone method and with music tonally conceived. The Piano Fantasy is by no means rigorously controlled twelve-tone music, but it does make liberal use of devices associated with that technique.

Orchestral Variations

The sleeve of Louisville Orchestra's LP with Orchestral Variations provides these notes. (S.S.)

The Orchestral Variations were completed on December 31, 1957. The work is an orchestral transcription of my Piano Variations composed in 1930. The notion of transcribing the Piano Variations for orchestral performance had been a recurrent thought of mine for some years past. The offer of a commission from the Louisville Orchestra provided the incentive for carrying out the project.

My purpose was not to create orchestral sounds reminiscent of the quality of a piano, but rather to re-think the sonorous possibilities of the composition in terms of orchestral color. This would have been impossible for me to do when the work was new, for at that time the piano tone was an integral part of its conception. With the perspective of twenty-seven years it was a comparatively simple matter to orchestrate as I have in the past, using the original as a piano sketch with orchestral possibilities.

The over-all plan of the work remains as it was: an eleven-measure theme, dramatic in character, followed by a series of twenty variations and a Coda. The intention was to make each variation cumulative in effect, with the Coda as a kind of summation of the emotional content of the work.

Nothing has been added to the notes themselves except a few imitative voices. These were needed in an occasional variation to fill out what might otherwise have been too thin a texture. Although the rhythms have remained the same, the bar lines have been shifted in some cases to facilitate orchestral performance.

The Piano Variations were dedicated to my friend, the American writer, Gerald Sykes.

The theme is eleven bars long, but the core of it is a four note figure, E-C-E Flat-C sharp which is heard in every variation and is inescapable to the attentive listener. The figure may be played by brass, winds, or strings, the value of the notes varies, but it is always there. The composition is a unified whole, there is no feeling that it is broken into separate variations, to be analyzed separately, and as individual variations are mentioned by number, it is only to indicate distance passed, as milestones.

The brass, in subdued tones, open the work and the theme is presented in a restrained vein. This quietness continues until Variation VII when the mood becomes emboldened: singing tones of the strings in VIII and IX predominate; in No. XI the oboe's pleading tone is in duet with the solo flute. From Variation XII on there is a steadily building climax, with an increasing use of brass, while No. XVIII is a Scherzo, with flute and clarinet in the lead. An ingenious section for drums closed the last Variation and leads to the Coda which is brilliant.

Dance Panels

Copland's comments about *Dance Panels* appear both in the Boosey & Hawkes score and on the 1975 CBS LP's sleeve. (S.S.)

Dance Panels was conceived as a ballet without a story. The published score is not a suite from the ballet but the entire music. Stylistically *Dance Panels* is direct and comparatively simple—some parts are very diatonic, 'white-notey,' one might say. The lyrical music is certainly plain, without complexities of texture. Portions of the score are quite lively and bouncy.

The introduction, with long, sustained notes, is in slow waltz tempo. The second section continues the waltz rhythm and is followed by the third, a light transparent scherzando. The fourth part is a melancholy and nostalgic pas de trois, while the fifth is characterized by brisk rhythms and jazzy drum patterns. The sixth section is a lyrical episode and, after a finale in jagged, irregular rhythms, the work ends as quietly as it began.

The music of the ballet was conceived as dance music, but without any specific 'story' in mind. The choreographer may present it as an 'abstract' ballet or as a 'story' ballet, according to his own ideas.

In concert performance, *Dance Panels* is to be played as one extended movement with only brief pauses between the separate sections.

Note that in ballet performances the fermata in the measure that precedes rehearsal numbers 1, 2, 3, and 8 is intended to last a considerable time during which the dance proceeds in silence. When performed in concert, however, each fermata should last for only the normal time span.

Something Wild

Copland composed the score for Jack Garfein's 1961 movie *Something Wild*. (S.S.)

Everyone is aware by now that composing for films is the most lucrative form of composition available to a composer. Because of that the acceptance of a film assignment automatically puts the composer under suspicion of merely taking on a well-paid job. But actually there is considerable craftsman satisfaction in writing for films on any level. It is the satisfaction that comes from knowing in advance that one's work may add something essential to the kind of group effort that a film represents. To work on the most serious level implies a motion picture on an equivalent plane of seriousness. That's what makes the choosing of a film script so important. For it is obvious that unless one is dealing with a film that really says something the composer will find it impossible to induce music from himself that fully engages his emotions. But more than that the composer would want to be convinced that by its nature the film was wide open for musical treatment and that his score would serve the picture in an important way.

Something Wild is that kind of film. Its theme is basic—how one young girl learns to live with violence. The picture tells its story with a minimum of dialogue, for which a composer is always grateful. The lengthy stretches of silent action invite musical comment in a way that imbues the whole picture with a certain musical 'tone.' It goes without saying that one must have an absolutely free hand in these matters, and this was assured me by Jack Garfein and George Justin, respectively the director and producer of the film.

An added zest came from the fact that it was twelve years since I had worked on a film score. As was true in the case of the five other Hollywood films that I had scored, this one also set up its own special problems.

Something Wild takes place in New York City and its action is interspersed with scenes of streets and subways, all of which were shot 'live' in the city. As a result the sound cameras picked up every variety of city noise: the trucks, the taxis, the subway trains, the police sirens, the slum kids' shouting. These present a serious threat to a composer intent on portraying the inner emotions of his characters. In one scene I tried for a while to outshout the bulldozer and the bridge traffic, but it proved a hopeless task. Since I couldn't fight the noise I decided to join it. In this instance the interweaving of noise and musical tension makes for a playing with sound that is perhaps more moving (and disturbing) than music alone could possibly be.

Bucolic scenes that are set in New York's Central Park can also be something of a trial for the composer's ingenuity. Charles Ives found an imaginative solution in his tone poem *Central Park in the Dark*. In *Something Wild*, our star Miss Carroll Baker is discovered asleep in the park in the early hours with a background of sky-scraper apartments. What I tried for were pastoral sounds that are edged with a steely quality, hoping thereby to suggest the country in the midst of the city.

It is a comparatively easy matter to reflect physical action in musical terms. More challenging are those moments when one attempts to think musically with the unspoken thoughts of the principal protagonists. *Something Wild* posed a related question: what does one do when the character is clearly unable to think consecutive thoughts? Such a scene occurs when Ralph Meeker returns to his apartment one night completely drunk. The natural continuity of music seemed wrong for the obviously foggy, disjointed nature of his mental processes. By using unexpected silences in a disconnected musical texture I hope to have suggested a somewhat unconventional solution. The musicians who recorded the score with me—there were fifty-six of us in all—had reason to wonder why the musical discourse stopped and started so fitfully. If they see the film (an unlikely supposition) I trust they will consider the discontinuities justified.

The most troublesome hurdle of all in *Something Wild* arises from the circumstance that the audience is kept guessing much of the time as to the underlying emotions and intentions of Miss Baker and Mr. Meeker. The trouble with music is that when it speaks it tells too much. In a motion picture like the Russian *Ballad of a Soldier* no such problem exists because we know that the instant that the boy meets the girl that love music is called for. That is not so in *Something Wild*. For a good third of the film we are in a quandary as to what the relationship really implies and that is part of the picture's fascination. Because of that I found myself exercising continual discretion in order not to give away too soon the real motives of my characters.

In most films the composer's prime opportunity comes at the very beginning of the picture, the so-called title music. The composer is supposed to do his best work accompanying a long list of screen credits before the audience knows anything about the film except its name. In the case of *Something Wild* I was given something a good deal more tangible to work with. The title and screen credits are superimposed on a background of shots of the city, some of them action shots and some abstractions created by Saul Bass. These cried out for musical enlivenment, giving me the chance to compose a sequence that may be thought of as the equivalent of a big city profile. The opening chord, taken alone, should give one a sense of the power and tensions inherent in the life of any metropolis. That one chord, in a way, should sum up what the picture is all about.

Connotations

The offer of a commission from the New York Philharmonic to compose a work for performance at the opening concert in its new home, Philharmonic Hall in Lincoln Center, sparked the writing of my *Connotations* for Orchestra. I began sketches for the composition early in 1961 and completed it in September 1962. After some consideration, I concluded that the classical masters would undoubtedly provide the festive and dedicatory tone appropriate to such an occasion. For my own part I decided to compose a work that would bring to the opening exercises a contemporary note, expressing something of the tensions, aspirations, and drama inherent in the world of today.

The *Connotations* for Orchestra is the first purely symphonic work I have composed since completing my Third Symphony in 1946. I have produced other works for orchestra since that time—the Orchestral Suite from my opera, *The Tender Land*, the revised version of my *Symphonic Ode*, the Orchestral Variations based on the Piano Variations of 1950 and the as yet unproduced Ballet in Seven Movements (1959). None of these (with the exception of the *Ode*) were composed in the first instance for orchestral performance.

Connotations also represents the first orchestral work in which I make use of twelve-tone principles. My first venture along Schoenbergian lines may be found in my Piano Quartet of 1950. This was further developed seven years later in my *Piano Fantasy*. Some critics have discerned earlier traces of these methods in my Piano Variations and in the earlier Song on an E. E. Cummings text, written in 1927. In the Quartet and the *Fantasy* the row is first presented as a theme. In the *Connotations* the row is first heard vertically in terms of three four-voiced chords with, needless to add, no common tones. When spelled out horizontally, these chords supply me with various versions of a more lyrical discourse.

The dictionary states that the verb *connote* means "to imply," to signify meanings "in addition to the primary meaning." In this case the skeletal frame of the row is the "primary meaning;" it denotes the area of exploration. The subsequent treatment seeks out other implications—connotations that come in a flash or connotations that the composer himself may only gradually uncover. The listener, on the other hand, is free to discover his or her own connotative meanings, including perhaps some not suspected by the author.

Structurally the composition comes closest to a free treatment of the baroque form of the chaconne. A succession of variations, based on the opening chords and their implied melodic intervals, supplies the basic framework. The variations are sometimes recognizably separate from one another, sometimes not. The problem, as in my Orchestral Variations, was to construct an overall line that had continuity, dramatic force, and an inherent unity. As has been pointed out many times, the dodecaphonic method supplies the building blocks, but it does not create the edifice. The composer must do that.

On the title page, *Connotations* for Orchestra bears the inscription: "Commissioned by the New York Philharmonic in celebration of its opening season in the Lincoln Center for the Performing Arts, and dedicated to the members of the orchestra and its music director, Leonard Bernstein."

The work is scored for large orchestra: three flutes, piccolo, two oboes, English horn, four clarinets (including E-flat and bass clarinets), two bassoons, contrabassoon, four horns, four trumpets, four trombones, tuba, timpani, piano, celesta, a large percussion group of instruments (played by five performers), and the usual strings.

Emblems

Boosey & Hawkes's score has these notes about *Emblems*. (S.S.)

In May, 1963, I received a letter from Keith Wilson, president of the College Band Directors National Association, asking me to accept a commission from that organization to compose a work for band. He wrote. "The purpose of this commission is to enrich the band repertory with music that is representative of the composer's best work, and not one written with all sorts of technical or practical limitations." That was the origin of *Emblems*.

I began work on the piece in the summer of 1964 and completed it in November of that year. It was first played at the CBDNA National Convention in Tempe, Arizona, on December 18, 1964, by the Trojan Band of the University of Southern California, conducted by William Schaefer.

Keeping Mr. Wilson's injunction in mind, I wanted to write a work that was challenging to young players without overstraining their technical abilities. The work is tripartite in form: slow-fast-slow, with the return of the first part varied. Embedded in the quiet, slow music the listener may hear a brief quotation of a well known hymn tune, "Amazing Grace," published by William Walker in *The Southern Harmony* in 1835. Curiously enough, the accompanying harmonies had been conceived first, without reference to any tune. It was only a chance perusal of a recent anthology of old "Music in America" that made me realize a connection existed between my harmonies and the old hymn tune.

An emblem stands for something—it is a symbol. I called the work *Emblems* because it seemed to me to suggest musical states of being: noble or aspirational feelings, playful or spirited feelings. The exact nature of these emblematic sounds must be determined for himself by each listener.

Music for a Great City

In 1962, the London Symphony Orchestra asked me to compose a symphonic work in celebration of its sixtieth anniversary season, inviting me to conduct the première performance with the Orchestra at London's Festival Hall on May 26, 1964.

I began work on the score during the latter part of 1963, completing it in April of 1964. The musical materials are derived in part from a film score I composed in 1961. The film starred Carroll Baker and was directed by Jack Garfein. The script was based on a novel by Alex Karmel called *Mary-Ann*. The picture was released for distribution in December 1961, under the title *Something Wild*.

The action of the story takes place in New York where all of the film was shot "live." Indoor scenes of tense personal drama were interspersed with the realistic sights and sounds of a great metropolis.

The nature of the music in the film seemed to me to justify extended concert treatment. No attempt has been made in *Music for a Great City* to follow the cinematic action of *Something Wild*. The four movements of the work alternate between evocations of big city life, with its external stimuli, and the more personal reactions of any sensitive nature in the varied experiences associated with urban living. *Music for a Great City* reflects both of these aspects of the contemporary scene.

The orchestral score has the following instrumentation: 3 flutes doubling on piccolos and alto flute, 2 oboes, English horn, 2 clarinets, bass clarinet, 2 bassoons, contra-bassoon, 4 horns, 3 trumpets, 3 trombones, timpani, 5 percussionists (playing a wide assortment of instruments), harp, piano, celesta, and the usual strings.

The title page of the work bears the inscription: Commissioned by the London Symphony Orchestra in celebration of its sixtieth anniversary season and dedicated to the members of the Orchestra.

Inscape

Copland's comments about *Inscape* appear in the liner notes of a Columbia LP with Leonard Bernstein conducting. (S.S.)

Two different series of twelve tones provide the materials from which is derived a major proportion of the entire composition. One of these dodecaphonic tone-rows, heard as a twelve-tone chord, opens and closes the piece. Another feature of *Inscape* is a greater leaning toward tonal orientation than is customary in serial composition.

The title is borrowed from the nineteenth-century English poet-priest Gerard Manley Hopkins. To the uninitiated, the word "inscape" may suggest a kind of shorthand for "inner landscape." But Hopkins meant to signify a more universal experience by his privately invented word. W. H. Gardner, his editor, described the sensation of inscape (or "instress of inscape," as Hopkins termed it) as a "quasi-mystical illumination, a sudden perception of that deeper pattern, order, and unity, which gives meaning to external forms." This description, it seems to me, applies more truly to the creation of music than to any of the other arts. Hopkins himself, incidentally, tried his hand more than once at musical composition.

Three Latin American Sketches

I would describe the character of the *Three Latin American Sketches* as being just what the title says. The tunes, the rhythms, and the temperament of the pieces are folksy, while the orchestration is bright and snappy and the music sizzles along—or at least it seems to me that it does. Nevertheless, the *Sketches* are not so light as to be pop-concert material, although certainly they would be a light number in a regular concert, much in the same way as *El Salón México*.

The first piece, *Paisaje Mexicano*, is poetic and lyrical. The second, *Danza de Jalisco*, is bouncy, contrasting the rhythms of $\frac{6}{8}$ and $\frac{3}{4}$. The final piece, *Estribillo*, is based on Venezuelan popular materials and is very vigorous.

Midday Thoughts

The liner notes of an LP on Etcetera Records contain these comments about *Midday Thoughts* and *Proclamation* for Piano. (S.S.)

Midday Thoughts is based on sketches for the slow movement of a projected *Ballade* for piano and orchestra dating from early 1944, when I was finishing *Appalachian Spring.* I had completely forgotten this music, which is very much in the manner of *Appalachian Spring.* A pianist friend, Bennett Lerner, called it to my attention and suggested that I consider fashioning a brief lyric piece from the materials. As I decided I liked the tune, this was a congenial idea, and *Midday Thoughts* was written in November 1982. Mr. Lerner gave the first performance at Carnegie Recital Hall, New York City, on February 28, 1983.

Proclamation

Proclamation for Piano (Duration: ca. 2 minutes) owes its existence to the urging of two friends, the composer Phillip Ramey and the pianist Bennett Lerner. They had noticed in my studio a sketch for a piano work begun in 1973, and they enthusiastically encouraged me to finish it. This was done in November 1982, and the rather stern-sounding piece, in what has not inappropriately been termed my "laying-down-the-law" style, was titled *Proclamation*. Mr. Lerner gave the world premiere on February 28, 1983 at Carnegie Recital Hall, New York City.

VII
Personal

Some of Copland's sharpest writing appeared in texts he labeled "Journals." Two selections appeared in his lifetime—the first in the periodical *Modern Music*, the other in his book *Copland on Music* (1960).

From a Composer's Notebook (1929)

"Inspire par la Muse de Tchaikovsky." This phrase, to be found on the title page of Stravinsky's latest score, will surely cause havoc among the musical "elite." Automatically these few words do away with the well-known theory which explains the newest manner of Stravinsky as a neo-classic revival brought on by a return to the ideals of Bach's day. But obviously one can't go back to Bach and to Tchaikovsky at the same time. This was first suspected when Stravinsky "returned," as they say, to Handel and Bellini in *Oedipus Rex*, and to Gluck and Johann Strauss in *Apollo*. The "Back to Bach" phrase had caught on, however, and nothing—not even Bellini and Strauss—seemed able to stop it. But I feel sure Tchaikovsky will.

No one has yet put forward an adequate explanation which covers all the works written by Stravinsky from the *Octuor* to *Le Baiser de la Fée*. Moreover, it is just because it is so difficult to penetrate the inner meaning of these new works that they are so rich in possibilities for the future.

Let me point out here three significant, though fairly obvious facts:

1. The one factor common to all the new works is Stravinsky's attitude towards the material he uses.
2. That attitude is an objective one, though not necessarily classically objective as was formerly believed.
3. The material he chooses to work with is not of great importance; it can be anything, banal or borrowed, from the sixteenth or from the nineteenth centuries; the only thing that counts is what he does with it. This has engendered an extreme elegance of style owing nothing to mere brilliance or cleverness.

My own guess is that these new works, far from being a throwback to any former period, tend towards a synthesis of the classic and romantic

285

periods that will result in a new style for which a new name will have to be found.

The American Composer Again

The weakness of American music, according to George Jean Nathan, "lies in the circumstance that its hopeful composers are in the aggregate trivial men. Two or three of them are pretty sound artists in a technical direction but as men, that is, as human beings, the bulk of them are psychically, mentally and—this in particular—emotionally commonplace." No doubt the bulk of our composers are trivial men, but so are the bulk of painters, poets, novelists, and critics. Mr. Nathan must agree that it is entirely within the bounds of probability that nature has endowed at least a *few* of our composers with heart, intellect, and depth of emotion. It is the failure of these few, not the commonplaceness of the many, which accounts for the weakness of American music.

Furthermore, it cannot be mere chance that the few exceptional men have thus far always failed. As I see it, the only adequate explanation is the nature of the environment in which they were placed. To take an extreme instance: at a time when America produced creators like Emerson, Poe, Melville, Whitman, there must have been one man of equal stature who was gifted along musical lines. But such a man, if he existed, was doomed. The environment killed him. Without the possibility of acquiring a technique, without orchestras, interpreters, publishers, listeners, in short without an organized musical life, it is impossible to develop composers. Mr. Nathan will tell you that we have had these things for the past fifty years. We have, but even today one cannot say that they are really at the disposal of the American composer.

The truth of the matter is that, musically speaking, America is very young, ridiculously young. It may take no one knows how long to grow up. Mr. Nathan must curb his impatience.

The Mahler Question

Those who most violently object to Mahler imagine they do so because he is trite, bombastic, long-winded. Why are they so sensitive to Mahler's faults? Is it because they are close to him and feel ashamed of his weakness, as if he were a spiritual half-brother? But Mahler is no relative of mine! To me it does not matter that he sometimes plagiarizes, sometimes lacks taste. I am willing to overlook his shortcomings for the sake of those real qualities which are also his: an apocalyptic grandeur, with its concomitant, a child-like naïveté greater than that of any other composer before him; an amazing contrapuntal mastery; an original orchestration thirty years in advance of his time. These things are not to be brushed aside. . . .

A Common-Sense Critic

A well-known Italian composer once told me that he thought the critical articles of Ernest Newman would retard the acceptance of modern music by fifty years. This is exaggerated, of course; but it is nevertheless true that because Mr. Newman is widely read and is published in "smart" magazines (and particularly because he never departs from good English horse-sense), he has had a more pernicious influence on public opinion than other critics of his generation. His process of reasoning is something like this:

> A number of people managed to persuade themselves about the time the war broke out, that we needed a new heaven and a new earth in music. From 1913 to 1923 new geniuses were being discovered every month. Of Malipiero, for instance, in 1918, one enthusiastic gentleman wrote that here was a man who was certain to produce "works of the first order." Here we are in 1929 and where is Malipiero now? And where are Ornstein and all the other geniuses, in this country and that, who were hailed as heralds of the new dawn? Personally, I am becoming exceedingly tired of the game; there are more profitable ways of spending one's energy than to trouble about what comes from the printing press of the "new music" etc. . . .

Mr. Newman is so plausible that I should be inclined to believe him myself, if I knew as little about new music as his readers.

Music and Words

Virgil Thomson can teach us all how to set English to music. If you insist on combining words and music you must be prepared to sacrifice one or the other. There is no such thing as equality of words and music, the few exceptions to this rule are special cases. To Thomson, words come first; so, in the manner of Satie's *Socrate*, he merely draws a frame of music around the words. In his setting of texts by Gertrude Stein—in the opera *Four Saints in Three Acts*, in *Capital, Capitals*, in his numerous songs—he has caught the rhythms and inflections which make the English language different from any other. Without the complexities of the English madrigalists, he manages to superimpose over an elementary accompaniment an amazing variety of rhythms merely because he allows the words to have the naturalness of speech. It would be impossible to translate these compositions into any other language; what better test of their fitness could be asked?

Modern Music Made Easy

Annually one of our symphony orchestras plays a new composition which leads the public and critics to think that at last they are beginning to get something out of modern music. As a rule such a work must be clear in form, brilliant in character, without obvious borrowings from Stravinsky or Schönberg, yet with plenty of dissonances (so that no mistake can be made as to its modernity). The success of this kind of work is assured; public and critics enjoy the sensation of adventuring in new tonal fields without losing their sense of direction, for in spite of all the strange foliage, they subconsciously recognize the land of old, familiar "heart-music." In some curious fashion, these compositions, though worthless in themselves, pave the way for a better appreciation of the real thing when it comes along.

Perhaps I had better add that this year's thrill was provided by Ernest Toch's Piano Concerto.

Signs of the Times

I quote from a letter recently received from Europe, written by a young American composer who is generally counted among the "radicals." "I can't say our season here has been thrilling, though I have had interesting impressions. First of all, Bloch's Quintet moved me in a way which was a real and great surprise . . . Secondly, *Tristan*, fairly well given at the opera, I found *great* and, in a curious way, disturbing, in spite of the fact that I have lived over every note in the score many times. Disturbing, I mean, because I am certainly no Wagnerian, am on the contrary aware of faults, weaknesses, etc.—and yet, when all this is said over and over again, where is the single work written since this that can be compared with it for a moment, in real force, in essential significance, in necessity, in importance, not to musicians, but to life as a whole? I must admit that in spite of *Pelléas*, in spite of *Les Noces* and *Oedipus*, it makes *la musique moderne* seems like *bien peu de chose*; and this not by virtue of what it (Wagner's music) pretends to be, but by virtue of what it really is. Not that one should be depressed; this has nothing to do with any movement or esthetic theory. It is, rather, because modern composers have not been big enough, not perhaps as musicians, but as human beings. And one cannot blame anyone for not having more personal force, more depth and strength and grandeur of vision than God gives him. I come more and more to believe that this is the essential thing, though I have always believed it to a pretty thorough extent."

If one of the second-line critics had written this, it would mean very little. Coming from the source it does, it is distinctly a sign of the changing times. . . . I cannot help adding that in a sense it is unfair to compare a work like *Tristan* with *Le Sacre du Printemps* and *Pierrot Lunaire*. *Tristan* is the crowning masterpiece of one hundred years of German romantic music while these later works are the masterpieces of a period of change, of experiment. Our *Tristan*, that is, the definitive work of our new musical era, has yet to be written. . . .

From a Composer's Journal
(1960)

La Forme Fatale

It seems to me now that there are two kinds of composers of opera. This thought occurred when I heard Henry Barraud explain his reluctance to plunge into a second opera after the performance of his first, *Numance*, at the Paris Opéra. His hesitation rang a bell and echoed my own thoughts. The fact that we can reasonably balance the thought of the labor and possible returns of an opera and decide calmly whether to launch into one again indicates that we are both different from the composer who is hopelessly attached to this *forme fatale*. We *play* at writing operas, but the operatic repertory is made up of works by men who could do little else: Verdi, Wagner, Puccini, Bizet, Rossini. It is some consolation to recall that we have precedent among the great dead who "played at it" too: *Fidelio*, *Pelléas*, *Pénélope*. (Mozart is, as always, a law unto himself.)

Ravel as Orchestrator

Georges Auric tells me that Ravel said to him that he would have liked to write a brochure on orchestration, illustrated by examples from his own work that did *not* come off. In other words, the reverse of Rimsky-Korsakoff's treatise, in which he illustrates only his successes. Auric also claims that Ravel told him he was dissatisfied with the final orchestral crescendo of *La Valse*. When I told this to Nadia Boulanger, she said that the morning after the première of *Bolero* she called to compliment Ravel on the perfection of his orchestral know-how. She reports that Ravel replied rather sadly, "If only the *Chansons madécasses* had come off as well." Curious, isn't it, that this humble approach to the arcana of instru-

ments combined should be the mark of the virtuoso orchestrator. (Schönberg quotes Mahler and Strauss to the same effect.)

The Soigné Approach

If there is anything more deadly to musical interpretation than the *soigné*
approach, I don't know what it is. (Thought of this during X's concert last
night.) When the emphasis is all on sheen, on beauty of sound, on suavity
and elegance, the nature of the composer's expressive idea goes right out
the window. Composers simply do not think their music in that way. Before all else, they want their music to have *character*—and when this is all
smoothed away by removing the outward marks of personality—furrowed
brow and gnarled hands and wrinkled neck—we get nothing but a simu-
lacrum of beautiful (in themselves) sonorities. When that happens in a
concert hall, you might as well go home. No music will be made there that
night.

Composer Reactions

Nothing pleases the composer so much as to have people disagree as to the
movements of his piece that they liked best. If there is enough disagree-
ment, it means that everyone liked something best—which is just what the
composer wants to hear. The fact that this might include other parts that
no one liked never seems to matter.

Music and the Man of Letters

The literary man and the art of music: subject for an essay. Ever since I saw
Ezra Pound turn pages for George Antheil's concert in the Paris of the
twenties, I have puzzled over what music means to the literary man. For
one thing, when he takes to it at all, which is none too often, he rarely
seems able to hear it for itself alone. It isn't that he sees literal images, as
one might suspect, or that he reads into music meanings that aren't there.
It's just that he seldom seems *comfortable* with it. In some curious way it escapes him. Confronted with the sound of music, we are all mystified by its
precise nature, and react differently to that mystery: the medical doctor has
an easy familiarity with it, often using it as a means of moving back quickly
to the world of health; the mathematician looks upon it as the sounding
proof of hidden truths still to be uncovered; the minister utilizes it as
handmaiden in the Lord's work . . . But the literary man, he seems mostly
to be uncomfortable with it, and when he puts two words together to characterize a musical experience, one of them is almost certain to be wrong. If

he uses an adjective to describe a flute, it is likely to be the one word a musician would never connect with the flute. A recent quotation from the letter of a dramatist: "If there is incidental music in the play, it should sing on the romantic instruments and forswear brass and tympany.[!]" For one G.B.S. [George Bernard Shaw] or one [Marcel] Proust or one [Thomas] Mann there are dozens of literature's great who rarely if ever venture a mention of music in the length and breadth of their work. These are the wise ones; the others, gingerly stepping amid the notes, are likely to fall flat on their faces. These others are the ones who puzzle me—and arouse a benign and secret sympathy.

Composer Psychology

At lunch with Poulenc, who recounted at great length the libretto of his new opera, *Les Dialogues des Carmélites*—it was easy to see how much the fate of this work, still to be heard, means to him. A little frightening to contemplate what his disappointment will be if the opera doesn't "go over." And yet he is giving it to La Scala of Milan for its world première—La Scala, famous for making mincemeat of new operas. There is something very composerish about all of this, for we would all willingly put our heads into the same noose. (Postscriptum: Poulenc won out this time!)

In Baden-Baden

Today I was reminded of my intention to write someday an orchestral work entitled *Extravaganza*. It seems a long long time since anyone has written an *España* or *Bolero*—the kind of brilliant orchestral piece that everyone loves.

The Orchestral Musician

Conducting the Sudwestfunk Orchestra, a particularly intelligent bunch of musicians, put me in mind of how curious a creature the typical orchestral musician is. Being the underdog in a feudal setup, he quickly develops a sort of imperturbability, especially as regards music. One can almost say that he flatly refuses to get excited about it. He is being paid to do a job— "Now let's get on with it, and no nonsense about it" is the implied attitude. You cannot play an instrument in an orchestra and admit openly a love for music. The rare symphonic instrumentalist who has managed to retain his original zest for music generally finds some means for expressing it outside his orchestral job. In thirty years of back-stage wandering I have never yet caught a musician with a book on music under his arm. As for reading program notes about the pieces he plays, or attending a lecture on the aesthetics of music—all that is unthinkable.

Something is wrong somewhere. Someone must find a way to make of the orchestral performer the self-respecting citizen of the musical community he would like to be.

Film Scores

The touchstone for judging a Hollywood score: Was the composer moved in the first instance by what he saw happening on the screen? If there is too much sheen, he wasn't; if there are too many different styles used, he wasn't; if the score is over-socko, he wasn't; if the music obtrudes, he wasn't. It is rare to hear a score that strikes one as touching because of the fact that the composer himself was moved by the action of the film.

Schönberg as Interpreter

I once heard *Pierrot Lunaire* conducted by its composer. It was a revelation of the value of understatement in interpretation—an element in interpretation that is little discussed nowadays. I was reminded of this by a quotation from Richard Strauss on the subject of his heroine Salome: "Salome, being a chaste virgin and an oriental princess, must be played with the simplest and most restrained of gestures. . . . " Schönberg underplayed the inherent hysteria of his lunar Pierrot—normalized it, so that it took its place alongside other musics instead of existing as the hysterical musical curiosity of a tortured mind.

Tempi

Of all the subtle qualities needed by a conductor, none is more essential than an instinct for adopting correct tempi. A gifted band of musicians can, if need be, balance itself (at least in repertory works); the solo instruments can project satisfactorily on their own; stylistic purity can be achieved naturally—but with the flick of a wrist a conductor can hurry a movement needlessly, drag a movement interminably, and in so doing distort formal lines, while the orchestra plays on helplessly. Conductors, in matters of tempi, are really on their own. Composers rarely can be depended upon to know the correct tempi at which their music should proceed—they lack a dispassionate heartbeat. The proof is simple: Ask any composer if he believes his own freely chosen metronome marks are rigidly to be adhered to, and he will promptly say, "Of course not." A composer listening to a performance of his music when the pacing is inept is a sorry spectacle indeed! He may be unable to set the right speed but he certainly can recognize the wrong one.

Voices

I hate an emotion-drenched voice.

The Young Conductor

After watching young student conductors for many years at Tanglewood I have decided that few things are more difficult than to judge adequately young talent in the conducting field. On the other hand, observing them at work helps to clarify what conducting really is. No man has the right to stand before an orchestra unless he has a complete conception in his mind of what he is about to transmit. In addition, he must possess a natural and easy authority, one that imposes itself without effort on each player. Without a conception there is, of course, nothing to impose. If one adds to this a natural facility of gesture, and a certain dramatic flair, then the visual aspect is taken care of. One needs, besides, an infallible ear, plus the ability to feel at home in many different styles. No wonder the student conductor often presents a pitiful spectacle. He cannot know, until it is put to the test, whether he has the right to be standing where he stands. But by the time he reaches the podium, it is too late. Unless he has "the gift," he is in for a rough time. Few experiences can be so unnerving; and at the same time, few successes more genuinely rewarding.

Musical Arousal

In a certain mood reading about music can excite one at the prospect of hearing some in rather the same way that reading about sex arouses one's lubricity.

Genius in a Small World

It takes a long time for a small country to get over a great man—witness Finland and Sibelius. Norway has taken fifty years to get over Grieg, and it looks as if Denmark would need as long a time to get beyond Carl Neilsen. If I were any of these men, it would not make me happy to know that my own work engendered sterility in my progeny.

The Teacher and the Pupil (1960)

This comment, archived among his papers at the Library of Congress, appeared in Copland's rough version of "From a Composer's Journal," but not in his final version in *Copland on Music*. (S. S.)

The teacher-pupil relationship in music is a mysterious one. I say this because I have yet to read a convincing account of a student attempting to convey what it is he or she imbibed from a music teacher. There must be subtle forces at work—too subtle to withstand close examination. I myself would have the same difficulty if I tried to explain what I learned from [Nadia Boulanger]. Perhaps the secret lies in the *ambiance* of learning a good teacher sets up, so that the simplest 'rules' or principles take on a magical quality. One cannot describe the instant and unspoken empathies between teacher and pupil within the framework of which all creative teaching is carried on.

Journal from
Venezuela Visit (1954)

In the course of his professional travels, Copland frequently kept a hand-written journal in which he recorded mostly musical experiences. For his visit to Caracas, Venezuela, in November and December 1954, for the First Latin-American Festival of Contemporary Music, he wrote by hand in a notebook with horizontal lines, whose cover reads "Cuaderno De Una Raya." He took similar notes on unlined paper during his 1963 return to Latin America. For photocopies of both journals, we are grateful to Prof. Elizabeth Crist of the University of Texas.

Typically, Copland pays attention to a large number of individuals. As in other passages from his journals reprinted here, he reveals his more critical side with grittier prose. This bluntness contrasts with the kinder public presentation of the same trip to Venezuela found in *The New York Times* article "Festival in Caracas." [When unsure of transcriptions, we have added a question mark between brackets, which were likewise used when we inserted additional names.] (R. K. & S. S.)

Non-stop flight in 7 hrs 50 min. Happy reception in the swanky Hotel T. (on the outskirts of town) by old friends: [Carlos] Chávez, Domingo Santa Cruz, [Jesús Maria] Sanromá, Villa-Lobos, J. J. Castro's, [Guillermo] Espinosa. Also four 5 former Tanglewood compostion students here— [Blas] Galindo [Dimas] from Mexico, [Harold] Gramatges and [Julián] Orbón from Cuba, [Héctor] Tosar [Errecart] from Uruguay, [Héctor] Campos-Parsi from Puerto Rico. (Also here: Edgardo Martin from Cuba. The Venezuelan composer: Antonio Esteves.) Virgil Thomson and I represented the U.S.A.

I missed the 1st two concerts, but heard tape recordings of some of the work: Of these, best impression was made on V.T. and myself by José-

María Castro's Preludes and Toccata. The Prelude was especially good—feelingful, harmonically expressive, rounded. The Toccata considerably less so.

Charming dance *Perion* by Luis Gianneo, perhaps too heavily orchestrated, but with plenty of flavor.

[Alberto] Ginastera's *Overture para el Fausto Criallo* is effective in its separate sections, but it doesn't add up to a piece.

Overtura del Salmo de Alegna by Jacobo Ficher had nothing of interest—operatic style, bombastic 'alegna,' obvious Russianisms of the old school.

Santa Cruz's Sinfonía concertate (para flauta solista, piano y cuerdas) is typical of his neo-classic style. Nice man—poor composer. The harmonies are haphazard, justified, I suppose, by the polyphonic independence. Result: dry and unrewarding.

Arturo Esteves' Concerto for Orchestra left a poor impression. It dates from 1950 and may no longer be typical of his present manner. It seemed inept—a badly digested version of [Paul] Hindemith. His *Cantata Criollo* will give another chance to judge his talent.

First concert I heard was all Brazilian under Villa-Lobos. It was a poorly chosen program—poorly conducted. At a week's distance, it is impossible to remember different contours of the various pieces. They all belonged to the folklore-inspired piece, done in such as manner as to be indistinguishable from one another. In another setting, they separately might have made a different—and better—impression.

Claudio Santoro's *O Café* had some Americanisms (del norte) in the 1st part but seemed poorly sustained in the later sections.

There was a *Xango* by Burke Marx, pieces by Cosme and Mignone, 2 movements from *Sononia* No. 2 by O[scar] Lorenzo Fernandez; the best known of the V-L *Bachiana Brasileiras,* and a colorful hodgepodge by V-L to end the program called *Papagais de Moleque* [?]. This man V-L is the pride and despair of all Latin-American musicians. [Camargo] Guarinieri, who should have been given the program to conduct, was unable to come due to his regular job as a conductor in São Paolo.

The Mexican program under Chávez was well presented. Again the program seemed over-similar in content. It began with a neo-classic *Obertura Festiva* of Rodolfo Halffter—no great shakes. Seemed thin and poverty-stricken in musical ideas—tho well orchestrated. [Manuel] Ponce's *Terial* has some pretty spots but is naïvely sewed together, dispelling whatever charms it possesses by formal repetitions and inadequacies. [Silvestre] Revultas' *Cuauhnahuac* leaves a sharp, but fragmentary impression. The [Candelerio] Huízar *Pueblerinas* did not seem to warrant exhortation. Chávez walked off with the honors easily with *Antigona* and *Sinfonía India.* (Galindo was not represented).

The next concert was divided between J. J. Castro and Villa-Lobos. It began with 2 more pieces by V-L—*Erosion* and Chôros No. 9. Inexcusable—both of them—and for the same reason: an absolutely chaotic juxtaposition of the good, bad, and indifferent. One wonders how he justifies the form to himself and to what extent he imagines he is getting away with murder. His participation in the Festival has had a depressing effect—and this is paradoxical, because of his pre-eminent position in Latin-American music.

Juan José Castro's Piano Concerto, brilliantly played by Jesús María Sanromá, was precisely what I expected: an honest piece, professionally done, with a certain superficial brilliance and an old-fashioned facture [sic], but essentially empty. Castro is not a real composer because he has nothing of his own to contribute. It is music that wins prizes, but that's all.

Tosar's early Toccata seemed especially fine in this company. Written at 17, it stands up well and promises more than he has fulfilled to date.

At a private séance (with V.T. at the home of the critic Alejo Carpentier), Tosar played records of a Suite for Strings, a Piano Sonatina, a movement sinfónica, and excerpts from another orchestral work. He seems not to have made much progress since his Tanglewood days. His music has sincerity and mood, and even line. But his loveliest music is [?] by a pianistic conception which he cannot translate into satisfactory orchestral terms. Thick basses that don't sound and, in general, an over-thick texture gives everything he does a kind of leaden quality. His intelligence seems slow—which is a great pity, for he is a very musical fellow. His Piano Sonata made the best impression, but here again—an over-consistency of style ends up by becoming oppressive.

Working on the "Freedom" piece each afternoon in the studio of Esteves, with a sensational view of Caracas down below. It is gradually shaping itself.

Many (too many) social reunions. One to the so-called Junto Country Club. Scary ride up into the mountains. Everything covered in mist when we got there. Coming back it took 45 min. to pass through the city because of traffic conditions.

Round table discussion about the advantages and weaknesses of the nationalistic trend. I was persuaded—by acclamation—to speak in Spanish extempore. (Sanromá told me later I referred several times to los jovenes compositores.) My point was that we, the older generation, had gone thru the nationalist-conscious phrase and had now emerged with Mexican, Brazilian, U.S. music. Problem is different for the younger generation—since they by now have a tradition to look up into or react against. I warned them against looking toward quotations of folk themes as an easy solution for their problems. (V-Lobos makes fiery speeches—just like an actor.)

Latin American Tour Journal (1963)

Sept. 7—Oct. 20, 1963

Sept 7—All night flight to Rio. V saw me off.

Sept 8—Arrival at the Gloria. After 3 hours sleep I moved to the Copacabana Palace Apts. Management of concert seems completely disorganized, as usual. At 6:30 PM, on the receiving line at a reception at the Residence of Ambassador Gordon (with Richard Tucker). Later, concert at the Candelaria Church (with Mary Orem) to see 81 year old Stravinsky conduct his mass. Performance *very* tentative. Piece sounded *very* chaste.

Sept 9—Chilean Ballet in the evening doing a danced version of [Carl Orff's] *Carmina Burana*. Not bad, but not too good. Me & Schoenberg's great nephew and Roberto Barry from B.A.—who is 'mad' at me. Supper afterwards with the Orems, who seem discouraged with the Brazilians and their situation.

Sept 10—Went book hunting in Rio. Poor game. Worked on my B.A. lectures.

Sept 11—Re-visited the Botanical Gardens. Impressive trees from all tropical countries (Too bad Mr. Harpin can't see them.) Went to the Chilean Ballet again with the Orems (Frank & Mary). Saw a revival of [Kurt Jooss' ballet] *The Green Table*—has aged considerably.

Sept 12—Lecture in the afternoon at the Universidad de Guanabára. Much ceremony and awarding of certificate as *musicólogo. Muito simpatico,* etc.—but I doubt whether anyone in the audience of 35 knew a single note of my music! Tea afterwards with Amer. C.A.O. Ed Borufs *chez lui.* Worked on my lectures at night. Not a very amusing life.

Sept 13—Brandaõ came to see me with music—most of it old stuff. Seemed to want to hear me tell him it was N.G. I obliged, and he seemed relieved, and ready to turn over a new leaf. Dr. Zins, an Austrian refugee, and wife entertained me at 5. Walked home on the Av. De Copacabana. It was a lovely walk. It's been a long time since I felt so little needed.

Sept 14—Flight to B.A. in 3 hours. Met at airport by 'Ghata' Ginastera and the Director of the di Tella Foundation, Enrique Oteiza. Dinner in the evening with the Juan José Castros, the Ginasteras, and the Oteizas. Talk of 16 years ago, when I was last here.

Sept 15—Afternoon drive to San Isidro to visit Victoria Ocampo, where I had been in 1947. Beautiful house owned by a real 'grande dame'. Discussion with JJ Castro about the new music, with Mrs. Ocampo clearly on my side, and seemingy quite taken with me!

Sept 16—First rehearsal with Orquestra Filharmonica. They are a willing group, with mixed elements, as is usual in S. A. Worked at the di Tella Institute in the afternoon on my lectures. Dinner with the Ginasteras, after which we went to orchestral concert at the Colón, conducted by Hamburg's Schmitt-Isserstedt.

Sept 17—Morning rehearsal. (Parts of Diamond and *Billy* not arrived!) Worked *four* hours in the afternoon on the 1st lecture script with an Ecuadorean student. Squeezed in radio interview, and 2 newspaper interviews. 'Home' exhausted!

Sept 18—Morning rehearsal. First lecture at 6:30 PM. Full house, receptive crowd, everybody seemed pleased. My Spanish reading ability has gained in ease.

Sept 19—More rehearsals—more work on lectures. It's *endless*. A monk's life with Lavalle St. around the corner.

Sept 20—Two rehearsals with 2 orchestras, morning the Filharmonica at the Colón, afternoon the Radio Orch. at the Law School. (Horrible acoustics at the school—how do the musicians stand it?) (written on plane, Quito to Bogota—10/12/63)

Sept 21—Dress rehearsal in the Colón. Spent the afternoon working on lectures for the di Tella series. At 5 spent a pleasant hour being photographed for a Sunday Supplement of *La Nación* ("A.C. in the Quiet City") by 2 bright youngsters. Evening, more lecture work.

Sept 22—Quiet day. Concert at 6:30. I was concerned about the size of the audience in the opera house. But it turned out to be OK. The orchestra was at its best; which was only pretty good. Audience seemed pleased. But for some strange reason they did not seem to know *Billy the Kid* was finished when we got to the end. Supper later as the guest of Jacobo Ficher & Señora (quelle bloody bore). Ginasteras & Mrs. Bautista were there (wife of the composer Julian Bautista).

Sept 23—Rehearsal with the Radio Orch. in the Facultad de Derechos Auditorium. *Ghastly* acoustics. (sounds like Notre Dame.) No p- possible. Once again, how do the musicians stand it? With only an hour's interlude, off to my second lecture. Big crowd again, which held out to the end of my 6 talks. After a quick supper alone I stopped in to hear a Piano Concerto by the Argentine composer Arizaba, conducted by Roberto Kinsky. The piece never discerned its own reason for being.

Sept 24—Two rehearsals, aft. and eve.—5 hours in all; es mucho in such a hall. The orchestra is more mature than the Colón group, but slower in learning things. Sometimes I think I've 'had it' in these parts, as far as orchestras go.

Sept 25—Rehearsal in the aft. Another dash to an 'Acto' at 6:30 PM, where I was solemnly inducted as Honorary Member of the Academia de Bellas Artes. All the music friends came—JJ Castro, Ficher, Giannio, etc. A supper party afterwards in my honor at the home of Jennette Irede, patron of the Mozarteum Society. Pleasant and ambitious French woman with a one track mind. Large and talkative party. (My tummy is shaky!)

Spet 26—Rehearsal in after and concert at 9:30 PM (always a tough assignment) at the Facultad de Derechos. Packed house of students, mostly—and like students, very enthusiastic (much autographing afterwards). But the acoustics of the hall still made it impossible to get a p' int of the orchestra. Probably the noisiest concert ever given anywhere!

Sept 27—Lunch with the Ginasteras and JJ Castro *chez* a rich Argentinian amateur of the arts. ? Shaw. Very Park Av. Apt overlooking the river. Third lecture at 6:30. Afterwards we drove in the rain to Belgrano for a supper with Mrs. di Tella and family. A nice lady—Mrs. di Tella—humane and sensible. The C.A.O. (Cultural Affairs Office) officers & wife, Dr. Grupps, was there.

Sept 28—Spent the day writing lecture VI. But delivered Lecture IV at 6:30. Crowd there despite Sat. after. Afterwards we went for supper to the home of a Mr. Civitas, Italian refugee who has made good in the publishing field. An atmosphere of the self-made man hung about the place, in strong contrast to the di Tella mansion, but it was rather more interesting.

Sept 29—A day spent on nothing but finishing sixth lecture. *Finally*, they were done. *Ojalá*.

Sept 30—Met with my first 'students' at the di Tella Foundation. Have a bad conscience at not being able to see more of them; so much time spent on orchestral rehearsals, concerts, and finishing the lectures. (No outward sign of resentment, however). See further on in this notebook for report on each student. In the evening, Lecture V.

Oct 1—More students. I also listened to a tape of a work by Ricardo Malipiero, colleague from Italy on the staff of the school. I recognized my own kind of 12 tone treatment. Piece seemed over-difficult for its content. In the evening, final lecture (VI) followed by a party chez the Ginasteras for all the 12 composer-students. I played the tape of the *Connotations* for them—couldn't tell what they thought.

Oct 2—More students' works examined—all day long. At 8 I was 'interviewed' by a dumb female who wanted to know what I thought of the difference between 'ethos y pethos', et al. I left her to entertain friends at a dinner party at Valerio's Restaurant: Fichers, Gianneos, Malipiero, Mrs. Julian Bautista, and the Ginasteras. It didn't come off too well. They all knew each other for too long and too well.

Oct 3—More students. Packed in afternoon. Left for Santiago at 7:10 PM. Mercedes Ginastera and Mrs. Erede saw me off. Smooth trip to Chile in 1 hr 50 min. Marvellous view of the Andes in the moonlight with snow covered tops of mts. and deep black crevices between. Was met at the airport by Domingo Santa Cruz, Celso Garrido Lecca, and Leon Schidlowsky; also the C. A. O. in Santiago, Philip Turner. After dropping my things at the Carrera Hotel I took off with the Chilean musicians named above for a Chinese restaurant. Much excited talk about music, such as I hadn't heard for some time.

Oct 4—Local situation with C.A.O.; not much liked by local musicians. No tact, apparently. Plotted my activities with him for the week in the morning and met Ambassador Cole, nice guy—former Pres. of Amherst College. Press conference at 12:30 was packed (Embassy people impressed with the turn-out; said I pulled more people than Tito!) At 7 reception for me at the Residencia. Large crowd of musicians with much undercover talk about the fact that a number of leftist musicians were present. Pumped hands until I was exhausted (Tummy shaky, any way.) Afterwards I went to Domingo's house for supper (his wife Filomena was pitiful to watch—has Parkinson's disease) He drove me back to the hotel.

Oct 5—Back to Domingo's house in the afternoon to hear some of his music (his idea). Similar impression ot the one I had years ago; a hard worker with only moderate musical gift. Tends to overdo logic, hammering away, pattern-wise, without much sensitivity to actual music-making. A fautly harmonic sense and little feeling for [??] then. It is surprising what he has accomplished for Chilean music, given his modest musical equipment. At 7 my first lecture at the Biblioteca Nacional (a gloomy lecture hall) for the Ass. Nacional de Compositiones. Pablo Garrido [not to be confused with composer Garrido-Lecca] presided. Afterwards a formal dinner given me by the composers. The Amer. Ambassador and his wife came. Speeches and toasts. Later Garrido insisted on taking me to a 'boite', where he idiotically had me 'announced' to the crowd. The young Chilean composer & German wife, José Asuar, was at our table. Ended up at 3:30 AM having coffee in Garrido's crowded little apartment.

Oct 6—At 8 AM awakened by the Banda del Ejercito playing in the Square under my window. At noon interview with Ariel Dorfman, 21-year old journalist, who seemed very bright. At 3 I went out to visit Carlos Riesco in his lovely old (and falling apart) hacienda outside Santiago. His wife and 2 children are charming, his compositions only fair. Before that I had had lunch with Garrido-Lecca and his wife Raquel at the Golf Club. Much talk about his forthcoming Guggenheim year in N.Y.

Oct 7—First rehearsal with the orchestra. Lots of enthusiasm—we get on fine. From 3 to 5 I listened to tapes of music by Chilean composers in the Instituto.

Leon Schidlowsky: *Triptico for Orch* ('59) Explosive, dramatic, no tunes—seems like stage music without the stage. Not my dish (very Jewish personality)

Carlos Botto—*Canos al Amor y a la Muerte* ('56) Sensitive; but the sentiment too ordinary.

Ten Preludes: Ten Piano Pieces—better, more varied

Gustavo Becerra[-Schmidt]—Quartet No. VI (1961) Lots of impulse, imagination, sounds well. (a little Bartok-y). Playable abroad. I was surprised it was so good. A Kouss. F. [Koussevitzky Foundation] award?

Sinfonía I (1956) Compact and imaginative. Poor final mvt—(lasts 10½ min in all)

Oct 8—Rehearsal A.M. Felt slightly tummy-sick afterwards. Lunch with Pablo Garricco. Took to my bed afterwards and had the doctor to re-assure me it was superficial. Stayed in all day.

Oct 9—Rehearsal AM (Garrido-Lecca attends them all.) In the afternoon I listened to more tapes of Chilean composers:

Eduardo Madurano—10 miro-piezas for str. Quartet short playable pieces. Also another work by him: *Gamma limo*—a disjointed, unsuccessful ballet (badly played)

Enrique Rivera—*La Ausencia* for tenor and instrumental ensemble. This 22 year old composer, still a student in the conservatory, impressed me as the most gifted youngster I have met on the trip. The music is à la page, but not too much so. He is very sure of himself, technically; and knows what he wants to do artistically. A fine talent, and a sympathetic kid.

Fernando Garcia—*American Insurrection*—a cantata for reciter, chorus, & orchestra Spotty in musical interest—lacks any real organization, superficially effective.

In the evening a lecture at the Catholic University. Large and attentive crowd. I spoke on Los Placeres de la Musica. Afterwards supper with the Pablo Izquierdas, head of the Univ. Music Dept, the Garrido-Leccas, Schidlovskys, and Philip Turner. (Latter is definitely a dumb-bell)

Oct 10—Rehearsal in the A.M. Distributed music to local musicians at the Embassy offices. Met the young composers class at the Conservatory in the afternoon. Becerra, as head teacher, was there. A sympathetic group, interested in newest trends, but anxious to add a social purpose to their music.

Once again Rivera struck me as the bright boy in the group. Dinner at Turner's house. Point of this was to entertain the rival faction of the Filharmonia Orch. under Juan Matteucci. *Ghastly* evening with ersatz guests and dinner served at 11 PM, and the Turners full of apologies, which didn't help.

Oct 11—Dress rehearsal. I dashed away at 12 noon to receive an honorary professorship from the Rector of the Univ. of Chile. All the composers attended in solemn session, and Domingo Santa Cruz made a touching speech. The concert went off well. Afterwards to Domingo's house for a small supper party including Amb. Cole and wife. He told me that in his 2 year stay in Santiago they had never had a U.S. Cultural event to match the concert and activities. Nice to know!

Oct 12—Up at 6 AM to take the plane to Bogotá. The Ambassador and his wife were also traveling. During a one hour stop at Lima, Peru, a large contingent received me at the airport—Americans and Peruvians. Itwiriaga and Sanchea Maloga, the composers and also the head of local orchestra was there. Felt sorry to have to pass them by, but the musical ambiente is too sickly to warrant a visit. Met at Bogotá by Embassy staff, and Otto de Greif (also at airport in 1941!) critic, with a younger critic, Manuel Drezner. Obviously, nothing much planned except the concerts. After resting up— (much needed)—I walked around the town a bit and recognized practically nothing from 1941. (Turns out my hotel of 1941 had been burned down by revolutionary riots in 1948.) Dinner alone and early to bed.

Oct 13—Jack Heidelberg, pianist, rang up and we lunched together. A local music-loving couple, the Theo Hermanns drove me out of town to the famous cathedral, inside the Salt Mine Mountain. Fantastic sight—especially as a Mass was being celebrated while we were there. We got back to the Hotel Tequiendama just in time for my dinner chez Ambassador Freeman. Before going had a talk with the C.A.O. and arranged for more activity: press conference, lecture, etc. (He made some lame excuses about the altitude and not wanting to overwork me.) The Ambassador is a music-lover; proved it by turning on my Piano Quartet as background for cocktail pleasantries. But he's a nice guy (career man).

Oct 14—First rehearsal with the Bogotá orchestra. The stage of the ancient Colón Theatre is tiny, the orchestra not as good as Chávez reported (2 years ago). Not a full complement of strings, and a poor percussion section. Thank heavens, the program is comparatively easy.

P.M.—various chores, interviews, etc. Had dinner with Luis Antonio Escobar, leading composer in Colombia. He is being very helpful in manoeuvering me around.

Oct 15—2nd rehearsal A.M. Olaf Roots, the permanent conductor, seems to be enjoying the rehearsals more than I am. Lunched with Escobar, after which we went to see some paintings by Colombian artists—Obregon,

Maxus, Widermann, etc. At 4, a well attended press conference, but the questions were none too bright. Dinner at 8 chez the Theo Hermanns with the Roots and another couple. Excellent food, which I much appreciated after all the restaurant stuff I've been having.

Oct 16—Rehearsal A.M. In the P.M. interview (in Spanish) for the National Radio of Colombia. At 6:30 a lecture to the public of the Museum of Modern Art, a sort of local 'New School', left-wing-ish, according to the Embassy ??. Full house, but my tape didn't work! (Did Santiago copying erase it?) Dinner with Jack H and young Colombian composer Larkas Estrada.

Oct 17—Final rehearsal. Dashed off at noon to do a TV interview with Escobar in Spanish. The studio people seemed very pleased. Rested in the P.M. On the way to the concert at 6:30 P.M. Roots told me that one of our cellists had died of a heart attack that afternoon. Since his wife played at same stand, we had 4 cellists for the concert. This unfortunate event colored the 1st half of the concert (We played the Coda of *App. Spr.* in memory of him.) But the Colón Theatre was packed—(unprecedented, they told me) and much enthusiasm engendered. Big party for me afterwards chez Escobar. The Americans present seemed especially pleased. A group of university students sang some chorsuses—the glee club movement just getting under way down here.

Oct 18—Went to the Gold Museum with the Escobars. Unique show. Rested up in the afternoon. Repeat concert, free to students, at the Ciné Colombia. The 2300 seats were full. But the acoustics were horrible, so the orchestra sounded muerto. Dull party afterwards chez Milton Leavitt, head of the local Bi-National Center.

Oct 19—Took it easy all day. J.H and Estrada came to say good-bye, also Oscar Buenaventura. Escobar took me to a tea chez Wiedermann, painter, who seemed delighted with my visit—so much so that he gave me a water-color. Dinner with Hermanns and Roots. The Israeli Ambassador came by.

Oct. 20—Up at 6:30 for a 9 AM plane. Seven gentlemen saw me off: the composers Roberto Pineda, Oscar Buenaventura, critic Otto de Greif, 3 Embassy staff—C.A.O. David Garth, ass't John Griffiths, Milton Leavitt, and Theo Hermann. This was meant as a compliment to me. Ojalá!

Letters (1923–1944)

Preternaturally mature, Copland was able at the age of twenty-two to write like an adult professional to his Parisian teacher, initially in a mixture of French and English. This book's editors here and elsewhere have identified certain names within brackets—[ ].

July 25, 1923
Dear Mademoiselle Boulanger,—

Nothing of very great importance has happened to me since I left Paris. But I want to write you at least a few words so that you may have no cause for thinking that I have forgotten you. No! I most certainly haven't forgotten you. In fact, if I liked, I might get really sentimental about the Rue Ballu and all that it has meant and still means to me. Mais, après tout, vous le savez aussi bien que moi, et puis—n'est-ce pas, c'est vous qui a dit—"Copland n'est pas romantique du tout"!? Not being romantic, I mustn't get "sentimental" about anything, must I? But I am sure you will understand what I feel I owe you after two years of work, just as you understood the emotion in my apparently cold Passacaglia. (Est-ce que, vraiment, vous comprenez quelque chose dans cet anglais un peu "tordu"?)

Next week I am going to Salzburg with my friend M. [Harold] Clurman. Six successive evenings of modern music should prove a big enough feast for even so insatiable a gourmand as myself. I suppose you have seen the programmes, but to be sure, I am enclosing a copy. I am particularly interested in hearing [Nikolai] Miaskowsky's work, because Boris de Schloezer, whose opinions are generally reliable, has spoken very well of him. Bartók's second violin sonata—(the first is already published); Hindemith's Clarinet quintette and the works by Bliss, Prokofieff, & Krenek should be especially worthwhile. Then there are the unknown names of [Leos] Janacek, [Othmar] Shoeck, [Philipp] Jarnach, etc. which sound tempting. All in all, the programmes are satisfying, but I wonder why they thought it necessary to give Roussel's *Divertimento*, or Szymanowski's early *Hafislieder* or Lord Berners' rather silly *Valses bourgeoises*. Et Sem Dresden—je me demande ce que ça peut être! (I have noticed with regret that Mlle. [Marcelle] de Manziarly's Trio is not included on the list.) I shall write you an account of the Festival and we shall hear what we shall hear.

After spending five weeks in Vienna, I can only say that it is "pas mal,"—beaucoup plus sympathique que Berlin, mais loin d'être Paris. It lacks, perhaps due to the war, a certain care-free atmosphere—"la joie de vivre." But of course, these are first impressions, and I will be able to judge it better when I am here longer.

I have found excellent surroundings in which to work and spend most of my time on composition and learning German. Thru an abonnement I am enabled to read over lots of new music and I am specializing in Bruckner, Reger and Mahler! (Vous savez que Reger est pour les Allemands ce que Fauré est pour les Français!) I have played a Violin Sonata by Reger (op 72) which is surprisingly good and encourages me to get more familiar with his work. On the other hand, for me, Bruckner is "carrément mauvais"!

Pour le ballet, il n'y a qu'une chose à dire: je fais mon possible—qui est quelque fois cinq heures par jour. So even if I don't accomplish anything I have the satisfaction of knowing that I worked hard!

Et Gargenville? Et Fontainebleau? Et Madame Boulanger et [Kurt] Hesselberg et Mary Sanders et tout le monde va bien j'espère.

Sincerely,

Vienne le 12 aôut, 1923 [12 August 1923]
Chère Mademoiselle,—

D'abord, on n'a pas joué le Myaskowsky. Ça, vous savez——! Et puis, le Prokofieff n'était pas du tout intérressant. Une ouvre de jeunesse probablement. Le Ravel et le Stravinsky que vous et moi—je veux dire nous—(nous autres Français!)—connaissons depuis longtemps, ont été acclamés par toute la salle. They were the "hit" of the festival. Mais le Milhaud, le Poulenc et même le sonate pour l'alto de Honegger était assez peu gouté. Pourquoi? Je n'en sais rien!

Il y avait beaucoup d'internationalisme mais, malheureusement, pas beaucoup de choses extraordinaires. Je suis bien sûr qu'on a joué [Yrjö] Kilpinen parce qu'il est finlandais et [Emerson] Whithorne parce qu'il est américain et de même pour plusieurs autres. Naturellement, le monde ayant tant besoin d'internationalisme en ces jours-ci, on peut le supporter; mais c'est de la mauvaise musique tout de même!

Peut-être croyez-vous que je regrette d'être allé à Salzbourg? Pas le moins du monde. D'abord il y a la ville elle-même,—une joie pour l'esprit, et les environs avec ces montagnes qui vous attraient tellement. Et on monte jusqu'aux hauteurs vertigineuses et on admire "the Old World"—(comme on dit chez nous)—qui a l'air tout à fait neuf. Les montagnes—ça vous interesse aussi, j'en suis certain; mais revenons à la musique ou je me sens plus à mon aise.

C'était par les ouvres de Hindemith, de Krenek, et de Hába que j'étais le plus frappé. Vous savez, je suppose, que tout le monde ici parle de Hindemith—on le joue partout, on l'appelle "le jeune Reger," on attend beaucoup de lui. Il a commencé par faisant du Brahms, mais il est bien loin de ça maintenant. Sa musique est extrêmement vigoreuse—d'un élan irrésistible. Ce que je lui reproche le plus est son manque d'idées fraîches. Il est le plus original dans ces scherzos qui sont quelquefois vraiment diaboliques. C'est drôle, n'est-ce pas, qu'avec de telles qualités il écrit de la musique de chambre? (Il y a aussi trois opéras d'un acte que je ne connais pas.)

La réputation de Krenek était établie tout récemment. Son troisieme quatuor à cordes était donné à Salzbourg: je le trouve inégal, mais rempli de belles choses, malgré des moments d'une laideur affreuse. On appelle Krenek un néo-classique, mais je vous previens qu'il écrit des dissonances atroces! Alois Hába est moins hardi, malgré son système de quart de ton. Mais son quatuor aussi m'a laissé avec une impression très favorable. Je peux dire beaucoup plus des oeuvres de Schoenberg, de Bartók, de Kodály ou de Janacek, mais je m'arrête parce que je crains de vous ennuyer.

Your little note in English gave me the idea of writing to you in French and I hope the result has not been too awful. But it is so much easier to write English that I will finish off that way.

During my stay in Salzburg I read André Gide's new book on Dostoievsky. (I must explain to you that my friend [Harold] Clurman and myself are ardent 'disciples' of Gide.) He says many interesting things concerning the Frenchman's need of logic and its relation to 'la grande ligne.' I must tell you one quotation he makes from the German, Rathenau, which I think eminently true. Rathenau says that it is because she has never consented either to sin or to suffering that America has no soul . . . .

Can I hope for another letter from you soon?

Sincerely,

[Brooklyn, New York]
Aug 26, 1924
Dear Mademoiselle Boulanger,—

Thank you so much for the program. I can very easily imagine all the work it must have been to prepare five of my things to be played at Fontainebleau and I am extremely grateful to you for having taken so much trouble upon yourself.

I have been a little reluctant to write to you this time because I have nothing very glorious to tell about myself. Two weeks ago I politely resigned my position as jazz pianist at Milford. I found it impossible to work on the organ sinfonietta because I could get no piano in a quiet place. As the time was getting short, I thought it best to leave. During the six weeks I was there I got very fat (dîtes-le, au moins, à Marion Sarles!) and I made an ink copy of the *Cortège Macabre*.

Just now I am in Brooklyn, living at my sister's house—but by the middle of September I hope to find a room for myself where I can work. I spend all of my time now, working on the organ composition. Let me tell you how far it is advanced.—For several reasons I have decided to make it in three movements instead of four. The first movement will be a short andante (the andante I wrote in May), then the scherzo, and lastly will come the most important movement with which I originally thought I would begin the work. It will take about twenty minutes altogether. (Honegger's first violin sonata has three movements arranged something like that.)

So far I have completely finished only the first movement, which is also orchestrated. But the other two movements are, pour ainsi dire, finished— that is, they are clear in my mind, but I must still write them down and orchestrate them and fill in the details. If I send it to you by October 1st, you will still have two full months to prepare it. It goes without saying that any corrections you make, I approve of, a priori. I am so glad Smiss is coming here—as soon as I have shown him the first movement, I will send it to you before the other two movements. If you have anything to suggest, please, by all means, write me immediately.

Now that my score is ready for [Boston orchestra conductor Serge] Koussevitzky I have been wondering just what to do about having the parts copied. It is terribly expensive here, but I suppose it must be done, and I shall manage to get the necessary money somehow.

Forgive me for making this a "business letter." I should have preferred telling you about other things—our jazz-bands, for instance, or Gide's *Corydon*, but I'll leave it for another letter.

Now that Smith has gone, Gargenville must be very quiet. Clurman and I expect to make him talk for hours and hours about everything that has happened since our departure. (By the way, did you receive Clurman's letter?)

I hope Madame Boulanger is in the best of health and hasn't completely forgotten me as yet. Remember me to everyone else I know in France!

With best regards from Clurman

Your devoted friend

135 W. 74 St.
April 3, 1925
Dear Mademoiselle,—

It was a great relief to know you were back safe. From the silence, I take it for granted you are never coming back here. I suspected as much. Is there time yet to change your mind?

I have many little things to write you about. First, the Guggenheim Foundation. This was organized recently to give scholarships to young men like myself. Mr. [Thomas Whitney] Surette is on the Board of Trustees and has asked me for letters from my teachers. Must I bother you with this stupid business? I'm afraid I must. Please send me a letter of recommendation as soon as you can find time. Mr. Damrosch has already sent me one. The scholarship is for [$] 2,500, is to begin in October, and can be used anywhere.

I suppose Miss Wolff told you about Rochester. It will be a good opportunity to hear the *Cortège*. I shall write you my impressions later. I had a rendez-vous with Koussevitsky here in New York. It came about in this manner. The League of Composers have asked me to compose a work for small chamber orchestra, which they will have performed next season. Because [Leopold] Stokowski conducts 2 concerts of the other Guild, they wanted to get Koussevitsky for 2 concerts for their League. I was chosen to see Koussevitsky about it. He is delighted and has accepted. (But it is still a secret so do not mention it too much. Dieu sait pourquoi!) At first, I thought of setting part of Rimbaud's *Saison en Enfer*, but I have changed my mind and now I think I will write a series of pieces to be called "Incidental Music for an Imaginary Drama." I think that is a better idea. I even have a few themes already. While talking to Koussevitsky, he said that he was willing to play anything I gave him next season, and had even announced over the radio that he would repeat my Symphony at the end of this season on an all-American program. But since time is too short, the all-American program will not be given until next winter. (Who will play the organ part, I wonder?)

Puisqu'il est si emballé que ça, it occurred to me only today that perhaps I can get him to perform the entire ballet, divided into three movements like this:

 I Cortège Macabre
 II Three Danses
 III Fourth Danse and Finale.

It is all no longer than an ordinary symphony and I believe is well contrasted. Of course, if this is too much for him to swallow I shall give him only the Three Dances.

So much for possible performances, for all of which I have only you to thank. I have written letters to [Ernest] Bloch and to [Nikolai] Sokoloff. I received two lovely ones from Marcelle and from [Edouard Gregory] Hesselberg. They gave the flute and clarinet song here and G. Laurent wants to give it in Boston in April. The performance here was quite bad—I think I shall add two more songs to Elizabethan words and make a group as you suggested long ago.

[Wilhelm] Mengelberg gave the Second Symphony with chorus of Mahler. How very modern the orchestration is! Thirty years ahead of its time. How I wish I could hear all the others, especially the Seventh. The music critics treat Mahler badly in New York. I shall write an article "In Defense of Mahler." Once more I have you to thank for discovering Mahler for me!

Yours

P.S. Please don't forget the Guggenheim letter. And the score of the Symphony? Is it being copied? I have "un peu d'argent" now so give it to a copyist and send me the bill. Also please have a second copy made of the organ part and send the bill also.

France—July 12 [1926]

Dear Israel [Citkowitz],—

I could write you a young book. So very many things have taken place since my last letter, that merely to mention them would fill a page. Since you last heard from me, I've taken my little turn around Europe: Zurich, Münich, Strassburg, and Paris; and then off again here to this ideal séjour on the southwest coast of France – Guéthary. Not bad for a quiet boy like myself.

But to really treat you properly, I should begin even further back—on a certain Saturday afternoon in the middle of June. The scene is a beautiful theatre off the Champs-Elysées, filled to the last strapontin, with an audience of more than 2,000 people among whom one can distinguish James Joyce, Serge Koussevitzky, Ezra Pound, Darius Milhaud, Nadia Boulanger, Marcel Duchamp, Alfred Knopf, Boris de Schloezer etc. etc, each and everyone buzzing with the excitement and expectation of hearing for the first time anywhere a program which contained—oh marvel of marvels—two new works from the pen of that young genius, your only true rival—George Antheil! Must I say more? To say more is to spoil all. The proud possessor of this very extraordinary audience fed it on Hashed Potpourri of almost every 19th century composer mentioned in the music histories (Symphony in F) and then proceeded to out-sack the *Sacre* with the aid of a Pleyela and amplifiers, ventilators, buzzers and other what-nots (*Ballet Mécanique*). No ordinary concert as you can see. The Symphony was a disappointment even to such Antheilians as myself, but the *Ballet Mécanique* brought forth the usual near-riot so everyone went home content. Though it gives you your usual attack of apoplexy, I am in all honesty bound to repeat my unshakeable conviction—the boy is a genius. Need I add that he has yet to write a work which shows it. If he keeps on exactly as he has started, the sum total of all his genius will be exactly nothing. Voilà!

The following day we left for Zurich and spent three pleasant days there, hob-nobbing with the musical celebrities of Europe, Asia, and Africa. There was only one composition that you should have heard (and that you will probably not hear soon) Anton Webern's Five Orchestral Pieces. The orchestral sonorities he manages to get are magical, nothing less. There was nothing insufferable at the festival, but on the other hand, nothing except Webern's pieces seemed strikingly original, and they were written in 1913.

While in Zurich, I was able to play some of my stuff for the Universal Edition people and something may come of it. Which reminds me to tell you that only to-day I have received the proofs of *The House on the Hill* and the *Immorality* from "my" Boston publishers, E. C. Schirmer, who now possess the signal honor of being the first gentlemen to print my music in America. We poor American composers—(you ought to hear Louis Gruenberg elaborate on that subject)—no conductors and no publishers and no nothing.

Damrosch is going to repeat the *Music for the Theatre*! I wonder why. He wrote me a letter asking me to come with the score—I came—he glanced at it casually—we exchanged politenesses—and that's all there was to it. Simple, n'est-ce pas? Who said it was difficult to get played in N.Y.

I was back from Germany before I received your letter, so the books you asked me to send must wait. But you can borrow my [copy of Arnold Schoenberg's] *Harmonielehre* [Treatise on Harmony, 1911] for as long as you like. Think twice before you write a "Socrate." Satie's work is highly serious and its genius lies in its discreetness: he simply makes the music a frame in which to fit a literary masterpiece. It seems the only setting possible for literary masterpieces.

Its nice to hear you are working so well. So am I. But it would be a crime not to work, given the ideal conditions I have. We have settled for the summer in a little villa all our own, which is exactly what we needed. Guéthary is in the Basque country, a small village built on the hills which rise up from the sea. On our right, half an hour away, we have Biarritz, the hang-out of Michael Arlen and his crowd and on the left nothing less than Spain. (Before the summer is out we have promised ourselves a bullfight!) I am working steadily on the piano and orchestra affair, which is now only a matter of time. For relaxation, a duck in the sea. We intend staying here till Sept. 1st (Harold sails Aug 18 and will probably see you before I do.)

You wrote some sort of mish-mash in your letter about being neglected or something. May I be allowed to point out that I have received 3 letters from you and am now sending my third? I know I should have answered sooner and I wanted to answer sooner, but um Gottes willen, when one is a promising young composer, can one do what one wants? Certainly not. You'll see!

Yours

Thurs. [Feb. 10, 1927]
Dear Kolya [Nicholas Slonimsky, a performer/writer], —

You're a darling to have sent all those delightful write-ups. After reading them I went to the mirror to see if I could recognize myself.

How flattering it was to read that the "Listener" can understand Strauss, Debussy, Stravinsky—but not poor me. How instructive to learn that there is "no rhythm in this so-called Concerto." And how badly I felt for Mrs. Gardner of Bridgeport when I thought how badly she must have felt when she discovered her mistake in the title. Only one thing got my nanny: how dare H.T.P. [H.T. Parker] talk of reducing me to my level, when I am waiting to be raised to my level. And all that really worries me is whether or not the Maestro will ever have sufficient courage to perform me anywhere.

I've seen Gerald [Sykes, his writer lover] half a dozen times and we always—do your ears burn these days?

If you think of it next time you write, tell the dates of K's Paris concerts.

When the Concerto is played again ("O horrid thought"!) we must see if we can't get the police to raid the concert hall to give a little added interest to this "horrible" experiment.

Till soon

New York—March 18 [1927]
Dear Roger [Sessions, fellow composer], —

I was delighted with your letter, the idea of your being in America and the thought that we shall see each other soon (which, incidentally, will save me from writing at great length now). And how delightfully silly of you to have imagined that there was any shadow of a misunderstanding between us when my not writing to you is quite simply explained by the Concerto, that is finishing it and playing it. That was in February, and then of course I thought it was too late to write, since Teddy [Chanler] had been announcing your arrival for the last month and a half.

It goes without saying that I am very keen to see the Symphony. As far as I know Koussie [Serge Koussevitzky] expects to do it in April—he even told me he might do an All-American program, though he didn't say whether or not he thought of doing the Symphony then. Anyway I know he is favorably disposed towards you and that an eventual performance is certain. I would even say it was certain for April if one could say that any conductor's plans are certain. Let's hope that Fate wills me in Boston at that time; otherwise I will have to be satisfied with a muddled version over the radio.

You are apparently not aware of the fact that I am returning to Europe this Spring due to the fact that they are doing the *Music for the Theatre* at the Festival in Frankfort. Wouldn't it be nice if we could sail together? I am thinking of going on the *Homeric,* April 30th but have made no reservations yet. If you know the boat you are taking, do let me know it. (I travel 2nd class as a rule, but am considering 3rd tourist . . . and you?) I shall be in Paris until the end of June—then to Frankfort—and then somewhere for the summer in Germany or Italy.

I'm glad you liked the Jazz article. It has helped considerably to get the whole business out of my system. You will find me a young man admirably stripped of all theories now. Let's hope it lasts.

Here's to seeing you soon

Königstein i. Taunus
July 14, 1927
Dear Kolya, —
I'm a pig! I'm a pig and a sinner and a wretch. But apparently I'd rather be all those things than write a letter. I detest writing letters and it is my great ambition in this world to find a friend who'll love me so that he'll be willing to write me letters without ever expecting an answer. (Did ever selfishness go further?) But even a pig has a conscience and my conscience has been giving me no rest for the past week saying "Aaron my boy, you simply got to write to your old friend Kolya." Whereupon, here I am.

For the summer I am tucked away all by my lonesome in this little German country resort, one hour outside of Frankfort. I drink large quantities of "poer" for the sake of my inspiration. For two months it's an ideal life, particularly since I know that on Sept 10th I set sail once more for the crowds and excitements of New York.

The Festival in Frankfurt was more notable for its banquets and lunches than for the music presented. My own piece came last in a three hour program which finished the Fest and the poor fagged-out public could only be roused from its lethargy by the pin-pricks of a jazz mute. But the infamous viola solo put everyone to sleep; that is, everyone except Hertzka who seemed to like the piece and stayed awake. So much for Frankfurt. Undismayed, I am going to Baden-Baden to-morrow to more Festivals—chamber operas by our fat friend Darius [Milhaud], Hindemith, [Ernst] Toch, Kurt Weill.

In Paris, I visited [Alexandre] Tansman convalescent at a Roman Catholic hospital. The talk turns invariably to the American tour with its wonders and marvels. Sascha is doing much better than Ravel it seems, with contracts pouring in from all sides. I also saw Sanromá chez K————. Why is he always so gay? We spoke of you and bemoaned the fact that you were so far away. Oh yes, and once K———— himself spoke of you—not exactly in the same tone I admit—but still he did speak of you, your name passed his lips, which fact alone I find distinctly encouraging.

Did I tell you I got a job as lecturer next season at the New School for Social Research in N.Y.? Twelve lectures, once a week, beginning Sept 30.

I hope to come home with a Trio on Jewish Themes and have a piece for large orchestra under way. Unfortunately the chamber orchestra ideas seem to have gone up in smoke. (Perhaps I am suffering under an inhibition in that direction . . . !)

Where are you in the world? Breaking the hearts of what young ladies at what summer hotel? (I wish you could have seen [Vernon Duke] Dukelsky's outfit when his Sonate pour Orchestre was played. The boy has missed his vocation. He really should be editing a fashion sheet for the well-dressed man.)

If I don't like to write letters, I adore receiving them especially when I'm all alone in Germany . . .

As ever,

P.S. For your Eagle Eye and the clippings may Heaven reward you.

Haus Leopoldine
Am Hainenberg[?]
Königstein i/T
Aug 18 [1927]
Dear Barbara & Roger [Sessions], —

I meant to write weeks ago to bless both of you for the leniency with which my deplorable conduct was overlooked. (Barbara's coals of fire particularly were a balm.) But, as you have probably discovered by now, I am a most efficient creature in everything except letter-writing. I remember your letters arrived just before I left for the festival at Baden-Baden—which, by the way, was much more interesting than the one at Frankfurt.

The decision of the Sessions family to return to America has caused much excitement in France if I can judge by the letters coming from Juziers. Both Israel and Roy Harris devoted a paragraph to the subject. I, for one, am delighted and shall do everything in my power to make America seem so nice that you'll want to stay for good. (The first thing being to start our Young Composers Society . . . !)

My own days in Europe are numbered. I sail the 10th. Königstein has been very nice indeed, but the summer has seemed so frightfully short. I have been able to do little more than get a half dozen new things under way: a Trio on Jewish Themes, a string quartet movement, a new orchestral piece, some E. E. Cummings songs, some piano pieces. And now, back to America, to fight for every half hour I can devote to composition—besides the enormous amount of time to be wasted on "lectures'" on modern music. These are mere details—what I mustn't neglect to tell you is that Königstein hasn't been at all warm—nor so very lovely at that!

I am to hear [Richard Strauss's] *Electra* on Tuesday. Roger, mon cher, you had better be satisfied with your thrills of 10 years ago and not take a chance hearing a real performance in 1927 if I can judge by playing over the score. How naïve and sympathetic the banality in Mahler is, compared to the empty, heartless banality of Strauss. Though I must admit Strauss's harmonic sense is extremely acute and he never fails one at the most dramatic moments. I have been spending much time over *Oedipus Rex*—a very different story indeed and I look forward to the discussions we are to have concerning it.

I hope all has been going well with both of you—that Barbara is completely restored to health and Roger has his Violin Concerto almost finished. Let me know when you expect to sail.

Faithfully, as ever,

P.S. The Irony of Fate. Now that I am done with jazz an article by I. [Isaac] Goldberg is to appear in the Sept. *[American] Mercury* on "A.C. and his Jazz."

[To Nadia Boulanger]
Oct. 16, 1927
Dear Mademoiselle,—

Unfortunately I am too rushed at the present moment to answer your letter as it deserves but anyhow the main point is that I want to thank you for the letter to [conductor Wilhelm] Mengelberg and for having arranged the affair with [Heinrich Josef] Strecker so beautifully. I do hope you are taking good care of your health—the end of your letter made me not a little concerned about you.

I wrote to Strecker immediately accepting. Also to Universal to send you back "As it fell. . . ." I'll send you a copy of the new song alone but it should not be published that way. As for the Concerto it is difficult to send it now, but perhaps a little later. Also, by the way, I won't bother sending parts of the Symphony until you write and ask for them—that is, when a performance becomes certain.

I have not sent the letter to Mengelberg because the situation has changed since we talked together. Then, I had two scores unplayed, but now one has already been performed last Wednesday—the *Cortège Macabre*—and the other, the Scherzo from the Symphony is to be given by Fritz Reiner and the Philadelphia Orchestra on Nov. 4th & 5th in Philie and on the 8th in New York. So you see when your letter came I no longer had anything absolutely new to offer Mengelberg—but I will visit him nevertheless and play him the Symphony and Concerto, if possible. At any rate we should become acquainted. And moreover, the purpose of being performed by someone besides Koussevitsky is achieved. But isn't it the irony of Fate, that altho I haven't composed a note in months I am to have three first performances (with the Three Dances) this winter.

The playing of the *Cortège* last week was miserable—a conductor no one ever heard of—Zaslavsky—and a mediocre orchestra. I expect more from Reiner—who was really enthusiastic about the Scherzo when I played it for him—and the famous Philadelphia Orchestra.

My lectures are going brilliantly. I have a class of about 125 people each week—which I find extraordinary and inexplicable. I have already played *Oedipus, Création du Monde*, Hindemith op. 37, etc. etc. If I weren't a composer it would be very amusing. But as it is, it is even difficult for me to give up three months of the year to merely making money; and it is practically impossible to do any concentrated work on composition unless I devote my entire energies to it. This is a problem which only a life-subsidy from some kind soul will solve. But simply from having given three lectures I am certain that my job in this world is composing and nothing else.

I am so glad to hear that everything is well with Israel—he writes me beautiful letters and seems content. I shall do my utmost to raise money for two more years and will let you know how successful I've been by the end of November if not before.

With my best thoughts for yourself and Madame

As ever

[Nadia Boulanger]
New York
Dec. 19, 1927
Dear Mademoiselle,—

It seems like years since I wrote you last. I have nothing of any real importance to write you—I've written no new works hélàs—but I have an irresistible desire to speak with you again after this long silence.

First let me list the various tragedies. (1) I have word from the Universal Edition from Vienna that they never did receive the "As it fell upon a day" you sent to them. I suspected as much. Would there be any way of your tracing it at this late date? (I have a copy here of course.) (2) I am mystified by the fact that I have never heard a word from Strecker about the violin pieces. Do you know anything about it? I wrote as you told me to do, but have received no answer whatsoever so far. What should be done? (3) I sent your letter to Mengelberg 3 weeks ago. No reply yet. This looks ominous! To balance these evil tidings perhaps you should know that I have (1) a request from M. Hettich for a vocalize-etude which I shall be glad to do if I can discover a model to go by, i.e., the books already published as a guide to what is wanted. (2) I have news from the Universal that the *Music for the Theatre* is now transformed into *Tragödie im Süden,* ein Ballet im Fünf Sätze. The ballet story is appallingly melodramatic, but the action has been well put to the music, and I have no doubt that the good German opera public will be delighted. The Universal assures me that a production is certain; even possibly this season yet. For once, it is pleasant to sit back and watch a formidable organization like the Universal do the unpleasant business of finding performances.

Roy [Harris] is here making the winter more lively. I am astounded by his business-like efficiency—I never realized he had it in him. Imagine, he has seen and played his music to everyone of any importance in New York from Edgard Varèse to dieu soit qui. And his activities in behalf of a good performance of his Sextet are amazing. But seriously, when I think of him, and think now of the choruses, I can't help but marvel at the progress he has made—and marvel at you too, who made it possible. He plans to return in February and he seems truly anxious to get back.

I have only one more lecture to give in my course. They offered me a second series of 12, but I refused because I wish to have all my time for composition after Jan 1. When I think that I have produced no work signed 1927, I assure you I have a sinking feeling of the heart. It is as if the entire year were wasted. This won't happen again if I can help it! Nevertheless I have agreed to give a second course next October. We are ending the season with a concert—I am enclosing a program to amuse you. I am extremely impatient to get back to work once again.

Mrs. Wertheim gave me $160. for Israel [Citkowitz]. Is he behaving himself? I often have bad visions of him causing you untold trouble and annoyance. Reassure me, please!

The seasons greetings to you and Madame.

Devotedly

Monday [March? 1928]

Dear Roger [Sessions], —

Something has come up which needs your immediate advice. The International Society for Contemporary Music suggests that we give our concerts under their auspices. There are several pros and cons. We are given absolute freedom in every way. The I.S.C.M. will concern itself with the practical end—get the hall, print programs etc. We can probably get more publicity for the concerts because of their name and possibly make surer of having the critics also. The I.S.C.M. (Alfred Human is president) is what sends the music for the International Festivals in Europe as I suppose you know. They have never had any other activity, such as sponsoring concerts etc., but, as I had known, from earlier in the winter, are anxious to be more active. This offer came thru Mrs. [Claire] Reis who is on the board of the I.S.C.M.! (I suppose she would get a certain satisfaction from dragging along in this precarious way with us rather than be left out altogether from the "Youth Movement.") I don't think this matters if our purposes are better served, however. There are several other advantages—composers who are played will be probably more impressed by a long title than an anonymous society, etc. etc.

My idea would be to announce the concerts thus: R.S. and A.C. present so and so and so and so under the auspices of the I.S.C.M.

The principal objection seems [to be] that we don't start that way with as complete a sense of freedom. There is almost certain to be a little confusion in the beginning as to what society is what in the mind of the public. Second, God knows what complications may arise.

One reason and one reason only makes me consider this offer very seriously and that is the fact that you will probably be gone for 3 years. If we start now, I want absolutely to continue. But I don't feel able to swing such a thing all by myself, without at least your moral support in America. I think it would look presumptuous on my part to want to run a society entirely alone—and it would look thus in the eyes of the public.

Tell me what you think. If you decide it would be better to go it alone, I'm willing. Only write within 24 hours after getting this if you can.

Autre chose. Have any overtures been made to Quincy Porter?

Have you asked Teddy [Chanler] to cable a reply? Perhaps we can do his violin sonata if he has nothing new. After all, it's never been given in public in its entirety.

Will Barbara please ask the Warfield-Bonine combination if they will help perform one or two violin sonatas for us? With my very best to you both and in haste

[March 1928? To Roger Sessions]

. . . I went to see Human to-day about the I.S.C.M. backing us. Our talk was anything but satisfactory. On the one hand, he agrees to our being czars and on the other he offers suggestions as to what we should play. He is afraid of our giving programs made up entirely of left-wingers in spite of all my reassurances. In a word, he's an ass and I have no desire to work with him. Besides he has no financial aid to offer and seems so busy that he'd have no time to run our very important affairs. I think we can just drop the idea and go ahead as before, alone. Tonight, I feel as if something would turn up for next year, if absolutely necessary.

I've talked to Minna L[ederman] about the wherewithal for photostating, etc. She was very nice about it and promised a definite answer in a day or two. I'll let you know as soon as I know what's what.

I sent the U.S.A. $1.20 income tax! Can you say as much?
Yours efficiently

Monday eve. [April 1928]
Dear Barbara and Roger, —

I'm too tired and too sleepy to give you an adequate report of our debut [?? Copland ?? concerts] but I'm rather happy about how it all panned out. I'm really sorry you weren't with us—I should have liked you [to] have been there so that we could have discussed the music (particularly Chávez'), so that you could have passed on the spirit of the concert which I didn't think quite satisfactory, so that you could have helped out at the party which was a dismal affair etc. etc. People asked for you both and the moral responsibility for the occasion was rather heavy on my slim shoulders. But I'm a man to accept the inevitable—and everything that happens in connection with the two of you I always place in that category! Margy Naumberg tells me you won't sail until after the 6th so you will be at one concert anyhow and that evens matters up considerably. As it happens, the Sonata will be an invaluable aid in bracing up the second program which had been weakish in its original form.

To me the most surprising thing that took place was the way the critics turned out. I think is an indication of what the concerts mean to the musical life here generally. Mary C. is sending you all of the clippings. They all damned Chávez which I think is a sign of the real excellence of his music . . . Anyhow the critics were there and we seemed like a very important organization! (Mrs Reis was astounded but very pleasant about it.) The audience seemed more literary and theatrical than musical. I don't quite understand why it was so; ["but" crossed out] The enthusiasm, which was greater than at similar functions of the League, did not quite reach my expectations—does that surprise you?

Ruth Warfield, looking marvellously, played Teddy's Sonata rather badly which wasn't surprising considering her recent illness and the short time she had to prepare it. Piston was here for his final rehearsal and the concert and bowed in response to much applause—the audience liked the Three Pieces though they seemed to me to be little more than well written. I don't know what the Thomson sounded like because I played the percussion part to the astonishment of Henry Cowell. I won't go into Chávez' stuff now. I have copies of his music to play for you as soon as I can get you near a piano and my article on him is appearing in the N.R. [*New Republic*] this Friday.

Mary has been extremely efficient throughout, tho new problems have arisen which seem almost insoluble. The only wrong thing she did was to lose your telegram before I saw it, but I heard it from memory and if I hadn't been such an excited ass I would have sent one in return.

Yours, "tired but happy"

Santa Fe,
New Mexico
June 1 [1928]
Dear Nadia [Boulanger],—

I should have written you these past many months, but there were so many things to write about I became paralyzed at the mere thought of transcribing them all to paper. And it always seems useless to write you unless I can write you everything. Now that I am 2,000 miles away from New York and our musical season is over all these things that seemed so important to write you then do not seem so any longer. Anyway you must have heard many of them from Roy when he came back and recently from Roger, perhaps also from Israel to whom I write regularly knowing how much he needs my moral support.

When I look back at the winter it seems to me that the only real thing accomplished was the fact that I have finished my slow movement for string quartet. I have just made a copy for you because I am most anxious to know what you think of it. Please show it to Roy and to Israel. (I dedicated it to Roy because it was his enthusiasm for the opening phrase which gave me the incentive to finish it.) The rest of the winter was spent in giving lectures and giving concerts. I should so much have liked to discuss both of these activities of mine with you, particularly the concerts. They went off surprisingly well—particularly from the standpoint of the press. The difficulty will always be to find good music by Americans. But we want also to play the young Europeans who are just beginning to be known in Europe like Conrad Beck or [Nikolai] Lopatnikoff. That's where you can help us (not to mention the Americans!). Please ask Beck to send us one or two of his recent chamber music works so we can introduce him to N.Y. next season. Also if you know of anyone else who is writing really worth while things, do let me know. We expect to give three concerts next season.

I am spending two months here in this old Spanish town of Santa Fé. I have a room and a piano and am hard at work thus making the summer six weeks longer than usual. There will be an interruption of two weeks in July when I play my Concerto at the Hollywood Bowl under [Albert] Coates. (I don't look forward with much pleasure to this because the time for rehearsal—these being summer concerts—is necessarily too short to hope for a good performance.) In August and September I will be back at the MacDowell Colony in Peterboro where conditions are ideal for work. I wish very much to turn out a large piece for orchestra this summer—and it is on this that I am working principally. Secondly, I should like to do a Trio—piano, violin, cello—for our concerts. As I have the thematic material already it shouldn't be impossible. It becomes increasingly difficult to work during the winters in New York. I have stopped answering the telephone and see as few people as possible—but still it is difficult. But as long as I must give lectures to make money and as long as I feel that the concerts can become important in our musical life I don't see very well what can be done.

I was very much relieved by what you said about Israel's work in your letter of last January. I hope he has continued to improve. Your letter induced Frederick Jacobi to help again with financial aid so that Israel has enough money until the end of October. Just now I don't see who I can turn to for more money then, but I suppose someone will occur to me. Hasn't Israel met anyone at your house who might be induced to help him—even if only for a few months? Since I shall probably be in Paris next Spring I should certainly like to have him stay at least until the fall of '29.

It seems strange to be so far away from Paris at this time of the year. Still, I suppose, it is good for me to see America a little, and then of course, playing at the Bowl is an excellent introduction to the Pacific Coast. Still, I do miss the rue Ballu very much. Now that Katherine isn't there to write me all the little details about what is going on I feel very much out of it. Perhaps, during the summer you will be able to find a little time to write me. (Address: 223 W. 78 St. always.)

Give my best regards to Madame Boulanger. Tell her I miss her taquinage as to how "célèbre" I have become. With deep affection, as ever

Sunday [1929?]
Dear Roger [Sessions], —

Last week, when no letter came saying the "Sonata" was finished, I naturally began to suspect trouble. Your letter therefore was reassuring. Don't worry, twice underlined, should satisfy anyone. However, you most certainly have my sympathy. I think writing a work to order for a set date excellent—when one has finished it. But, of course, the situation you are now in is horrible and my feelings as a fellow-composer and as a concert-manager are at war with one another. As the former, I should like to say, don't you worry; after all it's the Sonata which is important and not its being ready by a set date. But, as co-director of the C—S—Concerts I should like to see the public get what it is promised. (As the other co-director, I know you feel the same.) O Hell,—I hope I don't sound as if I were worried. I refuse to be like the famous cook who blew out his brains because the fish didn't arrive in time for the king's dinner.

All things considered, it would seem highly desirable that the Sonata be finished, however. You have until five minutes before the concert—24 hours a day.

I was delighted to hear you are coming to Washington.

Thank heavens, you have at last found something of which you can disapprove. Naturally, I agree with you. Putting the importance on "modern" and "novel" is stupid—it simply happened because of a series of events which I can explain when I see you. I think, in general, tho, the publicity hasn't been bad. We already have about 30 subscribers for both concerts. Mary C. calls me up in the greatest excitement every time a new subscription comes in. You're really missing half the fun.

There's been talk of a party after the concert. My idea was to ask people we like and the participants to go to some place after the concert. Mary C. was willing to stand the costs but I prefer it to be à la Boulanger, everyone paying for themselves. This will be a real innovation in modern music societies.

By the way, I hear thru dark channels that the L. of C. has decided to invite the two of us to join their board! Don't breathe a word of this, whatever you do.

There's nothing else.

[Richard] Buhlig is playing at our second concert nine pieces by [Dane] Rudhyar (*Three Paeans*), Adolf Weiss, a pupil of Schoenberg's, and Ruth Crawford, a girl who lives in Chicago. He refused to do the Elwell and I can't blame him (that I believe is my first real error as to music) so John Kirkpatrick is doing them instead. (Keep this under your hat too.)

Affectionately

May 28, 1929
Dear Carlos [Chávez],—

I was so glad to hear from you at last. But your letter came during my last few days here before sailing for Europe. I am leaving for Paris to-morrow and will be back again on Oct. 1st. That's why it has taken me so long to answer.

Now I have only time for essentials and not for the kind of letter I should like to write you.

1. Please finish the Four Horn Sonata so that we can have it ready for next season at the Copland–Sessions Concerts.

2. Since you will make a tour in South America you will meet composers—will you please keep a look-out for material for our concerts and ask composers to send us material.

3. I am arranging a concert in Paris about June 15th at which your Piano Sonata will be played at the same time as Roy's "Sextet'" and my new Trio and the two string quartet pieces. I will send you clippings if there are any interesting ones. Perhaps you will want to let some friends in Paris know about this.

4. Sessions' Symphony was played in Geneva at the International Festival of C[ontemporary] M[usic]. It has been accepted for publication by Mrs. Wertheim [Cos Cob Press] so that she has the entire rights on score and parts. Write for more information (when they will publish it, performance fees etc.) either direct to Mrs. Wertheim or [to] her manager Edwin Kalmus, 209 W. 57 St. N.Y.

5. As for my own "latest" orchestral piece I did not yet finish it. But I expect to finish it this summer. I have promised M. Koussevitzky already the first performance. Whenever he is finished with it (probably by December) you are very welcome to it. I know this is vague but what else can I tell you. With only one set of parts and one score performances are necessarily difficult to arrange as you well know. For the tour of South America I suggest that you use the *Music for the Theatre*. In Mexico City if you do not get the new piece in time, I suggest that you use the new version I am preparing for my Symphony for organ & orchestra for orchestra alone. This piece is nearer my newest manner than the jazz period.

Yours with love

[To Israel Citkowitz]
May 29 [1930]
Dear Israö

The sight of your handwriting on an envelope becomes thank God less strange. After the long drought it is especailly good to see it again. I'm sorry if you've ever worried about leaving me in the dark about your "vie intérieure." Your long silence was almost self-explanatory—I guessed that important things were happening to you, too important to write about, and contented myself with waiting for that distant day when they belonged to the past and I should undoubtedly hear about them. I think of our relation as being in a state of equilibrium—we can always take it up whenever we please and go on from where we left off without any sense of a gap or a separation. At any rate, so it seems to me.

As a matter of fact it's been a strange year in relation to friends. There's been a general overhauling, a revaluation of values. It amuses me to think how imperceptibly these changes take place—and yet, one day there they are. For example, Gerald [Sykes] seems much closer now, due partly to our living together in Bedford [N.Y.] for several months. Gerald understands me well ["now" inked over]—he makes up in perception what he lacks in sympathy (tho in relation to myself he has had sufficient on both scores.) Harold, on the other hand, has begun what might be termed almost a new life in which I play a much more modest role than in the old one. His love affair has made a man of him—he has developed a whole set of new friends who believe in him fervently and he has moments of real megalomania. And so he's on his way to being one of the really important critics in America. Of course the fact that he is also going to Yaddo this summer will bring us together again and will help to change our present relations.

Roy's stock is extremely low. I suspect he has me pretty much in the same class as N.B. now, a well-meaning but pernicious influence. That ruins everything because, as you know, I only thrive on sympathetic contacts. He attached while in N.Y. (He has gone to Cal. now) to a very impressionable young man by the name of Paul Rosenfeld and together they went over the situation pretty thoroughly. We none of us came out very well—but we'll survive I hope. His Quartet is his best piece so far and makes me wish I only knew him thru his music.

Something in me makes me welcome all such changes. Not, however, until they have happened. But when they have happened I embrace them.

My stay in Bedford will be over in another two weeks. I spend a month in town before going to Yaddo. Whether or not I go to Mexico this September is still a question. But I will almost certainly go to Europe next Spring for an extended stay of two years or so. I am seriously considering applying for a Prix de Rome. But principally I am interested in Germany, where I want to get some works played. (I might also do a bit of propaganda there for American music.) The wanderlust has me—I want to see Algiers, London for a longer stay, Marseilles, Capri, Constantinople . . .

Your own plans sound feasible enough. However much or little composing you do I advise you to finish the String quartet and W.W. Quintette you wrote about. They will prove great helps to your rep. Also let me warn you that you will not be pleased with America unless you have a room & piano of your own. You're used to different things now and I feel sure it will be difficult to live at home for any extended period of time. Have you thought of that? To be quite truthful I only take your plans half seriously! As far as I can see your next five years are one big question mark—and if there have been upheavals in the past there will certainly be upheavals in the future to upset the best laid plans.

I finally heard the *Ode*. I conducted it myself one morning at a rehearsal in Boston while K——listened from the auditorium. I only really heard the slow parts, the fast parts were ruined by being played too slow. The end sounded gloriously. It was a revealing experience. The upshot was that I have for all time given up trying to make music look on paper what it actually sounds like. Applied to the *Ode* it means that I must completely rewrite the barring of the fast parts throughout. I'm working on it now and have discovered how much easier some sections might have been written. For example, one part which originally had 13 changes of time—$\frac{3}{4}$, $\frac{7}{8}$, $\frac{5}{8}$ etc.—is now entirely $\frac{4}{4}$. I never believed it could be done till I tried. So that not a note of the piece will be changed but it will look entirely different on paper. When I think of the loss of time and money (the parts must be completely recopied and recorrected) I could weep. On top of this, I played it at the piano for Hertzka, head of Universal Ed[ition], who happened to be at Alma's one night and when he heard it was scored for a Mahlerian orchestra he advised her against publishing it. (Not that she'll take his advice.) "Why you're crazy man," says he, "there are not ten orchestras in all Europe that can supply 18 brass instruments." This darling *Ode* seems to be having a hard time in a cruel world.

I'm very pleased with the piano piece I am doing. It is a big work both in dimensions and meaning. For the moment its called "Theme and Variations." It's a new form for me and lends itself beautifully to my particular kind of development from a single germ. But it needs time to fully flower and won't be done probably until the end of the Summer. Then if I can get [Walter] Gieseking to play it I'll be satisfied. He's the only one who can.

I've had two very sympathetic letters from Carl B. I want you to write me your impressions of him as a person. He also sent me his Wylie songs which I find not so sympathetic. In a way it's tragic that he should want to compose. Unless I am badly mistaken, his stuff is terribly old-fashioned and without a real spark. (Don't breathe a word of this to him, of course.) I've told him more or less the same thing already, but it does little good. How do you feel about it?

Now that the ice is broken—keep in touch, if and when, you can.

Affectionately

Aug 15 '30

Dear Carlos [Chávez]—

I can't tell you how happy it made me to receive your very affectionate letter. Sometimes I could not help feeling that you had become so absorbed in your work in Mexico that you forgot me and all the friends you have here. But now I see it is not true—now I see you do miss me and the rest, which makes me very glad. Your letter made me feel very close to you, as if all the time we were separated was very little. Carlos, my boy, you really must try to come to New York in January. I have a great desire to see you again—and letters are such poor substitutes.

I have always had one principal concern for you—because of your half a dozen activities as director, conductor etc. you would stop composing. Now I see it begins to worry you also and—that is good! Is there no solution for this difficult problem? Is there no-one in Mexico who can help you run the school so that you have some time for your composition work? Before everything else, you are a composer. Which means you will never be happy until you have the time to compose. Of course, you know all this. But I want you to know that I know it too and that I am waiting impatiently for you to find the solution. So I was glad to hear that you had made a beginning with the two more "Mexican Pieces" and the new orchestral work . . .

It's clear you are hungry for news so I will put you au courant of what has been doing. As for myself, more and more I have been able to put aside every other consideration but composing. I have stopped writing articles, given as few lectures as possible, and lived in the country outside N.Y. from January to June so as to have time for myself. The only activity I have continued is the C——Sessions Concerts. The result has been not that I have written any more than usual, but that I have the necessary peace of mind for writing.

The work that I was writing for the [RCA] Victor Prize (it's called "Symphonic Ode") is finished, but I finished it too late to send it in for the prize. Instead, I sent in a work called "A Dance Symphony" which I quickly put together from my early ballet. The prize has been decided recently (though not announced publicly yet)—the $25,000 was divided among 5 composers and I was one of them! So with $5,000 I feel rich. I don't know yet who the other 4 composers are, but there is a rumor that Bloch is one of them. This means that I am free for several years and do not have to lecture any more.

Koussevitzky was to perform the Ode in March. Two weeks before the concert he told me the piece was so difficult rhythmically that he would need a summer to study it properly. So it was put off to this season and will probably be given in N.Y. in January. I am very anxious to hear it because I am sure it is by far the best thing I have done.

Just now I am working on a long piece for piano in the form of a Theme and Variations and am very pleased with the way it is going.

As for the others: Roy Harris is in California now, where he is married to a new wife. We performed his most recent work—a string quartet—at our concerts. It's probably his best work so far. He has a Symphony in 3 movements which you should see. It is uneven I think, but has excellent things in it.

Sessions is to be in Rome one more year. He hasn't written much, but the Piano Sonata—you remember?—is now finished and the Symphony is published by the Cos Cob Press. Paul Rosenfeld is spending the summer with [the photographer and gallerist Alfred] Stieglitz at Lake George, only an hour from here. I will see him soon and bring him news of you.

I suppose you must be wondering what Yaddo is! I came here to spend the summer, but I like it so much that I will stay until November. It is a very large private estate which is given over to creative artists—something like the MacDowell Colony. I have a wonderful studio in the woods—a Stone Tower which would make a perfect setting for an outdoor performance of the Tower Scene from *Pelléas*. Harold Clurman is here too.

If Yaddo had not turned out so perfectly, I should certainly have come to Mexico for Sept. and Oct. But with conditions so ideal for work (and costing nothing!) it would be a mistake to leave. You must not think that because the orchestra could not offer me a paid engagement I stay away. It would have been a pleasure to play for nothing, particularly now that I have the money for the trip. But the advantages of staying at Yaddo are so apparent that I must put the trip off for a while again. Don't despair, Carlos, it will surely happen some day.

Which reminds me to tell you—I played the "Concerto" as recently as last week at the Stadium Concerts in N.Y. [Albert] Coates conducted and did a good job. He speaks of arranging a performance in London in April. I expect to go to Berlin in March to see some of the new operas and to try to arrange some performances of my works in Germany—where they have never been given. If I like it well enough I may even stay a year.

This is news enough for one letter.

Affectionately

Tanger Maroc
Sept 22 [1931]
Dear Israö [Citkowitz]——

I was awfully glad to get your note. I was on the point of having very lugubrious thoughts on the subject of our relations, the kind of thoughts you had (apparently) last summer, and which I was now really feeling only for the first time. I was on the point of writing you, not to make playful approaches, but to tell you seriously how sad it made me feel to think you were slipping away and that we were gradually losing all sense of contact the moment we were separated. I'm sure that this habit we've gotten into of not corresponding any longer is bad. I don't even mean the writing of honest-to-God letters because I know they need a certain amount of "inspiration" about which one can do nothing. But it's the lack of any word at all which creates the vacuum and discourages the writing of any serious letters ever. N.B. and I never correspond but that is an entirely different matter, because our relationship is more or less static and will always remain what it is now. But our case is different and we can't go on for two years, as we just have, with impunity. I don't mean that it's your fault that we haven't written each other; I suppose if I kept writing letters, you'd reply. Je constate, c'est tout. It's both our faults,—and here is a beginning, in a new direction . . .

Paris isn't on my itinerary, which is now practically settled. I'm leaving here on Oct 1st and gradually working my way back to Berlin by way of Fez, Algiers, Marseilles, Genoa, Innsbruck, München. That gets me to Berlin about the 10th. There are several reasons for my going back,—Roger & Barbara will be living there, and the I.S.C.M. is intending to give the all American orchestral concert I told you about. I plan to stay until about Dec 15, and then go directly to London and sail for home from there. There may be a chamber music concert to arrange in London if the English section of the I.S.C.M. will further the idea. (I wrote Edward Evans suggesting your songs as a part of the program.) Anyway, I want to be home by about Jan 1, in order to hear Koussie do the Ode (endlich!).

If I stay at Strub's again, as I hope to do, and if the extra bed is still there, you must come to visit me for a week or so. All you'll need is carfare. We'll time your visit well, so that it comes at some special time, when some special event is being given. Though I imagine Germany will be special event enough all by itself. (I wonder if you know that Fred Jacobi's wife is giving a violin Sonata Recital there in Nov. with [Orchestre de] Ribaupierre.)

Tanger has been an experience. I can't say it's been very good for my work; so that I'll be glad to get back to civilization and piano tuners, but I feel I've seen something. The Oriental part of the World, in short. For instance, Paul [Bowles] and I were invited to an Arab's home for lunch. The women disappear at the sound of a stranger and one eats with one's hands out of a common dish with the male members of the family. I mention this because I get much more of a kick out of seeing one interior than seeing the outsides of a dozen villages. Nevertheless, they say Tanger is too international, and that one must go further South to see the real Arabian Cities—so I'm going to spend a few days at Fez on my way back. Fez, they say, hasn't been open to Europeans very long.

It gave me a "coup" to see you at a Paris address. Have you actually moved from Juziers, bag and baggage? The paragraph about that miscreant Teddy Chanler made me think you are just like the Queen in *Alice in Wonderland* who goes about crying "Off with his head!" about everyone she sees or knows. It made me tremble for my own. Of course you're right, but what did poor Teddy do?

The only music I have with me is the volume of Mozart's Quartets and Quintets. I'm getting to know it well, all of it, and will leave Morocco understanding him 100% better.

My address is American Legation here until Oct 1—after that Am. Express in Berlin.

Always, A——

Mexico City
Sept. 3, 1932
Dear Ma & Pa, —

Here I am, at last in Mexico City. The trip from San Antonio took two nights and a day on the train and was absolutely uneventful. We just arrived in San Antonio in time to catch the train that would bring us here in time for the all-Copland program.

Well, we arrived on the morning of the concert and were met at the station and have been very well taken care of ever since. An apartment had already been found for me in a quiet but central part of the city. Not long after my arrival people from the newspapers came and I am sending you some of the results. The article is too long to translate and says mostly things that you already know.

The concert took place yesterday evening. There was a rumor that the American Ambassador would come, but he didn't show up. It was an interesting experience to hear a whole program made up of my own works. The newspaper criticisms will come out later.

In the morning, Chávez took me to meet one of the Cabinet ministers, so that I feel I'm already a friend of the Government! No one seems to mind the change of president which I suppose you read about in the papers.

The City itself reminds me much more of Europe than of America. It's hard to believe I haven't crossed any water to get here. It's a great help having so many friends here, tho I must say, the Mexicans I see in the streets seem to have little relation to the Mexicans who are my friends. The city is a great mixture of magnificence and of poverty. But it has great charm too. I know you must have been disappointed that I didn't see the folks in Dallas but there just wasn't time if that concert was to be made.

Tell Leon that the car stood up under the strain so he can be proud of it. We had only two punctures in all, and one break in the gas line which occurred in the mountains at night in Tennessee and might have forced us to spend the night where we were stuck, if we weren't rescued by a farmer-mechanic who happened along by chance.

That's all for the moment. Write me at the address I gave you.

Love to all.

100 W 55 St.
New York
April 7 [1933]
Dear Carlos [Chávez]———-

I should have written you a week ago—just after the performance. I liked your work very much myself—and so did many others. It was well performed—all the men [were] first players at the Philharmonic and [Alexander] Smallens conducted. It was very clear and sharp. At the rehearsal it was more difficult to follow—the single voices without accompaniment—one must get used to—and the somewhat fragmentary nature of each movement. But at the performance I felt comfortable with the work—I felt your presence there—and Mexico. The difference between our works and those of the Europeans was striking. Theirs were so smooth and refined—so very much within a particular tradition, and ours quite jagged and angular. No "important" critics came—I don't know why I send you these clippings since they are completely negligible.

Perhaps it will surprise you to hear that I have joined the Board of the League of Composers for next season. Four years ago I turned down a similar invitation from them. But now I feel that because I join it it will be a different—and I hope—better organization. Anyhow, if I can't put new life into it I shall get out. (When [Henry] Cowell heard of this he asked me to join the Pan-Americans also. It was difficult to refuse. I told him in the end that I could take no active part in the affairs of the Society.)

Vivian Fine played your Sonata at a Pan American Concert. I turned pages for her! For some peculiar reason which I cannot fathom, it still continues to mystify the listening public. Or such was my impression.

You'll be glad to hear that I have finished the 3rd movement of the Partita and that I'm orchestrating it now.

Koussevitzky is playing the *Music for the Theatre* in Washington at Mrs Coolidge's Festival at the end of April. Poor programs but I'm going anyway.

The "Variations" were chosen for the Amsterdam Festival but I'm not going abroad.

Tell Silvestre [Revueltas] that Mrs. Wertheim has the quartet under consideration now, but that *Colorines* is in [Nicolas] Slonimsky's hands at the moment, because he is to do it in Havana soon. After he returns it I will submit it to her also.

Is Paul still there? My best regards, if he is. Remember me in fact to all the friends.

Love

Lavinia, Minn
[Sept (?) 1934]
Dear Israel [Citkowitz]———-

I couldn't figure out from your letter whether or not you realized that my question to Minna [Lederman] about you was just a joke. It never occurred to me that there was any serious danger of your becoming a fascist! Anyhow, I was awfully glad to have you write me at such length, and I must say the contents of your letter interested me enormously, particularly the Mass. part and the arguments with Roger [Sessions]. When I think of Roger and communism I immediately think of Elie [Siegmeister], who is I fear the symbol of Communism to Roger—whereupon all is lost there and then! He'll be "confused," as you say, just so long as he neglects to read the "classics." Then at least he'll have a real basis for a choice, whatever that may be.

I've had an interesting summer from that angle myself. I can't write all about it now, as I should like, because I should be writing a ballet for Ruth Page at this moment. But anyway—it began when Victor [Kraft, his lover] spied a little wizened woman selling a *Daily Worker* on the street corners of Bemidji [Minnesota]. From that, we learned to know the farmers who were Reds around these parts, attended an all-day election campaign meeting of the C.P. unit, partook of their picnic supper and made my first political speech! If they were a strange sight to me, I was no less of a one to them. It was the first time that many of them had seen an "intellectual" I was being drawn, you see, into the political struggle with the peasantry! I wish you could have seen them—the true Third Estate, the very material that makes revolution. What struck me particularly was the fact that there is no "type-communist" among them, such as we see on 14th St. They look like any of the other farmers around here, all of them individuals, clearly etched in my mind. And desperately poor. None can afford more than a 10¢ pamphlet. (With that in mind I appealed to the Group for funds and they sent me a collection of $30, which I presented to the unit here for their literature fund.) When S. K. Davis, Communist candidate for Gov. in Minn. came to town and spoke in the public park, the farmers asked me to talk to the crowd. It's one thing to think revolution, or talk about it to one's friends, but to preach it from the streets—OUT LOUD—Well, I made my speech (Victor says it was a good one) and I'll probably never be the same! Now, when we go to town, there are friendly nods from sympathizers, and farmers come up and talk as one red to another. One feels very much at home and not at all like a mere summer boarder. I'll be sorry to leave here with the thought of probably never seeing them again.

I expect to spend the month of October in Chicago. This ballet of mine that the Chicago Opera plans to produce on Nov 16 will keep me desperately busy until then. In times like these, having a definite objective to one's music is best—is easier anyhow.

I look forward to seeing you too.

Fraternally

Chicago, Ill
Oct 15 1934
Dear Carlos [Chávez]——

I too have been thinking of you! and reading about you and the theatre—(the Palace, rather)—and your new work (*Llamadas*)—and everything—and I could easily imagine how terrifically busy you have been and still are. So your letter (which came today) and the programs were very exciting.

I am writing to Kalmus today to tell him to send you a score of the *Music for the Theatre.*

I am sending you also today the score of the Short Symphony. This is a copy I made especially for you which I want you to keep. Some day, if your copyist has time I should like to have a copy of the score made for me. The performance of the work Koussevitzky was to have done last season was postponed because of what he told me was the extreme difficulty of the work. He expects to do it here this season, but as yet, it has never been played. (Kouss—has his own copy of the score.) Are you sure you can prepare the performance in so short a time? Otherwise perhaps it would be better to wait—as I am afraid that with this work a shaky performance would give an incoherent impression to the public. Of course, I leave it absolutely in your hands to do as you like.

I almost had two new orchestral works finished (I was working in Minnesota) when I had to interrupt them to do a ballet to be performed at the Chicago Opera in November. I have written it very quickly and included some old jazz of mine, but perhaps it will "go over" as they say.

The two orchestral pieces are "Seven Statement"? (very simple—for me anyhow—of which five are finished) and a ten minute "light piece" called *Salón México* which only needs to be orchestrated. I am terribly afraid of what you will say of the *Salón México*—perhaps it is not Mexican at all and I would look so foolish. But in America del Norte it may sound Mexican!

I will be in Chicago until about Nov 1 and then N.Y. Please come in Dec. and Jan.—I am sure it will rest you and I am very anxious to see you. If you don't come I'll have to come to Mexico soon again.

Victor wants to be remembered to you and Revueltas———
Always affectionately

Hubbard Woods, Ill.
Oct 24 '34
Dear P[aul Bowles]
The card that came this morning was the coup de grâce. For weeks I'd been telling V. how we were neglecting you frightfully. And he agreed. Every day I've been saying that we really must write. And he agreed. Why we didn't will be clear presently. It had nothing to do with Africa. I understand the attractions of Africa and I'm sure you know the disadvantages, so I took it for granted that you went with both eyes open. These are difficult times for young composers, and I'm sure it's better to eat in Africa than starve in N.Y. So there's no reason for "disapproving" as you seem to suggest—only the natural desire to have you back soon where I can look at you.

The reason for the long spell of silence was a ballet. Out of a clear sky, toward the end of August, Ruth Page, who is a dancer in Chicago, asked me to do a ballet for her to be ready by Nov 1. To talk it over V and I drove to Duluth and took a train from there to Chi. After a week, I had signed on the dotted line and have been working like a Trojan ever since. We dashed back to Bemidji and stayed there until about Oct 4. In those 5 weeks the music was done almost entirely. You can see I worked fast. It's 40 minutes long—not all new—I've used some of the early ballet in it. Now we are staying out at Miss Page's country place on Lake Michigan and I'm orchestrating and orchestrating. The ballet is to be put on at the Chicago Opera on Nov 23. Page did the scenario and a Russian by the name of [Nicholas] Remisoff the sets and costumes. The scene is a law court—the first dance that of the Prosecuting Attorney. The whole thing is a satire on justice and how she functions. If it goes over they'll take it on tour to lots of small cities, which would be fun.

That's why, you see, there was no time to write anyone. And you being so far away . . . I received the Stein songs. I'm curious to know how they happened to be published. You never wrote a word about all that. Why, I wonder, of all your things, did you print those two little things. I have no doubt Kalmus will "handle" some for you. That is, he'll put them on his counter probably, and they'll collect dust with all the Cos Cob things. Its surprising how little "modern" music he does sell. I doubt whether Schirmers would take many copies. Write to Kalmus if you like and say I suggested it. Or should I talk to him for you?

The Cos Cob Song Volume has been delayed by my not being in N.Y. When I get back—which should be around Nov. 1—I'll try to get it out finally. But you have never written a word about whether or not you got permission to use that poem of yours. Dare I go ahead just the same?

I've just reread all your letters and p.cards. But they only tell what you have been doing—and I'd like to know what you're doing now. Write me a nice, long, explicit, letter and say what you're up to in Fez. Describe your "duties," as your mother called them. Have you a piano there? Are you writing anything new? As soon as this damn ballet is finished I promise you a really long letter in return.

Chicago is all agog about the opening of *Four Saints [in Three Acts]* which takes place on the 7th. I hear Virgil [Thomson] is coming, and perhaps G[ertrude]. S[tein].

Love and kisses

Chicago Ill
Dec 13 1934
Paul Cheri—

What on earth are you doing in the jungles of Colombia? And did you ever receive the letter I sent you in October (a long one, sent to Fez (!), explaining why I've not written oftener, and why you shouldn't have and never should feel neglected etc. etc.) I had no idea you'd be down there this long or I would have written again sooner.

I've been in Chicago for the past few weeks a propos of the ballet I wrote you about. It's being given a second time to-morrow night at the Chicago Opera. It was fun for me to have done it so fast and Victor says the music is good. Incidentally I've been wining and dining all over town with the "best people"—a strong contrast to our Minnesota farmer friends of the summer. (While I write this, V is at the piano doing his own version of Ainsi parfois. By the way, did you know that thanks to Virgil we finally did have word from St. Leger about the poem and so the song is being published in the volume and will be out in another month or so. Where should we send it to you when it does finally appear?)

I saw Stein and Toklas here. They immediately asked for "Freddy." I told them the little I knew. Toklas seems to have the upper hand in management, Stein looks a bit vague as if a bit dizzied by all the furore around them. Now that they are the property de tout le monde I suppose you're not interested. You needn't be. (It's my great consolation for not being famous.) Listen—what are you doing down there anyhow? This letter is the equivalent of 16 of your postal cards so sit down and write me all, and be explicit. God how I love explicissity.

You asked about the Short Symphony. Koussie turned it down after a year and a half. I asked him "is it too difficult?" "Now," says he, "c'est n'est pas difficile, c'est impossible." Exactly one week later Chávez gave the world premiere in Mexico City. So there! He sent me a te[r]ribly enthusiastic letter which set me up considerably.

Where do you go next—

63 West 55 St
New York
Dec. 31 '34
Dear Carlos [Chávez]——

It was very exciting to get your letter and the programs and your music. What you said about the Short Symphony naturally made me very happy. Only a week before your performance, I had a conversation with Koussevitzky in which he told me that he regretted it very much but he could not play the Short Symphony as he had promised. "What's the matter," I said, "is it too difficult." "No," he said, "not too difficult, but just impossible." This week I will be seeing him again and I will be able to tell him that in Mexico they do the "impossible"! How I wish I could have heard it. And what a strange feeling it gives me when I think that you have heard a piece of mine which I have not yet heard. I will probably try to get [Leopold] Stokowski to play it, but it is too late for this season of course.

I was glad to hear of your determination to do some conducting outside of Mexico. It seems to me it should be quite possible. Almost every orchestra we have has guest conductors now and then, and besides there are radio hours available, such as [Ernest] Ansermet conducted this season. If you could succeed in getting a man like Arthur Judson to manage you it should be comparatively easy to arrange guest appearances. Naturally I'd be glad to talk to Koussevitzky for you, if you wish me to.

I have played over *Llamadas* many times but each time I feel the need of an actual performance to get a real idea of the music. Certainly I enjoy the directness and the plainness of the music, but I cannot "hear" the sonority from the piano version. The records of *H.P.* have not come as yet but I look forward keenly to receiving them as I now own a phonograph. Perhaps next season I will give lectures in conjunction with "Concerts of Recorded Music" and I will be able to play *H.P.* and [Silvestre] Revueltas' record also for a public.

You ask me about the Cos Cob Press. Mrs. Wertheim has given me the entire artistic control of the Press (altho the practical end is still in her hands). But the trouble is that there is a Depression and in October, Mrs. Wertheim (who has changed husbands and is now Mrs Wiener) announced that the Press would have to suspend all activities for a year, until Oct. 1935. I had hoped that we could arrange some plan whereby we could publish works by Mexican composers, if the Mexican Government might guarantee to cover the costs of publication, or perhaps to guarantee the sale of a certain number of copies which would cover the costs of publication. As a rule we do not engrave orchestral works, and the process we use, lithography, is about the cheapest that can be had in America. You see, Carlos, the Cos Cob Press is really so small, and is run on such a small amount of money each year, that out of five or six works published each year, only one Mexican work could be included if published in the regular way. But if there was a small subsidy to work on, we could bring out as many works as you see fit, and right away. Think this over. It's the most practical plan I can think of for making a real impression, and no one need know it is done outside of ourselves.

I have had a job offered to me—to take over the class in composition at Harvard [illegible] money so I accepted. It will be my debut as teacher and I will probably live in Boston during May and April. Koussevitzky promises to repeat the First Symphony, in Feb., I think. In Chicago they produced my ballet which I wrote you about. It was an experience for me to hear my music with stage action. Now I should like to write an opera, or at any rate, more music for the stage.

We have been reading a lot about Mexico in *The New York Times* lately, in relation to the religious question. I have wondered several times whether this affects your work in any way. My best regards to everybody—Silvestre, Paul, Lenora Ortega, Sandi, Agea, Armando, Contreras, Ayala——I think of them all, and of you, with warm affection.

Always

Jan 8 [1935]
63 W 55
Dear P. F. [Paul Bowles]

Here's the [Rouben] Mamoulian letter you ask for. I hope it's a help. I liked the picture of yourself you sent me and the letter. Apparently Hollywood can be lived in. When you do come back, and stop in Chicago, I think you should play some of your music for Ruth Page as she is looking for a composer for next year. She's awfully dumb (entre nous) but she does need music for ballets. She's in Jamaica (W.I.) now, but I think will be in Chicago the first three weeks in Feb. They still talk of bringing her in my ballet to N.Y. in April.

The only news is about me and Harvard. I'm taking over [Walter] Piston's composition class for the second term of this year—Feb to May. It's only three hours of teaching a week—on Tuesdays and Thursdays—and as I am practically broke—and the job is well paid—I couldn't very well refuse. I think it was very brave of them to have me, don't you? I'll probably commute for Feb and March and live in Cambridge in the Spring. You know my weakness for college "atmosphere"!

Last night the League started its season with a reception for Stravinsky. Virgil and everybody was there and I missed you badly. There's no doubt about it—you do something "indicible" to the N.Y. air which makes it more potentially exciting when you're here than when you're not.

It's hopeless to expect performances if you don't stay around here a while. All the young composers are in Roger's "crib" (with the exception of Jerry Moross) and you'd have the field to yourself. You can spend 9 months of the year anywhere you like but I think you ought to plan to be here for at least 3 during each season if you want to feel like a composer. Oh well, I feel so foolish giving you advice, & you seem like such a big boy now.

Write soon

MacDowell Colony
Peterboro, New Hampshire
Aug 28, 1935
Dear Carlos [Chávez] ——

I was so pleased to be given your envelope this morning—and so surprised and upset when I opened it and read "my dear Copland." But naturally I didn't receive the first letter you sent me c/o the League or you would have heard from me before this. Is it possible that only because you got no letter from me in reply to the first one you sent you should be so offended—or have I unknowingly offended you in some other way?

I'm sure you must know how dear you are to me in every way—how close I feel to you mentally and spiritually and musically—and the idea that anything whatever should mar our friendship even temporarily is very painful to me. Even tho I may not write for long periods you are always in my thoughts,—people are always asking me how you are—and I never feel really separated from you. This is particularly true when I realize that you must have been going through a very difficult period of your life. [The photographer] Paul Strand came back last June with news of your struggles and since then I have often wondered [how] the new political situation in Mexico has been affecting you and your plans. I have always remembered our conversation on top of the pyramids of Tlotihuacan when you told me that the future—whatever it was to be—did not frighten you. I believed you then—and it has given me confidence that you will know how to manage even in these difficult times.

We have been going through a difficult period here also—though of course not in the same way as you have. It becomes increasingly difficult for instance to have that sense that there is any public for our music—in any case, the public that can afford to pay for concerts is quite simply not interested. Its impossible to have one's music played (on the rare occasions when it is played) before a "dead" public without getting a feeling of isolation—which is so bad for an artist to have. In a period of such economic and general social tension music itself seems unimportant—at least to those middle class people who up to now have been our audiences. Is it the same in Mexico?

All this has personal repercussions too. It is no longer easy to be published (The Cos Cob Press has discontinued publishing for a year already and I don't know when they will resume)—I must make some money in order to live which uses up much valuable time and energy. I mention all these things not to give you the idea that I am "discouraged" in any essential way, but merely to show you that I have good reasons to feel sympathetic with your own struggles. It is just in such times as these that friends like we are should encourage and sustain each other. I can tell from your letter that you have felt I was too distant. Please know better now.

This winter I will lecture again at the New School using records as illustrations. As you see from the enclosed list I am using the *H.P.* set you sent me. But in order to make a musical analysis and perhaps play themes for the audience I really need the piano arrangement. Could you possibly send it to me? I will take good care of it and return it. Also can you tell me who in N.Y. would have the Revueltas record *El Rennacuajo Paseador*? The copy you sent me has been cracked. If no one has it in N.Y. could you possibly send me another copy? And if anyone in the audience should want to buy the records are they on sale? By the way, the Columbia Phonograph Co. is about to issue a recording of my "Variations." Later they will bring out the *Vitebsk* Trio and the Violin Pieces. I should like to send you these when they come out.

In June I finished my *Statements*—six short movements for orchestra. It is to be done by [Eugene] Ormandy and the Minneapolis Symphony this winter. As soon as I have an available copy of the score I will send it to you as I am anxious for you to see it. Just now I am finishing up the orchestration of *El Salón México* which I wrote you about last summer. What it would sound like in Mexico I can't imagine, but everyone here for whom I have played it seems to think it is very gay and amusing!

I wonder what you have been composing recently? I saw "The Spiral" piece in New Music [Editions] and liked it very much. I will arrange to have it performed in N.Y. this winter. If there is any new music by Mexicans which we should hear in N.Y. I wish you would send it to me and I will do my best to arrange performances either at the League or elsewhere.

The only permanent address I have just now is c/o E. F. Kalmus, 209 West 57th St. N.Y.C. I will be in N.Y. around Sept. 1.

Does Ansermet remember my First Symphony from the performance he gave in Berlin? I will have the scores you ask for sent to him as soon as I can. But I wish I could send some of my more recent things. (By the way, Stokowski has the Short Symphony now and I hope he will perform it this season. I want to hear it enfin!) Also you shall have your First Symphony score. I am certain that I have no copy of the cello sonatina because we corresponded about that once before and I examined all my music carefully but without success. I hope it is not lost. I am hoping for a long letter from you. With much love

Sept 30 1935
Dear Carlos [Chávez] ——

I was so glad to have your letter from Tlaxcala which explained everything. It is just such little incidents which make one realize how necessary a friend can be.

The League finally traced your original letter and the programs. I was so pleased to see that you had given some of the *Musica para Theatro* again. The programs in general looked interesting,—more interesting than those we have here certainly. I noticed that you are beginning to play music from Soviet Russia. I should like very much to make a trip there. (Have you seen my communist song "Into the Streets May First"? It has been republished in Russia.) I suppose it is too late now to give you information about new orchestral scores. Kalmus told me he had sent you some Cos Cob scores to examine. There is a new score of Piston's called Concerto for orchestra which is very able, though influenced by Hindemith. Sessions has a new Violin Concerto, not yet played here or published. Its extremely difficult—almost too difficult I should say. (The slow movement of his early Symphony is worth playing I think.) Roy Harris has two Symphonies—the first is recorded by Victor. You can write him c/o G. Schirmer. Piston can be reached at 92 Somerset St., Belmont, Mass. R. Bennett is published by Harms, 62 West 45.

Please get in touch with Minna [Lederman] about your book of essays. I am sure she can use one or two essays in *Modern Music*. Suggest which would be the best for her to use.

Stokowski has announced my Short Symphony for a first performance this fall. You can imagine how I am anxious to hear it at last.

I am anxious to have your answers to my requests in my last letter. If anyone should want to buy the records of *H.P.* what should I tell them?

Always affectionately

May 18 '37

Dear Carlos [Chávez] ——

Two days ago I mailed you the score of the *Salón México* by parcel post. I hope you get it safely. Today came Agea's letter asking for program notes— so I see we are thinking of the same thing! As for the orchestral parts, they will be ready by about June 15th. I hope that is not too late. I will leave instructions here to have them sent directly to you.

I am still in N.Y., as you see. First, I decided to put off my sailing so as to be present when they broadcasted the opera on May 9th. Then Harold sent an offer from Hollywood for me—$3,000 for a picture. I said I would come for $5000, not less. So I am waiting to hear what will happen. If nothing happens—I will sail for Europe around May 25. But just think—if they should accept my terms I will be seeing you at the Hollywood Bowl! So it's either Moscow or Hollywood for me.

I was so sorry you missed the opera. It seemed to go off very well—even better than I had hoped—considering how quickly it was all put together. [Writer Herbert] Weinstock heard it twice—perhaps he's written you about it. When I first heard the chorus and orchestra together I said "My God, it sounds like the Ninth Symphony"! By that I meant it had a surprisingly big sound, and a highly dramatic one. Also, the end has something of the same "Freude, Freude" feeling, tho in completely different terms. Of course the kids had everyone completely interested. Kids are like Negroes, you can't go wrong if they are on the stage. Well, someday I hope you'll hear it. C. C. Birchard is publishing it.

I suppose you must have wondered how I happened to write that piece for *The N.Y. Times* on Silvestre. As a matter of fact I had no idea the *Times* would use it. The publicity secretary of the Filmarte Theatre where Redes was playing called me up and asked if I would not give some publicity material on Redes in order to bring customers to the show. I did it rather hastily—and was very surprised when she called to tell me she had sold it to the *Times*. Apparently anything about Mexico is of interest now.

Nothing very much has happened since you left. I went up to Boston to hear Koussie read thru the *Statements* [for Orchestra] as a rehearsal. He said that the orchestration was "masterly," but the [bottom line of page missing] he is right, but I liked it anyway. He says he will "surely" do it next season, and this time I believe him, because he's actually heard it.

Mrs Reis is still muy tonta on the subject of electrical instruments of the future. Dukelsky is being very active with an idea for putting on 3 concerts of "entertaining" modern music for the fashionable people next season. I am thinking about the Composers Union we must definitely get started next season.

I hope the Festival will be a big success. Also, that you'll enjoy working on the *Salón México*. Be sure to have Armando send me all the reviews— even those of Señor Pollares!

Remember me to all the amigos. I hope that Ortega is all recovered by this time.

Love

Tepoztlan,
Morelos,
Mexico.
Oct. 6, 1944.
Dear Mink [Minna Lederman]:

If this reply seems late, try to remember that your letter, mailed on the 26th, only reached here two days ago. I hope this one goes a bit faster so that my measly suggestions may be of some help for issue no. I.

I do feel kind of swamped by the variety of questions you fling at me. Don't forget that I am rather rusty—not having been in the center of activities for a good many months. So—take all this for what its worth:

1. About Latin America: I don't get the impression that very much has been happening in Mexico. Still if you want a round-up of events I'd suggest you ask Salvador Moreno. He's a young composer in the Chávez camp, a Mexican of Spanish antecedents. He's bright and amusing, and has recently been writing criticism for one of the Mexican dailies. The catch is that he is ill at the moment with some sort of eye disease, and I have no way of knowing whether he will be up to turning out an article right away. He can be addressed care of the Orquesta Sinfonica.

I recently had news of a new "Grupo Renovacion Musical" that has been formed in Cuba. They gave two concerts of works by the new generation of composers. I doubt whether the works are very significant, but I think it's worth reporting on. José Ardévol could write an article about it. You could address him care of the Grupo at Compostela 156, altos, La Habana, Cuba.

Argentina's season is just over and I think we ought to have a report on the new works introduced. It could be written by Roberto Garcia Morillo, who is assistant critic on *La Nacion* of Buenos Aires. You can write him care of that paper.

From Chile I think you might have a study of Domingo Santa Cruz's new Piano Concerto. I spoke with [Cuban pianist Claudio] Arrau here and he seemed very impressed by it. Santa Cruz writes the sort of music that analyses well. The article should have some musical illustrations. I think you could take a chance again on young Juan Orrego, who once flopped on a round-up of the season. This is more in his line, I think. Write him care of Santa Cruz, if you don't have his own address in the files.

From Brazil I think Carleton S[prague] Smith ought to have a thousand words inside him about life on São Paulo, where I understand he is cultural attache to our consulate. Also I have just heard that Everett Helm, a young composer pupil of Piston, is being sent down to Brazil on a travel grant from the State Dep't to "write a book about Brazilian music." You might contact him for a piece for a later issue. His US address is: 702 East 17 St., Santa Ana, Cal. I don't know whether he is still there or has already left for Brazil.

I also wish that we could have a note from Montevideo but I don't know who could write it. Even Curt Lange has left, and is now living in Brazil. My only idea would be to write to the Uruguayan pianist Hugo Balzo, care of the S.O.D.R.E. Orchestra in Montevideo, and he undoubtedly could suggest someone intelligent for the job.

If you want something from Lima why not go back to the man who wrote so amusingly last time. Wasn't it Raygada?

2. About Europe: The only composer I've heard about is in Rome. He is Nino Rota, who once studied at Curtis and is a good friend of Sam Barber. (Barber would supply his address.) I'm not sure of the kind of article he'd write—he's the delicate rather than the forceful type; but I know he's gone through a lot, and recently communicated with Barber.

I should think that one good source for material would now be Switzerland, since they'd know more than before, and would probably be more ready to tell what they know. But I don't have names to suggest.

As for Paris I'm stumped. Why don't you ask Milhaud if he doesn't know of someone who could write for you. You might even persuade Poulenc to say what it was like, since according to *Time*, he wasn't a collaborator.

Too bad about London being such a pain in the neck. But I think it's time that Marc came across with a piece. Or you might even attack Benjamin Britten again. After all, he once wrote for you. I don't have other ideas because most of the younger men are in the Army now—fellows like Humphrey Searle or Henry Boys. If you are desperate you might ask Erwin Stein, who works in an editorial capacity for Boosey & Hawkes' London office. He's an experienced writer but I don't know how unbiased. ([Music editor Hans] Heinsheimer would probably be willing to discuss his capabilities frankly with you.) There's another fellow in the B&H office by the name of Campbell—forgotten his first name. He also has written—but he's a rabid Bloch fan, and I don't know whether anything else pleases him. Heinsheimer would know about him too.

For a stab in the dark about Brussels, you might ask Désiré Defauw whether he knows of any musician in Belgium capable of writing for you.

I wish we had someone in Spain who could send some dope. I'll ask Salazar whether he has any suggestions about that.

3. About the Harris article by [Robert] Evett, I'm all for it. Everybody knows that Roy has a harmonic system, and nobody knows what it is. It should be an article with illustrations that completely satisfies the curiosity.

4. About the Portrait series: if you are to have Quincy Porter don't have Hans Nathan do it. He's a dyed in the wool European and I don't think Quincy would like being written up by him. Douglas [Moore?] would know whom to suggest for Quincy. For a new name in the series I'd be for an article on Burrill Phillips' work. I think its significant, and has character. Robert Palmer knows the work well, but whether he can organize an article about it I don't know.

5. I have heard the new Sonata for 2 pianos of Stravinsky. Its a charming but slight work. Whether it rates a whole separate article for itself I doubt, but if you're hard up for material it would pass. I don't happen to know Prof. Tangeman.

6. About correspondents from American cities: Boston should be written up by Irving Fine of the Harvard Music faculty. They've had a new Hindemith *Uraufführung* during the summer. Also private hearings of new piano works by Harold Shapero. Fine is fine for those things. His address: 15 Everett St., Cambridge 38, Mass. (There were other things too, of course.) I think [Vincent] Persichetti is OK from Philie, but have nobody better to suggest from Pittsburgh and Cleveland than the people you already know. When I am in Washington I'll keep my eye open for somebody to recommend from there.

I assume you'll be writing up the Musicians' Congress concerts on the campus of UCLA, in Sept.

7. About general articles my mind is blank, mostly because I have had little contact with musicians these last months, and therefore no stimulation. Why not try to get Sam Barber to write an article. His last symphony showed him to be getting less stuffy. He is very articulate with the pen and might have something he wants to write about. Anyway, I'm sure he would like being asked.

Later on I might want to do one myself—something about the men who have come "back from the wars." A kind of welcome home article that would give them a send-off into civilian life. But it's too soon yet—so forget it. [in ink]: (Just an idea, anyhow!)

I'm planning to fly up to Washington for the Coolidge Festival and then on home to N.Y. No one has seen a public announcement of the event, but [Harold] Spivacke keeps saying it will come off at the end of Oct. In any case I am coming back then. That's just around the corner so there's no sense in prolonging this already long letter.

I sent a letter to Claire [Reis] urging her to close up shop at the end of this season. I haven't heard her reaction, but am curious.

Glad you've been writing and selling things. But what things??

I leave Tepoztlan and the primitive life on the 23rd, and I ought to be back in New York by Nov. 1st.

Love and all that,

Conversation with
Edward T. Cone (1967)

This extended interview with the Princeton University musicologist Edward T. Cone is a summing up, recapitulating autobiography that touches upon many steps in his composing career. Perhaps out of respect for Professor Cone, a generation younger and thus familiar with the older composer for his entire professional life, Copland provided longer, more thoughtful answers than were customary for him.

E.T.C.: *There is a frequently quoted legend to the effect that the name Copland originated on Ellis Island, when an immigration officer misunderstood your father's pronunciation of Kaplan. Is that true?*
A.C.: I'm not sure I know the real answer. My father did not come directly from Russia to the U.S.; he probably didn't have enough money to make the trip all the way, a typical situation in those days. In such cases Scotland, especially Glasgow, was a known stopping-over place. You had enough money to get from Lithuania (where he started) to Glasgow, and then you got a job there and earned enough money to go on to the U.S. So my father was in Scotland for about two or three years.

In 1964, when I was conducting in Glasgow, I noticed that there were more Coplands in the telephone book spelt without an *e* than with an *e*. One of the reasons, it seemed to me, was that *o* in Scotland is pronounced like *u*. They don't say Scotland, they say Scutland. And they would say Cupland, not Copland. In Glasgow everybody called me Cupland; and to this day David Adams, who is the European head of Boosey & Hawkes, and who is Scottish, always refers to me as Cupland. Now if you pronounce the name Kaplan in a Jewish or Russian way, you get almost exactly the same sound, and I suspect that the transliteration was made there in Scotland, and that my father simply took the spelling they gave him.

Then the story about the immigration officer is a myth?
I guess it is—I might have started it myself. This idea about Scotland only struck me when I was told there, "Your name isn't spelt peculiarly from our standpoint; it's more usual than the other way."

I might add here that nobody in our family ever, to my knowledge, mentioned the name Kaplan to me. The first time it occurred to me that the name might originally have been Kaplan was when I went to visit my grandfather, who was the last of the family to be brought over. Of seven children, my father had been the first to come, and he gradually brought over all the others, one at a time. His parents were the last to leave the old country. When I was taken to visit them, I was astonished to see on their name-plate the name Kaplan. At that moment I realized that this must have been the original name.

Were you brought up as an Orthodox Jew?
Well, my father was president of the oldest synagogue in Brooklyn—it used to be off Court Street, down near Borough Hall. I was born on Washington Avenue, possibly half an hour away, so it wasn't a question of going there every Saturday; but on the High Holidays, naturally, we went. Nevertheless I can't say it was anything more than a conventional religious association.

Were you Bar Mitzvah?
Oh, yes, it was a big affair! I never mastered Hebrew properly, though. I merely learned how to read it, with only a hazy understanding of its meaning. I'm sorry to say I can't speak a word of it today.

What was Rubin Goldmark like as a teacher?
He was top man of his time for composition—everybody studied with him. With the founding of the Juilliard School he was named head of the Composition Department, although I studied with him before Juilliard existed. He was recommended to me by my piano teacher, Leopold Wolfsohn, with whom I studied for about four years in Brooklyn. When I was about seventeen, I decided that I needed harmony lessons. (I had begun by trying to study harmony through a correspondence course, but that didn't work.) When I went to see Goldmark, I realized that I was going to a highly recommended man who must be pretty good.

He *was* good—what he knew he knew very well indeed. *His* Stravinsky was Wagner: he had gone up and down the country giving lectures on Wagner's operas. But he had very little sympathy with or understanding for contemporary music, so that it would have been useless for me to hope to get anything from him on that score. We went through regular harmony and counterpoint. His be-all and end-all was the sonata-form. You hadn't finished your studies, he thought, until you could write a proper sonata in three movements with the first and second themes and developments all in the right places.

Have you kept those exercises?
Yes, I have. I have the Sonata still—it's awful. Just what you'd expect, and I knew at the time it wasn't very good.

Where you writing your own music on the side?
Yes, I was. I brought him my innocent little *Cat and Mouse* piece. He said, "I can't tell you anything about this. I don't understand how you go about it or what the harmonies are all about."

The *Cat and the Mouse* was rather like Debussy. It still sells rather well—about a thousand copies a year! Durand published it, a fact of which I was very proud. Monsieur Durand himself heard me play it at the graduation exercises at Fontainebleu that first summer. He came backstage and said he liked it and asked me to come to see him in Paris. And when I did, he took the piece. That was the first thing I ever had published, and the exciting thing to me was that it was Debussy's publisher who had accepted it. I still remember the thrill of that—you know, seeing that familiar Durand cover on my first published piece!

At what point did you feel that you needed something that Goldmark couldn't give you?
I had been thinking about France from the time I was eighteen or nineteen. In those days, it was clear that you had to be "finished" in Europe. You couldn't be "finished" in America. Remember that I was an adolescent during the First World War, when Germany and German music were very unpopular. The new thing in music was Debussy and Ravel—also Scriabin. (I was very Scriabin-conscious in those days.) It seemed obvious that if you went to Europe you would want to study in France. Also I had met an older fellow, a Johns Hopkins graduate named Aaron Schaffer, who had gone there just after the war, in 1918. (He lived in Baltimore and later became the head of the Romance Languages Department at the University of Texas. He died a few years ago.) He was a strong influence for France, because he went to study at the Sorbonne, and wrote fiery letters about all the wonderful things he was hearing in the concert halls. Germany seemed like that old-fashioned place where composers used to study music in Leipzig. All the new things seemed to be coming from Paris—even before I knew the name of Stravinsky.

This seems to have remained a lifelong prejudice with you.
I suppose it has sort of stuck. I did spend the summer of 1922 in Berlin, though. You know who told me to go there? Boulanger! She felt I should have some contact with German musical culture. The following year I spent the summer of 1923 in Vienna. In that way I tried to counterbalance my strong French orientation.

How did you find out about Nadia Boulanger? You didn't go to her straight-away, did you?
No, I certainly didn't. I had never heard of her. It was by sheer chance that I learned about the establishment of the Fontainebleau school. This was its first year, 1921. I read about it in *Musical America,* of all places. I was ex-cited about the idea of having somewhere specific to go—after all, I didn't know anybody in France, and I was hesitant at the age of twenty to go there cold. The idea that a school was being started in the summer, just for Americans, made me think that in that way I might have the chance to get to meet more people. I headed for the school's office in New York so fast that they told me I was the very first student to sign up.

I was very lucky to have gone there. I studied with Paul Vidal. He was the Goldmark of the Paris Conservatory—the man to study with, it was said—but he turned out in fact to be another version of Goldmark. He was very conventional in his tastes. Also I couldn't understand his French. He spoke a kind of patois that was very hard to catch. (I had only high-school French at the time, so this was a real problem.) But they kept telling me about a teacher—

Who was "they," other students?
Yes, especially an attractive student harpist, Djina Ostrowska. (She died a few years ago, too.) When she enthused about her harmony teacher, I said, "I'm not interested in harmony, I'm studying composition." But she said, "Come anyhow, just to visit the class." And I did, finally. I remember Boulanger was analyzing something out of *Boris Godunov.* The enthusiasm with which she was doing it, the sense of her knowing the work cold—but mostly her enthusiasm, her relationship to music as an exciting thing—registered strongly with me.

Then Mademoiselle Boulanger did a very nice thing. She invited me to visit her in her home with the harmony class; in that way I got to know her better. At any rate, it suddenly struck me one day that here was the person I wanted to study composition with. (Looking back, I think it was a very brave decision, because I knew perfectly well at the time that there had never been any great women composers. This should have been a deter-rent, but wasn't.) She wasn't teaching composition at Fontainebleau—just harmony (which was what she taught at the Conservatoire, the school and the Conservatoire being closely connected), so I studied composition with her privately when I settled in Paris in the fall. I remember bringing some piano pieces to her at the beginning. She said, "Why don't you make a ballet out of these?" I said, rather skeptically, "Do you really think I could?" But I did, and that turned out to be the main project during the three years I studied with her.

In addition I attended the Wednesday afternoon *déchiffrage* classes. We looked at lots of contemporary music at those meetings. The analysis wasn't detailed, it was a way of getting to know the work by performing it at two pianos or reading it from the score. The principal model she held up at all times was Fauré, and the idea of the long line: starting a piece at the first note and going straight on until the end in some connected fashion. We also looked at Debussy, and Stravinsky scores too, as soon as they came out (or sometimes before they came out, because she knew Stravinsky personally and borrowed the scores from him). No Schoenberg that I remember—no emphasis on the contemporary Germans. Don't forget that this was 1921. Twelve-tone music, of course, we didn't know about until 1924. I don't know when she herself first became aware of Schoenberg.

How did she teach composition?
I would bring her stuff that I was writing, and the exciting thing was that you had the feeling that her musical instinct was so sure that she could immediately point out the weak spot and tell you why it was weak, why it didn't seem to belong there, why it seemed to stop the flow, or whatever else was the matter with it. All that was very valuable: the sense that you were with someone who knew all the answers, who could relate them to general principles—and who was enthusiastic about what you were doing! *That* was the main thing. Mr. Goldmark had been a very nice man, but he lacked enthusiasm—it was just a job. To her it was an art, it was music, it was exciting!

Did she ask you to do specific analysis on your own?
I don't remember bringing in things I had analyzed. I remember hours of reading Mahler scores, painfully reading them at the piano—especially *Das Lied von der Erde*. It didn't matter how slowly you went, you had to go on!

Did she give you any orchestration?
Yes. I was orchestrating my own ballet, which turned out to be a 35-minute work in the end. It has never been performed in its entirety, but a 16-minute excerpt ultimately furnished the music for my *Dance Symphony*.

Just before I left France in 1924, she told me of her engagement to appear in America the following season as organ soloist with the Boston

Symphony and also with Walter Damrosch's orchestra, and she asked me if I would like to write a concerto for her. I protested that I didn't know anything about the organ. "Oh, you can do it!" she said—she was always saying "You can do it!" Also, I had never heard any of my own orchestration, so I was very chary about what I might turn out. But she insisted, and so I did.

Was it your influence that persuaded a number of other young Americans to go to Nadia Boulanger?
I think it was. I wasn't literally the first American to study with her, but I was the first to study composition with her. Melville Smith had been studying organ with her, and I believe that Marion Bauer had studied harmony shortly before. Then there was Herbert Elwell. He had been with me at Fontainebleau but had hated it and "escaped" to London in the middle of the term—much to the distress of the Director! When he returned to Paris later in the winter, he went to Boulanger after hearing me enthuse. Roy Harris, Walter Piston, and Marc Blitzstein didn't come until later, after I had returned to the States. (Virgil Thomson learned of her through Melville Smith.)

Boulanger had been known as a teacher of organ and harmony and counterpoint, but the idea of studying composition with her was mine. I like to think so anyway.

When you returned from Europe, how did you see yourself making a living?
I thought I'd teach, like everybody else. In those days, one wasn't thinking about the universities, or even the conservatories. You would just send out cards to interested people and then hope for the best, which is precisely what I did. I took a studio on West 74th Street and waited for something to happen. I thought my announcement reading "recently back from Paris" would do the trick but unfortunately nobody answered!

By January I realized my position was getting pretty desperate. I went to see the writer, Paul Rosenfeld. (He was an important personality in those days, and I'm very sorry that he is forgotten as much as he is today.) I asked him if he knew some wealthy patron who would like to support a young composer for a year, and he mentioned Mrs. Alma Wertheim, a sister of Henry Morgenthau, as a possibility. She very kindly agreed to give me $1,000.

About four months later the Guggenheim Fellowships were established. They started with a preliminary trial year, during which time no applications were accepted; they chose candidates themselves, and they delightfully picked me to be the first Guggenheim Fellow in music. The fellowship was renewed the following year as well. I used to go to Europe in the spring, from April to September, returning for the winter in New York.

Was it about this time that the League of Composers was started?
No, that was founded in 1922, during my student years in Europe. You evidently don't know the whole history. That brings up something that I find very troubling: namely, that composers nowadays seem to have no sense of history whatsoever, and practically no interest in where they came from, or how they got here, or why we are where we are now. You can't imagine how distressing to me that is. It makes our younger men seem so primitive, like savages on an island who have no conception of how anything happened, and couldn't care less. It may have a healthy side to it, of course, but it seems to me somewhat poverty-stricken to have no curiosity at all as to your own historical background.

I remember once, when I was at Harvard in 1952 on the Norton Professorship, getting curious about the music of George Chadwick. I had always thought of him as being very German-oriented, but something I had recently read made me think that perhaps he had changed his mind during his later years, around 1910. I took out some of his scores from Widener. When I had one of them in hand, I noted that the last borrower had had it out in 1896! There's an alarming lack of curiosity today.

Were you illuminated about Chadwick, by the way?
I was quite surprised by how smoothly written his scores were. The technique was really first class. It wasn't very original, but it was certainly good music of its time. I don't think it would hurt us occasionally to hear some piece from that period. Who knows, there may be some dark masterpiece, rotting away, waiting to be rediscovered! But clearly it wasn't a very rich period, except for Ives, of course.

The Twenties, on the other hand, began something that carries over right into today, so that a little curiosity as to how it all began might be of some value to the young. It was Varèse who sparked the organization of our modern-music-performing societies with the formation of the International Composers' Guild. Soon there was a breakup on the board caused by some difference of opinion. The reason generally given is that Varèse didn't want to repeat premiere performances, while other members wanted to give second and third performances of things they liked. Actually I think it was more a clash of personality than anything else. Anyway, the splinter group called itself the League of Composers and was perhaps somewhat less radical in ideas than Varèse himself. Varèse and [the harpist] Carlos Salzedo (who was important to the development of new music here, from the standpoint of propaganda and performance) continued with their own ideas; the splinter group was led largely by Louis Gruenberg and, I think, Lazare Saminsky. They were greatly helped by Mrs. Claire Reis, who was the very active chairman of the League for more than twenty years. The establishment by the League of the magazine first called *The League of Composers Review*, and then renamed *Modern Music*, under the keen editorship of Miss Minna Lederman, was very important. It not only helped to keep everyone aware of what was going on but helped to develop writers. That was where Virgil Thomson began writing, where I began—where practically everybody began. (That's not quite true. My first article was published in *The Musical Quarterly*. It was a long study of Gabriel Fauré—naturally.)

The real critic of the movement was Paul Rosenfeld. He was in neither camp; he was a friend of both camps. But he had great admiration for Varèse. He wrote the first significant book on the American movement, called *One Hour with American Music*. It's very brief, but it states some basic things. The chapter on Varèse is still very readable. I wish that with all the reprinting of books in paperback somebody would have the bright idea of picking the best of Rosenfeld and bringing him out again. He did write in a kind of prose that was too highly flavored—that was his main weakness. But he was a sensitive fellow; and when his reaction was sound, he had insights which would bear rereading nowadays. Besides, it's always interesting to learn how the newer things seemed to listeners who were making contact with them for the first time.

I remember his articles on Sessions's Black Maskers *and on your Piano Variations.*
Yes, I thought at the time that he was very brave, for the Variations didn't get good criticisms from the press in general; it seemed from the standpoint of idiom and expressive character very odd and strange, and hard as nails.

Do you see your music as falling into definite periods? I think of the Variations, for instance, as inaugurating a new one.
Yes, different interests came along at different times, which resulted in music of different character. There was a distinct break around 1930 with the Variations. Why it came I can't tell you. The period of the Twenties had been definitely colored by the notion that Americans needed a kind of music they could recognize as their own. The jazz came by way of wanting to write this more immediately recognizable American music. It's a very unpopular idea now but seemed very much in the cards then. Don't forget that it was the Hungarianness of Bartók that seemed so fascinating: not only was he writing good modern music, but it was Hungarian in quality. Stravinsky was very Russian—a Russian composer, not just a modern composer. (No one could have forecast his neoclassic development.) I was just thinking along the line that seemed the ordinary line to think along,

simply applying the same principle to America and trying to find an American solution.

There was a second thing working in me at that time, if I can analyze it myself. In addition to the sense of the Americanness, the need to find a musical language that would have American quality, I had also a—shall we say Hebraic—idea of the grandiose, of the dramatic and the tragic, which was expressed to a certain extent in the Organ Symphony, and very much in the *Symphonic Ode,* which very few people know nowadays. The *Ode* was a major effort, on which I worked for several years. It really seemed like a culminating work, so that I had to do something different after that. But I certainly didn't visualize doing a work like the Piano Variations! I think now, however, that the Variations was another version of the grandiose, except that it had changed to a very dry and bare grandiosity, instead of the fat grandiosity of a big orchestral work that lasted twenty minutes.

Couldn't one say that in the Thirties, with the Variations and the Short Symphony, your music became more international in style?
Perhaps, but nonetheless I like to think of them as being in some way American. Their rhythmic life is definitely American, and influenced by jazz, although there are no literal quotations. I wouldn't have thought of those rhythms, particularly in the Short Symphony, if I hadn't had a jazz orientation. When I say that I had a jazz orientation, most people think I mean that I played jazz. Actually I didn't play jazz at all. I did read popular music, of course, but I never could improvise in the jazz manner.

How long would you say the new style lasted?
Primarily through the Variations, the Short Symphony, and *Statements.* In *Vitebsk,* which preceded these works, the sharpness and dryness of the harmonies might fit into this period too. But I think of it primarily as a *morceau caractéristique,* a piece that just happened. I don't know why, except that I had heard the Jewish theme I made use of in a stage production of *The Dybbuk,* and liked it. After that, during the early Thirties, I went to Mexico. That explains *El Salón México* and my interest in Mexican tunes.

The late Twenties were rather rough going, as it was difficult to earn a living. By the fall of 1927 I had used up my two Guggenheim Fellowships but through Rosenfeld I inherited a course of lectures he gave on contemporary music at the New School for Social Research. He had tried lecturing for a winter and hadn't enjoyed it, not being a public speaker in any sense; audiences made him nervous. He asked me whether I would like to take over. I began talking to perhaps fifty people and found that you could earn money faster by talking to fifty than by talking to an individual student. So I fell into lecturing, without ever having dreamt that I was going to. Later I began to speak on the subject of music in general, which was the origin of *What to Listen for in Music.* I found the audience tripled as soon as I announced my subject as Music rather than Modern Music. So economically I was in a fairly good position up to about 1937. Then—I don't remember why, either the audience dwindled or I grew bored with lecturing—anyway, I gave it up. Perhaps the depression hit the audience. At any rate, the lectures ended, and those years between 1937 and 1939 were rather "grimmy."

Fortunately, toward the end of the Thirties, American composers began to interest entrepreneurs whose projects required music specially written for them. One of the first was Lincoln Kirstein, whose Ballet Caravan introduced American themes which demanded American music. The movie companies, especially those making documentary films about the American scene, began to feel the need of a music that would reflect what they were showing on the screen. I suppose my music was considered sufficiently American—I don't remember how some of them happened to come around to me, but they did. That provided not only a source of income but also the new feeling of being asked to write music for a functional purpose. Before that we wrote for ourselves; nobody was asking for it.

I suppose this was the origin of what you have sometimes called your vernacular style.

Yes, a more accessible style. I don't think I ever deliberately sat down to write something in a style that everybody could understand. In the first place you can't be sure that everybody will fall in love with your music even if it is written in such a language. There is no guarantee that the audience is going to want it any more than they would a dissonant piece. I think a more accessible style was brought on by the nature of the things I was asked to do: a ballet score implies that you are looking at something while you are listening to the music, so that you can't give your undivided attention to the music. This suggests a simpler style. The same is true of movie music. As I stress in the new edition of *Our New Music* [reprinted in *The New Music*, 1968], it was unfortunate that I wrote my little autobiographical sketch in the first edition just when I was writing these more accessible things, for I gave the false impression that this was the direction I was going to head for in the future. I was just all keyed up by the fact that finally here was a need for our music!

After the war, you gradually moved toward serial or twelve-tone writing. How did that come about?

When I look back now, it seems to me that the Piano Variations was the start of my interest in serial writing. It was Eric Salzman, I think, who said it was almost Webernesque in its concentration on a few notes. Although it doesn't use all twelve tones, it does use seven, and it stays with them throughout in what I hope is a consistently logical way. Also I wrote a song in 1927, recently republished under the title "Poet's Song," which is quite twelve-tony and shows that I was thinking in those terms then. Schoenberg's greater fame after the end of the last war and the continual talk and writing about the technique brought the whole matter to the front of my mind again.

I'd like to explain here one thing about Schoenberg in relation to myself: in the early years, in my own mind, he and Berg and Webern were under something of a cloud for the reason that they were still writing German music, and German music was the thing we were trying to get out from under. The expressive quality of their music took precedence over their method, which wasn't clearly understood until much later anyway. (Even Roger [Sessions], with all his sympathies, didn't come to it until much later.) No matter how significant the method may have seemed, it never occurred to anybody to disconnect the method from the esthetic, which seemed to be basically an old Wagnerian one. The later works of Webern hadn't been written. His cool approach was completely unknown. So it isn't strange that I didn't feel sympathetic. I didn't need the method at the time, for I was busy exploring for myself. It was only later, at the end of the Second World War, the younger fellows, Boulez and such, made it clear that you could keep the method while throwing away the esthetic. This came as a brand new idea to us. Why we didn't think of it for ourselves, I'll never understand.

By 1950, I was involved. The attraction of the method for me was that I began to hear chords that I wouldn't have heard otherwise. Heretofore I had been thinking tonally, but this was a new way of moving tones about. It freshened up one's technique and one's approach. To this very day that remains its main attraction for me.

Do you use it exclusively?
Not necessarily. I wrote an orchestral work this summer entitled *Inscape* in which I used it in a rather more tonal way than I did in my *Connotations*. It still seems to me full of possibilities.

This might be a good point at which to bring up something I've always been curious about, yet oddly enough have never asked you. The first time I met you was at a reception after some concert or other in 1946. I had submitted an orchestral work for the Gershwin prize, and had been turned down. I was greatly flattered when you told me that you had been on the jury and had been very favorably impressed by my piece. You even described the piece very accurately. "But," you went on to say, "I voted against it. Its melodic line was too

German." What did you mean by that? And what did you mean, some years later, when you told me it would be a good idea for me to look at the works of—that name again—Fauré?

Did I say that? I suppose I was thinking about the chromaticism of Germanic expressivity, as against a more tonally oriented line—a kind of weltschmerzy quality German music has with its high chromatic content.

And you would say that even in your twelve-tone music your line is not essentially chromatic?

I don't think anybody would ever imagine it as having been written by a German composer. I try to do my own thing using an extended language. Still, there is a difference, even in my own work, because I think of twelve-tone music as having a built-in tenseness. I like to think that the way I use it, it has a certain drama about it, a sense of strain or tension which is inherent in the use of the chromatic. These are new kinds of tensions, different from what I would have dreamt up if I had been thinking tonally.

Do you think of a series ahead of time, or do you think up a theme and develop your series from it?

I'm very much in the Schoenberg line: I always think of a theme. It wouldn't occur to me to pick a series deliberately and then build a theme out of it. I can imagine that being done, but it seems to me quite hard and chancy.

When you construct the music, do you think of combinatoriality, derivations, etc., or do you proceed more or less intuitively?

I've never made any extensive study of current methods, and I'm very vague as to how they all work. The new terminology is Greek to me. I haven't been through the [Milton] Babbitt school: I haven't that kind of brain. I feel lucky enough if I can add properly. From that standpoint, I'm very much of the old school. But I don't think recent developments are essential to making use of the method as it first developed. No, I am interested in the simple outlines of the theory, and in adapting them to my own purposes.

Suppose you were commissioned now to write a movie or a ballet score. Would you attempt to use your new idiom, or would you feel that you ought to write something simpler and perhaps more tonal?

I couldn't decide in advance; I'd have to know the subject matter. I would want to write a kind of music that seemed appropriate. I'm not married to twelve-tone, and I haven't necessarily given up all contact with tonal music in the usual sense. As always, I would say that any functional music must be influenced by the need you are trying to fulfill.

You said that in the late Thirties you had a rather rough time until along came the ballets and the movies. But since then you have never wanted for musical commissions, so that you have never had to depend on teaching for a livelihood.
No, but I did teach briefly at Harvard, twice, during Walter Piston's sabbaticals, for a half-term in 1934 and again in 1944. True, my film scores helped a lot. Then, in 1938, Boosey and Hawkes became my publishers, guaranteeing me a certain sum each year, so that I wasn't dependent on teaching. Also don't forget that I was at Tanglewood for 21 summers, starting in 1940 and lasting over a span of 25 years. That was income derived from teaching, although it may not be very serious to teach students for just two months of the year. But I did have contact with a great many composition students during that time, perhaps some 400 in all, and I found it very stimulating.

One of the reasons I never thought about teaching in a university is that I had no degree. I graduated from high school and decided not to go to college in order to devote all my time to music. I didn't have the requirements I supposed one needed to teach in a college. Nowadays it's probably freer.

How do you feel about the fact that today many, perhaps most, young composers look on university teaching as the normal thing to do? They seem to think of this first of all, and even look with wonder on the few who decide against the university career and try to make a go of it in the world at large.
It's partly a matter of individual temperament. Certain people are at home and happy within the university, whereas others would not feel comfortable there and shouldn't be there in the first place. If that's the only place they can make a living, so much the worse, for it means a lot of strain. Speaking generally, without relation to personal temperament, I don't think it is healthy for the whole composing community to move within university walls. The protected feeling and the small field of reference are a little worrying. At some point I should think one would want to test everything one does outside, in the big world. Too long and too exclusive a settling into the university musical ambiance might be in individual cases rather upsetting, and as a general trend perhaps not healthy for the musical situation in the country at large—and certainly not healthy for the future of our symphony orchestras. I realize that a good many young composers are not interested in the symphony orchestra, nowadays, but I hope they will be again.

Do you see any signs, in the kind of music that young composers are now writing, of their university training and orientation?
Certainly the orientation has had a serious influence. The concentration on analysis of the innards of all works seems rather special to the present

period. There was always analysis going on, but not the kind one is familiar with in the pages of *Perspectives*. That's a new manifestation.

I gather from your tone that you would add, "not an entirely happy one."
Well, it's lovely if you like to read the stuff! I don't mind that there's a lot of analysis going on, but I wish it were balanced with a little more interest in, shall we say, the musical content without reference to the analysis content. If a piece gives off absolutely nothing to talk about except the way it's put together, there's something a little funny about the piece. One ought to be able to get some sort of charge out of it just by sitting there and listening to it in a dumb fashion. I think that basically we all listen to music in a rather dumb way, especially when we are presented with a new piece about which we know absolutely nothing. Too often you get the feeling, when reading an analysis, that there isn't much point to the music except the way the darn thing's put together. Well, that's very unsympathetic to me. It worries me a little bit that one doesn't meet up now with the kind of composer we used to think of as being "musical." If you said of someone, "He is terribly musical," that was the highest compliment you could pay. Nowadays, to stress the "musicality" of a composer would seem to be somehow pinning a bad name on him or making him seem lesser or limited or not so interesting.

What is your own approach to the teaching of composition?
I don't think of myself as a teacher in the usual sense. I've never taken anybody from the beginning right straight through to the end. What I try to do is what I used to find valuable in Boulanger: I react. I try to point out what I think are the good things and where the piece seems to flounder or not carry on or to get off the rails. That's very good for summer teaching, but it wouldn't work if you wanted to give a student a four-year course.

How do you feel now about your association with the MacDowell Colony? Do you think that such places still have something to offer young composers?
My interest in the MacDowell Colony was aroused by Paul Rosenfeld. I had received a commission from the League of Composers to write a piece for a concert Koussevitzky was to conduct for the League in the Fall of 1925. I was very anxious to go someplace where I could concentrate on writing this piece, and Rosenfeld suggested the Colony. That was the first I had heard about it.

What it provided, more than the mere place to work, beautiful as it was, was face-to-face contact with people in the other arts. This was new for me. People in New York artistic circles had a chance of meeting one another, but I was pretty naïve and didn't know many people. I had never seen an American poet before I saw Edward Arlington Robinson there that first

summer—and William Rose Benêt, and Elinor Wylie, and Louis Unter-
meyer and his wife, Jean. I had never talked with American painters. I knew
some American composers but not many. I met Henry Gilbert and Roy
Harris there. The Colony was an eye-opener for me. It was immensely
stimulating to hear other people talk about their problems in poetry or
painting.

I went back four or five times during the Twenties and Thirties, each
time meeting different people, and each time being provided with a studio
in the woods that was absolutely my own—quiet during the entire day and
night (although we didn't work at night, for in those days there were no
lights in the studios). I found it invaluable, and I don't see why it wouldn't
be invaluable in the same way right now. Not everybody has the perfect situation for writing, and also going away from home for two months and
settling down in a new environment can be quite stimulating.

Young composers can get that at Tanglewood, too.
Yes, but not the contact with artists of other kinds. It's one thing to meet
casually, at a party, someone who writes poetry. It's another thing to live
with him for two months, to see him at breakfast and dinner every day, to
talk with him each time. That's much more than a casual encounter. What
Tanglewood does, by contrast, is to give you professional stimulation in
your own art, with other people working in the same field, which one gets
in a broader sense at a place like the Colony or at Yaddo.

I would like to see every state in the Union establish a MacDowell
Colony. I don't know why they shouldn't. They've set up these Arts Councils now wanting to do things for their own states, they have affluent citizens with properties who want to do something valuable with them but
don't know what, so why not have a colony in every state?

*It's a very good idea. What else might the Arts Councils or foundations do to
help us?*
The best thing would be to get more unplayed music performed. But
there's another point that I often think about. I've spent quite a lot of time
being what you might call a good citizen of the Republic of Music. I don't
find that composers think much about that—about music as an international concern. Take our relations with South America. I had never thought
about our southern neighbors until I was offered a trip down there as a
kind of cultural ambassador for an official committee set up by Nelson
Rockefeller during the war years, in 1941. It was a real eye-opener to go
there and make friends with the composers: to see them having the same
problems we had up here, to an exaggerated degree, and to see how they
understood the problem of their relationship to native musical materials.

It extended my idea of what goes into the making of music to find out how it worked in countries like Argentina, Chile, or Brazil; not only was the situation different in each of these countries, but also the types of composers were different. Such an experience enlarges one's field of vision.

I wish there were more of that: moving composers around, letting them bang up against other ideas different from the ones that are current—or even agreeing with the ones that are current. It should be valuable for mature composers and students alike. Look at the influence of French culture on American artists: the fact that so many American artists went to France had an enormous effect. In the same way, it wouldn't hurt anybody to spend a couple of months in Rio—a delightful experience, or an awful experience, but it would be an experience. You wouldn't be left cold by it. I'm a little concerned by a kind of high-class provincialism that seems to be typical of the present-day musical scene. Everybody gets encouragement from a small circle. I realize that encouragement is important, and there are plenty of examples of composers who began with a small circle of admirers; but one can overdo it. The tendency to lean back and depend upon that small-circle encouragement is, I fear, a lessening rather than an enlarging of one's capacities.

I would like to see an extensive foundation program foster this kind of moving about. After all, the Rockefeller and the Ford Foundations do send people abroad all the time. I myself went again to South America, six years later, in 1947, for the State Department. I spent two months in Rio and wrote most of my Clarinet Concerto there.

Perhaps we can see that copies of this interview fall into the right hands. But, speaking of this interview, it's too bad that we're doing it today and not tomorrow. That would have been very appropriate.
Why? Oh, yes, I see. Tomorrow is November 14. No, I'm trying to forget that!

Well, Happy Birthday to you anyway.

—**November 13, 1967**

Bibliography

Books by Copland

What to Listen for in Music. New York: Whittlesey House, 1939. New York: Mentor, 1953. Revised ed. New York: McGraw-Hill, 1957. New York: Mentor, 1957. New York: Quality Paperback Book Club, 1988. Introduction by William Schuman. New York: McGraw-Hill, 1988. Introduction by Alan Rich: New York: Penguin, 1999.

Our New Music. New York: Whittlesey House, 1941.

Music and Imagination. Cambridge, MA: Harvard University Press, 1952. New York: New American Library, 1959.

Copland on Music. Garden City, NY: Doubleday, 1960. New York: Norton, 1963.

The New Music 1900–1960. New York: W. W. Norton, 1968.

Copland 1900–1942, and Vivian Perlis. New York: St. Martin's Press, 1984.

Copland Since 1943, and Vivian Perlis. New York: St. Martin's Press, 1989.

Books about Copland

Berger, Arthur. *Aaron Copland.* New York: Oxford University Press, 1953. Westport, CT: Greenwood, 1976. New York: Da Capo, 1990.

Smith, Julia F. *Aaron Copland: His Work and Contribution of American Music.* New York: Dutton, 1955.

Dobrin, Arnold. *Aaron Copland: His Life and Times.* New York: Crowell, 1967.

Peare, Catherine. *Aaron Copland: His Life.* New York: Holt, 1969.

Skowronski, Joann. *Aaron Copland: A Bio-Bibliography.* Westport, CT: Greenwood, 1985.

Butterworth, Neil. *The Music of Aaron Copland.* London: Toccata, 1983. New York: Universe, 1985.

Venizia, Mike. *Aaron Copland.* New York: Children's Press, 1995

Perlis, Vivian. *Annotations: A Guide to the Music of Aaron Copland.* NY: Boosey & Hawkes, 1997.

Shirley, Wayne D. *Ballet for Martha: The commissioning of Appalachian Spring;* and *Ballets for Martha: The creation of Appalachian Spring, Jeux de Printemps, and Hérodiade.* Washington, DC: Library of Congress, 1997.

Pollack, Howard. *Aaron Copland.* New York: Holt, 1999. Urbana, IL: Univ. of Illinois, 2000.

Robertson, Marta, and Robin Armstrong. *Aaron Copland: A Guide to Research.* London and New York: Routledge, 2001.

Dickinson, Peter, ed. *Copland Connotations.* Suffolk, UK, and Rochester, NY: Boydell & Brewer, 2002.

Elizabeth Crist and Wayne Shirley are preparing a selection of Aaron Copland's letters.

361

Index